Paddling to Where I Stand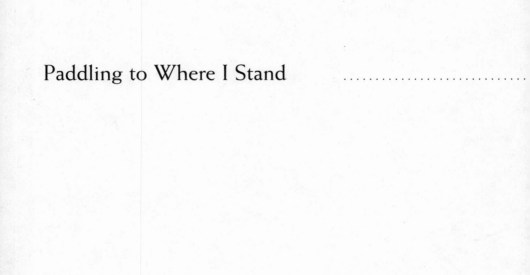

Paddling to Where I Stand

AGNES ALFRED, QʷIQʷASUṮINUX̌ʷ NOBLEWOMAN

As told to Martine J. Reid and Daisy Sewid-Smith

Edited and annotated with an Introduction
by Martine J. Reid

Translated by Daisy Sewid-Smith

UBC Press / Vancouver and Toronto

15 14 13 12 11 10 09 08 07 06 05 04   5 4 3 2 1

Printed in Canada on acid-free paper.

National Library of Canada Cataloguing in Publication

Alfred, Agnes
    Paddling to where I stand : Agnes Alfred, Qwiqwasutinuxw noblewoman /
as told to Martine J. Reid and Daisy Sewid-Smith ; edited and annotated
with an introduction by Martine J. Reid ; translated by Daisy Sewid-Smith.

    Includes bibliographical references and index.
    ISBN 0-7748-0912-4

    1. Alfred, Agnes. 2. Kwakiutl Indians – Biography. 3. Kwakiutl women –
Biography. 4. Kwakiutl Indians – Social life and customs. I. Sewid-Smith,
Daisy. II. Reid, Martine Jeanne, 1945- III. Title.

E99.K9A43 2004   971.1'00497953'0092   C2004-900838-2

Canadä

UBC Press gratefully acknowledges the financial support for our publishing
program of the Government of Canada through the Book Publishing
Industry Development Program (BPIDP), and of the Canada Council for
the Arts, and the British Columbia Arts Council.

This book has been published with the help of a grant from the Heritage
Cultures and Languages Program, Multiculturalism and Citizenship Canada,
Department of Canadian Heritage.

UBC Press
The University of British Columbia
2029 West Mall
Vancouver, BC V6T 1Z2
604-822-5959 / Fax: 604-822-6083
E-mail: info@ubcpress.ca
www.ubcpress.ca

Contents

Preface

I was there before I came.
– Martine Reid

Paddling to Where I Stand has been long in realization. In the fall of 1975 I came to Vancouver as a French PhD student in the field of anthropology, having been granted a Canada Council fellowship as part of a cultural exchange program between Canada and France. I had just completed my "mémoire" (the equivalent of a master's degree) for the Diplôme de l'École des Hautes Études en Sciences Sociales. The subject of my research was the nineteenth- and twentieth-century Kʷakʷakəwakʷ, specifically, the role of salmon in all areas of their lives. This was probably one of the first theses on these people to be written in French (de Widerspach-Thor 1975).

What first attracted me to these people was a feeling I had while reading Franz Boas and the extensive anthropological literature of the twentieth century. The Kʷakʷakəwakʷ were not merely another colourful population, rich in ritual and ceremony: they were perhaps the most elaborate theatrical group ever to have strutted their brief hour on a small corner of the world's stage. At that time, I was a student in one of Paris's dramatic art schools, and this brief encounter with the Kʷakʷakəwakʷ triggered in me an impulse to change to a new field of endeavour: anthropology. I also began to attend the lectures of Professor Claude Lévi-Strauss at the Collège de France. One of his main interests then was the relationship between myth and iconography, and, more particularly, the relationships between Dᶻunuq̓ʷa (Kʷakʷakəwakʷ), X̌ʷix̌ʷiỷ (Kʷakʷakəwakʷ), and Sx̌ʷayx̌ʷəy (Salish) myths, along with the whole complex of masks and rituals attached to them. This eventually led to his publication of *La Voie des masques* (1975), which was later expanded (1979) and finally translated as *The Way of the Masks* (1982).[1]

Having spent a lonely time tracking the Kʷakʷakəwakʷ through the twisting trails of Paris libraries, I was anxious to encounter the real, living, contemporary

people. During my first academic year at the University of British Columbia
I wanted to be able to communicate with the Kʷakʷakəwakʷ people in their native
tongue, so my first goal was to learn Kʷakʷala. My advisor, the late Wilson Duff,
introduced me to the late Mrs. Katherine Ferry Adams,[2] a Kʷakʷakəwakʷ woman
who lived in Vancouver. A very alert woman in her early seventies, she was part
Gʷasəlla (Smith Inlet) and part Nakʷaxdax̌ʷ (Seymour Inlet), and she spoke
Kʷakʷala and a number of regional dialects as well as excellent English. As for
me, my knowledge of English was more academic and literary than functional.
While I was taking international phonetics at UBC's linguistic laboratory, Kitty
Ferry introduced me to Kʷakʷala as well as its English equivalents.

As my knowledge of Kʷakʷala language and culture grew, I realized how much
I owed Kitty Ferry. In introducing me to her language and her culture, she also
introduced me to her worldview. "We will start with the human body," she once
said, "and all its anatomical parts; then we will create sentences. After that we
will deal with what is outside the human body: the sky, the land, the sea, and the
underworld." In this way, she disclosed to me the four realms of Kʷakʷakəwakʷ
cosmology. As our mutual trust and friendship developed, Kitty Ferry adopted
me into her family and bestowed upon me a Kʷakʷala name, ʔĺxċəmǧa (Abalone
Shell Woman), during a potlatch ceremony performed at Yəlis,[3] Alert Bay, in 1978.

In May 1976 the late Kʷakʷakəwakʷ chief James Sewid,[4] whose daily or secular
name was Poogleedee (Guests Never Leave Hungry), invited me to attend a
week of potlatches that were going to take place at Alert Bay (see Introduction,
"Orthography," for information regarding Kʷakʷakəwakʷ names). Kathy Ferry had
arranged for me to stay with Mrs. Agnes Cranmer, whose daily Kʷakʷala name
was Ǧʷəntilakʷ (Heavy with Property). She was the granddaughter of George
Hunt, anthropologist Franz Boas's well known and long-time collaborator. Upon
George Hunt's death in 1933,[5] Ǧʷəntilakʷ's husband, Daniel Cranmer (whose
potlatch name was Pəlnəkʷala Wakəs), succeeded Hunt as Boas's interpreter.[6]
Clearly, I could not have been in better company to start my journey among the
Kʷakʷakəwakʷ.

The small town of Alert Bay, situated on crescent-shaped Cormorant Island
at the northeast end of Vancouver Island and on Kʷakʷakəwakʷ land, is now the
home of two distinct, although geographically adjacent, ethnic communities:
Yəlis and Alert Bay. Yəlis is now the home of the Nəmǧis Band, which derives its
name from the mythic halibut, Ńəmkalagým, the Only Halibut on the Ocean
Floor.[7] In 1964 the Nəmǧis Reserve population of Alert Bay was 686 (Wilson
Duff 1964: 21); by the time I arrived there it had increased considerably to around
800. The same could be said for the non–First Nations population of the island.

During the 1970s there was increasing awareness among both Aboriginal
peoples and scholars that unwritten languages were facing extinction. North-

west Coast Aboriginal languages and all their associated cultural knowledge were disappearing, along with their practitioners. In response to this disaster, the Urgent Ethnology Program of the Museum of Man in Ottawa (now the Canadian Museum of Civilization) financed scholars to record languages and customs in order to preserve them for study and to return to Aboriginal peoples an irreplaceable part of their heritage and culture. I was one of those so financed. I wanted to work with whomever possessed the most complete store of traditional knowledge, and all my evidence pointed to one individual: Mrs. Agnes Alfred, known by her Kʷakʷala daily name as ʔAx̌uw̓ (or ʔAx̌uw̓aw, which is a more affectionate term), whom I had met on several occasions at G̓ʷəntilakʷ's. ʔAx̌uw̓ and G̓ʷəntilakʷ had a special relationship that had been nurtured by a long history of shared life circumstances, and, as I learned later, G̓ʷəntilakʷ's late husband, Dan Cranmer,[8] who was part Qʷiqʷasutinux̌ʷ and part Nəmǧis, was related to ʔAx̌uw̓. It is said that her mother and his mother were sisters. ʔAx̌uw̓ and Dan were first cousins but, in accordance with Kʷakʷakəwakʷ kinship terminology (see Chapter 2), they referred to each other as brother and sister.

ʔAx̌uw̓ was a respected, non-literate, octogenarian woman who had witnessed undreamed-of changes in the condition of her people while retaining her position as a noble (*noxsola*)[9] Kʷakʷakəwakʷ matriarch. She had virtually no Western education and did not speak English, although she could understand a few words. She was one of the few individuals still fluent in Kʷakʷala, in both its classical and everyday forms (see Introduction), and was recognized by her peers as a talented storyteller with a long memory. From my base at G̓ʷəntilakʷ's house, where I was given room and board, I started working with ʔAx̌uw̓.

So began a sometimes frustrating, sometimes exhilarating, period of my life – an exciting and, in the end, incredibly rewarding voyage of discovery. The journey began, appropriately enough, with my recording ethnographic material pertaining to the Kʷakʷakəwakʷ view of the sea. The work involved recording myths and beliefs pertaining to aquatic mythic creatures as well as to the sea itself, the type of knowledge that quickly disappears when a language is not in daily use (de Widerspach-Thor 1978).

During the years between 1976 and 1978 I attended a large number of potlatches at Alert Bay and elsewhere in the area and was struck both emotionally and aesthetically by the Kʷakʷakəwakʷ *hamaċa* (Man-Eater) ritual. This rite of passage enacts a universal drama reaffirming and celebrating humanity's ascendance over the forces of chaos. People who are entitled to perform it speak of it with great pride. I started to work with a group of elderly chiefs who had been initiated into the *hamaċa* society, among them Chiefs James Sewid (Poogleedee), Tommy Hunt, Jim King (x̱aqʷagila, Copper Maker), Bob Wilson, and Jim Wallace (Wallas: The Great One). An analysis of the *haṁaċa* ritual, from its first descriptions in the late 1800s to its most recent performances, later became the subject of my doctoral dissertation (Reid 1981).

The Kʷakʷakəwakʷ have been the subject of considerable study in the anthropological literature, as our References demonstrate. However, most of the nineteenth- and early-twentieth-century ethnographic accounts of these peoples were conducted by male ethnographers and focused upon the roles and activities of male individuals, especially chiefs and their deeds. Similar data on women were incidental and incomplete.[10]

As I immersed myself more and more into Kʷakʷakəwakʷ culture, I became aware of the real and symbolic powers of women – powers that go beyond being the perpetuators of the lineages. I realized the significant role that noble women have in Kʷakʷakəwakʷ society, in which men's power and standing rely considerably on women, who, through their dowries, supply men with highly valuable tangible and intangible privileges. These privileges are constantly reasserted, reaffirmed, and deployed, and their provenance is clearly cited during each potlatch ceremony. I also witnessed the significant role that noble women played in the *haṁaċa* ritual, where they functioned as mediators between the natural-human-profane realm and the supernatural-sacred realm.[11] As I realized women's role in keeping many aspects of their culture alive, I started to ask myself many questions concerning the female domain – questions that had never before been addressed.[12]

At the time I started my research, ethnographic material on North American First Nations women was rare; only a few biographical accounts existed in the literature (e.g., Anauta, qtd. in Washburne 1976; Alice Lee Marriott 1948; Nancy Lurie 1961). Although a growing body of anthropological literature has since attempted to correct the male viewpoint so pervasive in the discipline,[13] this bias, so frequently lamented in the anthropological literature on women, was then typical of the Northwest Coast ethnological material. There was a lacuna in this field that I hoped that my collaboration with the Kʷakʷakəwakʷ and ʔAx̌uw̓ would fill.

ʔAx̌uw̓ was very independent, still living alone at the approximate age of eighty in the sizeable house that her late husband, Kʷaguł Moses Alfred, had built for her and their large family. When this house was first built it stood right in the centre of Yəlis, on Kʷaguł land. During the fall and winter she would visit her relatives, going, like a migratory bird, to Campbell River and other places on a regular annual cycle. As our trust and friendship developed, I followed her seasonal migrations and eventually met the whole family, including one of her granddaughters, Daisy (Mayanił: Precious One),[14] the daughter of Chief James Sewid and Flora Alfred, ʔAx̌uw̓'s second offspring. Since her early childhood,

Daisy has been fascinated by her culture and its history. Fluent in her mother tongue, Kʷakʷ̓ala, she has written and lectured on a wide range of topics pertaining to the Kʷakʷ̓akəwakʷ (Sewid-Smith 1979; 1988; 1991; 1995; 1996; 1997).

Our encounter was fortunate. As our friendship grew stronger, the three of us decided to record everything ʔAx̌uw̓ might be willing to tell us. ʔAx̌uw̓ herself urgently felt the need to pass on her knowledge to younger generations. More important, we wanted to record the narratives in which she was particularly interested and to write them down in her own literary style. Her memoirs would be told in the following setting: a Kʷakʷ̓akəwakʷ woman discussing her culture with her adult Kʷakʷ̓akəwakʷ granddaughter, with whom she had a close relationship. This would bypass the serious problem of attempting to communicate with an alien collaborator who was illiterate or clumsy in ʔAx̌uw̓'s native tongue (a situation that is the rule rather than the exception in the ethnographic and life-story literature). We conducted the recordings and partially completed the translation of the tapes during 1979 and 1980, with the support of a grant from the Crestview Foundation. Further recording was done in 1983, and some video recording was conducted in 1985. Subsequent support for translating was provided in the 1980s by the Secretary of State (1988) and the Association for Canadian Studies (1989). All original material, tapes, and transcriptions were deposited at the archives of the UBC Museum of Anthropology, and copies were made for ʔAx̌uw̓'s family.

Most of our translating took place during weekends and long nights, when Daisy's late husband, Lorne Smith, a noble x̌awid̓is man from Turnour Island, was out fishing and when their children and grandchildren were asleep. Sometimes we would translate in the presence of Daisy's sisters, brothers, and in-laws. After we listened to the recording together, Daisy would give a continuous verbal translation from Kʷakʷ̓ala to English. I took dictation, helped find the appropriate wording, offered alternative translations for the wording, whether factual, descriptive, or cognitive, and tried to make the translation a continuous flow of clear English using the punctuation for normal written prose. Together we reread and edited the text several times, always keeping in mind our commitment to privilege her voice and intent. (For more details on our method, see Introduction, beginning on page xvii, especially pages xxii to xxv.)

Listening to ʔAx̌uw̓ was always an enriching experience. She constantly amazed us with her knowledge, her sense of precision and detail, and her eloquence. The measure of the respect we all felt was reflected in the silence that possessed us whenever we heard her rich, deep voice. We would all listen attentively and respectfully, caught in the flow of wisdom, information, and humour. Here was the voice of an eloquent elder.

As I was deeply interested in the relationship between gesture and speech during storytelling (a relationship that is lost once oral literature is written down), I decided one day to preserve ʔAx̌uw̓'s gestures for further study by videotaping her as she spoke.[15] She was sitting in the living room of her daughter, Flora Sewid, with Daisy seated next to her. A nervous and inexperienced camera operator, I had been kneeling for a long time, hoping ʔAx̌uw̓ would stop, catch her breath, sigh, do anything so I could get up and stretch. I did not dare to interrupt her. But no, the myth of the White Seagull Woman, a story of which she was particularly fond, was unfolding so beautifully that it held me immobile and spellbound for hours.

The reader should know that, throughout these recordings, like a bright path through a dense woodland, there was always laughter. I remember vividly, on one particular day, the suppressed giggles of her daughter Libby and her grand-daughters Louise and Vera. Timidly, unsure of whether or not she should speak of such a thing at a time when *bibax̌ʷk̓əm*[16] (i.e., First Nations peoples) could still be perceived as "savages," ʔAx̌uw̓ confessed with embarrassment: "Our soap was ... Shall I tell?" The soap was, as we shall see in her recollections, urine – something not too funny in retrospect, but, at the time, it was enough to make us all burst into laughter.

After completing the recording and part of the translation of ʔAx̌uw̓'s narratives, both Daisy and I, for personal and familial reasons, had to set aside our work until circumstances allowed us to resume it in the late 1990s. During this long hiatus, Daisy became one of the leading linguistic experts in her community, teaching her native language and developing a method to transcribe it. Inspired by ʔAx̌uw̓'s wisdom she acquired an even greater sense of purpose and became a linguistic consultant to her own people by translating some of Boas's texts in the context of land claims issues. She also contributed an Aboriginal perspective in the religious dimensions of childhood and family life as part of the UN convention on the rights of the child (Sewid-Smith 1996). Expanding on ʔAx̌uw̓'s teaching model, she collaborated with Nancy Turner and Kʷakʷakəwakʷ elder, Chief Adam Dick, on the sacred aspects of the cedar tree (Turner and Kuhnlein 1998), and with Bouchard and Kennedy (2002) on the annotations of their most recent book on Northwest Coast mythology by providing valuable commentary on hundreds of rather complex Kʷak̓ʷala expressions that had been first translated in German and required clarification in their new English form.

During my brief lecturing career at the UBC Department of Anthropology (1979-83) I taught basic and advanced courses pertaining to the anthropology and ethnography of Northwest Coast cultures and in the areas of First Nations studies. Several art-related projects followed (mainly in the form of exhibitions of ancient and modern Northwest Coast art with their accompanying essays [1987; 1989; 1993; 2000]). I consulted and did research for the Ministry of Indian and Northern Affairs to review the land claim submitted by the Council of the Tsimshian Nation (1984b). Another consulting project was to organize for the Native Investment Trade Association (NITA) their Nexus '92 International Arts Conference: "Revival and After," which contributed a great deal of discourse on the so-called Northwest Coast cultural revival phenomenon. All these research activities served to broaden our educational perspectives. In addition, a fairly substantial body of autobiographical material had been published in these intervening years with which I became familiar. When we resumed our work, Daisy and I had better ideas on how to articulate and present our raw material in a publishable form.

ꓱAx̌uw̓ lived a full and, I think, happy life. She grew up in a stratified society, and her high social and ceremonial standing gave her access to a certain education and knowledge shared only between her equals. Before adolescence, ꓱAx̌uw̓ was married to an older man who had been chosen for her, and thus she was spared the inhumane treatment concomitant with most residential schools. As a young child she did go to the local school, but her time there was too short to deprive her of her cultural and human identity. During her long married life, she gave birth to thirteen children and also had several miscarriages. In accordance with the responsibilities of her rank, she was involved in potlatching during the years when potlatching and related activities were prohibited and punished with imprisonment. Until her final days, ꓱAx̌uw̓ continued to play a vital role in carrying on the business of potlatching, as may be seen in Appendix D, which recounts Daisy's traditional potlatch wedding ceremony.

Near the end of her long life, ꓱAx̌uw̓ looked very frail, like a tiny, fragile bird. But in spite of her delicate appearance, she was as strong as a rock. She often wondered why she was still part of the realm of this world, having outlived many of her children. Nearly blind, she still wove small red cedar baskets that she promptly gave away. She had shown her determination and strength of character all her life and eagerly wanted to document her life experiences and knowledge for the future generations. Most particularly, she wanted them to know who they are and where they came from.

Paddling to Where I Stand is the first published memoirs of a Qʷiqʷasutinux̌ʷ woman. The three of us – ꓱAx̌uw̓, Daisy, and I – have attempted to lead you through the magic of myth time, along the rocky roads of daily survival, to the present (not necessarily in that order), providing a glimpse of First Nations life on the Northwest Coast during the period of its most rapid change. ꓱAx̌uw̓'s memoirs bring to life the changing culture of the Kʷakʷakəwakʷ and show us how a First Nations woman managed to quietly fulfill her role as a matriarch in her ever-changing society, thus providing a model for younger generations.

Paddling to Where I Stand was not written from the perspective of the outsider seeking to fit the facts into the framework of established general Western ethnographic and literary conventions. ʔAx̌uw̓'s memoirs remain her own. Her narratives document in amazing detail the enduring pulse of a living culture and convey the Kʷakʷakəwakʷ tradition even when they recount postcontact events. In presenting this rare material we have tried to be faithful to ʔAx̌uw̓'s voice and, thus, to her mind. Our goal was to hear and to discover ʔAx̌uw̓, her life, and her culture as she saw them and lived them.

Paddling to Where I Stand contributes to the fields of First Nations studies, women's studies, oral history and tradition, the anthropology of memory and cultural change, and the sociology of aging. It addresses readers interested in seeing the world through ʔAx̌uw̓'s eyes, readers who are willing to attempt to embrace her life experience told in her way. We see her memoirs as a chance to come to know her and her culture from within.

Acknowledgments

ʔAx̱uw̓ is the author of this book. We were merely her scribes. Clearly, the first person whom we wish to thank is ʔAx̱uw̓, for sharing with us her knowledge and experiences, her wit and laughter, her wisdom and earnest passion to pass on her knowledge to future generations.

Writing down ʔAx̱uw̓'s memoirs on her behalf was also a family affair that could not have taken place without the collaboration of all her immediate and extended family members who shared their "granny" so enthusiastically with us. We cannot name them all here, but among them were all her children and their families and all her grandchildren and their families.

There are other people whom we would also like to thank, especially the Kʷakʷakəwakʷ elders, who generously offered their knowledge when we sought it, many of whom, we are sad to say, are no longer with us. We acknowledge the teachings of hereditary chiefs Henry Bell, Tommy Hunt, James Sewid, Jim Wallace, Lorne Smith, Harry Assu, James Henderson, Harry Walkus, James Dick, Herbert Martin, James Roberts, Moses Alfred, James King. Among the women, we acknowledge Mrs. Flora Sewid, Lucy Brown, Agnes Cranmer, Emma Beans, Mary (Frank) Clifton, Ida (Dick) Assu, Emma (Alfred) Beans, Sarah Johnson, Daisy Moon, Mrs. James Knox, Daisy Roberts, Mary Dick, and Kitty Ferry.

A very special thanks goes to contemporary Kʷakʷakəwakʷ chief Adam Dick for his invaluable assistance, as well as to Dora (Sewid) Cook, Mitzi (Roberts) Assu, Helen Beans, and Colleen Hemphill.

We are also grateful to the following academic colleagues for their valuable assistance: Michael Ames, who, as director of the Museum of Anthropology at UBC, administered the Crestview Foundation grant that supported the early phase of our work. George MacDonald and Michael Kew gave their intellectual and academic support early in the project. Marie Mauzé, Michael Harkin, and Sergei Kan provided collegial encouragement and many helpful comments. Dell Hymes made valuable editorial and general comments on the Introduction.

Judith Berman offered her helpful comments and professional opinion regarding Kʷakʷʼala orthography and linguistics. We are grateful to Randall Bouchard and Dorothy Kennedy, who shared very generously and with such enthusiasm their work on the translation of Franz Boas's 1895 *Indianische Sagen der nordpacifischen Küste Amerikas* before it was published. Nancy Turner, William White, and Vicky Wyatt showed encouragement and sustained interest in our research. Joanne Richardson kindly proofread the manuscript at an earlier stage, and David Neel, Kʷakʷʼakəwakʷ artist and photographer, granted permission to use his very sensitive portrait of ʔAx̱uẃ.

Several greatly supportive friends generously made many valuable contributions of their time and energy to help us along the way. Edith Daly-Iglauer provided unlimited encouragement and proofread earlier drafts of the Preface and Introduction with a sharp pencil and the keen, professional eye of an accomplished author. Cynthia Reid typed the manuscript at a very early stage; Dian Weimer helped create the kinship diagrams on the computer; and Gloria Smith was particularly helpful with her instructions on the Kʷakʷʼala keyboard. Daisy Sewid-Smith's children, Gloria and Todd Smith are thanked for being so patient all these years. We especially thank Jean Wilson, Associate Director of UBC Press, for believing in our project since its inception, and for her great patience in helping us through the publishing process. Darcy Cullen and Deborah Kerr were particularly helpful in the final stages of the book.

Our deep gratitude also goes to the late Canadian Haida artist and story-teller, Bill Reid, who recognized another talented storyteller in ʔAx̱uẃ and gave us the poetic rendering for the title. He, who also "wrote aloud" so eloquently, has been a continuing source of inspiration.

Finally I would like to thank Professor Emeritus Rodney Allan Badger for his academic and proofreading assistance, and unconditional support.

The financial support of the Crestview Foundation, Secretariat of State, and the Association for Canadian Studies, helped us in the earliest phases of this project and is gratefully acknowledged.

Introduction

In recent years autobiography as a genre has come under a good deal of scrutiny. Is an autobiography a fiction of the self (Mandel 1968; Heilbrun 1988)? A story of a story? "A novel that dares not speak its name" (Barthes 1994)? North American First Nations autobiographical material, especially, has been the subject of much discussion in anthropological literature. Even treated as "a culturally specific narrative genre" (Cruikshank 1990: x), autobiographies still raise many issues, as we shall see in this book, which attempts a new way of writing down (textualizing) the verbal art of a non-literate First Nations individual.[1]

Autobiography

There are several ways to record a person's life. The subject may tell it and write it, in a self-written first-person narrative, an autobiography. A biographer may write a person's life from direct or indirect sources in what is called a biography. Pre-literate North American First Nations individuals have narrated their lives (or episodes of their lives) through such intermediaries as ethnographers, missionaries, ethnologists, historians, and doctors, and these life-history narratives form another category of writings, known as "as-told-to autobiographies." Georg Misch (1951) and Karl Weintraub (1975; 1978) have described their histories of Western autobiography "as the history of the rise of the idea of the individual in the West" (David Brumble III 1988: 4). Although the history of Western autobiography spans some 4,500 years, starting with the ancient Greeks,[2] this genre, as we know it in its most popular form, is relatively recent and began to be common only after the eighteenth century.[3] Since then, it has become so well entrenched, so structured by convention, that Western readers now consider it to be a "natural" genre not requiring explanation. The familiar model comes from written autobiography, a first-person narrative that purports to describe the narrator's life or episodes in that life, customarily with some chronological reflections about individual growth and development.

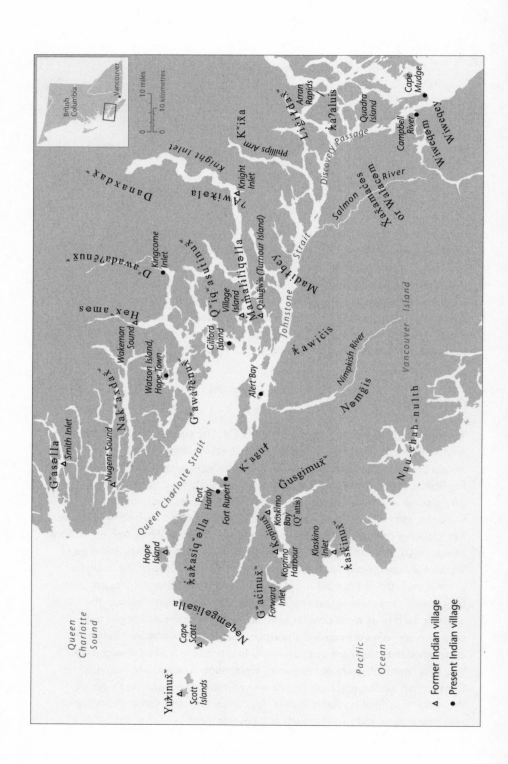

Queen
Charlotte
Sound

British Columbia
Vancouver

10 miles
10 kilometres

Yux̌inux̌ʷ
Scott Islands
Cape Scott

Naⱪₑmǥₑlisₑlla

Gʷaⱪinux̌ʷ
Forward Inlet
Koprino Harbour
Koskimo Bay (Qʼatis)
X̌ⱪopinux̌ʷ
Klaskino Inlet
ⱪaskinux̌ʷ

Hope Island
ⱪaⱪasiqʷella
Port Hardy
Fort Rupert

Kʷaguⱡ

Ǧusgimux̌ʷ

Nimkish River

Nemǥis

Nuu-chah-nulth

Vancouver Island

Gʷasɛlla
Smith Inlet
Nugent Sound

Nakʷax̌daⱪ
Wakeman Sound
Watson Island, Hope Town
Gʷawaʔenux̌ʷ

Hax̌ʷamas

Dzawadaʔenux̌ʷ
Kingcome Inlet

Qʷiqʷasutinux̌ʷ
Gilford Island
Village Island
Mamaliliqₑlla
ʔawikʼala
Alert Bay
Qalugwis (Turnour Island)

Danaxdaxʷ

Knight Inlet
Kʼʷix̌a
Phillips Arm

Liǧiⱡdax̌ʷ
Arran Rapids
ⱪaʔaluis
Quadra Island
Campbell River
Ǧwaǥₑm̓
Cape Mudge
Wiweqₑy

Madiⱡbey

Xaⱪⱪamaȼes or Waⱡaȼₑm
Salmon River

Discovery Passage

Johnstone Strait

ⱪawiȼis

Queen Charlotte Strait

Pacific Ocean

△ Former Indian village
● Present Indian village

In *Le Pacte autobiographique* Phillippe Lejeune (1975: 14) defines autobiography as a "retrospective account that an actual person makes in prose of
his own existence, stressing his individual life and particularly the history of his/
her personality." In her narratives, ʔAx̌uw̓, the subject of *Paddling to Where I
Stand*, was not explicit about the history of her personality. Nevertheless, her
telling of her life and social roles offers an unparalleled insight into her personality
and how she saw herself. Roy Pascal (1960) insists that in "true" autobiography
we must find some "coherent shaping of the past." This presupposes a clear
understanding of the subject's notion of time and how it is experienced, lived,
and expressed. How did ʔAx̌uw̓'s concepts of time compare with those of
individuals who do not share her culture? It seems that ʔAx̌uw̓'s sense of time
and temporal flow had something to do with her personal experiences. For
example, she told us that she "was baptized not long ago," or that her "father
had died not long ago." Both events, which she witnessed, had actually taken
place some fifty or sixty years earlier, during a period of time that Westerners
would refer to as the past. For ʔAx̌uw̓, however, this time belonged to her present,
her lived reality. What ʔAx̌uw̓ had not witnessed and had not experienced
personally was referred to as happening "long ago" and did not belong to her
field of lived experiences. Such events may have taken place in mythical times
(e.g., before or after the Flood) or in historical time (e.g., with reference to a type
of food she did not eat because it was no longer prepared, or to events of which
she had heard but had not experienced).[4]

Life histories provide a method of assessing the individual in society and the
relationship between self and community. The use of First Nations life histories
as ethnographic documents can be traced back to Franz Boas, the putative
founder of modern scientific anthropology in North America, whose intensive
relationship with the Kʷakʷakəwak̓ʷ and emphasis upon the collection of Native
texts and their personal interpretations led him to regard descriptions cast in
the imagery of the people themselves as the "true" and "authentic" rendering of
culture (Blackman 1981: 65; Goldman 1975: xi). Scholars who followed Boas's
intellectual path continued to value the life-history document. One example
among many is Paul Radin's (1983 [1926]) *Crashing Thunder: The Autobiography
of an American Indian*, perhaps one of the most popular narrated Indian
autobiographies presented by an anthropologist.[5]

The methods and theories of the personal narrative have been applied and
debated in anthropology for some time. North American literature on the subject
is vast, and we offer only a brief review. Some anthropologists recorded life
stories either to "salvage" elements of "disappearing races" (see Krupat 1985;
Brumble III 1988) or to add a "human" dimension to anthropological science by
presenting the individual "informant's" perspectives on his/her "worldview" or

"culture" (see Langness 1965: 8). By the middle of the twentieth century, the debates in anthropology centred primarily on the verification of the life story or on the validity of an individual's perspective vis-à-vis the ethnographer's "objective" observations from a range of other sources (Kluckhohn 1945; L. Langness 1965). In *For Those Who Came After* Arnold Krupat (1985) points out that, if they are going to begin to understand the nature and consequence of their work, then collaborators in any cross-cultural project must see themselves as individuals existing in a particular time and place. At the boundary of the discipline, First Nations women involved in personal narrative groups "have found that personal narratives provide insights into culture and society not afforded by conventional anthropological methods" (Howard-Bobiwash 1999: 117-18).[6]

The past twenty years have seen an upsurge in the use of autobiographical material, while, at the same time, "anthropology's claim to provide authoritative interpretations of culture is being challenged from both inside and outside the discipline" (Cruikshank 1990: 1).[7] Audiences for ethnological writings are changing and have become multiple as members of the described cultures have, increasingly, become critical readers of ethnography. Debates about how to represent cultural experience may be partly responsible for recent scholarly attention to orally narrated life stories; however, there may also be other reasons for the recent proliferation of such documents. For example, some "ethnic biographers have produced brilliant explorations aimed at rediscovering the sources of language, and thereby also the nature of modern reality" (Fisher 1986: 199). Also, renewed anthropological interest in life histories coincides with increasing attention to analysis of symbolism, meaning, and text. Much of the contemporary philosophical mood (in literary criticism and anthropology as well as in philosophy)[8] involves inquiring into what is hidden in language, what is conveyed by signs, what is pointed out, what is repressed, implied, or mediated. What initially seem to be individualistic autobiographical accounts are often considered to be revelations of traditions and recollections of disseminated identities (Fisher 1986).

In "Ethnicity and the Post-Modern Arts of Memory," Fisher (1986: 197) discusses the phenomenon of contemporary reinvention, or re-creation of ethnic identity through remembering, as a reaction to globalization and the fear of becoming levelled into identical "hominids." Furthermore, if First Nations (and especially those who are literate) are going to be portrayed in the anthropological literature, then they want to be the ones doing the portraying.

The debate about autobiography as fiction is not new, and it comes down to this: who writes what, about whom, and how?

Why is autobiography a fiction? Many factors are at play. In the case of a literate person, her/his autobiography is a self-written fiction, a construction of the self. Of course, no autobiography can be a "true" representation of the self in any absolute sense, but self-written autobiography is at least the subject's own fiction. With the as-told-to autobiographies of non-literate First Nations persons, on the other hand, it is the recorder-editor who decides what is to be the final shape of the subject's "autobiography." Therefore, the roles of the editors must be disclosed. As-told-to autobiographies should be considered "bicultural documents, texts in which the assumptions of Indian autobiographers *and* Anglo editors are at work" (Brumble III 1988: 11).

Various authors have noted the natural human tendency for an autobiographer to select those experiences and events from his/her life that conform to or substantiate a fictional or mythic view of the self. We agree on this point of selection when we see that ʔAx̣uw̓ has on several occasions consciously omitted some relevant information. In one particular instance, at the end of a Raven myth (M 18), she said: "I have discreetly removed an episode that I consider inappropriate."[9] Some silences may indicate the witholding of information that she considered embarrassing to herself or her kin, that was a "guarded truth," or that properly brought-up people simply "did not talk about."[10] ʔAx̣uw̓ has, consciously or unconsciously, deleted some elements of her narratives. Knowledge is power and consequently, she may have decided not to reveal all of what she knew (e.g., sacred notions or taboos, which can be harmful if revealed). That intentional withholding of information would have been consistent with her view of what her life story was or should have been. There are always some silences that are inherent to a particular life in a particular culture. ʔAx̣uw̓'s tellings as well as her silences will have to be interpreted accordingly. This brings up a question of ethics. Do we reveal, if we happen to know from other sources, what the narrator, for whatever reasons, chose not to tell? Do we or do we not respect these forms of silence?

Writing Down As-Told-To Autobiographies

Writing down another culture has its problems: a recorder-editor records, transcribes, and translates what the First Nations subject gives orally. Sally McClusky (1972), in her critique of John Neihardt's *Black Elk Speaks* (1932), is the first North American literary scholar to draw attention to the problem of editor-narrator relationships. David Brumble III (1988), Greg Sarris (1993), and many other life-history critics have concurred with her.

We are all aware of the problems of life history. Ethnologists have approached informants to relate their life histories, asking questions along the way to guide them and to ensure adequate details. Ethnologists then edit these great bundles of material (now usually in translation) into something like chronological order, selecting content and making other changes necessary to transform a collection of transcripts of individual oral performances into a single, more or less continuous, narrative, often editing out repetitions that are, in fact, important stylistic and rhetorical features (Dauenhauer 1999). The new imposed chronology distorts the narrator's sense of time. As David Brumble III (1988: 66) points out, "the whole process is a construction of the Western mind with Western habits of mind." According to him, the published version of an Aboriginal autobiography that does not include the hand of a non-Aboriginal editor is very rare. Of the 600 published American Indian texts that are autobiographical, more than 83 percent were narrated. Of these, 43 percent were collected and edited by anthropologists, and the other 40 percent were collected and edited by non-Aboriginals from other disciplines.

Whether narrated or written, autobiography is not someone's life but, rather, an account or story of his/her life. ʔAx̌uw̓'s narrated life story is an account of an account, a story of a story. As Greg Sarris (1993: 85) points out elsewhere, ʔAx̌uw̓'s story would be, as it were, doubly edited: first during the encounter between herself, as narrator, and us, as recorder-editors; and second during the literary reencounter of the translation and editing process.[11] In the encounter between ʔAx̌uw̓ and us, it is important to remember that, for whatever personal or cultural reasons, she may have edited and shaped her oral narrative in certain ways.[12] Her memory may have been intentionally selective.

All autobiography is shaped by narrative convention, and, in many ways, the history of American Indian autobiography parallels the history of Western literary tradition (Brumble III 1988: 4-5). Among those researchers who followed Boas to the Northwest Coast and who valued the utility of life-history documents were Edward Sapir (1921), whose studies focused on a Nootka man; Diamond Jenness (1955), whose studies focused on a Katzie man; and Marius Barbeau (1957), whose studies focused on Haida carvers. Four Northwest Coast life-history documents span four successive generations of Southern Kʷakʷakəwakʷ cultural history and are particularly valuable for their documentation of cultural continuity and change. In 1940 Kʷaguł chief Charlie Nowell dictated his life to Clellan Ford (1941) and, following him, Qʷiqʷasutinux̌ʷ chief James Sewid, the father of Daisy Sewid-Smith, related his personal history to, and with the editorial assistance of, anthropologist James Spradley (1969). Finally, in the 1980s, Gʷacinux̌ʷ chief James Wallas told Kʷakʷakəwakʷ legends to Pamela Whitaker (1981), whose book includes a very short portrait of this elderly man; and Lig̱iłdax̌ʷ chief Harry Assu (1989) of Cape Mudge collaborated on his life history with anthropologist Joy Inglis. With the exception of the important life history of Haida elder Florence Davidson by Margaret Blackman (1982), the recent works by Julie Cruikshank

(1990, 1998), and the life histories of First Nations women from the Yukon by Nora Dauenhauer and Richard Dauenhauer (1994), most other documents of the lives of Northwest Coast Aboriginals concern male individuals. As Marc Augé (1982: 6) writes, "anthropology is produced and received by men of a particular epoch and society, in a determinate intellectual political conjuncture."

Some twenty years ago Margaret Blackman (1982: 65) pointed out that there has been a familiar pattern of shortcomings in ethnographic accounts. Male ethnographers who were interested in life histories focused upon the roles and activities of First Nations men, while similar data on women were incidental and incomplete, limited to discussions of the crises of a normal life cycle: birth, puberty, marriage, and death. As we mentioned in our Preface, anthropological literature on Aboriginal North Americans includes only a few examples of women's biographical accounts; through the early 1970s, when we began our research, very few First Nations women had written their own autobiographies. (Maria Campbell [1973] and Jane Willis [1973] were among the exceptions.) Northwest Coast ethnology, which is relatively rich in accounts of men's lives, was still deficient in accounts of women's lives.

Aware of this deficit in the anthropological literature and the pressing need for biographical material on women, as well as for more personal reasons, Daisy and I began to work with her grandmother, Mrs. Agnes Alfred, known as ʔAx̌uw̓, a non-literate elderly Qʷiqʷasutinux̌ʷ woman of Alert Bay. She was in her eighties when we started our work in 1978, and she died in 1992 at the approximate age of 98 to 102.

What were our objectives and methods? Our primary objective was also ʔAx̌uw̓'s primary objective – that is, to fulfill her desire to record everything she was willing to tell for the written record. ʔAx̌uw̓ was acutely aware that the younger generations of Kʷakʷakəwakʷ people needed her help, as well as that of other elders, to ensure the continuity of cultural identity and traditions. We wanted to capture her verbal art in her native tongue, Kʷakʷala, and ensure the accuracy of the transcripts by having them translated by someone fluent in her language and culture. That person was her granddaughter Daisy (Mayaniɬ: Precious One), the daughter of Chief Jimmy Sewid and Flora Alfred, ʔAx̌uw̓'s second offspring. Given the growing interest of younger Kʷakʷakəwakʷ people in reclaiming their native language, we intend to transcribe phonetically the unedited original recordings at a later time.[13]

We wanted to hear from ʔAx̌uw̓ what it was like to live the life of a Qʷiqʷasutinux̌ʷ woman who had seen the end of the nineteenth century. We wanted to render the portrait of this five-times great-grandmother, who happened to be one of the last great storytellers of the Kʷakʷakəwakʷ people, as she would like to be remembered – in terms of her knowledge and life experiences, through the workings of her memory, and by mounting a memorial in words. Thus our work is an homage to ʔAx̆uw̓ and to all the talented Kʷakʷakəwakʷ storytellers for whom remembering meant not just drawing on rote or fossilized memory but engaging in an awesome creative activity. *Paddling to Where I Stand* represents our endeavour to capture, as accurately as possible, both ʔAx̆uw̓'s sparkling verbal waves and her equally intense moments of deep creative silence.

Our objective was *not* to write another anthropological interpretation of Kʷakʷakəwakʷ culture but, rather, to privilege ʔAx̆uw̓'s voice and ways of seeing, thereby providing a route to Kʷakʷakəwakʷ meaning. Through her words we also gain a better understanding of her awareness of the world. Our less immediate objective was to examine ʔAx̆uw̓'s sense of self, her identity. We know from previous studies in this field that pre-literate autobiographies put before us conceptions of the self that are often foreign to modern, individualistic societies. At a later date, in another publication, we will piece together a sense of who ʔAx̆uw̓ was, the substance of her self, both from her stories and from her narrative style.

In *Paddling to Where I Stand*, ʔAx̆uw̓'s narratives mean much more than "the course of a lifetime," and therefore we prefer the term "memoirs," her remember-ings (to remember: m̓əlqʷəla; memory: m̓əlg̓ʷəɬ). Her narratives allow us to see the remarkable complexity of Kʷakʷakəwakʷ life from the point of view of a Qʷiqʷasutinux̆ʷ woman and an accomplished storyteller – a life told through myth (n̓uy̓əm), chants, tribal and personal history, and episodes from other people's lives. The n̓uy̓əm include several versions of the Bax̆ʷbakʷalanux̆ʷsiwēy̓ (Man-Eating Spirit) paradigm[14] and several other myths, some of which could be considered as educational narratives (glix̆sʔalayuw̓) routinely told to young boys and girls (see Chapter 1). Historical accounts or news of particular events (c̓əkaləm) include, for example, the last deadly raid by the Bella Coola on the Qʷiqʷasutinux̆ʷ, which took place around 1850 at G̓ʷayasdəms on Gilford Island – a raid for which, ʔAx̆uw̓ confessed (thereby breaking decades of silence), her great-aunt might have been responsible. The consequences of the raid for the Mam̓aliliqəlla, G̓ʷawaʔēnux̆ʷ, D̓zawadaʔēnux̆ʷ, and Qʷiqʷasutinux̆ʷ continue to this day (see Chapter 2).

ʔAx̆uw̓ related intricate genealogies, making sure we understood the complex kinship relationships of the people about whom she talked. She recounted personal and tribal collective life experiences, such as her arrest (along with her husband Moses) for illegally participating in the notorious 1921 Village Island potlatch (see Appendix B). She shared her knowledge of culturally specific traits surrounding the complexity of the potlatch (see Chapter 7). Although ʔAx̆uw̓ spoke some Chinook,[15] she never used the word "potlatch" in her narratives as a "single named taxonomy category" (Berman 1996: 246), although this is common usage nowadays not only among Kʷakʷakəwakʷ people but also among the peoples of all other Northwest Coast cultures. Instead she used a variety of terms that referred to specific events that took place at specific times and for specific audiences. Examples of these include *pəsa* (to invest within your own tribal group), *ẏaqʷa* (to give upon witnessing rites of passage), and *maxʷa* (to invest among several tribal groups). She also told of the practice of witchcraft, its effects, and remedies.

Marriages took a prominent place in ʔAx̌uw̓'s narratives, with their complex formalities involving dowry and bride-price, as well as the usage of Coppers (see Chapters 5 and 6). Several types of marriages were described, such as the pre-arranged marriage performed for her future husband, Moses, when, as a child, he was married to a dead girl from the west coast of Vancouver Island (see Chapter 5). She related several episodes of other lives, including those pertaining to her two close relatives, one of whom was taken captive by the Bella Coola and later escaped and returned among her people, while the other was ransomed back immediately after her capture (see Chapter 2). ʔAx̌uw̓'s own life was revealed in her telling of important events, such as how she was married before having menstruated and how she had thirteen children (see Chapter 5). She revealed her intimate knowledge of the land and place-names of the Qʷiqʷasutinux̌ʷ (with their fishing sites, digging gardens, and hunting grounds) as well as her daily activities, her personal fears, joys, and emotions (see Chapter 3).

Who Was ʔAx̌uw̓ and Why Was She the Subject of Our Collaboration?

We do not know precisely when ʔAx̌uw̓ was born as there were no birth certificates for any First Nations children born in the late 1800s (i.e., before the arrival of a federal agency for the administration of Indian affairs). However, we do know that she gave birth to her first child, Alvin, in 1910, several years after her marriage to Moses Alfred, a union that occurred a few years before she had menstruated. Assuming that she married at the age of twelve or thirteen and gave birth to Alvin perhaps three years later, as she guessed, her birthdate might have been around 1894.[16] ʔAx̌uw̓'s father, G̓ʷutəlas, was a Mamaliliqəlla (both his parents were from Mimk̓ʷəmlis, Village Island); her mother, Puʌas, was part Nəmǧis (from Yəlis, or Alert Bay) and part Qʷiqʷasutinux̌ʷ (on her mother's side; from G̓ʷayasdəms, Gilford Island) (see Plates 1 and 2). She married Moses Alfred, Kodiẏ, a Kʷaguł from Fort Rupert, conferring upon her what she referred to as the fourth component of her identity. ʔAx̌uw̓ identified herself as a Qʷiqʷasutinux̌ʷ rather than a Mamaliliqəlla, thus stressing her matrilineage.[17]

Most of what we know about the Kʷakʷakəwakʷ comes from Boas and his disciples. His contribution to Kʷakʷakəwakʷ ethnography and ethnology is enormous, but he was also responsible for making a huge, somewhat confusing, generalization.[18] The people whom he visited on the northern tip and western corner of Vancouver Island and the adjacent mainland, and on the many islands situated in between, belonged to about twenty-eight well-defined local groups that he referred to as "tribes" (see map). They all spoke a common language: Kʷakʷala. As a nation, they called themselves then, as now, the Kʷakʷakəwakʷ; that is, the Kʷakʷala speakers. Because Boas worked mostly with the Kʷaguł of Fort Rupert[19] (home of the Kʷaguł proper) through his informant-interpreter George Hunt,[20] the whole nation became known as the "Kwakiutl" ("ancient smoke that brought people together at Qaluǧʷis"),[21] after the most common Anglophone spelling. But many of Boas's publications on the ethnology and ethnography of the Kʷakʷakəwakʷ people pertained not only to the Kʷaguł of Fort Rupert but also to the Nəmǧis of Alert Bay, the x̌awiċis of Turnour Island, the Qʷiqʷasutinux̌ʷ of Gilford Island, the Nakʷaxdax̌ʷ of Blunden Harbour, and so on. This also clarifies why ʔAx̌uw̓ called herself a Qʷiqʷasutinux̌ʷ and not a Kʷaguł. Whenever ʔAx̌uw̓ spoke about the Kʷaguł people as a tribe, she was referring specifically to the Fort Rupert people. In *Paddling to Where I Stand*, unless otherwise stated, we follow ʔAx̌uw̓'s use of the term Kʷaguł.

As so much anthropological literature on the Kʷakʷakəwakʷ originated from and revolved around the Kʷaguł and derived mainly from George Hunt and his close relatives,[22] and also because knowledge is highly localized and often private property, we thought that it would be enlightening to hear about the Kʷakʷakəwakʷ people from a different source. Although ʔAx̌uw̓ was in some ways remotely related to the Hunts, she made clear her tribal affiliation and her personal identity. Furthermore, she had not been "trained" as a professional informant and therefore was not anticipating the random questions from us.

The most important reason for selecting ʔAx̌uw̓ was her willingness to speak out. Although ʔAx̌uw̓ did not know how to read, she grew to know the power of the written word.[23] She had been made aware of George Hunt's writings, which were conducted in collaboration with Boas; and she had seen and learned to sing Christian hymns translated into Kʷakʷala. Furthermore, all of her children's Christian names seem to have been selected from "a book" (see Chapter 4); and, finally, she had contributed information to some of her granddaughter's (i.e., Daisy's) publications, which she acknowledged. ʔAx̌uw̓ was eager to pass on her life experiences and knowledge to her descendants, and we thought that her story could be used in some applied strategies for cultural continuity among the Kʷakʷakəwakʷ people. Through the teaching of tribal names and affiliations, kinship ties and relationships, respect for proper etiquette and behaviour in social and ritual circumstances, and through storytelling, ꓥAx̌uw̓ informed her descendants and generations to come on how to behave, how to survive, and how to adapt in a changing world white retaining their Native identity.

Upon closer examination we found that, besides wanting to pass on her knowledge to younger generations, ꓥAx̌uw̓, whether consciously or not, took the opportunity to clear up community rumours and set the record straight about certain facts and their consequences. She conveyed her feelings about what happened to others, and she demonstrated, particularly to the lower class (x̌amala: commoners, lower class), how knowledgeable she was about her cultural and personal history. In other words, she was putting forth "the last word" on several controversial subjects, and she was doing so in a format that would outlast her.

Paddling to Where I Stand is ꓥAx̌uw̓'s book. She titled it after one of her favourite names, Six̌ʷasuw̓, a potlatch name meaning, "Many People Are Paddling towards Me," which implies that many guests attended many pot-latches that were given by family members who passed the name on to her.[24] And she added, "Today when I am old, people are still coming towards me, but this time they are seeking my knowledge about my people."

Except for Chapter 7 ("Fragments of Recollections"), for which Daisy did not hesitate to ask a series of direct questions having to do with her "modern, new" life, our questions to ꓥAx̌uw̓ were few. Some questions remained unanswered. We wanted her memoirs to be her own, with us interfering and suggesting as little as possible. ꓥAx̌uw̓ told only what she wanted to tell. Sometimes reflective, she often commented on specific points, making sure that we understood them. Whether ꓥAx̌uw̓ discussed genealogy, marriage, or potlatch "rules," her intention was to inform, to reveal, to educate. Her silences were respected. Her sense of humour, her laughter, and her wit were recorded.

Since ꓥAx̌uw̓'s granddaughter, Daisy, was the primary translator, we greatly reduced the risk of producing a fictional character. We were very much aware of the fact that "all translation involves the cognitive and semantic categories of another language and culture" (Berman 1996: 248; see also Rubel and Rosman 2003). With Daisy as principal translator we greatly reduced the risk of distortion. Daisy grew up immersed in her culture and speaking her grandmother's tongue; she has witnessed and "lived" oral performances and has experimented extensive-ly in oral rendition. We were both aware of the implicit and explicit knowledge inherent in Kʷakʷakǝw̓akʷ texts. Daisy had recorded several elderly relatives in the past, and this led her to write and publish several articles as well as the well known *Prosecution or Persecution* (Sewid-Smith 1979), which deals with the anti-potlatch law and its consequences for the Kʷakʷakǝw̓akʷ people. Having been a

First Nations instructor for twenty years in School District 72 in Campbell River, Daisy researched and wrote a grammar book in order to aid the teaching of Kʷakʷala (Sewid-Smith 1988).[25]

As for me, the ethnographic qualifications I brought to the collaboration combined graduate training in anthropology received at the Paris École des Hautes Études en Sciences Sociales and the University of British Columbia, followed by several long sojourns among Kʷakʷakəwakʷ people (beginning in 1976), some rudiments of Kʷakʷala and international phonetics, and considerable enthusiasm for recording oral tradition, which I did with ʔAx̌uw̓ and other elderly Kʷakʷala speakers prior to meeting Daisy.[26] As our friendship grew deeper, the three of us decided to collaborate on ʔAx̌uw̓'s memoirs.

Paddling to Where I Stand is neither a classic ethnography nor a literary autobiography, as documented by Bataille and Sands (1984) in *American Women: Telling Their Lives*. It is not organized according to Western literary conventions, which usually entail ordering material in a linear, chronological sequence. ʔAx̌uw̓ did not present her stories in this way; rather, she had them move in and out of different time frames, having Daisy, other family members, and/or me as captivated listeners.

The chronology presented in *Paddling to Where I Stand* unfolds according to how ʔAx̌uw̓ saw herself and her life. ʔAx̌uw̓ lived to be about 100 years old. This means that, preceding her own memory (which spanned at least four generations)[27] and the memory of her immediate ancestors (which spanned another few generations) was myth time. Then, all animals, birds, fish, monsters, and humans spoke a common tongue, lived in great houses, and were honoured as the forebears of the Kʷakʷakəwakʷ Nation, lending their iconic images to the crests of the great human families. As ʔAx̌uw̓ grew from childhood to womanhood as the wife of a Kʷaguɫ nobleman, myth time slipped even further into the background, but the bond that secured her to her past and formed a pattern for her present was never broken. Until the end, from her home in the small fishing village of Alert Bay, her connection to her mythic past and to her people remained strong.

When ʔAx̌uw̓ spoke, we confronted an awesome compression of time. She was born one generation after the practice of slavery had ended and two generations before storytellers came to rely upon the written word. She made a very clear distinction between the times of myth (ńuy̓əm) (see Chapter 1); the times she had heard about but not experienced (c̓ək̓aləm) (see Chapter 2), and the times she had lived and known personally (see Chapters 3 to 7). This sequence formed the basic chronology of her memoirs, but her stories often wove the three time periods together in a non-linear way.

Because this is ʔAx̌uw̓'s book, we did not interrupt her voice in the body of the text. Our comments are restricted to each chapter's introduction and endnotes, which establish the context and explain obscure or untranslatable concepts to non-Kʷakʷ̓ala readers.

Style and Translation

Translation is far from being an absolute and accurate process. Given that perfect translation is impossible and that all translation is at best relative and disputable, our duty was to be as faithful as possible to ʔAx̌uw̓'s original words and intended meaning. Our task was to represent clearly and accurately ʔAx̌uw̓'s voice and views by making her text accessible without drastically altering the cultural framework within which she existed.[28]

Converting oral narratives to written text raises many questions related to content and form. ʔAx̌uw̓ spoke with at least two voices. (Chanting could be considered a third voice.) In her formal voice she followed the tradition of pure oral literature, the classic style of oral myths, legends, and historical accounts. We have tried our best to retain as much of ʔAx̌uw̓'s formal voice as is possible in the context of translations. By "context of translations," and in agreement with Bauman (1984: 10), we mean a context "in which the words spoken are to be interpreted as the equivalent of the words originally spoken [in Kʷakʷ̓ala]." A question remained: How should ʔAx̌uw̓'s narratives be put on the page, what kind of format should we employ? Several scholars have devised experimental written forms that attempt to capture a sense of the actual performance (Hymes 1977; 1990: 85). Some linguists have used literal, word-by-word translation, a kind of strict morphemic gloss, a procedure that "tends to cast its light entirely on language and leave literature in the dark" (Bringhurst 1999: 19). We have retained the format and presentation of the text that Westerners normally associate with prose or autobiographical accounts, that is, with sentences in paragraph style rather than in the form of a continuous narrative.

ʔAx̌uw̓'s classical style of speech, as opposed to her everyday style of speech, was marked by certain stylistic features, such as repetitions and quotative markers, whose functions range from the aesthetic and structural to the emotional (Hendricks 1993: 78-9). For this reason we have not edited out repetitions, even though some readers may find them tedious. As Nora and Richard Dauenhauer (1987: 15-16) have pointed out with regard to Tlingit oral literature, good oral composition involves the constant use of repetition. This is because repetition emphasizes main ideas, lends the story a musical rhythm and balance, and/or simply gives listeners a break so that they need not receive too much new information all at once. ʔAx̆uw̓ also used repetitions to aid her in oral composition, to give her time to think, and to enable her to formulate what was to come next. She often repeated the name of a place or person or certain anecdote in order to underscore a theme or idea. Some names were repeated over and over again in order to achieve a certain response from us or simply because it was integral to the story as she understood it and remembered it.

ʔAx̆uw̓ often made use of the quotative markers *la laʔi*, or *laʔum laʔi*, which can be translated as "they," "they say," "so they say it goes."[29] These often occur at the beginning or the end of her story. As Robert Bringhurst (1999: 113) points out, "the quotative casts a statement into narrative relief. It can suggest that what is said has been tested by tradition and found true, or warn that it bears no guarantee because it lies outside the speaker's own experience." And, sometimes, in order to add weight to her statement (or to abolish whatever doubt that could still exist as to its veracity), she would mention the name of a person/witness who had been involved in, or somehow related to, what she was saying.[30]

ʔAx̆uw̓'s daily speech was informal, that is, it did not require the conventional style with its oratorical qualities and the use of sacred names, as in the context of myth. In this voice she told us where she was born, where she grew up, and what she did during her childhood and adulthood (Chapter 3). At times the more formal style overlapped with the informal style. For example, once we asked her if an individual could be reincarnated in a descent group (*n̓əmayəm̓*) different from her/his own. After a long, reflective pause, she said she did not think so and immediately started telling a myth to prove her point. (ʔAx̆uw̓ would often respond to questions with a myth or, sometimes, with a chant.)

We hope that no colloquialisms[31] appear in ʔAx̆uw̓'s memoirs. Unfortunately, some readers have become accustomed to reading impoverished and/or clumsily translated Aboriginal stories. Such translations tend to reflect the childish level of English spoken by early First Nations storytellers. There was nothing childish in ʔAx̆uw̓'s speech. We are convinced that her grasp of Kʷakʷala was no less strong than was Shakespeare's grasp of English and that her tellings of the old tales would have resonated in the Kʷakʷakəwakʷ consciousness much as Homer's tellings would have resonated in the pre-literate Greek consciousness. Indeed, at times some of her language was ancient, revealing concepts and words no longer used by contemporary Kʷakʷala speakers. On numerous occasions we had to check and cross-check with other Kʷakʷakəwakʷ elders in order to determine the exact meaning of her archaic expressions.

The most salient aspect of ʔAx̆uw̓'s tellings was that they were not dead and buried somewhere in what we call the past. On the contrary, her oral testimonies were alive for her in her immediate present, and they seemed to have a life of their own that, in the form of guiding principles/experiences, simultaneously reflected the continuity of past, present, and future. Consider, for example, the closing of the myth given to her by Ǧʷəmǧəmlilas:

This is the myth [ńuy̓əm] that Ǧʷəmǧəmlilas passed on to me. She told it to me when Cuxʷča⸱esa, Duda's brother, brought out this haṁaća pole at his potlatch. They gave it as a dowry to Peter Smith. This was a dowry for Duda, the haṁaća pole called Səmsəmsid. That is how the haṁaća pole came to his [Peter Smith's] family. This pole is now owned by Lorne Smith, as it was given to him by his uncle as a dowry. This is all I know. This is what Ǧʷəmǧəmlilas told me. (M12)[32]

We have tried to preserve much of the flavour of ⸱Aх̌uw̓'s storytelling as it moved back and forth from tribal history, to myth, and to personal reminiscences; consequently, the written text became the story of our hearing her stories. We very much want our readers to be able to share something of what it was like for us to listen to ⸱Aх̌uw̓ telling stories. In light of the constitutive features of narrated North American Indian autobiography and of critical work surrounding the genre, we hope that our holistically oriented approach will result in a portrait of ⸱Aх̌uw̓ that mirrors her life as she saw it. Of course we should ask ourselves, to what extent have we, like others, created a fictional portrait? And if, indeed, we have created a fictional portrait, then we hope that it is as close to ⸱Aх̌uw̓'s reality as we could possibly have made it. Finally, we hope that *Paddling to Where I Stand* will contribute to preserving and transforming Kʷakʷakəwakʷ culture and that ⸱Aх̌uw̓'s memoirs will attest to the endurance of First Nations storytelling, even as it is transformed into a new literary form that, in its turn, enlarges our sense of life's possibilities.

Historical Context

⸱Aх̌uw̓ was born at a time of great change for her people, and *Paddling to Where I Stand* should be understood against this background. Contact with the Whites[33] (ṁaṁatła) was minimal before 1849, a time that marks the beginning of the colonial period (1849-71). It had been preceded by the maritime fur trade period, which started in the late 1700s.[34] The Kʷakʷakəwakʷ took an active part in the trade.[35] Fur traders were not interested in radically altering First Nations ways of life but, rather, in conducting the business of trading. As both "Europeans and Natives shared a mutually beneficial economic system," that period brought prosperity to First Nations, "an increase in wealth in a society already organized around wealth" (Duff 1964: 57). Historians have described this period as one that involved few disruptive cultural consequences for First Nations as they could easily control and adapt to the changes (Fisher 1977: xiv; Cole and Darling 1990: 119-34).

The colonial period was of a different nature from the fur trade period, however. It saw the encroachment of settlements and the establishment of the basic features of Indian administration – a series of major cultural changes that were profoundly disruptive because they took place so rapidly that First Nations "began to lose control of their situation. Gold miners, settlers, missionaries, and government officials," all in their own different ways, "required the Natives to make major cultural changes, and the Whites now had the power to force change" (Fisher 1977: xv).

The date of 1849 is important to the Kʷakʷakəwakʷ for several political and socio-economic reasons. "As Vancouver Island and British Columbia were British colonies quite separate from Canada, the imperial government saw the necessity of colonizing Vancouver Island in order to confirm British Sovereignty in the area" (Duff 1964: 60). The government entrusted this task to the Hudson's Bay Company[36] (whose chief factor was James Douglas), temporarily granting title of Vancouver Island to the company. James Douglas was governor from 1851 until 1864. In 1866 the two colonies were united into one, which, in 1871, entered Confederation as the province of British Columbia. It was during these two important decades that the basic features of Indian administration were established. By the time Douglas retired (1864), he had negotiated fourteen treaties with First Nations living around Victoria, Nanaimo, and Fort Rupert, and he had set aside a large number of reserves on Vancouver Island. In the late 1880s "Commissioner P. O'Reilly established several reserves for some bands of the Kʷakʷakəwakʷ and in effect formalized the Crown's claim to the rest of their aboriginal territory" (Codere 1990: 363).[37]

In 1849 coal (*dˀəğʷˀət*) was discovered at the company's post at Beaver Harbour. Fort Rupert was established there and was maintained until the late 1870s, when it was sold[38] to its last factor, Robert Hunt, the father of George Hunt, Boas's collaborator (Healey 1958: 19). When the fort was established, four tribes – later known as the Kʷaguɬ Confederation – moved back to their original site, forming the largest Kʷakʷakəwakʷ settlement at that time. Before long, this group constituted the centre of ceremonial activity. Fort Rupert maintained its central position until about 1900, when Alert Bay superseded it as the centre for the people of Queen Charlotte Strait. Alert Bay had its start as a White settlement in 1870, when two Europeans, Huson and Spencer, established a salmon cannery there and sought First Nations labour.

Pre-contact Kʷakʷakəwakʷ society consisted of what amounted to a ranked noble minority with hereditary titles, a commoner majority, and a small group of slaves (who were war captives). Slavery ceased to be practised in the 1860s, concomitant with the decrease of inter-tribal warfare. Although many rules brought by the Whites conflicted with the old customs, ʔAx̱uw̓ sighed with relief at one particular change – peace instead of war. In her own words: "Our people used to always have wars in the early days and to enslave their captives. We are so fortunate to be a peaceful people now. *Ayoho!* Peace, is good!" (see Chapter 2).

Inhabiting in remote places such as Village Island and Gilford Island, ʔAx̱uw̓'s ancestors lived according to the rhythm of the seasons and the accompanying salmon migrations, staying in large, permanent houses in the winter and seasonal camps in the summer. Summer was a time for fishing, gathering, and preserving food; winter was a time for "winter dances," where initiations and numerous other ceremonies would take place. The all-encompassing social, economic, political, and religious institution was the potlatch (a word derived from the Chinook trade language, meaning "to give") – a complex and long-lasting ceremony that celebrated important events in their lives (e.g., naming of children, marriage, transfer of rights and privileges, and mourning the dead). Large amounts of food were consumed and gifts were given to the guests who had come to witness these events. In each tribe there was a graded series of ranked positions, which determined the standings of individuals within the potlatch system.

During the 1850s and 1860s several disasters struck the Kʷakʷakəwakʷ. One of them that occupies a significant place in ʔAx̱uw̓'s memoirs related to the dramatic events that occurred around 1857 or 1858 when the village of Ǧʷayasdəms was destroyed and its inhabitants massacred by a Bella Coola raiding party (see Chapter 2). Another disaster of dramatic proportions for the entire First Nations Coastal population took place shortly after, in 1862, when the entire region was devastated by smallpox brought north from Victoria. Other introduced European diseases resulted in a population decline from nearly 10,000 to less than 3,000 by 1880 (Codere 1961: 439).[39] As Helen Codere (1990: 363) has shown, potlatching decreased in importance and frequency during these depressing years, resulting in the significant alteration of the complex hierarchical social structure. The population decline led to confusion around inheritance patterns and competition for many vacant high-ranking positions.

Less than twenty years prior to ʔAx̱uw̓'s birth, the Kʷakʷakəwakʷ had been exposed to Christianity. In 1877 the Anglican missionary, the Reverend Alfred James Hall, began work at Fort Rupert, although he soon moved to Alert Bay (in 1879) (Plate 18). ʔAx̱uw̓'s husband, Moses Alfred, went to the school founded by Reverend Hall some time after its creation in 1881. (Moses was, in fact, named after the reverend). Hall's home was large enough to accommodate several young girls, one of whom was ʔAx̱uw̓; Mrs. Hall taught these children "domestic duties." In Chapter 7, ʔAx̌uw̓ recounts her impressions of Reverend Hall, particularly how good he seemed to have been to the Nəmǧis. She also recalls the feast song based on a Christian hymn that he had composed and had taught to them in Kʷakʷ̓ala, in an attempt to convert them. He baptized ʔAx̌uw̓ quite some time after her marriage to Moses. By 1888 Reverend Hall had built a sawmill to provide employment and lumber for single-family houses; ʔAx̌uw̓, along with many of her relatives, worked there. In 1881 the federal government established a Kwawkewlth[40] Agency at Fort Rupert, but this too soon moved to Alert Bay. In 1894 the Department of Indian Affairs opened an industrial school for boys at Alert Bay. Meanwhile, Mrs. Hall's program had grown into a residential school for girls, which ʔAx̌uw̓ attended for a very short time (Healy 1958: 24-31; Halliday 1935: 229-32; Canada 1882: 171; Canada 1883: 161; Canada 1895: 158, 160; Codere 1990: 363).

As the frequency and intensity of contact with non–First Nations increased, many changes took place in Kʷakʷ̓akəwakʷ ways of life. With the conversion of many Kʷakʷ̓akəwakʷ to Christianity, First Nations religious beliefs began to change. Initially, the main effect of the early contacts and trading with Whites was to stimulate potlatching to even greater vigour. It brought increased material wealth, which increased the size of potlatches and, to some degree, altered the functions of this cultural institution. For many years the missionaries and the Indian Agents saw the potlatch as an evil institution, and in 1876 it was suppressed under Section 149 of the Indian Act, which forbade potlatching and winter dancing (Canada 1876). But the potlatch continued to be practised "underground" in the form of simulated Christmas events. This is made very clear in ʔAx̌uw̓'s narratives when she tells us that, shortly after her marriage to Moses and once they were established at Alert Bay, potlatch presents were hidden under the mattress or in the bathroom under the guise of being "Christmas presents" (see Chapter 6). Cultural conflict appears to have reached a peak in 1921 with renewed enforcement of the law against First Nations ceremonies, along with a deepening economic depression. As a result of this, forty-five Kʷakʷ̓akəwakʷ people, among them ʔAx̌uw̓ and Moses, were arrested for attending and participating at a potlatch that was held at Village Island in December 1921 (see Appendix C). In spite of the repeated attempts of the dominant culture, however, potlatching and winter dancing never died.[41]

Many features of White technology were adopted by Kʷakʷ̓akəwakʷ peoples. In 1911 power boats began to replace carved dugout canoes; modern single-family houses replaced many large multi-family houses. Emphasis upon the traditional social structure (e.g., the descent group [n̓əm̓ay̓əm: one blood; of the same blood]) began to change to emphasis on the nuclear family, and children were sent to non-Aboriginal schools to learn new ways. In 1867 an ordinance was passed that forbade First Nations people from using liquor. In 1919 Indian Agent Halliday (see Plate 17) mentioned that Moses Alfred was known to have sold liquor. Despite ʔAx̌uw̓'s disapproval, Moses started a small business that consisted of selling hard or fermented cider; later, to ʔAx̌uw̓'s delight, the business collapsed (see Chapter 5). In 1951 the Indian Act was revised and no longer forbade potlatching and winter dancing. Also in 1951 First Nations gained the right to purchase liquor and to vote in elections.

Kʷakʷakəwakʷ material and economic life changed rapidly and continuously after contact. Iron and steel replaced stone, shell, and sinew; animal skins and woven red cedar-bark and mountain-goat wool robes were replaced by the Hudson's Bay Company blankets, which were acquired in great numbers for potlatching. By the time ʔAx̌uw̓ was born in her father's traditional big house at Village Island, European clothing was in general use, although ʔAx̌uw̓ admitted that as a child she was always barefoot and took quite a long time to adjust to wearing shoes (see Chapters 5 and 7). The Kʷakʷakəwakʷ also became involved in the Canadian economy and thus more dependent on money income. Moses, along with a few partners, engaged in a series of personal businesses, first work-ing in a logging camp and later acquiring a fishing licence to operate his own fishing boat. ʔAx̌uw̓ herself worked in several canneries.[42] This development led to a period of great prosperity for the Alfreds and other Kʷakʷakəwakʷ who were involved in a cash economy between 1900 and the mid-1920s. ʔAx̌uw̓ very proudly told us that one component of her dowry consisted of $1,000 in gold coins (in Chinook jargon, *gildala*: gold dollars). "Wealth became widespread, primarily because the old organization of production, knowledge of local resources, and industrious habits fit the new opportunities offered, particularly those of the commercial fishing industry, which needed seasonal labor" (Haw-thorn, Belshaw, and Jamieson 1958: 109-10, qtd. in Codere 1990: 363). The high incomes that resulted purchased more Euro-Canadian goods, many in quantities that were used in potlatching. Examples of items that ʔAx̌uw̓ mentioned as being given away as potlatch goods included tables, pool tables, gramophones, dressers, and beds (see Chapter 6). However, Kʷakʷakəwakʷ prosperity suffered a setback in the 1920s, with the difficulty of financing powerboats. Difficulties lasted through the Depression, but the boom in the fishing industry during the Second World War restored prosperity (Codere 1990: 364; Kew 1990: 164).

During the 1950s, through the Canadian government, the Kʷakʷakəwakʷ were permitted to elect their own political leader and representatives, thereby starting to manage their own affairs through the implementation of economic programs within their own bands. (This in turn created some tension between elderly hereditary chiefs and "modern" elected chief councillors.) At present there are fifteen bands, each of which functions as an independent political unit committed to community and economic development (Cranmer-Webster 1990: 387). Potlatches are held mainly in Alert Bay, Campbell River, Comox, and sometimes in the remote villages of Kingcome Inlet and at Ḡ"ayasdəms (Gilford Island).

Another Canadian government policy of that time emphasized the paternal line of descent and therefore had a direct impact on women: those who married non-Indian men would lose their membership in their band. Such women were removed from official records and lost their claim to what they were entitled to, such as land, resources, and funds. This policy was rescinded in 1986, leaving the bands to decide how these women and their families should be reintegrated and their rights returned to them.

The political and economic upheaval of the mid-twentieth century had a dramatic impact on the population. In 1962, 75 percent of the K"ak"akəwak" were under the age of thirty-two, the majority of these youths having regrouped to Alert Bay, Fort Rupert, Kingcome Inlet, and Cape Mudge.

In 1978, the National Museum of Man in Ottawa returned the ceremonial paraphernalia that had been surrendered by the K"ak"akəwak" in 1922 in a bargain to obtain reduced sentences for the forty-five people who had been arrested at the 1921 Village Island potlatch (see Appendix C). The collection was divided and housed in two museums, the Kwagiulth Museum at Cape Mudge and the U'mista Cultural Centre at Alert Bay. These institutions "provided a locus for systematic community attempts to document and revitalize cultural life by recording oral histories, producing language and culture curricula, preparing exhibits, organizing and administering classes on cultural projects" (Cranmer-Webster 1990: 389).

Orthography

The English word "Kwakiutl" for K"aguɬ has its origin in the writings of anthropologist Franz Boas's "Census and Reservations of the Kwakiutl Nation" (1887) and is still in use today. According to Helen Codere (1990: 376), Boas used it to designate "four levels of classification":

1 The Kwakiutl group, those speaking the Kwakiutl language of the Kwakiutlan branch of the Wakashan family.[43]
2 The grouping of speakers of the Kwakiutl dialect (i.e., those who have been known to anthropology as the Southern Kwakiutl). See, for example, Wilson Duff 1964: 15.[44] The northern Kwakiutl are the Haisla, the Heiltsuk-speaking Haihais and Bella Bella, and the Owikeno. See Boas 1966: 37-41; Olson 1954.

3 The several groupings of the speakers of the Kwakiutl subdialect, which excluded the Nawitti and the Quatsino of the north and northwest of Vancouver Island.

4 The Kwakiutl tribe (Boas 1897: 330); that is, the four groupings of the speakers of the Kwakiutl subdialect, who had moved to Fort Rupert shortly after the Hudson's Bay Company established the fort in 1849.

To Boas's four classifications we should add a fifth: Kwakiutl also referred to the single subgrouping of those speakers of the Kwakiutl subdialect among the four groupings mentioned in 4 above, as their name was Walas Kwakiutl (the Great Kwakiutl). The name "Kwakiutl," for which, according to Helen Codere (1990: 376), there are more than twenty synonyms, has come to refer to more than it should; specifically, it has come to refer to the whole nation instead of to one subgroup. To avoid confusion, except when designating the Kʷaguł of Fort Rupert and the Walas Kʷaguł, the name Kʷaguł will be replaced by the term Kʷakʷakəwakʷ, which means Kʷakʷala speakers.

Kʷakʷala language uses many sounds that do not occur in English. More than half of the consonant sounds of Kʷakʷala have no counterparts in English. However, as linguist Wayne Suttles (1991a: 15) points out, "these different sounds make the distinction between one word and another, and therefore if Kʷakʷala is to be written so it can be read, its different sounds must be differentiated and represented in a consistent system of spelling." There are several ways of spelling Kʷakʷala, depending on which phonemic system we choose. Throughout this book (except in quotes taken from previously published material), words and names in Kʷakʷala are spelled according to the system used by the language program at the Carihi Secondary School in Campbell River. The University of Victoria initiated this language program, and this is the system that translator Daisy Sewid-Smith (1988), a Kʷakʷala speaker and teacher of the fundamentals of this language, has used in her teaching.

The forty-eight distinct sounds (not counting the glottal stop ʔ) of the Kʷakʷala language are symbolically represented as follows:

b	c	c̓	d	dᶻ	g	gʷ	ǧ	ǧʷ
h	k	k̓	kʷ	k̓ʷ	l	i̓	ł	
λ	ƛ	ƛ̓	m	m̓	n	n̓		
p	p̓	q	qʷ	q̓	q̓ʷ	s	t	t̓
w	w̓	x	xʷ	x̄	x̄ʷ	y	y̓	ʔ

The seven vowels are: a, e, i, o, u, ə, ē.

Appendix A presents a detailed linguistic key to the alphabet and to the Ḵʷak̓ʷala spelling used in this book. It also describes some of the sounds of this language in order to help with pronunciation.

At times, *Paddling to Where I Stand* may be difficult to read because of the many Ḵʷak̓ʷala names and words. This difficulty is exacerbated by the fact that Ḵʷak̓ʷakəwak̓ʷ people bear many names during their lives, depending on time and circumstances. These names are not mere tags but, rather, true epithets, which are descriptive of an individual's attributes and that offer revealing examples of how Ḵʷak̓ʷakəwak̓ʷ individuals see themselves. Individuals take a series of names of higher and higher rank as they grow older,[45] and each one usually reveals the person's sex, age group, descent group, rank or status, and (sometimes) role (e.g., chief or successor to the chief). Furthermore, for each individual, ʔAx̱uw̓ (Agnes Alfred's Ḵʷak̓ʷala daily, or secular, name as opposed to her ceremonial names) often remembered at least two and sometimes more Ḵʷak̓ʷala names in addition to her/his Christian name. As we wanted neither to dilute the flavour of the narratives nor to reduce the richness of ʔAx̱uw̓'s knowledge, we have used the Ḵʷak̓ʷala names for places and people as often as she did.

To enable the reader to follow ʔAx̱uw̓'s narratives easily, especially when she mentions relatives and other relevant persons, we present a cast of characters in the form of kinship diagrams (see Appendix E). ʔAx̱uw̓'s father, Ǧʷutəlas (People Coming towards His House for a Potlatch), was a full-blooded M̓am̓aliliqəlla; her mother, Puλas (Place Where You Are Satiated), was part Nəmǧis and part Qʷiqʷasutinux̱ʷ. ʔAx̱uw̓ was married to Moses Alfred (Kodiẏ), a Ḵʷaguł from Fort Rupert whose mother was Nəmǧis. The M̓am̓aliliqəlla are indigenous to M̓im̓kʷəmlis, Village Island; the Nəmǧis are indigenous to Yəlis, Alert Bay; the Qʷiqʷasutinux̱ʷ are indigenous to Ǧʷayasdəms, Gilford Island; and the Ḵʷaguł are indigenous to Fort Rupert (see map).

Kʷakʷakəẃakʷ Peoples in the Nineteenth Century

Presented in geographical order from north to south (see map).

1	Gʷasəlla	Smith Inlet
2	Nakʷaxdax̌ʷ	Nugent Sound
3	Gʷawaʔēnux̌ʷ	Watson Island, Hope Town
4	Həx̌ʷaməs	Wakeman Sound
5	Dᶻawadaʔēnux̌ʷ	Kingcome Inlet
6	Qʷiqʷasutinux̌ʷ	Gilford Island
7	Danaxdax̌ʷ	Knight Inlet
8	ʔAwiƛəla	Knight Inlet
9	Maṁaliliqəlla	Village Island
10	Madiłbey (or Maʔəmtagila)	Qaluǧwis (Turnour Island)
11	Nəmǧis	Nimpkish River
12	ƛawičis	Turnour Island

Kʷaguł from Fort Rupert

13	Gʷitəlla or Kʷix̌amut
14	Q̇umuẏoʔiẏ or Kʷix̌a
15	Walas Kʷaguł
16	Qʷəmk̇utəs

Nəwidiẏ People

17	ƛaƛasiqʷəlla	Hope Island
18	Nəqəmgəlisəlla	Cape Scott
19	Yuƛinux̌ʷ	Scott Islands (Cox and Lanz)

Gʷaċinux̌ʷ Sound People

20	Ǧusgimux̌ʷ	Koskimo Bay (Qʷattis)
21	Gʷaċinux̌ʷ	Forward Inlet
22	K̇op̓inux̌ʷ	Koprino Harbour
23	ƛaskinux̌ʷ	Klaskino Inlet

Liǧiłdax̌ʷ People: Cape Mudge and Campbell River

24	Wiweqey	Topaze Harbour (Cape Mudge)
25	Wiweqəm	Topaze Harbour (Campbell River)
26	Kʷix̌a	Phillips Arm
27	ƛaʔaluis	Arran Rapids
28	X̌ax̌amaċəs	Salmon River
or		
28	Walacəm	Campbell River, Comox

Paddling to Where I Stand

1

Myth Time

Introduction

Kʷakʷakəwakʷ mythology is both rich and complex. During his fifty years of research on the Kʷakʷakəwakʷ, Franz Boas collected and published what Helen Codere (1966: 299) refers to as "the entire corpus of Kwakiutl mythology in Kwakiutl text and English translation." This statement may sound rather excessive, especially if Codere is referring to the mythology of not only the Fort Rupert Kʷaguł but also of the whole Kʷakʷakəwakʷ nation. Boas's major publications on Kʷakʷakəwakʷ mythologies include: *Indianishe Sagen von der nordpacifischen Küste Amerikas* (1895; 2002);[1] *Social Organization and Secret Societies of the Kwakiutl Indians* (1897), which contains a large amount of mythological material; *Kwakiutl Texts* (Boas and Hunt 1902-5); *Kwakiutl Texts* (Boas and Hunt 1906); *Kwakiutl Tales* (1910); *Kwakiutl Tales, New Series* (translation 1935, texts 1943). His final work on the Northwest Coast was on Kʷakʷakəwakʷ mythology and was entitled *Kwakiutl Culture as Reflected in Mythology* (1935). Boas also collected some other myths and material from linguistically related neighbouring groups such as the Bella Bella (*Bella Bella Texts* 1928; *Bella Bella Tales* 1932a) – material that sheds some light on particular features of myths, especially those that were introduced into Kʷakʷakəwakʷ mythology either through marriage or war.

As has previously been said, women are far from having equal representation in the overall record of Native North American oral literature, a fact corroborated by Margaret Blackman (1982: 6) and Robert Bringhurst (1999: 205). When it comes to oral literature, we are faced with a dearth of material about Kʷakʷakəwakʷ women. Most of the Kʷakʷakəwakʷ oral literature recorded by Franz Boas originated from George Hunt, and later material was also obtained from male informants (Charles Nowell, edited by Clellan Ford [1941]; James Sewid, edited by James Spradley [1969]; and James Wallas, edited by Whitaker [1981]). However, there exist a few rare cases of Kʷakʷakəwakʷ[2] stories that were told by women, the recordings of which took place far away from their home base. It seems that, in earlier times, male storytellers spoke more freely to visiting male linguists than did women. Women were reluctant to speak to foreigners as such behaviour would have been considered to be improper, especially if the foreigners were male. Furthermore, it is said that family traditions were secretly guarded, and their telling was the prerogative of the eldest daughter of a family.

This perhaps also explains why, when a woman was the source of ethnographic information, her identity was not always made clear. According to recent information from Randall Bouchard and Dorothy Kennedy (2002: 351), some of Boas's early collection of myths (1895), which were told by George Hunt, actually "came from George Hunt's sister, who was married to Mr. Spencer, a cannery owner at Alert Bay." Very little information was given about Mrs. Spencer except that her mother was an "Indian."[3] During the same period, another Kʷaguɫ woman was recorded at Alert Bay; she told Boas "the heroic deeds of the Mink" (Rohner 1969: 45; see "Mink Legend" in Bouchard and Kennedy 2002: 353-7). Another Kʷakʷakəwakʷ woman storyteller to be recorded in Kʷakʷala was named Qasalas. She told her "family story" to George Hunt. The story (both transcript and translation) is in Boas (1910: 400-13). Ten years later Hunt reported to Boas on how he came by a rare example of a woman's storytelling in "The Wail of Llal!Eqwaila, a GwaʔsEla Woman," which was published with transcript in Boas and Hunt (1921: 836-85). Hunt took notes on her "cry song" (*laḡʷaləm*),[4] a kind of recitative. According to George Hunt's 4 July 1916 letter to Franz Boas:

I hear a woman crying for the Death of her Brother. and in her crying she start to tell the whole History of her family. she Began from the Whale before it turn into a man. and this man came to marrie to the Kwaguɫ tribe. She kept on crying or singing from 7 o clock until nearly 3 o clock. and after she finished. I went to her and asked her if I could write the story of her cry song. she said that she would be proud of it ... no Body is allowed to sing it But the oldest Daughter of the family she Belongst to. (Hunt 1916)

According to Judith Berman (1996: 233), "Hunt reported that he obtained seventeen generations of the genealogy in the song while the woman was in Fort Rupert, and then undertook a journey to Smith Inlet to obtain the remaining five generations from her after she had returned home."[5] Hunt transcribed two other stories by two other Kʷakʷala-speaking women, K'amax̱alas and 'Man'manliqalas (Boas 1930, vol. 1: 246-50, vol. 2: 241-6; Boas 1935-43, vol. 1:

17-23, 58-61, 219-27, and vol. 2: 15-21, 59-61, 209-18). One might ask if there was formerly a distinct women's tradition of narrative art in the Kʷakʷala language.

The following small corpus of myths (ńuẏəm), far from exhausting ʔAx̌uw̓'s repertoire, is the result of two phases of fieldwork and corresponds to two sets of recordings. The first set was recorded at Agnes Cranmer's house at Alert Bay in 1977-8, always in her presence; on several occasions other persons, friends, or relatives would witness the storytelling and recording. The second set was recorded in the context of her memoirs but as part of an audiovisual recording session that was conducted in the presence of Daisy Sewid-Smith in Campbell River in 1985 at the house of her mother, Flora Sewid, ʔAx̌uw̓'s second offspring. As mentioned earlier, the first recordings were conducted before the decision had been taken to record and transcribe ʔAx̌uw̓'s memoirs. Our initial interest had been to record and research myths and beliefs pertaining to the aquatic realm. For easy reference we identify the myths as M1, M2, M3, M4, and so on, and we present them in the order in which they were told. As we shall see, the aquatic mythic landscape reveals Q̓umugʷēẏ (Lord of the Sea), the custodian of the wealth of the ocean, which includes Copper and abalone shell (M8), and a wide range of different supernatural creatures in some way associated with the ocean (M1, M5, M10).

The second set was videotaped so as to record ʔAx̌uw̓'s body language[6] in the context of storytelling. Both sets were translated by Daisy Sewid-Smith. Several of these myths echo those that were collected by Boas a century before. For those interested in comparing this material with earlier versions, we identify the latter in endnotes.

The myths that ʔAx̌uw̓ told us in the context of her life story have been left in the body of the narratives forming her memoirs. Therefore, this chapter, which we have entitled "Myth Time," stands on its own and offers the reader an insight into ʔAx̌uw̓'s vision and experience of the mythic world, her traditions and beliefs, her narrative style, and the sounds of Kʷakʷala words and names.

It seems that, according to Boas, events described in ńuẏəm took place before the end of the so-called myth age (Boas and Hunt 1902-05: 111; Berman 1992). What Boas referred to as myth, tradition, tale, legend, and history belongs to the Kʷakʷakəwakʷ ethnoliterary category of ńuẏəm,[7] a very diverse category with several subdivisions, all of which had different functions in social life (Berman 1992: 148).

One of those subdivisions was sometimes called ńuẏəmił, literally, "tradition in the house" (Boas 1947: 250).[8] According to Berman (1992: 148), "house stories describe how a descent group ancestor acquired certain names, crests, and other important privileges in the myth age. House stories are owned by the descent group (or by the chiefly lines within the descent group) in the same way that chiefly names and crests are." Therefore they formed an important component of Kʷakʷakǝwakʷ cultural property (see Myth 8). Such ńuẏǝmił, particularly those of Chiefs Henry Bell and Jimmy Sewid, were recorded during Daisy's wedding ceremony and are provided in Appendix D. Another type of house story (M10 and M15) features an adolescent hero who journeys across the sea into the mountains to encounter a supernatural being. This being will eventually yield to the hero the treasure he seeks (J. Berman 1992: 148).

A second major subdivision of ńuẏǝm involves the animal stories. In these the actors are the ńuxʷnińis, or "Story People," animal beings who possess odd powers and abilities, such as the buffoon-like Mink, x̌isǝlagilakʷ, son of the Sun (M3; M7; M15).[9] The Story People linger on the threshold between human and animal form and live in beachside villages, more or less like humans. According to Berman (1992: 148), "the narratives about them do not name crests or descent groups or often even tribal names, though many refer to particular village sites. If they have an etiological theme, it generally refers to something, which affects a wide range of creatures: wind and weather, fish, and so on" (M3; M17). According to Berman (1992: 148):

These two subdivisions stand in opposition to each other. House stories explain the public symbols of rank, wealth, and privilege, while the audience of animal stories is usually informal and domestic. Etiologies in the animal stories describe change. The outcomes of these stories – the barrenness of mountain summits, the cyclical rhythm of the tides – are stages of existence, which did not exist at the beginning of time, but were brought about by the narrated events. In contrast, the etiologies in the house stories describe continuity. The chiefly crests and privileges acquired in the stories existed at the beginning of time, and have been handed down to the present unchanged. At most they were merely transferred from spirit to human ancestor. That is probably the reason house stories are sometimes also called ńuẏǝmbalis, "stories from the (beginning) end of the world." (See also Boas 1921: 1351-52.)

A third subdivision consists of stories about Ɋaniqilakʷ,[10] a fabulous, supernatural being with bird-like wings and extraordinary properties. Ɋaniqilakʷ is the Transformer, whose actions bring an end to the myth age. "Ɋaniqilakʷ journeys from village to village, in a north-south direction, encountering all kinds of characters on his way, including the animal-people and descent group ancestors" (Berman 1992: 148). According to Daisy Sewid-Smith, Ɋaniqilakʷ transformed people with evil thoughts into compassionate people; he is also responsible for the present shape of the ratfish who, originally, was an insolent man and who, after transformation, became useless to human beings (except for providing them with hair oil).[11]

The reader will identify myths that share several themes. They typically portray a named individual, usually male, who seeks supernatural creatures' abodes in the wilderness, confronts them, and receives supernatural treasures, or ƛugʷéy̓ (M15). These treasures often come as a set of four – four being the privileged number in Kʷakʷakawakʷ thought.[12] These treasures are all-powerful and take different forms: the water of life (q̓ʷəlasta, deriving from q̓ʷəla: alive) has the power to restore the dead to life, and the mortally wounded are resuscitated after being sprinkled with it; the supernatural wand is a never-failing harpoon (səgayu mastuw̓); and the death bringer (halayuw̓) is a formidable weapon (M10).[13] The last given treasure is wealth in the forms of inexhaustible provisions of food and animal pelts. The forms of supernatural beings are as diverse as are their powers. Sometimes the encounter results in the individual receiving a crest. Some myths establish the right to a particular dance and the paraphernalia attached to it, as they are transferred to their rightful owner (M8).

ʔAx̌uw̓ recounted legends that could be considered educational narratives (glix̌sʔalayuw̓), stories that were routinely told to young children. The hunting myth (M15) could have been intended for young boys, while the Nəmǥis story (M1) could have been intended for girls as well as for boys. It portrays a female child who, after throwing a tantrum, is taken to the underworld where she meets frightening monsters whom she later discovers are the Halibut People. The aquatic landscape reveals the underworld, its inhabitants, and the rituals of proper eating, namely, how to properly treat food remains. In everyday life the Kʷakʷakawakʷ always respectfully disposed of fish remains by throwing them back into the ocean – an action that they believed guaranteed the reincarnation of the Fish People in their fish form so that they would return to the rivers and streams year after year and offer themselves to people as food.

A fundamental belief held by the Kʷakʷakawakʷ and all First Nations on the Northwest Coast relates to the concept of transformation. In myth time, humans and animals were said to have shared the same faculties. Not only were they capable of communicating with each other, but they were also able to exchange physical forms. Animals depicted in myths have a social and ritual existence parallel to that of human beings: they live in villages and houses, celebrate the winter dances, and wear masks. ʔAx̌uw̓'s narratives give us convincing descriptions of her supernatural universe (M5) and, at times, have a surreal quality (M1, M5). Typical transformations include changing from being dead to being alive, being sick to being healthy, being poor to being rich, being animal to being human, being human to being animal, being animal to being things (e.g., a rock, a pine needle, a wedge, etc.).

Some myths seem to have what we would call a moral ending: M5 shows an unfaithful wife and her lover being killed by her husband. Rivalry between elder and younger siblings is also a common theme to several of the myths told by ʔAx̆uw̓. Adultery (or, more specifically, incest with a first cousin) and jealousy between elder and younger brothers leading to a murder is the theme of another (M6). In M2 a boy who is deserted by his father and stepmother because his body is covered with sores survives and becomes prosperous thanks to his compassionate grandmother's help, while the very people who neglected him are left dying of hunger.

The Raven and the Mink play the role of trickster, or catalyst, embodying human characteristics such as cleverness, curiosity, wit, foolishness, humour, dignity, and despair (M3; M17; M18). Some myths tell of acquiring power and gifts from supernatural beings. A self-moving canoe is given to a man who marries the daughter of a chief. (This woman is said to have a strong copper scent.) Interestingly, the Copper Chief lives in a country completely lacking any kind of wood (M16). Other stories portray Mouse Woman as the messenger of supernatural beings (M8; M9).

ʔAx̆uw̓ told several versions of the Baxʷbakʷalanuxʷsiwēy̓ myth,[14] all of which share common features: A lazy boy struck by his father leaves for the forest and encounters Baxʷbakʷalanuxʷsiwēy̓, an ogre referred to as the Man-Eating Spirit, from whom he will acquire the hamaċa ritual. Considerable attention has been given to the etiology of the ogre's name. Baxʷbakʷalanuxʷsiwēy̓ (Boas: "Cannibal at the river mouth") is based on a folk etymology that interprets baxʷbakʷala as "eating humans" and the suffix -xsiu as "river mouth."[15] The spirit name comes from the northern neighbouring and related language Owikeno, in which baxʷbakʷala means "becoming increasingly human" and the suffix -xsiu means "passing through an aperture" (Hilton and Rath 1982; Berman 1992: 128), probably in reference to the process of initiation. As has been pointed out by Martine Reid (1981), in order to be a cannibal, Baxʷbakʷalanuxʷsiwēy̓ would have had to be human; being non-human, he is merely a predator. Boas (1966: 173) literally translates Baxʷbakʷalanuxʷsiwēy̓ as "having the eating of men at the mouth of the river, who resides with his relatives in the high mountains"; another of his translations is "Cannibal-at-the-North-End-of-the-World." A better gloss of the Kʷakʷakəwakʷ etymology of Baxʷbakʷalanuxʷsiwēy̓ might be "Man-Eating Spirit at the Mouth of the River."

Below is the list of ńuy̓əm in the order they were told by ʔAx̆uw̓.

M1 — Ṗoy̓: The Halibut People (Nəmǧis)
M2 — x̓əmqisəla: The Boy Whose Body Was Covered with Scabs (ʔAwiẋinux̆ʷ)

The following myths were narrated by ʔAx̌uw̓ and recorded in 1977 and 1978 at the house of Agnes Cranmer, Alert Bay. Interestingly, ʔAx̌uw̓ began talking about beliefs surrounding the killer whales:

M̓im̓ax̌ʔinux̌ʷ: Killer Whales

Our ancestors respected the *m̓im̓ax̌ʔinux̌ʷ* (killer whales)[16] very highly. They never teased them as people do today. Nowadays they shoot them and abuse them. In the early days they believed in the world of the *m̓im̓ax̌ʔinux̌ʷ*. They would not dare to kill them. If they teased them, they would not forget. The *m̓im̓ax̌ʔinux̌ʷ* would not forget. If you treat them well, they will treat you well.

One day, a friend of the *m̓im̓ax̌ʔinux̌ʷ* drowned. A *m̓ax̌ʔinux̌ʷ* knew he was under the sea. He was the only one who knew the drowned man was under the sea. So the *m̓ax̌ʔinux̌ʷ* decided it would be better to get him to the shore, so that his relatives would know what had happened. That was the *m̓ax̌ʔinux̌ʷ*'s idea. Because the *m̓im̓ax̌ʔinux̌ʷ* are people, they have minds like people. This *m̓ax̌ʔinux̌ʷ* wanted to make sure that his friend's body received a proper funeral from his people, if they wanted to give him one. The *m̓ax̌ʔinux̌ʷ* did not put him right on the shore. He and other *m̓im̓ax̌ʔinux̌ʷ* brought him to the surface and waited for the incoming tide. They kept pushing the body up until the waves washed it ashore. That is what they say. This is not a *n̓uy̓əm* [myth]; it is just *q̓aʔy̓uɫ*.[17] That is it.

M1 – P̓oy̓: The Halibut People

Nəmǧis Version

There was a little girl living at ʔUdᶻolas, a village located up the Nəmǧis River. One night she threw a tantrum. Her parents went to bed and called her to join them. But she would not go to bed. She continued her tantrum, so they left her sitting up all night alone. Sometime during the night she was dragged into the underworld [*bibəṅaǧaw̓ey̓*].

When her parents woke up they could hear her crying. As they went to look for her, to their surprise she was not there. But they could still hear her sobbing. It seemed to them that her cries were coming from underground.

The father started to dig, following the cries of his daughter. As he was digging deeper and deeper, her cries became fainter and fainter. The little girl had been taken deep into the underworld. There she cried all the more when she saw the people surrounding her. Their faces were all twisted and ugly. There was not one that was not ugly. They had twisted mouths and they were cross-eyed. The little girl kept crying because, by now, she was terrified.

The ugly people introduced her to a little girl who was about the same age as she was. She was not as frightening as the others were because her face was not as horrible as theirs and eyes were not crossed. The little girl took her by the hand and led her into the underworld. She was dragged into the underworld because she threw a tantrum, for it was said that children would go to the underworld if they threw tantrums. She was there for many years, and she got to enjoy it because she became fond of her little friend, whose eyes were not really crossed. Her friend was about the same age as she was and was the one who looked after her in the underworld.

The underworld people lived in a house that was built like our own traditional houses. One day, there was a great thunder-like noise on the roof of the house. The people grabbed some poles to push open the roof of the house. When they opened the roof, many fishing lines appeared, with things attached to their ends, and reached the floor of the house. The little girl looked at the lines. She was asked if she could recognize her father's halibut hooks. "Yes, of course I can recognize them," said the little girl. The underworld people then picked up a line and smelled it and cast it aside, saying it stank. All of a sudden the little girl pointed at one of the lines. "These are the ones," she said, "these are my father's halibut hooks. I recognize them." Two underworld people were told to grab hold of the hooks and hang on. The father pulled up his lines and dragged on board two huge halibut. He cast the two lines again, and two more underworld people were told to grab hold of the lines.

Suddenly the little girl realized that all these years she had been living among the Halibut People. Her father had, by then, four great big halibut. You could hardly see the top of his head emerging from his canoe for all the halibut he had caught.

"Come here," the people said to the little girl. "You will be next with your friend. She is going to return you to where you belong. Your parents certainly miss you very much. You are going to go home," they said to the little girl. "Your little friend is going to return with you to your home. Whatever you do, take good care of her flesh. Save every one of her bones. Do not lose one piece of bone. You will cast her bones very carefully into the sea near where you live," they said to the little girl. She grabbed hold of one of her father's halibut hooks and her little friend did the same. The father pulled the line up and almost fell into the sea from shock when he saw his daughter at the end of the line. He picked up his daughter and made her comfortable in his canoe. "Please do not club my friend," she said to her father. He took the little halibut gently off the hook. The little girl sat at the bow of the canoe, and her little halibut friend came flapping to where she was sitting.

When the father returned to the village, the mother could not believe her eyes when she came down to meet him and found that her daughter was part of her husband's catch.

They say that the little girl had been gone for four years; but in her mind she had only been gone for a short time. She carried her little halibut friend up to her house and said that no one but her was to eat the flesh, for that was the order given to her by the Halibut People. She laid a mat down, a mat that they used to use long ago when they were eating or feasting. They call the eating mat yəbəluẃ. And on this mat she placed every bone. When she was finished, she picked up the mat and went down to the sea, to say farewell to her friend. As soon as she cast the bones of her little friend into the sea they came back together as a little halibut, who swam home to her people. This is a Nəmǧis story, for this was supposed to have happened at ʔUdˀolas.

M2 – λ̓əmqisəla: The Boy Whose Body Was Covered with Scabs[18]

ʔAwikinux̌ʷ Version

There was a child living with his stepmother, and his name was λ̓əmqisəla, meaning filthy or dirty body. This was the name that his stepmother gave him because his body was covered with scabs and sores. Because of this she did not like him very much and she did not feed him properly. When she fed him, she only gave him fish bones with a bit of flesh on them. Whenever his stepmother gave him these bones, he hid them and did not eat them. He suffered so much from his scabs. He would go down to the river to fish and every day he would catch a lot of fish and leave them on the shore. Every day he would leave the fish lying there on the shore.

One day, when he came back from fishing, he noticed that of those fish he had caught earlier there was not one left. He did not know who had taken them. He had to catch his own fish because he was hungry and because his stepmother did not feed him properly. Four times this happened to him. Four times his fish disappeared after he had left them lying on the shore. By the fourth time, he felt very sorrowful – more so because his stepmother hated him so bitterly.

The stepmother started urging his father and everyone else to abandon the village and leave the boy behind. The father cared more for his wife than he did for his own son, so he went and told everybody to leave their village; they all left by canoes and settled down at another village site. The boy, whose body was covered with scabs, had a grandmother, and before she left, she went to get what they call *saǥəm*, a substance that works like coal. It would burn for a long time, not just for a few hours. The grandmother went over to the fire to burn some of her personal things that she would not need, and, when no one was looking, she took the *saǥəm*, and put it in a clamshell. She closed the clamshell and put it near a post. She whispered to her grandson and told him what she had done so that, after they had left, he could use the *saǥəm* whenever he wanted to start a fire. She told him that she did not want to leave him alone. She even tried, at the last minute, to stay behind with him, but the others would not listen, and they seized her and put her in one of the canoes. When the canoes were out of sight, the boy went to the clamshell his grandmother had mentioned. He opened it and started blowing at the *saǥəm* to get it to burn. Then he went into the forest and got some logs, from which he split some planks to build himself a shelter. That night he went to sleep.

He woke up at the sound of an eagle and found that he was living in a big traditional house. Something magical had happened. The house was huge and superbly built with totem poles standing in front of it. An eagle was perched on top of one of the poles. Lying on the beach was a halibut that the eagle had recently caught and dragged ashore. The bird was very much alive, sitting on top of this boy's supernatural gift [ƛugʷéy]. The totem pole was supernaturally bestowed upon this unfortunate boy.

The boy's scabs got worse. He went down to the beach and dragged up from the shore the big slimy halibut that had been left there. He scraped the slime off the halibut's body and rubbed it all over himself. As soon as he did this, his scabs vanished. He cut a piece of halibut and prepared it for his meal. From that day on, he never wanted for food. Whenever he needed food the eagle would fly down from his perch and, with no effort, catch whatever the boy wanted. He would catch ǧ^wəy̓əm [whale], m̓igʷat [seal] – all the rich traditional foods that they ate long ago. In a short time the boy became quite prosperous, and the scabs that used to cover his body were completely healed.

Meanwhile, the boy's father and his people were very impoverished in their new village, while he, the one they had deserted, never wanted for anything. He always had cooked seal on hand. After each meal he would throw his scraps on the ground. One day, as he was sitting on the threshold of his house, the Raven appeared and started eating his scraps. The boy noticed the Raven and spoke to him, saying, "I wish you were human and could talk, for I would ask you about the old woman. I would ask you about my grandmother, for I would like to know where she is and how she is doing." The Raven answered: "I am human. And your grandmother is suffering because she is living in a state of poverty where she is now. She always has to go to the back of the island on which she lives in search of food. And she is sobbing constantly. Every day she goes to the back of the island to try to dig a few clams. Your father and his people have no food. They are starving." The boy said to the Raven: "You had better come in, and I will give you something to eat." After the bird had finished his meal, the boy tied four containers full of seal meat on the Raven's back and instructed him to deliver them to his grandmother.

The Raven flew away until he came in sight of the old woman; he landed near her, carrying the precious load the boy had tied to his back. He came closer to the old woman and started picking at the few clams she had dug up. She picked up rocks and threw them at the Raven to chase him away. The Raven spoke to the old woman: "Do not throw rocks at me," he said. "Come over and untie what has been sent to you by the boy you deserted. He has plenty of everything now; he is overburdened with wealth. He has everything he needs where he is staying. He was fortunate to have had bestowed upon him a huge house embellished by two heraldic poles. An eagle is always perched on top of one of the poles and is always catching whatever the boy needs in the way of food." The old woman ran to the Raven, stumbling as she went, and untied the parcel containing the seal meat. She started to eat it, for she was very hungry. She put what was left over in her basket and covered it with the few clams that she had gathered. When she reached home, she went directly to the mat she had been weaving, and she turned her back to her family.

She had a grandchild, the daughter of her son's hateful wife. The granddaughter noted that the old woman seemed to be eating something. "What is the matter with the old lady?" she said. "I think she is eating something." The old woman got angry with her and said: "What could I have been eating?" The granddaughter decided to scrupulously watch the old woman, who soon tried to sneak a bite of food. The girl ran up to her and searched her. "I told you she was eating something," she said. "Look at the seal meat that she has been eating!" The old woman became so angry that she took the fire tongs and started beating the girl on the head. "These provisions were sent by the boy whose body was covered with scabs," she said to her granddaughter, "the boy you deserted, the boy you left behind."

The boy had received many more supernatural treasures [ƛ́ugʷēẏ]. Among them were q̓ʷəlasta, the water of life, and the halaẏuʷ, the death bringer. These are the treasures he was fortunate enough to have received. When the father heard how wealthy his son had become, he told his people that they should all return to their original village. His son was now prosperous and completely healed of all his scabs.

The boy was standing outside his house when he saw his father and his people approaching in their canoes. The boy turned to the eagle sitting on the top of the heraldic pole and told him to go ahead and fetch his father, his stepmother, and his stepsister. The eagle returned, holding the boy's stepmother in his claws and then placing her on the shore. The boy retrieved from his house all the fish bones that his stepmother had given him for food. He ran down to his stepmother and threw into her face the very bones with which she used to feed him. This was how he repaid her for the way she had treated him. He had the eagle pick her up and throw her into the sea. She was being repaid for all the things she had done to him.

He realized that it was the eagle who was now making him prosperous and who had been eating his freshly caught fish early on. He saved his grandmother and his people from starvation, but, because of their wickedness, he had the eagle throw his father and stepsister into the sea. He saved his people and lived among them.

M3 – ƛisəlagilakʷ [the Mink] and Dˀaq̓ʷalanukʷ [the Northwest Wind]

It is said that at one time, the forces of Dˀaq̓ʷalanukʷ,[19] the owner of the Northwest Wind, always beset our world. The Northwest Wind was always blowing. It never calmed down. The Mink, ƛisəlagilakʷ [Born-To-Be-the-Sun], was angered by this state of affairs and decided that he should have a little talk with the owner of the Northwest Wind. He hired Təq̓ʷa [the Octopus], Ṅən [the Grizzly Bear], X̌ʷəmdiẏ [the Land Otter], and P̓oẏ [the Halibut], to accompany him on his visit to the owner of the Northwest Wind. They were a party of four. As it was impossible to paddle a canoe because of the constant forces of the Northwest

Wind, they had to pull it along the cliff. So he hired these particular companions precisely for their respective qualities.

The Land Otter had a very strong grip, which is why x̣isəlagilakʷ hired him. He covered only one bay, and then the Grizzly Bear took over. He had very strong hands too, and managed to pull the party past two more bays. Next was the Octopus. He used only one of his eight arms at a time, gripping the cliff with his suction cups. When one arm got tired he would replace it with another. By these means x̣isəlagilakʷ and his team finally arrived at the house of the owner of the Northwest Wind. They took the Halibut and laid him flat in front of the door, with his tail still in the canoe. This was part of x̣isəlagilakʷ's plan. He called the owner of the Northwest Wind to come out. He told him to get up and come out. The owner of the Northwest Wind got up and peeked out of the front door. Then he stepped out onto the Halibut. As soon as he touched the Halibut, he slipped and fell into the canoe. This is why x̣isəlagilakʷ had hired the Halibut. He grabbed the owner of the Northwest Wind by the hair, holding his knife in one hand and the hair in the other, and said: "You are surely going to die." The owner of the Northwest Wind said: "Oh, nobleman [giǧaméy̓]! At least tell me why you are going to do this to me?" x̣isəlagilakʷ replied: "Your world is ƛumalagəlis [going to extremes]. You are overdoing it. It should be calm at least once in a while. You make it impossible for us to stay afloat in our canoes."

"Granted, nobleman," said the owner of the Northwest Wind. "Just ask me in a nice way, and I will see to it that your world never has a Northwest Wind again; it will never have a wind of any kind." "Ridiculous, ridiculous," answered x̣isəlagilakʷ. "It would be just fine if it blew once every four days. Yes, that is the way it should be." So that is what has happened ever since. The Northwest Wind never blows as much now as it did before. It is because x̣isəlagilakʷ went to the home of the owner of the Northwest Wind and threatened to cut his throat. He did not cut his throat because he promised not to allow the Northwest Wind to blow so much. He promised to blow only one out of every four days. This is what happened. This is the end.

M4 – Hemaskasʔuẇ and the m̓im̓ax̌ʔinux̌ʷ: The Raven and the Killer Whale People

ʔAwik̓inux̌ʷ Version

At Rivers Inlet [ʔAwik̓inux̌ʷ] there once lived a Raven called Hemaskasʔuẇ. He was always busy doing things. One day, he took off in his canoe and set out all by himself simply to see what he could find. He came, after a while, to a place called Max̌ʷa, a place known for the strange rocks that could only be found there.[20] These rocks were porous. Because the bow of his canoe was riding too far out of the water, Hemaskasʔuw̓ decided to stop at Max̌ʷa. He took four of these strange rocks and put them aboard to use as ballast. He then continued his course, and, as he rounded the next long point, he saw before him a large bay containing many canoes; the bay seemed to be filled with them. There were campfires all along the shore.

As he approached the bay, the people ran down the beach to greet him and invited him to join them. He beached his canoe and walked to a great fire and sat down. The chief, who was sitting there, spoke: "Let us find out the truth from our friend." This is what the chief said.

It soon became clear to Hemaskasʔuw̓ that these people were not ordinary human beings but m̓im̓ax̌ʔinux̌ʷ, killer whales, in their human forms. It also became clear that the many canoes drawn up on the shore were their whale-like outer trappings and that the man who spoke was the chief of the Killer Whale People. "Let us find out the truth from our friend. Let him go," said the chief, who was also called Max̌ʷa.

"I hear these rocks are good," said the people; "they get hot very quickly." They were referring to the strange rocks to be found at Max̌ʷa, for in those days they heated water for cooking by dropping hot rocks into it. "Yes, let our friend go," said Max̌ʷa. "Let him fetch these strange stones." Hemaskasʔuw̓ was known to go so fast that they said he was lalabax̌sala.[21] The Killer Whale People decided to challenge Hemaskasʔuw̓ to find out which of the two, the Killer Whale or Hemaskasʔuw̓, would be the fastest to go to Max̌ʷa and back. Each one would bring four porous rocks.

The Killer Whale People chose for Hemaskasʔuw̓ the oldest canoe, the kind they called d̓aguw̓, a very old and very slow canoe; that is, it was the slowest of the Killer Whales' outfits. They asked him to equip himself with this old m̓ax̌ʔinux̌ʷ gear – this old canoe, this d̓aguw̓ to go to this place they called Max̌ʷa in order to get the strange porous rocks so that they could use them for cooking.

Hemaskasʔuw̓ decided not to fly and did as they asked. As he started to go to sea, he was told to find one rock only. So he set out in the direction of this place they called Max̌ʷa. But, as you will remember, he had already put four rocks into his own canoe for ballast. So he just went around the corner of the bay, took one of these, and returned in the very slow canoe they had lent him. In the meantime, the lalabax̌sala [the fastest] of the m̓im̓ax̌ʔinux̌ʷ went directly to the place called Max̌ʷa. Shortly after, when the m̓im̓ax̌ʔinux̌ʷ who had stayed on shore saw a canoe returning, they exclaimed: "Our own is returning," for they thought it was the m̓im̓ax̌ʔinux̌ʷ they had sent. When they realized that it was Hemaskasʔuw̓, they were very embarrassed and ashamed.

The waves from Hemaskas?uẇ's canoe had not yet touched the shore when the Killer Whale who had left with him returned. He had gone to the faraway land called Maxᵂa, the land where these strange porous rocks can be found. Hemaskas?uẇtook the porous rock and put it on the shore.

The Killer Whale People were really ashamed because the slowest Killer Whale's gear they had given to Hemaskas?uẇ turned out to be the fastest. The chief spoke: "Go and get our *ƛawaẏuẇ* [22] [a pole]. Some young Killer Whale People picked up a large piece of driftwood and carried it down to the beach. There they started asking each other: "Where is it? Where is it?" Finally they seemed to have found what they were seeking, and Hemaskas?uẇ watched to see what they were doing. He saw that they were trying to lift something with the aid of the piece of driftwood. "I wonder what it is," he thought. "It must be a rock that is hardly showing, that is buried in the beach." Hemaskas?uẇ finally got up because he was annoyed that he could not see what they were trying to lift. "What are you doing?" he asked the Killer Whale People. "This is what we use for food," he was told.

What do you suppose it was?

It was a small *maẏus*, a small raccoon crouched between two rocks.

That is what those fools were trying to lift!

"Move over and let me get it," Hemaskas?uẇ said. He grasped the raccoon by the tail and walked up the beach with it.

The Killer Whale People were astonished that he was able to do this, that he was able to carry the raccoon by the tail. He learned that a raccoon is to the Killer Whale People what a big seal [*migᵂat*] is to us. And we know that nobody could lift a huge seal even with a large piece of driftwood.

The Killer Whale People prepared the raccoon just as we would a seal – by roasting it. They then put it on a mat and cut it into strips. The size of each strip was the width of the black mark on the raccoon's tail. This is how big the strips were, according to what Hemaskas?uẇ saw.

M5 – Ẇaẇalis [Myth That Took Place before the Flood – *yex̌ᵂəxsa*]

ƛawiċis Version

This is the story of Ẇaẇalis,[23] who was from Qaluǧᵂis [Turnour Island]. Ẇaẇalis was a seal hunter [*ṁaṁigᵂata*]. He and his little slave [*q̓akuẇ*] went out every day hunting seals. Every time they went out, Ẇaẇalis's wife met with her lover. Every month she had to isolate herself and stay in a little house during the time of her menstruation. Ẇaẇalis, her husband, believed she was an honest woman, and he trusted her.

One day W̓awalis came home and started to kick his little slave, whom he thought had done something wrong. The little man started to cry and said, "You should not do that to me. I try to do my best in performing my duties whenever we are out hunting." This is what he said as he continued to cry. "You should discipline your wife. Every time we go out, she is with another man." W̓awalis could not hear the little man and asked him to repeat what he had just said. The slave replied, "You kick me because I try to do my duty. I do everything I am told when we shoot and catch seals. You should go and kick your wife and give her a beating because she goes with another man every time we go out hunting."

W̓awalis wanted to have proof of this accusation. One day they were ready to go out hunting. W̓awalis did not say anything to his wife; he just left. They had a little girl called Qadᵊidala. She asked her father not to forget to bring some seal meat for her. "I'd love to eat seal," she said. Every day, he would bring home his seal catch and his wife would cook it for his lunch. There is a small box in the bow of the canoe where the seal hunters put their lunch when they go out hunting. Since they were hunting seals in the dark, W̓awalis and his slave were supposed to stay out all night. But that day they returned earlier than usual. Quietly, they went home, sneaking around the back of W̓awalis's wife's lover's house. W̓awalis heard his wife giggling, having a nice time in bed with her lover. W̓awalis and his slave started scratching, and it sounded like a rat wanting to come in. The wife shouted to her lover: "The rat should eat W̓awalis!" By the way she said it, you could tell that she wished for her husband's death. W̓awalis and his slave kept scratching while the couple continued frolicking in bed – laughing, giggling, carrying on, and having a fine time. The lover was a *giǧaméy̓* [a nobleman, a chief]. Soon everything was quiet, for the couple had fallen asleep. W̓awalis and his slave were preparing to kill his wife's lover. They lit a bunch of kindling to make a torch, pushed the door open, and saw his wife and this man asleep. W̓awalis did not touch his wife; he just took his knife and cut the man's head off. W̓awalis and his slave pulled the body out and put it in a sitting position on the platform in front of the house, the place they call ʔəwag̓ʷas. They placed the chief's hat on top of the headless body.

W̓awalis left with the head of his wife's lover and returned to his seal hunting. When his wife and the little girl woke up, they felt the cold blood around them and started to scream and cry. Someone in the big house asked: "What is happening? Who is crying?" "Maybe she soiled her bed," someone answered, "and that is why she is crying." It was not that. It was the blood of that man, the blood of her lover. W̓awalis's wife got very busy cleaning up the little girl; she later bathed herself.

The family of the lover, his sisters and nieces, were living in his house. His sister said to her daughter: "You had better go and tell your uncle to come and have breakfast." It was now morning. The daughter went out and called him, but he did not stir. She ran back to her mother and said: "Uncle never moved." "Well, touch him, wake him up." She went back and tried to touch her uncle again, but he remained still. She ran back to her mother and said: "Uncle never moved." "Touch his head and remove his hat," her mother said. She ran back and moved the hat. To her horror, there was no head under the hat. The little girl screamed and ran back to her mother, telling her what she saw. Soon after, the whole village found out what had happened.

W̓aw̓alis was still out seal hunting but returned later in the day. He was paddling in slowly. The people waved to W̓aw̓alis to make him hurry. His people kept waving, so W̓aw̓alis paddled faster. When he and his slave landed on the beach, all the people went down to see him, to meet him. The people did not know that W̓aw̓alis had killed the nobleman. Nobody knew exactly what had happened to the nobleman. W̓aw̓alis did not pay any attention. He just took his lunch box and went to his house. His wife was drying her hair by the open fire. She was a beautiful woman. Qadᶻidala was really anxious to see her father, but her mother said to her: "Do not bother your father. Let him eat first. Go and let him finish his meal." So W̓aw̓alis's wife fed them right away.

Qadᶻidala did not mention the seal meat, even though she was eager to eat some. Her mother knew this and went to get the seal meat that was in the lunch box. That is when the trouble began. She opened the box and saw that there was something in between the pieces of seal meat. Immediately, she recognized the head of her lover. W̓aw̓alis grabbed the head of his wife's lover and violently hit her with it. She died instantly.

He was really a supernatural man, this W̓aw̓alis. Horrified, his daughter panicked and started screaming. W̓aw̓alis grabbed the little girl and turned her into a sawbill duck.[24] W̓aw̓alis and his slave walked down the beach to his canoe and left. The little girl, transformed into a sawbill duck, was swimming around in the channel near Qaluǧʷis. This bird really looks like that little girl. Its face looks exactly like Qadᶻidala's face. Even today they can still recognize the pretty little duck swimming around the channel.

W̓aw̓alis took off and went up to Rivers Inlet in ʔAwiḱinux̌ʷ country, leaving Qaluǧʷis behind. Now there is a big tribe over there. This tribe is called ʔAwiḱinux̌ʷ. ʔAwiḱinux̌ʷ is the name of the tribe and W̓anukʷ [owner of a river] is the name of the river. They went right up the river. There were lots of houses there, but signs of smoke came from only one. They went right up to this house. A blind woman was trying to cook something, just as they used to do in the early days. They got hot rocks and placed them into the water in which the meat was to be cooked. The two men simply sat there and watched what the blind woman was doing. W̓aw̓alis did not know that she was blind. They took the seal meat from her just as she was searching for it with her hands. She called her granddaughter who was in her bedroom. "Come out and help me. I cannot find the seal meat that I was going to cook." "Maybe these two men took it," replied the young girl. "Those two men who are sitting there." She closed the door and went back to her bedroom. The old woman called out again to her granddaughter. As soon as the young girl went back to her bedroom, Ẇaẇalis gave the meat back to the old woman. She called out to the granddaughter again. "Come out and eat with the two people you were talking about." So the young girl came out.

She was the prettiest girl you ever saw! A really beautiful woman. Ẇaẇalis and the slave started to eat the seal meat with the young girl and her grandmother. They were eating seal meat. Ẇaẇalis became very thirsty. He asked the old woman about the water container. "Where is your water container, where is your pail? Go and get some water," Ẇaẇalis ordered his slave. But the old woman said: "No, never go near this river because a big monster [ẏagəm] lives in it. As you can see all these houses are empty. Every time people go near the river and try to get water, they are swallowed by that big ẏagəm."[25] "Well," Ẇaẇalis said to his slave, "go and get my belt." It was a *Sisayuɫ* belt, a Double-Headed Serpent belt. He gave his slave the belt to use and told him what to say should he be in danger of being devoured by the ẏagəm.

So the slave went out. As soon as he tried to put the pail in the water, the big ẏagəm came up and swallowed him. The big monster's belly was full of skeletons and people, some of them half alive. So the slave said, "*sisćalliɫ, sisćalliɫ, sisćalliɫ, sisćalliɫ*"[26] [to coil] four times. As soon as he repeated the word four times the big ẏagəm exploded. Ẇaẇalis took the life-giving water [q̓ʷəlasta] and sprinkled it over the skeletons and the people who were barely alive. They all came back to life. Ẇaẇalis and his slave went back to the house with the pail of water. But before returning, they took a little bit of clay from the ground in order to cure the blind woman. They put a little bit of clay in each eye and the blind woman was able to see again.

Then Ẇaẇalis and his slave went back to the village. The people were really good to Ẇaẇalis. He remarried and kept on doing what he had been doing before he left Qaluǧʷis [Turnour Island]: seal hunting. Ẇaẇalis and his new family went to the mouth of Rivers Inlet to dig clams. They went there and shot a white sea otter[27] [q̓assa]. The slave skinned it and Ẇaẇalis gave the skin to his wife to wash on the beach. However, the waves carried it out to sea. The woman tried to catch it, but two Killer Whales came by and carried her off. "Ẇaẇalis, the killer whales have kidnapped your wife," someone said on the beach. Ẇaẇalis and his slave ran to the beach but could not catch up to them. They walked back behind his house and found two bulrushes [k̓ak̓iƛama]. They cut four pieces out of them and left. After walking for a long time in a southeasterly direction, they examined the ground on the beach. They pushed all four of the sticks into the ground and Waẃalis turned into a wolf. He went straight down into the underworld.

The first people he saw there were the Crabs [q̓umʔis]. He went to the Crab People's house. "Maybe you know what has happened to my wife," he asked them. "She just passed by us. You will catch up with her if you keep following the Killer Whales who took her," the Crab People told him. So they continued their pursuit and passed by all the houses of the Sea People, including the Red Snapper [ƛaẋsəm]. All the Sea People understood each other and could communicate with Waẃalis. Finally, they came to the last house of the underworld village. They watched a slave splitting wood. He was working very hard. "You are sure a hard worker," said Waẃalis to this man. The slave said, "We will be needing lots of wood, for the chief has a new wife." "She is *my* wife," said Waẃalis. "I came to get her back." While he was talking to the slave, Waẃalis turned into something very small, penetrated the wood, and created an obstacle for the wood-splitter. The slave could not get his wedge out of the wood. The little man started to cry. "Oh! My master is going to be really mad at me! Oh! The old chief is really going to scold me! It was his best tool!" Waẃalis returned to human form. "If you promise to help me get my wife back, I will fix your wedge," said Waẃalis. "I can try," replied the slave. Waẃalis took the blade out of his mouth and put it back into the slave's pouch. Waẃalis had real supernatural power and so could do these things.

The slave said: "The Killer Whale People are going to have a feast and I have to start the fire and fill up the cooking containers with water in order to boil some food. I have to go out and bring lots of water into the house. I will go out three times and pour the water; the fourth time I will pour it on the fire." Waẃalis could see his wife in the big house under the sea. The fourth time the slave went in with the pail and poured water onto the fire, causing it to smoke. Under cover of the smoke, Waẃalis ran into the house, seized his wife, and escaped.

After Waẃalis had returned to dry land with his wife, he had a dream that the Killer Whale People were going to capture her again. And if they were not successful it would rain for forty days and forty nights, causing a real Flood – like in the Bible.[28] Since Waẃalis did not want to lose his wife again, he prepared some clay and cast her in it in order to keep her forever. Waẃalis and his wife both turned into stone just before the flood [yeẋʷəxsa] covered the earth. It was the Killer Whale People's doings. Waẃalis got his wife back and never lost her again as they were both transformed into stone forever. That is the end.

м6 – The Two Brothers

There was a nobleman [*gig̱amēẏ*], and his brother was committing adultery [*gisgas*] with his wife. *Gisgas*[29] refers to a man having an affair with his brother's wife [*gǝmp*]. The nobleman did not like this. He was always plotting the death of his brother, but his wife always managed to prevent it from happening.

One day, the nobleman sent his brother down to the beach to get some cockles [*dᶾoliẏ*]. There was a *ẏagǝm*[30] [monster] in the form of a gigantic cockle living nearby. The brother followed the chief's instructions. The wife told her lover to be careful: "You must keep this, so that you will use it when the giant cockle catches you." She gave *ʔux̌ʷsuliẏ* [false hellebore][31] to the man with whom she was having an affair.

When the nobleman's brother went to get some cockles at night, he encountered the giant cockle, the *ẏagǝm*. It opened its mouth and swallowed him. He started to eat the *ʔux̌ʷsuliẏ* and, at the same time, rubbed some of it inside the cockle. In a very short time, under the influence of the *ʔux̌ʷsuliẏ*, the giant cockle got drunk, opened its shell, and spat him out. Once more he was safe. The woman had given him *ʔux̌ʷsuliẏ* because she knew this would happen. The nobleman took the cockles he ordered to get and laid them at his older brother's feet. The nobleman was shocked to see that his brother was still alive. He thought that, by then, he should have been dead.

The noble husband made new plans for the death of his brother. There was another *ẏagǝm* on the roof of his house. "Go and check the leak on our roof," he said to his brother. "Go and look at it because it is really bad to have our house leaking this way," he said. The younger brother was sent out again, and the woman gave him a large stone hammer [*ńǝbaẏuw̓*]. The monster that was living on top of the older brother's roof used to feed on live human beings. Indeed, the roof was a very dangerous place to go. "He is sending you again to a place that is far from being safe; another monster lives there. Take this hammer with you." This hammer was made of stone; they used it long ago for cutting wood. "Hide it and use it to smash the mouth of the monster," said the woman.

He went onto the roof. As soon as he did so, the monster opened his mouth and tried to swallow him. The brother hit the monster's mouth with the stone hammer, and it went right through. The monster died instantly from the hammer blow. Once more the younger brother was safe, and he returned after repairing the leak in the roof.

The elder brother was getting discouraged because his younger brother had so far survived all the schemes to bring about his death. The older brother was full of jealousy. He then thought of what to do next. "Go to the place where they club *ⱡubańiẏ*, the cormorant, so that we can have some for supper," said his older brother. "Your brother is planning your death again," said the woman while giving her lover a pillow. "They are going to take you to a cliff where colonies of cormorants live. You will have to be let down by rope in order to catch them."

The younger brother had been selected by his elder brother to club a cormorant. He tied a rope around the waist of his younger sibling and sent him down the face of the cliff. At some point, the elder brother, who had come along to check the descent, said, "That is enough." The younger brother tied a cormorant to the end of the rope, and the elder brother began to pull them both up the cliff. As he started his ascent of the cliff, the younger brother tied the pillow onto his back, as the woman had instructed him. He had almost reached the upper edge of the cliff when his brother cut the rope. He fell down, but the pillow attached to his back softened his fall, so he was not hurt. He was safe once more and went back to his brother.

The elder brother was running out of ideas of ways to kill his younger brother. He did not try again for a long time, but then he got another idea. He had a chest decorated with abalone shells. The nobility usually owned this type of chest. The woman knew, of course, what her husband was planning. "You are on your own," she said to her lover. "I have run out of ideas about how to save you. This time I am going with you. He is going to place you in the chest and push you out to sea. I just do not know what to do for you. I will go with him when he takes you out to sea. As soon as the chest touches the water I will bang on top of it to make you aware that you are in the water," she said to him. The elder brother dressed him up in his finest. He put an ermine headdress on him and a blanket covered with abalone shells. Then he placed him in the chest. They left in a canoe and paddled far out to sea, among a group of islands. The older brother took hold of the chest and threw it into the water. With one of the paddles the woman banged on the lid of the chest four times.

The whole country was talking about it. An abalone-inlaid chest was set adrift. Whoever found it would be ʎugʷala [blessed; fortunate]. The younger brother drifted around at sea in a sitting position inside the chest.

Four sisters were playing on a beautiful island. The water was so smooth that they easily noticed what appeared to be a wave of sunlight on the horizon. The youngest of the four girls saw the shimmering chest floating on the surface of the sea. She went and told her older sisters. The surf was bringing it closer to the shore. The youngest girl ran down to the beach and watched it. The older girls just kept playing. The youngest girl knew that this was the chest that everyone was looking for – the chest that had been set adrift and was inlaid with abalone shells. The chest rode the surf as it came in. "It is going to be mine," said the eldest. She ran and grabbed it, trying to push it up on the shore. But she was not strong enough. The second-eldest sister tried also, but she was not strong enough either. So did the third sister, but she did not succeed. Finally, the youngest sister was able to reach the chest; she grabbed it and pulled it up onto the shore with ease. The youngest sister, who first sighted it, opened the chest and found a man sitting in it, and married him. She took him for her husband. He did not die. Everything turned out all right because he married the youngest of the four sisters.

M7 – x̄isəlagilakʷ: The Mink and How He Lost and Found His Bowels[32]

x̄isəlagilakʷ [Born-To-Be-the-Sun] was sitting on an island looking out to sea. Suddenly a fish jumped out of the water right in front of him. "Həy̓uẃ![33] I wish I were the one who was jumping out of the water! I would probably jump on the other side of that current!" So the fish jumped on the other side of the tidal current. "Həy̓uẃ! I wish I were the one who was jumping out of the water! I would probably jump on the other side of the kelp [ẃaẃadiy̓]," exclaimed x̄isəlagilakʷ. "Həy̓uẃ! I wish I were the one who was jumping out of the water! I would probably jump on the other side of the ƛ̓isƛ̓əkʷ [where sea grass grows], which is not very far from where I am sitting!" Finally, x̄isəlagilakʷ said: "Həy̓uẃ! I wish I were the one who was jumping out of the water! I would probably jump out of the water and glide onto the beach!" x̄isəlagilakʷ ran over to the fish and tried to catch it as it was flapping on the beach. He grabbed the fish and brought it up on to the shore to cook it. He barbecued the fish in the forest. He was sitting in the bushes. His barbecued salmon was quite tasty. x̄isəlagilakʷ was admiring his barbecued fish and started to chant to it:

> ʔəngʷa gʷa cana ʔən na wis sux̌ da pəƛəw wi ƛan na?
> Nus sa naganəm ƛaƛ ƛuẃ
> ʔəngʷa gʷa cana ʔən na wis sux̌ da ċeċix̌ ƛa na?
> Nus sa naganəm ƛaƛ ƛuẃ

He was naming all the edible parts of the fish at the end of the chant.

> I wonder to whom this fin will belong?
> I suppose it will belong to me.
> I wonder to whom this tail will belong?
> I suppose it will belong to me.

He then laid down on the ground to sleep, as he was very tired. Before he went to sleep under the trees, he said, "Trees of the forest, could you please look after my barbecue?" He wanted the trees to look after his barbecued fish. x̌isəlagilakʷ fell into a deep sleep. He slept ever so soundly.

A group of children came along to play where they usually played. There were many children, and they all saw x̌isəlagilakʷ's barbecued fish by the fire. The children took it and ate it. x̌isəlagilakʷ did not even stir. They ate up all his barbecued fish. The children took the cooked slime and rubbed it on his lips and then left him. They had eaten all his barbecued fish. He slept ever so soundly and for so long that his bowels came out. His bowels were lying on the ground because he slept too much.[34] The children took the bowels of x̌isəlagilakʷ away with them.

He woke up and started spitting. "To, to, to, to," such a bad taste was on his lips. "*Sisəl, sisəl*," he said. He cursed the people who took his barbecued salmon. The barbecued fish must have tasted really bad, he said to himself. He tried to stand up, but he could not walk because he did not have any bowels left in his belly. He sat on the ground but started to slide, so he moved to the rock where he had sat previously.

Along came several sailing canoes [*yawapiẏala*]. It is said that they were going to Dᶻaw̓adiẏ [Knight Inlet]. The *ńuẏəm* says that they were going up the inlet. "Have you any news?" x̌isəlagilakʷ asked the canoeists. "The one behind us has news," they told him. There was a party of four canoes. Along came the last canoe. "The only news we have heard is about x̌isəlagilakʷ's bowels," they said. x̌isəlagilakʷ repeated, "*Sisəl, sisəl, sisəl, sisəl*," cursing the children.

He started crawling as he went. He was looking for the children because they were kicking his bowels around like a ball. He could not walk because he no longer had his bowels. He wandered and found the children. They cheered happily as they ran around the field. They were using his bowels as a football. He sat down and waited for the right opportunity to sit on his bowels. When his bowels finally rolled around near him he ran and sat on them. This enabled him to return them to his body. The children started chanting to him: "I was trying to sit on my bowels." This is what they were chanting to him as he managed to sit on his bowels and return them to his body.

M8 – Nawalagʷaćiy: The Supernatural Cave Dance[35]
Origin: Qʷiqʷasut̓inux̌ʷ

All the birds and the land animals were having a gathering at the Nawalagʷaćiy.[36]

Note: At this point, ʔAx̌uw̓ felt that she had to explain something, and she started the story with the following prelude.

Nawalag̱ʷaċiy is the name of a supernatural cave located on the land of the Q̱ʷiq̱ʷasuṯinux̌ʷ [Gilford Island]. They say the cave had a hole in the roof. Not only did it have an opening in the roof but it also had a large root inside that the Animals used as a log drum. I have actually heard X̌aneyus talk about it.

The Nawalag̱ʷaċiy was a very dark place. When the Animals entered their cave they had to use a torch made of łaṅəm [salal berry branches], which they lit and waved around in a circle to give them some light. They were beating on the root, as this was their drum. This is what I have heard about the Animals. This was supposed to have happened at ʔəpsaguw̓.

Whenever they performed the Nawalag̱ʷaċiy, the Supernatural Cave Dance, they would do so with just one character – the Bək̓ʷəs, or the Wild Man of the Woods.[37] This is where the Bək̓ʷəs Dance originated. When men like Bondsound (Arthur Bondsound),[38] for example, were being initiated as a Bək̓ʷəs, they would just take this one character to represent the Supernatural Cave Dances. This is why the song says *"la ʔum ʎug̓ala nuk̓ʷ mi dᶻəms"*: "they have been blessed with these treasures."

In the early days, the Bək̓ʷəs would be the only dancer to represent the Supernatural Cave Dances. ʔAnus[39] was the fortunate man who saw the cave, and so the Bək̓ʷəs Dance belongs to him. Most of the people now do not know much about the Abalone Shell Covered House that came out of the sea. People, who now talk about the Supernatural Cave Dances never, never refer to this aspect of it.[40]

Note: At this point, ʔAx̌uw̓ returned to her main story.

The cave at ʔəpsaguw̓ was not far from the sea. One day a house came out of the water, near ʔəpsaguw̓. They say that the owner of the house was Q̓umug̓ʷeẏ, the Lord of the Sea [also called the Wealthy One]. The house emerged at high tide. Oh! It sparkled as the sun shone on it! It was completely covered with abalone shell! In the meantime, the Animals kept beating their root-drum so that Bək̓ʷəs could dance. When the house rose up to the surface of the sea, Bək̓ʷəs was outside waiting to hear the call of the drums. ʔAnus and his son ran towards the Abalone-Covered House and received it as a supernatural treasure [ʎug̓ʷeẏ]. Q̓umug̓ʷeẏ gave him the house and the names referring to the abalone shell. This is why we have the following names: ʔIxċəmg̱ałilak̓ʷ [Born To Be an Abalone Shell]; ʔIxċəmalag̱əlis [Abalone of the World]; ʔIxċəmg̱a [Abalone Shell Woman]. All these Abalone Shell names[41] came from Q̓umug̓ʷeẏ. ʔIxċəmg̱ałilak̓ʷ and ʔIxċəmxəmlił [You Look Like an Abalone Shell]. These are the names ʔAnus received when he encountered the house inlaid with abalone shell. He also received the house itself. He received all these supernatural treasures from Q̓umuẉ̌ey at ʔəpsaguẉ, when the house of the Lord of the Sea emerged from the water.

This is the ńuẏəm that the old man [Arthur Bondsound] told me. This is all I know about it.

M9 – The Animal Kingdom

As this particular version was not directly recorded from ʔAx̌uẉ but was adapted and dramatized by Jimmy Sewid and Daisy Sewid-Smith for public performances, we present it in Appendix B.

M10 – Nix̌ag̱amēẏ and Nik̓ʷix̌ag̱amēẏ: Day Hunter and Night Hunter[42]

Danaxdax̌ʷ Version
This happened at Knight Inlet. There were four brothers. Nix̌ag̱amēẏ (Day Hunter) and his younger brother always hunted seals during the day.[43] They used spears to hunt the seals, for it was before the time of the shotgun. Nik̓ʷix̌ag̱amēẏ (Night Hunter) and his other brother went out every night to spear seals; but they were not catching as many seals during the night as were Day Hunter and his brother [during the day]. There was much debate in the village as to why Day Hunter was having so much success hunting seals, for people argued that at that time of the day the seals should be able to see the hunters and escape swiftly. They were really wondering why Day Hunter was having such success.

There is a certain place at Knight Inlet where the seals congregate. This place is called qələs. There is a hole where the seals come out to rest, and that is where Day Hunter and his brother clubbed them. In this manner they caught many seals. Day Hunter would put a rope around the waist of his brother and send him down the hole to club the seals. Night Hunter began to wonder why these two were catching more seals than he was. He wanted to examine the seals more closely in order to tell how they were caught. Night Hunter looked at one of his brother's seals and noticed a little spruce needle in its mouth. The needle was there because the seals had been resting near a grove of spruce trees.

One day, Day Hunter and his younger brother went hunting for seals. They did not travel very far before pulling the canoe out of the water and continuing by land. Night Hunter and his younger brother were following them. They wanted to find out their secret. Something was strange, so they followed them. They saw Day Hunter putting the rope around his brother's waist. He let him down the hole to the pool where the seals were sleeping. He clubbed the seals and pulled them up. Since they were catching the seals near the woods instead of from the sea, the seals had spruce needles caught in their mouths. Night Hunter and his brother were watching. "I was watching what you were doing," said Night Hunter to Day Hunter. He had found out the secret of his brother's success. Meanwhile, Night Hunter's other brother was still watching and hiding. "So this is what you have been doing; this is your secret," he said to himself. "Now we have found out." When Day Hunter was about to pull up his brother, the third brother, who was still watching from behind the bush, ran up and cut the rope. Day Hunter's brother dropped down the hole and died among the seals. This brother also killed Day Hunter and threw him down the hole. Both were now in the *qəlas*, lying dead amongst the seals under the sea.

Night Hunter and his brother packed up all the seals. They did not count how many they had. They just filled up the canoe and went home. The other brothers were under the sea, dead – but not for very long.

In a corner was a pool. It was the house of the seals, and it was shared by all kinds of monsters. Every time they came up through the hole for air they made a large backwash. This receding wave went right to Day Hunter, who was lying there at the bottom of the hole. This brought him back to life. The first big monster was called *x̌əmdˀisbalis* [*x̌əmdiẏ*: land otter]; and the second big monster was *x̌əmdəmagustalagilakʷ* [mythical land otter]. The first monster took his monster costume off, hung it on the wall, and asked the other monster why Day Hunter was not moving yet. Day Hunter was just pretending that he was still dead. The next monster and all kinds of different animals who live under salt water came by, one by one, through the big hole. Before they came to this big hole they made a large backwash in order to help revive Day Hunter. This was also done every time the killer whales took their costumes off in order to become people. All the Sea People tried to revive Day Hunter when they entered their big house. They kept noticing him lying there. "What is the matter with this fellow human being [*bəxʷəs*]? This is somebody who obviously never had much sleep," one of them replied. They all tried to wake him up. "We will put his body on a board and cut him up," said another. Three times someone motioned to cut him up. The fourth time, as someone was going to make the cut, Day Hunter grabbed his hand. They all realized now that he was alive. He then saw all the different monsters' costumes hanging on the wall. He realized that he was among the Underwater People, who live under the sea. There were different kinds of *ẏagəm* [monsters], but they all had one chief. Day Hunter grabbed the wrist of the monster that was about to cut him into pieces. The monster people remained speechless for a long time. Some of them tried to get back into their monster outfits. A few of them showed both a human hand and a monster hand because they had not had enough time to get completely dressed.

The nobleman spoke up: "Ask our friend what he wants. Why did he come to our house? Ask him if he wants a supernatural gift [ƛ́ug"éý] from the seals or from the porpoises." Those porpoises have extremely good ears. They were there too, and their costumes were hanging on the wall. The porpoises are the only ones who can tell what you are thinking. They can see and hear what you think. Day Hunter was thinking how wonderful it would be if he could become more successful in his life thanks to the power of knowledge the Underwater People have. He already had a lot of luck hunting with his brother during the day. A porpoise spoke up because he knew what the man was thinking. So the chief of the Underwater People told his spokesman to ask the man if he wanted a *max̌"soyas,* as the porpoise had indicated. *Max̌"soyas* is a symbol that shows that you have given a potlatch [*max̌"a:* to give away]. It is a potlatch pole. This is exactly what the hunter was thinking that he wanted. "Ask him if he wants *səgayu mastuw̓,* the magic spear," said the porpoise. Again, this was what the hunter was thinking he wanted. "Ask our friend if he wants the *həlaýuw̓,*" said the porpoise. The *həlaýuw̓* is the magic hunting bow and arrow.[44] When used against the animals they turn into stone. This is what happened in the Nəmǧis *ńuýəm* [myth] of the Sisayuł. The hunter wanted the *həlaýuw̓.* This was his third wish. "Ask our friend if he wants the *q̓"əlasta,* the life-giving water. If you sprinkle this water over dead people, they will come back to life." The hunter was wishing for this also. So he received these four supernatural gifts to take home with him. He was to return home in his baby seal costume. They call the baby seal "*w̓aliý.*" A monster took Day Hunter home. This monster was very flat, and they put the baby seal right in the middle of him.

When they arrived in front of the village, Night Hunter and his brother saw the little seal in the water. It was bobbing up and down with the waves. Other people from the village wanted to catch the little seal, and it started to shout: "Drop! Drop!" The people were carrying their canoes down to the beach. They were not pulling them, for that would have damaged the bottoms. The little seal said: "I wish that you would drop the canoes. Drop! Drop! Drop! I wish that you would drop the canoes and wreck them!" So the first two men dropped their canoe. Another family was approaching the water's edge with its canoe. The little seal said the same thing: "Drop, drop, drop!" The seal did not want to be caught because he wanted to take revenge on his brother. He wanted to pay his brother back for killing him. Other families came with their canoes to the beach, and again the seal made the canoes fall. Their canoes split in two. They could not do a thing because their canoes were badly damaged.

Night Hunter was in the village. "Do not stay home, go out hunting," someone said to him. He was with his brother. They carried the canoe down to the beach and tried to spear the little seal. The spear went into the flat monster, taking Night Hunter with it. He did not know that the monster was carrying the little seal. So the little seal paid back his brother.

Day Hunter transformed back into his human form and came ashore with his four treasures: *maxʷsoyas, səgayu masɬuƚ, həlay̓uƚ,* and *q̓ʷəlasta.* He used them all and, as a result, did not have to go sea hunting anymore. With the *həlay̓uƚ* he caught many seals. He was a fortunate man now. He used the *həlay̓uƚ* to destroy anything he wanted by turning it into stone. Day Hunter became a powerful man in the village. He did not have to work hard in order to get what he wanted. We do not know where the monster took Night Hunter. He just took him away under the sea. Day Hunter settled down in the village. One day he went to see what had happened to his brother at the *qəlas.* His brother was reduced to a skeleton. Day Hunter sprinkled the life-giving water over him and brought him back to life. From this time on, the two brothers were powerful men in the village. This happened at ʔIwigalis, in Knight Inlet. We used to pass by this place on our way to the head of the inlet. This is the end.

M11 – Hudis: The Midgets[45]

The name of the village from which this story originated has been forgotten, but it was a very large village with an exceptionally fine beach. Each day a group of girls would hike to the other side of the village and swim. They would come home only to eat, and then they would return to the seashore. There was a large pine tree lying on the ground near the beach, with half of its roots exposed. A thunderstorm had probably taken this tree down, as its bark was partially burned. The girls went home, had dinner, and went to bed, unaware of impending events.

The next morning they went back to swim at the beach on the other side of the island. After swimming they were tired and laid down on the big log to rest. They slept all day and into the night. While they were sleeping the tide came in and carried the log out to sea. In the middle of the night, one of the girls woke up and discovered that they were floating out to sea. She found that there was a big hole at the end of the log. She called to the other children to come and hide in the hole so that they would be protected from ocean swells. The children soon became hungry and scared. They could hear seagulls landing on the log. They saw the seagulls' legs through the hole. By sticking their hands through the hole, they caught and killed lots of seagulls in a very short time. They ate them and used the feathers to make clothes.

They soon became very thirsty. So they peeled off the bark of the pine tree and sucked its juice to quench their thirst. They were floating around, drifting day after day, with no hope of being rescued.

One day they felt the big log bang up against something. They thought they had beached. They looked out of the hole but could not see a thing as the sun had not yet risen. Some of them jumped out and fell into the water. They were not on a beach as they had thought; rather, they had hit a large cedar log floating about on the sea. The girls who remained in the log were wise not to jump as those who did drowned and perished in the sea. Those who had jumped in the water tried to save themselves by grabbing the log, but the charred layer crumbled in their hands. Half of the girls drowned; the other half stayed in the log and floated around many more days, living on seagulls.

One morning they felt the big log rolling around. The first girl to awaken thought that this time they really were on a beach. It was a beautiful clear morning, and the sun was shining brightly. The girl who was first to awaken climbed out of the log and found a lovely village site situated on a fine beach. However, she did not notice any people in this village. She went back to the hole in the log to wake the others. "Wake up," she said. "We have landed and we should look for fresh water." They all left the log and started walking along the sandy beach. At one spot they noticed footprints. They followed the footprints, which led them to a very large village. The houses in the village were very much the same, except for one. There were people on the shore, and they approached the girls. However, they were not ordinary people; they were midgets. And they were very happy to see the girls. The small people were really a friendly tribe of halibut fishermen. They were bringing in a large catch of fresh halibut to the sides of their houses. Since these people had very small mouths, they had to wait for the halibut to have maggots [ʔabaṅiẏ; ʔaṗid: to have maggots], to be dried and rotten, before they could eat them.

The children started to feel lonely, thinking of their friends who had drowned in the sea and of those who had died of hunger and thirst, for only a few children from the original group had survived the journey.

Although they spoke different languages,[46] the midgets and the girls could understand each other. They overheard the midgets saying that people from another village were planning to raid and plunder them. The little people began frantically preparing themselves for the attack. In the meantime, the children wanted to enter the only house that did not look like the others. They went in and sat around the fire in the middle of the room. A great big man was also sitting there, facing away from the fire. The girls just sat there looking at the

great big man. A woman said to him: "Face this way, so you can see your visitors."
She continued: "ƛ́alaʔənxʔidas, ǧʷəmdʸiẏ, ƛ́aɬbēy, ƛ́aɬalis."[47] She was recalling all
the names of the whales. The girls realized that they were in the house of the
Killer Whale People and other Whale People. So the great big man turned around
and faced the girls. He shook his head and said: "Do you belong to these friendly
people? The little people living in this area are very kind. They are preparing
themselves for an attack from outsiders, who are going to try to kill them." The
woman said to the girls, "You should stay here until everything is over." The girls
agreed: "We are going to stay here until everything is over." "Pretty soon flocks
of ʔadəmǧʷaliẏ [surf scoters] will be arriving. These ducks are going to attack the
little people. They are going to fly around the little people's houses and use their
feathers as bows and arrows." Soon the birds arrived and attacked the midgets
by shooting at their faces and bodies. When the raid was over, the human girls
came out of the Whale house. They pulled out the feathers from the faces and
bodies of the midgets who had survived. The little people were very appreciative
of the girls' help and treated them very well in return. They provided the girls
with halibut for their travelling provisions. The Whale man said to them, "You
can go home now. We will give you a canoe and plenty of dried halibut, so you
will not get hungry. But you cannot stop to rest and sleep. You have to take turns
paddling and sleeping. You are going to paddle day and night until you reach
home. The first thing you have to do in the morning is to observe the sunrise
and to follow it. It will direct you to where you have to go. In the evening the
moon will be on the bow [ʔogiwēẏ] and you must keep paddling towards it. You
are going to go home to your village, and you must do what we tell you to do.
You have enough fish to get home safely. You will arrive right in front of your
village."

The next morning they left, following the direction of the sunrise. In the
evening, when the moon was on the bow, they continued paddling. They had
to paddle very hard in order to make it back. They cut and sun-dried the
halibut that the little people had given them. The midgets had their own way
of preparing fish by storing it for a certain time until it rotted and shrank.
The girls preferred their own way. They dried it in the sun and had enough
food to last their trip.

They paddled day and night, taking turns sleeping and eating, and they
arrived right in front of their village, as the Whale man had said. The people
there had forgotten about the girls. They had been lost for a very long time.
Some of their parents had died during their absence and the village had become
a ghost town. Only a few old people were still alive. The girls returned to the
small houses of the women. That is the end.

M12 – Baxʷbakʷalanuxʷsiwēẏ: The Man-Eater at the Mouth of the River

Danaxdax̱ʷ Version[48]
Peter Smith's mother, Ḡʷəmǧəmlilas, told me this story. Listen.

At one time, the *ćeqa*, the Red Cedar-Bark Ceremony, was an occasion for competition between chiefs. They called such an event *ʔəpsikəs*, which simply means "opposite side." Such an *ʔəpsikəs* was being held by the Danaxdax̱ʷ at Knight Inlet. For many days, guests had been arriving from faraway places in their canoes – places like Miṁkʷəmlis, Cax̱is, and so on.

One of the noblemen [*giǧamēẏ*] had a very lazy son. They both just stayed home while the other *giǧamēẏ*, his rival, held a big *ćeqa* – or dance, as they call it. The lazy boy would always sit like this [ʔAx̱uẇ imitates the boy's behaviour], with his legs stretched out and his head down between his knees. That is precisely what we were taught never to do. We, who were of high standing, were raised with manners and instructed in the difference between proper and improper behaviour.

The lazy boy and his father would hear the sounds from the nearby ceremonial house as their fellow villagers performed the *ćeqa*. Unable to attend these great occasions because of his son's delinquency, the enraged father would hit the youth on the knees with the fire tongs or some other handy object and, in violent tones, give vent to his anger and disappointment: "You should be over there dancing instead of sitting here uselessly, listening to the sounds of those great happenings with your head between your knees."

One day, during just such a quarrel over the boy's laziness, which prevented them from attending the *ćeqa* that was taking place at Knight Inlet, the boy, instead of sitting passively as usual, got up and went out into the forest. The lazy boy, wonderfully agile in spite of his indolent ways, moved easily through the dense forest at Knight Inlet, wandering deeper and deeper into the woods. It began to snow. Suddenly feeling cold, he started to look for shelter and found a hole created by the crossing of logs that they call *xʷəlkʷ*. He crawled into this hole for shelter, for he was getting very cold. He sat in this large hole in the red cedar logs until night came.

Someone spoke to him, but he could not see who it was. "Prepare yourself," the voice said, "for the one that will possess you is coming." This is what the unseen voice said to the lazy boy. The boy became very frightened. He felt suddenly completely different, as if something had entered him and transformed him. A supernatural force had taken hold of him. This is what the invisible voice had warned him would happen – that a supernatural being would enter him. They say that, he would be *ƛugʷala* – blessed with supernatural power. He now had been transformed into a *hamaċa*, as the supernatural being who possessed him was Baxʷbakʷalanuxʷsiwēy̓, the Man-Eater.

When daylight came, he left his home. It is said that he flew swiftly like the wind and caused great grief to his people because he was eating them. He had become a Man-Eater. This is also what they used to say about the earlier *hamaċa* – that they were Man-Eaters.

On top of his head was a little totem pole tied with a knot woven out of red cedar bark. This was his *ƛugʷēy̓*, his supernatural gift. It was a *hamspiq*, a miniature *hamaċa* pole. This was tied on top of his head because this was his *hamaċa* totem pole. He came and flew swiftly above his village and ate people. He would kidnap them and eat them. He had become very fierce. He brought great sorrow to his people because he would eat them. His parents became very concerned when they found out that the *hamaċa* was their son. They would gather the menstrual pads of the women and pour the blood at his favourite place, at a point near Knight Inlet. They used to say in the early days that the menstrual blood of a woman would bring the *hamaċa* back to his human condition. His fellow tribesmen tried to lasso him but they could not capture him. His younger siblings suggested that one of them must be sacrificed in order to trap him. They chose one of the younger brothers, killed him, and brought his body to the *hamaċa*'s favourite place. It did not take long until he ate his brother's entire corpse. And he flew swiftly like the wind to wherever he went. He would disappear for four days at a time. This is what he would do.

The time came for him to return. It was dawn when he came back, flying around and around, circling his father's house. They could hear him rattling on the roof of the house. He was bringing his *hamspiq* home, his miniature *hamaċa* pole, which was tied on top of his head. He brought it through the hole in the roof of his father's house. Səmsəmsid [many mouths; *səms:* mouth] was the name of his *hamaċa* pole. His *hamaċa* whistle made fantastic sounds. It had several voices, producing the sound of the Bəkʷʼəs [the Wild Man of the Woods], the Owl ["pəyup əyup"], and the Raven. His whistle made the sounds of all these birds. Another whistle sounded like Qʷaniq̓ʷala. This whistle had a very peculiar raven-like voice, which we call Qʷaniq̓ʷala. These were the sounds of his *mad̓is*, or *hamaċa* whistle. These were the voices that his whistle produced.

He finally landed on top of the roof of his father's house, and the father decided to perform a *ċeqa* in honour of his lazy son, who had been blessed with this great supernatural treasure. This was his lazy son. He was now sure that this would make him more powerful than the potlatch chief of the rival tribe.

The potlatch chief with the lazy son was now also the owner of a ćeqa because his son had encountered Baxʷbakʷalanuxʷsiwēẏ and had been blessed with the supernatural gift called Səmsəmsid – the haṁaća pole.

The son started his dance at the top of the pole, then appeared through the first mouth at the top of the carved column, and then went down, in and out of each mouth, right down to the bottom of the carved pole. This dance was performed right after he cast the pole on the ground, transforming it into his haṁspiq inside his father's house. The lazy boy's father had a great big ćeqa that day on account of the supernatural gift bestowed upon his lazy son, the son who had run into the forest at night. And it was at Knight Inlet that he encountered a spirit that possessed him. It was at Knight Inlet that he was bestowed with this great supernatural gift.

This is the myth (ńuẏəm) that Ḡʷəmḡəmlilas passed on to me. She told it to me when Cuxʷćaʔesa,[49] Duda's brother, brought out this haṁaća pole at his potlatch. They gave it as a dowry to Peter Smith. This was a dowry for Duda,[50] the haṁaća pole called Səmsəmsid. That is how the haṁaća pole came to his [Peter Smith's] family. This pole is now owned by Lorne Smith [Daisy's husband] as it was given to him by his uncle.[51] This is all I know. This is what Ḡʷəmḡəmlilas told me.

M13 – Baxʷbakʷalanuxʷsiwēẏ: The Man-Eater at the Mouth of the River

ʔAwiḱinux̌ʷ Version

This ńuẏəm [myth] is from the ʔAwiḱinux̌ʷ [Rivers Inlet people]. It is called Nənẇaqawēẏ [Wisest One; Man of Wisdom]. Nənẇaqawēẏ was a chief who had four children, all sons. According to the legend, they were very active, clever hunters and trappers. They were always hunting for animals. They used to go deep in the forest and high up the mountain to do their trapping and hunting.

One day they decided to go to this particular mountain. Nənẇaqawēẏ tried to warn his children, saying to them: "Be very careful. You can go to the house from which black smoke belches out of the smoke-hole; that is the house of the Grizzly Bear. Never enter the house whose smoke-hole expels the fiery colour of blood. It is said that the house from which blood-coloured smoke rises is the house of Baxʷbakʷalanuxʷsiwēẏ, the Man-Eater at the Mouth of the River. It is said that Baxʷbakʷalanuxʷsiwēẏ lives there. Do not enter. You can go to the house from which brown-coloured smoke belches out of the smoke-hole; that is the house of the Bear. You can go to the house from which light brown smoke rises out the smoke-hole; that is the house of the Deer. That is a safe place to go. The house with the smoke-hole expelling white smoke is also a safe place to go; that is the house of the Mountain Goat. These are the homes that you can go to. But do not go to the houses I have warned you about."

As a precaution, their father gave them four things: a *daṅax* [a special stone], *x̱ag̱əm* [a comb], *p̓aləms* [a ball of wool], and *ƛadəm* [hair oil]. Four things were given to them. "It will surely happen," he said, " Baxʷbakʷalanuxʷsiwēy̓ will come after you. If he does pursue you, never put the things in front of you. Put them always behind you. Always put each thing behind you when you throw it on the ground. Pour the hair oil behind you. Never in front of you." This is what their father said to them as he gave them the four things. "For he will surely come after you and pursue you," Nənẇaqawēy̓ warned them.

The boys left and walked up the mountain and sat at the very top. The youngest son had injured his knee. Some dry blood was still showing on his knee. Then they saw it. They saw a house where the smoke-hole expelled a fiery column of smoke and ashes towards the low-lying clouds. The four disobedient brothers [*nəṁiṁas*] entered the house they were warned not to go to. This was the house from which blood-coloured smoke was belching out of the smoke-hole. They argued before entering. "Our father told us to enter the house from which blood-coloured smoke rises out of the smoke-hole," said the eldest. "He did not," said the youngest. "That is the very house that he told us not to go to." The eldest insisted, arguing that it was the very house that their father told them to go to, the house with the blood-coloured smoke rising out of the smoke-hole.

They finally decided to go in. They saw a huge woman whose face was black. She was the wife of Baxʷbakʷalanuxʷsiwēy̓. This huge woman was fidgeting and licking her lips greedily. There was also a child wandering around in the house. The child was crying, pointing at the dry blood showing on the knee of the youngest son. The four brothers became very frightened for they now realized that they were in the house of the Man-Eaters. They could see that the man-eating child was hungry for the blood that had dripped out of the youngest brother's knee. The huge woman got up and walked towards him, carrying a stick. "Scrape off the blood on your knee for my son," she said to the youngest boy. The youngest son spat on his knee and started scraping the blood, for it had now dried and become hard. He gave the stick to the male infant, who ate the stick and the blood together.

The four brothers were now very frightened and devised a plan of escape. "Let us try to shoot arrows through the knothole in the wall," the youngest brother said. The youngest boy always seemed to have more sense than did his elder brothers. "You will shoot first," he said to the eldest of the four, for they still had their bows and arrows with them.

There was a knothole in the wall, and he asked them to try to shoot their arrows through it. The oldest brother shot first. His arrow went right through the knothole in the wall. The youngest brother said to the oldest one, "You go out and retrieve your arrow." The oldest brother jumped up and ran out of the house and never returned. The second brother shot his arrow right through the hole, and he too was told to go out and retrieve it. He also never returned. Likewise, the third brother shot his arrow through the knothole and ran outside to retrieve it. They were all very frightened.

The huge woman, whose face was black, fidgeted some more and continued licking her lips. She wanted so much to eat the four brothers, for it is said that the Baxʷbakʷalanuxʷsiwēẏ is a man-eater.

All the brothers had run out now, except for the youngest. He took his bow and arrow and shot through the hole. All his older brothers had already run for safety. When the youngest brother started to run, the huge woman tried to grab him. She had finally realized that the brothers were not going to return after retrieving their arrows. The whole building rumbled as she cried out, "Baxʷbakʷalanuxʷsiwēẏ, we would have feasted, Baxʷbakʷalanuxʷsiwēẏ!" The woman cried as she called to her husband to return from wherever he was.

The four boys ran as fast as they could down the mountainside. They could hear the sound of many whistles all over the mountain as Baxʷbakʷalanuxʷsiwēẏ swiftly pursued them. Baxʷbakʷalanuxʷsiwēẏ was catching up to them when they finally remembered the objects that their father had given them. They took the hair oil and poured it behind them. It turned instantly into a huge lake. Baxʷbakʷalanuxʷsiwēẏ was on the other shore, delayed by the lake. The four boys ran and ran as fast as they could.

Baxʷbakʷalanuxʷsiwēẏ managed to cross the lake by swimming and soon he had nearly caught up with the boys. Baxʷbakʷalanuxʷsiwēẏ was again close behind them. They took the ball of wool and threw it behind them, and it turned instantly into a very dense patch of fog. Baxʷbakʷalanuxʷsiwēẏ could not see, but there was no fog where the boys were because they had put the wool behind them. They were able to see ahead. Baxʷbakʷalanuxʷsiwēẏ eventually managed to find his way out of the wool that had turned into fog.

The boys' father heard the commotion as they were running down the mountain. He could hear Baxʷbakʷalanuxʷsiwēẏ sounding the craving for human flesh in the *haṁaċa* cry of "hap, hap, hap!" As Baxʷbakʷalanuxʷsiwēẏ had again nearly caught up with the four boys, they took the comb and threw it on the ground behind them, where it turned instantly into a thicket of small trees. Baxʷbakʷalanuxʷsiwēẏ had to struggle to get through because the trees had formed a fence [ḱakus] around him. When the trees are all very close together, they called it ḱakus. Baxʷbakʷalanuxʷsiwēẏ caught up to them again. And they had only one more object to throw: this was the *dənax*. They say it is shaped like a miniature mountain and is made out of stone. "I warned them," the father said to himself. "Tie our house down, Nənwaqawēy̓!" the boys screamed to their father. They threw the *dənax* behind them, where it turned instantly into a huge rock that stood in front of the Man-Eater. It was the last thing they could use to block the way of Baxʷbakʷalanuxʷsiwēy̓. They were now very close to their father's house.

Nənwaqawēy̓ had secured his house by tying it firmly down. The four sons ran swiftly into the house and bolted the door.

Baxʷbakʷalanuxʷsiwēy̓ came swiftly, pacing around the house and uttering his *haṁaċa* cry. "Why don't you calm yourself?" Nənwaqawēy̓ said to the Man-Eater. "Calm down." He said this to Baxʷbakʷalanuxʷsiwēy̓, who was pacing around the house sounding his whistles. "I do not want you to feast on my sons alone," he said to Baxʷbakʷalanuxʷsiwēy̓. "Go and fetch your wife and your child." He told Baxʷbakʷalanuxʷsiwēy̓ to return home and come back with his family so they could all feast on his sons together.

Baxʷbakʷalanuxʷsiwēy̓ went back up the mountain to fetch his wife and child. While he was gone, the father and his sons dug a hole behind the screen [*ṁawił*] at the back of the house. They took some rocks and heated them in the fire. Nənwaqawēy̓ killed four dogs and prepared them as food. He was going to tell Baxʷbakʷalanuxʷsiwēy̓ that these were his sons.

It was not long before he heard Baxʷbakʷalanuxʷsiwēy̓'s fantastic sounds. He came into the house with his family. The four boys were hidden behind the screen, two on each side. This was the very same screen that Baxʷbakʷalanuxʷsiwēy̓ and his wife would soon be leaning against. Nənwaqawēy̓ and his sons had dug a big pit behind the big screen and covered it with cedar mats.

Baxʷbakʷalanuxʷsiwēy̓ and his family sat down. The rocks were already in the fire, for Nənwaqawēy̓ was going to steam the dogs they had killed to take the place of the boys. Nənwaqawēy̓ led Baxʷbakʷalanuxʷsiwēy̓ to believe that these dogs were his sons. He suggested that he should tell a few stories before the food was cooked. Nənwaqawēy̓ took his talking stick and brought it forward. It had many figures carved on it, all of which were alive. Nənwaqawēy̓ pointed out the figures as he told the stories related to each one of them. The figures on the talking stick were all alive, and when Nənwaqawēy̓ struck the ground with his speaker's staff, the figures all moved and sounded their respective voices. The talking stick of Nənwaqawēy̓ was covered with creatures that were all moving – alive and sounding.

Baxʷbakʷalanuxʷsiwēy̓ and his family enjoyed the myths so much that they got sleepy and finally fell asleep. The screen against which they were leaning opened in the centre and the boys were hidden behind the screen, two on each end. The boys opened the screen in the centre and Baxᵂbakᵂalanuxᵂsiwēẏ and his family fell into the big pit that had been dug. Quickly the boys and their father grabbed all the hot stones from the fire and threw them into the pit, and then they poured water into it. The stones they threw in were red-hot, and they kept pouring water on them. Baxᵂbakᵂalanuxᵂsiwēẏ still kept sounding and did not fall silent for a long time. They kept hearing his *haṁaċa* whistle as well as his *haṁaċa* cry.

They did not check on Baxᵂbakᵂalanuxᵂsiwēẏ and his family for a long time because they wanted to be certain that they were dead. Finally they decided to check to see if they were really dead. Nənẇaqawēẏ and his sons dragged them out of the pit and cut them up. They were looking for what was making the sound of the Baxᵂbakᵂalanuxᵂsiwēẏ – that is, his *haṁaċa* whistle [*ṁədʔis*]. They did not know that the whistle was under his armpit. They tried to look in the stomach of the man-eating ogre. They cut his stomach for nothing, for it was not there. They finally found the whistle under his armpit. It was a bellows whistle, so whenever Baxᵂbakᵂalanuxᵂsiwēẏ pulled his arms up and down, it would sound. They killed Baxᵂbakᵂalanuxᵂsiwēẏ and found the *haṁaċa* whistle. They got it from Baxᵂbakᵂalanuxᵂsiwēẏ after they had killed him.

They also say that our present-day biting insects were created from the ashes of Baxᵂbakᵂalanuxᵂsiwēẏ's body as it was consumed by fire. These are the mosquitoes and the horseflies [*sadikᵂa*]. They say that these miniature blood-seekers were created from the ashes of Baxᵂbakᵂalanuxᵂsiwēẏ. That is what happened. They say that the ashes of Baxᵂbakᵂalanuxᵂsiwēẏ turned into blood-feeding insects. This is the end.

Note: The following myths were recorded and videotaped in 1985 at the house of Flora Sewid, ʔAx̌uẇ's daughter, in Campbell River.

M14 – Baxᵂbakᵂalanuxᵂsiwēẏ: The Man-Eater at the Mouth of the River

ʔAwiḱinux̌ᵂ Version

It is said that Nənẇaqawēẏ was a very wise man. He was also a very experienced man. He had travelled all over his country. He had four sons, all expert mountain goat hunters. *Təwixa* means to go hunting mountain goats up in the mountain. They always seemed to choose a mountain with many challenging obstacles whenever they went mountain goat hunting. "I really do not think you should go there," their father said to them. This was Nənẇaqawēẏ's warning. "The Baxᵂbakᵂalanuxᵂsiwēẏ lives there, at the very place on the mountain where you want to go. Don't go near any house from which red smoke rises out of the roof, because this is the house of Baxʷbakʷalanuxʷsiwēẏ. You will look for the house that has white smoke. This is the house of the Mountain Goat. On your way you may go to the house with light brown smoke. This is the house of the Deer. Don't go near the house with black smoke; this is the house of the Grizzly Bear. Every dangerous animal has black smoke rising out of its house." This is what the father said to his four sons.

Before they left home, their father gave them four things: some wool [ṗaləms], some hair oil [ƛadəm], a stone [dəṅax], and a comb [x̌aḡəm]. Their father had warned them, telling them that if Baxʷbakʷalanuxʷsiwēẏ came after them they would have to use these things that he had given them. They were told to place these objects between themselves and their pursuer. These were the instructions their father gave them.

The four boys left, and one of them, the youngest, injured his knee on the way. The blood ran down his leg and quickly dried up. He still had dried blood on his knee when they entered the house of Baxʷbakʷalanuxʷsiwēẏ.

The eldest of the four boys reminded them of what their father had told them: "Our father had told us to go to the house with the red smoke." The youngest tried to argue with him, saying: "No. I heard him forbid us to go near it." The oldest refused to listen to him and entered the house of Baxʷbakʷalanuxʷsiwēẏ.

The boys came in and sat opposite a big woman. The child of Baxʷbakʷalanuxʷsiwēẏ started crying and pointing at the youngest brother's knee, which was covered with dry blood. The huge wife of Baxʷbakʷalanuxʷsiwēẏ stood up and grabbed her child. He was licking his lips at the desirable thought of eating these boys. She picked up a stick and threw it at the youngest son, saying: "Scrape the blood off your knee." The youngest son of Nənẇaqaweẏ did as he was told and handed it back to her. She took it and passed the stick on to her son, who devoured the blood and the stick all at once.

He was crying because the Baxʷbakʷalanuxʷsiwēẏ were man-eaters and craving human blood.

They became very frightened. Then Q̇oyuweẏ,[52] the last boy before the youngest, spotted a knothole in one of the planks of the house wall and suggested a shooting contest. "Let us try to shoot our arrows through that knothole," said Q̇oyuweẏ to his brothers. "You shoot first," he said to the disobedient elder brother. The latter got up and shot the arrow right through the knothole. His brothers told him to go out to fetch his arrow. The second eldest brother was next. He also shot his arrow right through the knothole and went out to fetch it. One by one they did this, shooting right through the knothole and fetching the arrow without coming back. So every time one of the brothers succeeded in shooting an arrow through the knothole, he went out to fetch it and took the opportunity to run away. They all ran for their lives.

Suddenly the big woman started screaming for Baxʷbakʷalanuxʷsiwēy̓. Just as suddenly, Baxʷbakʷalanuxʷsiwēy̓ appeared, and you could hear the many sounds of his haṁaċa whistle [m̓əd̓is].

The four boys ran as fast as they could with Baxʷbakʷalanuxʷsiwēy̓ pursuing them. Just before the man-eating creature caught up to them, they took the hair oil and poured it on the ground. It turned into a great big lake that they hoped Baxʷbakʷalanuxʷsiwēy̓ could not cross. The boys were running towards their home as fast as they could, when Baxʷbakʷalanuxʷsiwēy̓ almost caught up to them again. They threw the comb on the path behind them. It became a dense entangled thicket. This stopped Baxʷbakʷalanuxʷsiwēy̓ for a while. The boys continued running, and just before Baxʷbakʷalanuxʷsiwēy̓ caught up to them, they used the rock, and it turned into a huge mountain with a cliff so steep that it was impossible to climb it. Now they were left with only one thing, the wool.

They finally reached the house of their father. He could hear the boys screaming, "Tie down the house with a rope so that Baxʷbakʷalanuxʷsiwēy̓ cannot get through!" The father came out and said, "I tried to warn you, you disobedient boys!" They kept screaming at Nənẇaqawēy̓ to tie the house down as the sounds of the man-eating ogre who was chasing them were getting nearer and nearer. Then the boys threw the wool down behind them, and it became a very thick fog patch. But Baxʷbakʷalanuxʷsiwēy̓ always managed to get around every obstacle that was put before him.

The boys ran into the house. They could hear Baxʷbakʷalanuxʷsiwēy̓ circling the house, and they could hear the sounds of his multiple whistles: "hap, hap, hap, hap!" The sounds of Baxʷbakʷalanuxʷsiwēy̓!

"Calm down for a while," said Nənẇaqawēy̓ to Baxʷbakʷalanuxʷsiwēy̓. "Calm down long enough for me to say something to you. I would like to suggest that you do not eat my sons just on your own. I think you should go fetch your wife and your son so that we can all feast on my sons." This is what Nənẇaqawēy̓ said to Baxʷbakʷalanuxʷsiwēy̓. The man-eating ogre took Nənẇaqawēy̓'s advice and went to fetch his wife and child.

In the meantime, Nənẇaqawēy̓ slaughtered his four dogs so that Baxʷbakʷalanuxʷsiwēy̓ would think that they were his sons. They would be ready for cooking by the time the man-eating creatures arrived.

Nənẇaqawēy̓ dug a hole and placed the backrest at its edge. The boys were hiding behind each end of the backrest, two on each side.

The huge Baxʷbakʷalanuxʷsiwēy̓ and his family entered the house. Nənẇaqawēy̓ heated some rocks to cook the four dogs he had killed. Baxʷbakʷalanuxʷsiwēy̓ came and sat down, leaning against the backrest.

Nənw̓aqaweỹ's wife suggested that he should tell stories before the feast. "Tell them stories of particular events that happened in your life," she said to Nənw̓aqaweỹ. He replied, "Go and get my speaker's staff [ỹaǧənp̓iq]." The talking stick looked like the one owned by N̓umas [Q̓ʷəmxuduw̓].[53] His staff appeared to be a replica of Nənw̓aqaweỹ's staff. All the figures carved on Nənw̓aqaweỹ's staff were alive. As he was telling the story he would hit the floor with it. The Baxʷbakʷalanuxʷsiweỹ family enjoyed the storytelling but soon fell asleep. As soon as they fell asleep, the boys released the props that were holding the backrest, and the man-eating creatures fell into the pit. Nənw̓aqaweỹ quickly grabbed the tongs and started throwing the hot rocks into the pit, while his four sons poured water into it. Baxʷbakʷalanuxʷsiweỹ and his family were killed by the boiling water. It is said that Baxʷbakʷalanuxʷsiweỹ was still making his whistling sound, even though he was covered with hot rocks and boiling water.

Nənw̓aqaweỹ and his family did not uncover them until the noise ceased; they did not check on them until they were silent for a long time. After they were dead, Nənw̓aqaweỹ and his boys cut them up in order to find the m̓əd̓is, the instruments making the whistling sounds. They did not find the whistle right away, but, sometime later, they found it where it had fallen out of Baxʷbakʷalanuxʷsiweỹ's armpit into the fire-pit. It was a bellows whistle. They had cut up Baxʷbakʷalanuxʷsiweỹ in vain because they thought that the noise was coming from his stomach. They had killed Baxʷbakʷalanuxʷsiweỹ and his family.

It is said that the horseflies and all the insects that bite and feed on human beings, such as horseflies [sadik̓ʷa] and mosquitoes [ƛisƛən], were born from the ashes of Baxʷbakʷalanuxʷsiweỹ. This is why the insects like to bite. That is all for now.

M15 – Nənw̓aqaweỹ's Sons and K̓uɬx̌eỹ

ʔAwik̓inux̌ʷ Version

The four boys wanted to go out again because they were good mountain goat hunters. They told their father they wanted to go to a very special place. Again, their father told them that they were choosing the worst place to go. "It is a very dangerous place, where you want to go. Let me warn you. Do not sleep where the ground is clear and level," he said to them. And of course the foolish eldest again made the same mistake by telling his younger brothers to go to a clearing: "This is the place our father told us to sleep in." They lay down and fell asleep. When they woke up, they found out that they were sleeping on top of a mountain, at the very edge of a steep cliff. This is why their father had warned them not to sleep there. They were really in trouble. They had taken cedar ropes with them to lasso mountain goats. This is what *təwixa* means, to lasso a mountain goat with a loop on a rope.

What could they do? They were just looking straight down the cliff. They had been sleeping on a ledge of solid rock. The youngest asked the oldest to give him his rope; then he asked his other brothers to give him their ropes too so that he could tie them together in the hope that they would reach the bottom of the cliff. He told the eldest to tie the rope about his waist and he lowered him down the cliff. He let the others down as well. Then the only one left on the ledge was the youngest. What could he do? He just dropped the rope and shouted at his brothers to go home. They were really in trouble because they had been told not to go to such a place.

When all his brothers had gone, the youngest, left alone, decided to go back to sleep. It was not long before someone came and shook him. He was told to get up and follow a path that had been made for him. He sat up and looked around but could not see anything or anyone. He thought that he must have been dreaming. This happened to him four times. Someone would come and shake him and tell him that there was a path that had been made for him. When it happened to him the third time, he decided that he would pretend to be asleep. He covered himself with *woẍsoẁ*, a woven cedar-bark cloak, and made a hole in it so that he could peek through it and see who was coming and shaking him.

It was not long before a little man appeared wearing a cedar-bark headdress. The youngest son knew that the little man was a white weasel, an ermine. "Get up and follow the path I have made for you," the little man said. The path they were travelling on was very narrow and it made the boy very nervous. The little man, noticing the boy's nervousness, turned to him and told him to put his palms up. He took them and placed them against his own palms. Then he told the boy to put his feet up, and he placed the soles of his own feet against those of the boy. The boy was amazed, as now the palms of his hands and the soles of his feet seemed to stick to the rocks; he could now climb up or down the mountain without difficulty.

Nənẁaqawēy̓ was very upset when his sons told him that the youngest son had not been able to come down the mountain with them. But the youngest son managed to get down the cliff safely with the help of the little man and finally returned home.

Next they decided to go to a place where everybody always feared to go. "You are just the most disobedient children," Nənẁaqawēy̓ said to them. "You have now chosen a place that is even more dangerous than the previous ones." They wanted to go to a trapping place owned by ẍuɬẍēy. ẍuɬẍēy is the name of the cougar [*ṁaṁisa*]. It was on a very slanted mountain where the boys could have disappeared, never to be heard of again. They reached the trapping place of ƛuɫx̌ēy, which was on the very top of the mountain, and here they fell over the smooth, slippery edge.

ƛuɫx̌ēy came to check his trap, and he saw that he had caught many things. He was so happy when he saw how much he had caught.

Nənwaqawēẏ knew that something serious had happened to his sons because they were gone for so long. He made an outfit out of ćaḡʷəmɫ [thimble-berry] and went looking for them. He knew where the traps of ƛuɫx̌ēy were. He arrived there wearing his thimbleberry outfit just as ƛuɫx̌ēy was emptying his trap. ƛuɫx̌ēy named each species as he took it out of his trap. He was very happy when he saw that he had caught some unusual species.

Wearing his thimbleberry outfit Nənwaqawēẏ went to the trap site, lay down, and fell asleep. ƛuɫx̌ēy came upon him and carried him out on his shoulders. He could feel that what he was carrying was breathing. He touched Nənwaqawēẏ again to see if he were breathing, but this time Nənwaqawēẏ held his breath. ƛuɫx̌ēy picked him up, carrying him over his shoulders again, and took him to his house. He threw Nənwaqawēẏ on his butchering table and went to get his knife. He pointed the knife at Nənwaqawēẏ four times; as he did it the fourth time, Nənwaqawēẏ grabbed his wrist. ƛuɫx̌ēy had taken his cougar outfit off and now tried to put it on again, but it was too late. Nənwaqawēẏ had seen him. The only part of the cougar outfit that ƛuɫx̌ēy was able to put on was the palms. The other cougars told ƛuɫx̌ēy not to feel bad but to negotiate with Nənwaqawēẏ. Nənwaqawēẏ demanded that his sons be returned to him. But the sons had broken their heads when they slipped against the rocks at the trap site of ƛuɫx̌ēy. That was the last thing that these boys ever did in their lives.

He did get his sons back, so I guess they were brought back to life.

That is the end.

M16 – The White Seagull Woman[54]

ʔAwiƙinux̌ʷ Version[55]

This happened during the Flood. Q̓ʷəmq̓ʷəmgila was an ʔAwiƙinux̌ʷ man [from Rivers Inlet]. He had four ʔaẏəlkʷ [servants]. I do not know what you call ʔaẏəlkʷ in English; it is not exactly a slave [ɉakuɫ]. Q̓ʷəmq̓ʷəmgila was beating his drum and singing for his four servants as they performed the ɫasəla [the Peace Dance]. His drum was a carved box drum,[56] in the northern style.

He told the boys to stop dancing when he finished his song. Then they went to this place called Nuxʷəns. This is where my mother's oldest brother went. This man's name was Hemaskən [Raven], and he lived at Nuxʷəns. It is said that a large eagle flew down to the water's edge, and, when the water of the incoming Flood touched the bird, it turned into stone. This happened at Nuxʷəns, not too far from a river.

The four servants were approaching this big rock. As they reached it, a beautiful white Seagull[57] appeared. The Seagull never showed any sign of fright at the sight of these four men walking around in the area. The four servants decided to try to catch it, which they did without much difficulty. It was a beautiful Seagull, with pure white, immaculate plumage. They captured it and went to get the carved box drum they had left on the rock. They put the white Seagull in it and covered it with a lid when they left.

They did not check on the box drum for four days. On the fourth day they came back, and, to their surprise, a beautiful woman was sitting beside the box. They looked at her, and, after some discussion among themselves, they agreed that Q̓ʷəmq̓ʷəmgila rather than one of them should take her for a wife. They brought her to him so that he could marry her. I guess these four men were like slaves, but they are not called slaves in this *ńuy̓əm*, they are called *ʔay̓əlkʷ*. These were the four servants who drifted into this area during the Flood.

Q̓ʷəmq̓ʷəmgila took this beautiful woman for his wife. She was so attractive, with her very long hair. There was something else about her as well: Q̓ʷəmq̓ʷəmgila noticed an unusual scent emanating from her. Very soon she became pregnant.

Q̓ʷəmq̓ʷəmgila would often ask her, "Please tell me your name; please give us your name or we will just continue to call you '*y̓ax y̓ax*'! Hey, you!" They did not know what to call her, so when they talked to her they would just say "Hey, you!" The woman refused to tell them her name. She had an unusual scent, and the men thought that it was a metal-like scent.[58] She became pregnant and gave birth to twins. One of the babies, a female, died. These were the children of Q̓ʷəmq̓ʷəmgila. The surviving child was a male.

The Seagull Woman said to Q̓ʷəmq̓ʷəmgila: "How do you feel about us going to ʔAlakilağamēy̓ and asking him for his daughter's hand so you could marry her." "If that is your wish dear," he replied to his wife, whom he really respected. The Seagull Woman had suggested to her husband that they proceed to get another wife for him.

They all left, travelling by foot. Their young son became exhausted and did not want to go on any further. He refused to go any further with his parents and the four servants. The father really did not want to leave his son behind. But the mother did not say a word. The Seagull Woman did not seem to care whether the child went with them or not. "We will just take turns carrying you on our shoulders," Q̓ʷəmq̓ʷəmgila said. The child rejected his father's offer and said to him: "Just simply build me a shelter here, and I will be fine." Q̓ʷəmq̓ʷəmgila gave in and built him a shelter. He was heartbroken about leaving his son behind, but after they had built him the shelter, they continued on towards their destination. When they reached a large lake, the Seagull Woman said to the servants, "Go and borrow a canoe so that we may cross the lake." One of the servants left, went somewhere around the lake, and returned with a rolled-up mat that was similar to our woven red cedar-bark mat. He gave it to the Seagull Woman, who spread it out. They all sat on this mat, which carried them magically across the lake. When they reached the other side of the lake, the woman folded it again and hid it. They crossed four lakes, and at each one they borrowed a special mat, which, after the crossing, she folded and hid.

They reached the village of ꞌAlakilaḡamēẏ. She told her husband to find out whether or not there were people living there. She asked him to shout, "Is there any human being living here?" Her husband did as she asked, repeating: "Is there any human being living here?" There was no reply. "I guess there is no one living here, dear," he said to his wife. "Do you expect to get a reply so soon?" she said. "You must shout four times before you get a reply." After the fourth call there appeared a woman with long braids and a head with two identical faces, one in front and one in back. This was Helaṁolaḡa, the Mouse Woman. "What do you want?" she asked. "We have come to ask to marry the princess [*ḱidit*] of ꞌAlakilaḡamēẏ," Q̓ʷəmq̓ʷəmgila replied. The Mouse Woman disappeared and went to ꞌAlakilaḡamēẏ. She stuck her head through a round hole so as to talk to ꞌAlakilaḡamēẏ. She returned to Q̓ʷəmq̓ʷəmgila and reported that ꞌAlakilaḡamēẏ had stated that he may now proceed with the wedding songs. Q̓ʷəmq̓ʷəmgila started singing with his four servants, who had earlier performed the *ⱡasəla* Dance. He kept singing for a while with the four servants, and then he told them that was enough.

Through a hole, ꞌAlakilaḡamēẏ handed a long strip of material made of something similar to mountain goat wool, which he called *ʔalagəm*.[59] This is where his name comes from. These are the names of the northern people:

> ꞌAlagəmit: Buckskin in the House
> ꞌAlagiloḡʷa: Buckskin Woman

These names refer to the white piece of buckskin put through the hole.

There were four strips in all, and each time one was handed through the hole, the Seagull Woman took it. She took it, folded it, and put it away as it was given to her. There was a total of four *ʔalagəm*. These were handed through the hole as part of the dowry for Q̓ʷəmq̓ʷəmgila's future wife.

The Mouse Woman repeated the process of calling ꞌAlakilaḡamēẏ. She had long braids and two identical faces – one in the front, one in the back.

ꞋAlakilağamēẏ appeared at the hole again and handed to the Seagull Woman
a little baby wrapped in *Ɂalagəm*. This female infant was the future bride of
Q̇ʷəmq̇ʷəmgila, for whom the Seagull Woman had come.

From the size of the child you could tell that it was a newborn. The baby was
handed over by ꞋAlakilağamēẏ and was accompanied by a small container [kʷéćiẏ;
like a small chamber pot]. The child bride-to-be and this small container came
together.

Q̇ʷəmq̇ʷəmgila held the child for a moment as he was trying to make a
decision regarding what to do. In the meantime, the Mouse Woman had
disappeared. Q̇ʷəmq̇ʷəmgila turned to his wife and said: "I do not want the
responsibility of taking this child. We would not travel too far before she died."
The Seagull Woman said to him, "What you decide to do with the child is your
responsibility."

He called out to someone to come and take the child back. As he did this,
ꞋAlakilağamēẏ came out to see him. Before, he would just send the Mouse
Woman to negotiate with Q̇ʷəmq̇ʷəmgila. Q̇ʷəmq̇ʷəmgila said to ꞋAlakilağamēẏ,
"ꞋAlakilağamēẏ, I do not want to take such a responsibility. What if something
happens to your child?" "You have made a major mistake, Q̇ʷəmq̇ʷəmgila," said
ꞋAlakilağamēẏ. "If you had accepted my child, your descendants would have died
but they would have been in their graves for only four days. That is the reason I
gave you the q̇ʷəlasta, the life-giving water, in this little container. You would have
just had to sprinkle the life-giving water on them to bring them back to life. You
have made a major mistake."

ꞋAlakilağamēẏ took his child and went back home, but the names that were
to come with it, as a dowry, were given to Q̇ʷəmq̇ʷəmgila. These are the names:
ꞋAlakilağamēẏ, ꞋAlagiloğʷa, ꞋAlagəmił. These are the names that were given to
him along with the *Ɂalagəm*. This was the dowry that came with the female
infant in spite of the fact that he did not marry her. And this is precisely the
dowry that the Seagull Woman wanted.

They quickly left and travelled with great speed to where their son had been
left in the shelter they had built for him. When they had to cross the four lakes
again, she repeated the same process as she had before – spreading the mats
and folding them – but she always returned them to the four original owners.
When they finally reached the place where they had left their son, they were
shocked to see a huge house exactly where they had built a small shelter. Their
son had received a supernatural treasure [ƛugʷēẏ]. There was a carved figure of
a man standing outside the house, who, judging from its body language, was
endlessly giving praise [cəlwaqa].⁶⁰ And on one side of the house was a big
canoe [xʷakʷəna]. These were the supernatural treasures their child – the
surviving twin – had received. On top of another carved pole was an eagle that

would catch fish, or anything edible from the sea (like seals and so forth), with which to feed this fortunate child. They decided to stay with their son and not to return to where they had lived before. They decided to stay with him as he had received several supernatural treasures.

The Seagull Woman told the servants to gather as much cedar bark as possible [təqəm: rope; dəwix: cedar rope]. So they did and filled the canoe with it. She had decided to visit her father. That is why she had asked them to gather enough cedar bark to make a long rope. They were going to need it. They left and reached the tunnel of x̌aqʷagila [Copper Maker]. This is what the ńuɏəm says. Before they went into the tunnel, the Seagull Woman draped the Ɂalagəm over the canoe and tied it with the ropes. When they reached the tunnel she stood up, but she did not ask the men to assist her. She seemed to know what she was doing. She said to the four servants, "When we go through the tunnel you must paddle with great speed. No one has ever survived the place in which we will find ourselves. Others have tried, but their canoes have capsized." This is what the Seagull Woman said to the men. The Seagull Woman took a toolbox and sat firmly on it with the child beside her as they started going through the tunnel. As they were advancing deeper into the tunnel, they saw many skeletons floating around them. These were the remains of those who had attempted to go through the tunnel of x̌aqʷagila. When they reached the end of the tunnel, they found themselves at the edge of a powerful waterfall. This waterfall was the reason other canoes had capsized and sunk. But the Ɂalagəm was draped over their canoe to prevent the water from getting into it and capsizing it. They went through the tunnel, and, as they paddled, the oars stirred up the bones floating around their canoe. These were the skeletons of all those who had drowned attempting to go through the tunnel of x̌aqʷagila. Finally, they safely reached the land of the Seagull Woman's father.

There was no vegetation growing in this country, in this land of x̌aqʷagila. When they arrived, x̌aqʷagila was standing outside his house. When he saw his daughter and child sitting on the toolbox, he went to meet them. He shouted: "So, that is where you disappeared to, x̌aqʷagiloǧʷa [Copper Woman]." He started to call out her names, all of which referred to copper. "So, that is where you disappeared to, x̌aqʷaǧalaǧēɏ, Q̓aq̓ənqalaǧa [a name referring to copper scent]." He would call all these names out, switching back and forth between the names referring to copper and the names referring to the scent of copper. This is why she refused to give her name. She had many copper names.

The father's servants came down and lifted the canoe with copper poles and brought it to the front of his house. They all got off the canoe and went into the house.

This is the part that is so foolish!

In the house were many little seals. They were moving around the floor of the house. The Seagull Woman said: "Don't feed the guests with *ł̓alsa* [filleted halibut]; kill one of the seals, one of these little brothers, and feed them with it." It happened that the seals were the people's dogs. That is what they did.[61]

They decided to return home. Q̓ʷəmq̓ʷəmgila gave to his father-in-law *təqəm* [rope] and *dəwix* [cedar rope] as a bride-price. He received all these things because, in the land of his father-in-law, everything was made of copper, even the canoes and the paddles, and he did not have the types of trees from which to manufacture ropes. That is also why the Seagull Woman insisted that they gather a lot of fibres, like *dəwix* and *təqəm* – to make a very long rope. Even ƛ̓aq̓ʷagila's fish trap had broken down because he had tried to make it out of copper. Now he was able to tie his traps with *dəwix*. That was the bride-price Q̓ʷəmq̓ʷəmgila paid to his father-in-law. The Seagull Woman went to Q̓ʷəmq̓ʷəmgila and told him that her father ƛ̓aq̓ʷagila [Copper Maker] wanted his wooden canoe. Q̓ʷəmq̓ʷəmgila said to his wife, "If I do give it to him, what will we use to return home?" ƛ̓aq̓ʷagila already had it in mind to give Q̓ʷəmq̓ʷəmgila a copper canoe as part of his daughter's dowry, and he would have this canoe ready before they left. This canoe was similar to what you now see, like the White man's boat, so he would not be without a canoe in which to return home. So Q̓ʷəmq̓ʷəmgila consented to let his own wooden canoe be given as a bride-price.

ƛ̓aq̓ʷagila filled the copper canoe with Coppers. Q̓ʷəmq̓ʷəmgila and the Seagull Woman left the land of ƛ̓aq̓ʷagila and travelled home. The copper canoe made an unusual sound because it had a copper covering. It looked like a modern boat that was covered in such a way that it would not sink when they went through the tunnel of ƛ̓aq̓ʷagila.

Q̓ʷəmq̓ʷəmgila decided to call the people together, and everybody was talking about how he was going to give away the Coppers he had received. Q̓ʷəmq̓ʷəmgila was going to gather the people together to show them what he had received as a dowry from his wife.

There is a song that Q̓ʷəmxuduẃ [ʔAx̌uẃ's uncle] used to sing. This is the song that Q̓ʷəmq̓ʷəmgila sang at this gathering. It is a *ƛasəla* [Peace Dance] song, and it is in the ʔAwiƙinux̌ʷ language. These are the words of this *ƛasəla* song:

kec̓ux̌ palax̌s dux̌ x̌as
wiwəna tusila ƙalux̌
sumax̌ala kasuʔuẃ

He would sing it for the *hilikələł* [the main dancers of the *ƛasəla*].[62] I recorded this song for my daughter Flora some time ago, and this is why I remember the words. Q̓ʷəmq̓ʷəmgila travelled down the coast. As he did so, he passed by a village and the people called out to him, saying: *wiwəna tusila ƙaluẋ.* "The people are calling out" is what the words of the song mean: *wiwəna tusila.* This song refers to the people who saw him from their village as he travelled down the coast in his copper canoe, making the sound of Coppers clanging against each other.

> *Səbəlƙala gəʔe:* You Are on the Water Making the Sounds of Coppers Clanging Together
> *Səbəlẋidʔəmǧa:* Coppers Clanging Together Woman
> *Səbəlẋawidʔəmǧa:* Clanging Copper Woman

This sound was coming from the many Coppers he had on board, and this is what he was going to give to these people when they gathered together. The people to whom he is referring as *wiwəna tusila* were the people living in villages along the coast who called out to him as he passed by. "Won't you spare us one Copper?" they would plead. And this is what the song says.

He did throw Coppers to people who asked for them.

[ʔAẋuw̓ sings the song.] All the people of the coast had heard that he was going to give away Coppers; this is why they were calling to him as he passed by. This was the dowry from his wife, the daughter of ƙaqʷagila.

This is the end. This is what the *ńuẏəm* says.

M17 – Hemaskasʔuw̓: The Raven and the Daylight Keeper

It is said that at one time there was no daylight, and, as a result, it was always dark. This caused great concern to all the people. They were trying to decide how to correct this state of affairs. It had something to do with the Daylight Keeper. Some of the people suggested that they should transform themselves into berries so that the Daylight Keeper would eat them. This is what some of them said, and I am merely following what the *ńuẏəm* says.

Some of the people said it was not a good idea because this was winter and there were no fresh berries available. Some others suggested that they could transform themselves into something edible that the Daylight Keeper's daughter would eat and then become impregnated.

Hemaskasʔuw̓, the Raven, got up and spoke: "I will volunteer my services. I will transform myself into a tiny pine needle and fall into the drinking water." It is true that whenever people fetch water, they always take a drink. They all agreed that Hemaskasʔuw̓ had a good idea.

So, this is what Hemaskasʔuw̓ did. He transformed himself into a pine needle, which was floating around in the drinking water of the Daylight Keeper.

His daughter did exactly as was predicted. She took a drink of water before she filled up her container, and almost immediately Hemaskasʔuw̓, in his tiny little pine-needle form, jumped into her drinking water.

A short while later the daughter of the Daylight Keeper became pregnant. The Daylight Keeper and his family were living all by themselves in this area, but they did not seem to be concerned by the fact that their daughter was pregnant. In time she gave birth to Hemaskasʔuw̓, a Raven boy in his human form, who was deeply loved and indulged by his grandfather. When it was time for Hemaskasʔuw̓ to make his move, he pointed at the container where the daylight was stored.

"I wonder what your grandson wants. He seems to be wanting the box of daylight," someone said. And of course Hemaskasʔuw̓ immediately nodded his head. Someone had guessed what he wanted. His grandfather gave him the box. Then he started pointing at the canoe that was beached in front of the house. "He seems to want to go sailing with it," said his grandfather. The child immediately nodded his head, as he did not yet know how to speak. He just cried whenever he wanted something. The grandfather yielded and put him in the canoe, tying it up with a cedar rope. Throughout history, Hemaskasʔuw̓'s best friend has always been Helamolaǧa, the Mouse Woman. She had accompanied Hemaskasʔuw̓. The grandfather pushed the canoe out and pulled it back and forth, again and again, to pacify the child.

Hemaskasʔuw̓ was so happy that his grandfather had found out what he wanted. The grandfather pushed him far out to sea and then pulled him back in again. When the grandfather pushed him far out, Helamolaǧa quickly chewed the cedar rope to make it break. They paddled away swiftly and escaped with the box of daylight. This was when there was no daylight on earth. Hemaskasʔuw̓ opened the box of daylight and the whole earth became flooded with light. This is what Hemaskasʔuw̓ did. This is not a very long story. This occurred when Hemaskasʔuw̓ challenged the Daylight Keeper, when the earth was in complete darkness, and he became the Raven-child of the Daylight Keeper's daughter. This is the end.

M18 – Hemaskasʔuw̓: The Raven and How He Lost His Daughter[63]

Hemaskasʔuw̓ was building a canoe in the forest. Every day he went into the forest. One day, as he was going to work on his canoe, his daughter insisted on going with him. He was reluctant to take her with him, but, as this was the first time the child had wanted to go with him, he yielded. Hemaskasʔuw̓'s daughter was an extraordinary child. She was extremely beautiful, made even more so by the elaborate tattoos around her ankles and wrists. She also wore her very long hair loose along her back.

On the day that the canoe was going to be completed they put hot rocks in the water inside the boat in order to steam it open. This is what he was going to do on this very important day, and that is why he did not want his daughter to accompany him. But the daughter just kept crying until she got her way.

When they arrived at the canoe-building site, he saw an unusually large chief's hat resting against his canoe. It had figures painted on it, and they were all alive and moving. "Don't you touch it," he warned his daughter. "This is the first time I have seen such a thing. This is the first time it has ever come here." After the steaming of the canoe was completed, he carried his daughter and put her in it to play. He was now getting ready to launch his vessel.

The girl was attracted to the large hat and wanted to play with it, but her father kept warning her not to get near it. She waited until her father's back was turned, and then she quickly put the hat on. As soon as she did this, the very large giqəmɬ [noble's hat] flew away with her into the sky.

Hemaskasʔuw̓ was so deeply saddened by the disappearance of his daughter that he sang his mourning song for her. (By the way, this is a song I sang for David Gladstone;[64] he is learning and recording Kʷakʷakəwakʷ mourning songs. I keep forgetting to tell ƛalis[65] to take this song so he can use it.)

Hemaskasʔuw̓ would go to the other side of where he lived and he would sing his song daily. [At this point ʔAx̌uw̓ sings the mourning song.] This was the mourning song Hemaskasʔuw̓ sang for his daughter. Q̓umala means mourning, the mourning[66] period for his daughter.

One day, his daughter reappeared and approached him, but he could not see her because of his tears. "Come with me, Hemaskasʔuw̓," she said. "I have now taken pity on you. So let us go home." Hemaskasʔuw̓ opened his eyes and looked at her. To his surprise she was completely bald. She no longer had any hair. Hemaskasʔuw̓ said, "You have no resemblance to my daughter at all," and he resumed crying. The daughter kept pleading for him to go home with her to her house. "If you would only see the place where I just came from, you would not believe the winds that blow there. That is where I lost all my hair! The only reason you do not recognize me any longer is because I no longer have any hair. That is where I lost all my hair," explained the girl. But Hemaskasʔuw̓ insisted she was not his daughter. She finally gave up trying to persuade him, put the large hat on, and flew away again. As she was flying away, Hemaskasʔuw̓ saw the ƛeqʷéy̓ [tattoos] on her ankles. Hemaskasʔuw̓ started screaming after her as he had recognized the tattoos on her ankles, on her legs, and on her body. He saw two rows of tattoos on each calf as his daughter flew away up into the sky. This is why he started screaming after her, because he realized that it was really his daughter. His daughter always said that if he had done as he was told, if he had gone home with her, all his descendants who had died would have come back to life. This is what happened. She was completely bald because of the winds in the sky. She never came back.

That is it.

I have discreetly removed an episode that I consider inappropriate.[67]

2

...... # War, Conflict, and Slavery

Introduction

Anthropologists seem to be unanimous in declaring the term "warfare" inappropriate for the kind of small-scale raiding or quick ambush parties, trophy head-hunting, and acts of revenge that were generally practised by the Kʷakʷakəwakʷ (Codere 1950: 99-117; 1961: 483-540; 1990: 360; Hawthorn, Belshaw, and Jamieson 1958: 37; Drucker 1965: 75). Where they disagree is with regard to the rationale for these assaults. Some scholars conclude their research by stating that these raids, which, although they resulted in securing booty (animal furs, boxes of bark, preserved food, canoes, and ritual paraphernalia) (Boas and Hunt 1902-5: 223) and capturing slaves, were not economically or politically motivated (Codere 1950: 127-8; Goldman 1975: 173-6). For Codere, the author of *Fighting with Property*, nineteenth-century Kʷakʷakəwakʷ inter-tribal fighting was an instrument for acquiring status and prestige. Goldman (1975: 176) argues that "fighting with property" did not substitute for war; rather, war financed "fighting with property." To Goldman, who followed a religious perspective, warfare was religious and ritualistic, an extension of the winter dances that was permeated with war-like symbolism embodied by Winalagilis (*wina:* to make war),[1] the Spirit of War, who was a central character in the winter ceremonial.

It seems that the most important conscious motivation for Kʷakʷakəwakʷ warfare was to avenge the death of a fellow group member, whether that person's death was through murder or accident. The person killed in revenge, who sometimes, but not always, was a slave, became "the pillow" of the deceased.[2] What was wanted was another death to balance and ease the pain of the group's loss (Donald 1997: 170; Boas 1966: 109). This act would take larger proportions and become an organized war party if the deceased were of high standing.

A somewhat different, economically oriented, view, held by Ferguson (1984: 301-7) and, more recently, Donald (1997), maintains that one important motive for warfare was the capture of slaves, whose labour, according to the latter's research, was central to the economy of these hunting-fishing-gathering and preserving societies. In addition, slaves were used as important items of exchange in the traditional potlatch system.[3]

Furthermore, we know that, in traditional Kʷakʷakəwakʷ society, noble names (i.e., titles of nobility) and ceremonial privileges were both inherited and acquired through marriage. However, it has been said that there was a less conventional but still proper means of acquiring supernatural powers and titles. This was through killing the owner, regardless of whether the victim was a community member or a stranger, especially if he/she was a title-holder. Boas and Hunt (1921: 1017) recorded a good example of an acquisition of a privilege by the killing of the owner. It was also said that the entire *hamaċa* ceremonial, which, by the late 1890s was the most important and highest-ranking of all Kʷakʷakəwakʷ winter dances, was not practised until about 1835, when it was obtained in a war with their northern linguistically related neighbours, the Heiltsuk (Bella Bella) and the Owikeno. And yet, various family histories give instances of *hamaċa* performances, at an earlier time, being transferred as marriage gifts (Codere 1961: 448; Suttles 1991b: 100).

Fighting between the Bella Coola and the Kʷakʷakəwakʷ and, more particularly, between the Kʷakʷakəwakʷ and the Qʷiqʷasutinuxʷ has been reported on several occasions (Boas 1966: 111-15). The Bella Coola, who speak a Coast Salish language, were northern neighbours of the Kʷakʷakəwakʷ. Traditionally, they lived in the Bella Coola Valley, north and south of Bentinck Arms, Dean Channel, and Kwatna Inlet. By the early 1900s most of them were living at the village of ʔAlqlaxl located at the mouth of the Bella Coola River (Kennedy and Bouchard 1990: 323). The raid waged by the Bella Coola on the Qʷiqʷasutinuxʷ, and the subsequent war party against the former aggressors (about which we are to hear from ʔAx̌uẇ), was probably the last of a long series of aggressive acts[4] of revenge carried on between the two ethnic groups.

The Qʷiqʷasutinuxʷ, or "People of the Opposite Shore," lived on Gilford Island. Their permanent winter village was Ḡʷayasdəms at Health Bay, and their traditional territory covered the area of Tribune Channel and some of the adjacent islands to the north and the west. In 1834 William Tolmie (1833-35) estimated the Qʷiqʷasutinuxʷ population to be at 250. During the mid-1850s Ḡʷayasdəms was destroyed by a Bella Coola raid, which, judging from several recorded accounts, was the most devastating event in the long history of the Qʷiqʷasutinuxʷ. These accounts, however, do not all agree on specific details (Rohner 1967; Douglas 1952). Franz Boas (1897: 427) refers to the raid as "one of the most famous ones" in the history of the Kʷakʷakəwakʷ people and certainly the best remembered today. Feelings of anger between the two groups have smouldered just below the surface until recent times. So persistent was the residual animosity between the Bella Coola and the Qʷiqʷasutinuxʷ that, in 1987, some 130 years after the raid, they signed a peace treaty during a potlatch given by ʔAxuw̓'s son-in-law, Chief James Sewid, at Campbell River – an event that we attended with ʔAxuw̓ and many of her relatives.[5] Representatives from all the Northwest Coast peoples, including a great number of Bella Coola (and even some Maori from New Zealand), came as guests to witness this historic happening.[6]

In 1962 anthropologist Ronald Rohner was visiting the Gilford Island people, and he provided a synopsis of the Bella Coola raid based on the information he was able to gather at that time:

A ranking Bella Coola man and his wife were at Bond Sound in the fall of the year, perhaps to catch herring, but more likely to collect clover roots and to trade. They were probably accompanied by several other Bella Coola families. Several Koeksotenok families were also at the site. A Koeksotenok woman stole a very valuable *hamatsa* whistle belonging to the ranking Bella Coola couple, but they did not retaliate at the time, even though the theft was a capital offence. The following season the Bella Coola attacked Gwayasdums in revenge, razing the buildings and killing most of the men, women, and children. (Rohner 1967: 30)

Two published accounts, differing somewhat in detail, describe the conflict. One version, given to Boas by George Hunt, presents the raid and its aftermath from the point of view of the Kʷakʷakəwakʷ (Boas 1897: 426-30). The second is told from a Bella Coola perspective (British Association for the Advancement of Science 1891: 16-17). Rohner (1967: 30) analyzes the two versions as follows:

According to the 1891 version, there were sixteen houses at Gwayasdums at the time of the raid, and all but five men and four women were killed. The survivors managed to escape. This version gives an entirely different reason for the raid from the one presented above, and it states that four Kwakiutl canoes overtook the Bella Coola as they tried to escape. Boas's account, on the other hand, states that the Kwakiutl Indians did not set out after the Bella Coola until several days after the raid and that the former were not able to catch them. The latter account agrees most closely with reports from my informants.

Rohner reported other information relevant to ʔAxuw̓'s version of the Qʷiqʷasutinuxʷ–Bella Coola war: "One man, Caribou Jack, had been taken as a

slave by the Bella Coola and later was allowed to escape. He was about sixty
years old when he returned to the Gilford area in 1908." Jack was probably
between eight and twelve years old at the time of the raid. So Rohner (1967: 31)
concluded that the raid must have occurred between 1856 and 1860, probably
closer to 1857. Caribou Jack is an important figure in ʔAx̌uw̓'s account as he was
her great-aunt's cousin or, as she puts it, her grandmother's brother.[7]

ʔAx̌uw̓'s Version of the War between the Qʷiqʷasutinux̌ʷ and the Bella Coola

We are going to talk about the reason we think the Qʷiqʷasutinux̌ʷ were attacked
and massacred by the Bəlx̌ʷəlla [*wina:* to declare war; to attack; to fight]. I will
reveal everything that was told to me by my grandmother [hereafter, grandmother
= great-aunt], Max̌ʷalog̓ʷa, for she was one of the survivors. She was Caribou
Jack's sister [hereafter, Caribou Jack's sister = Caribou Jack's cousin].

All the Qʷiqʷasutinux̌ʷ people used to go to Hada, a food-gathering site on
their land. Hada is a large open meadow where wild clover [t̓əx̌ʷsus] grows in
profusion. A long time ago they ate the wild clover roots, which are white and
stringy. Hada is a large open field. It is just like the White man's farmland, and
this is where they used to dig for clover roots. As was our way, many tribes went
there to collect or trade clover roots from the Qʷiqʷasutinux̌ʷ. Tribes like the
Mam̓aliliqəlla, the Nəmǧis, and all our Kʷakʷakəwakʷ tribes would gather at
Hada to trade this traditional delicacy, which was found only there. I imagine
that at one time the Qʷiqʷasutinux̌ʷ must have been associated in some way with
the Bəlx̌ʷəlla as the latter also came to Hada to trade for clover roots. They
owned really good clover roots, the Qʷiqʷasutinux̌ʷ. The Bəlx̌ʷəlla did not come to
harm us at that time; they just came to trade for clover roots.

When the Bəlx̌ʷəlla arrived, as was the custom, they were invited ashore.
Hada had four large traditional houses. A fort-like fence was built around the
village because, in those days, people had to protect themselves from their
enemies. As you know, the logs would be split in half. I actually saw it that way.
It looked like a fence sticking out of the ground. But by the time I saw it, the logs
had rotted away. There were four large houses there, and the fort-like fence was
built around them.

When the Bəlx̌ʷəlla arrived, they stayed at the house right at the end –
towards the north side of the camp. This was where our aunt, Kʷənx̌ʷalog̓ʷa's
mother,[8] lived. This is where the guests stayed.

The Bəlx̌ʷəlla had left their belongings in this house. They were there to trade
with the Qʷiqʷasutinux̌ʷ for clover roots. Shortly after their arrival, they were

invited to eat at someone's house. This is always what they did for those who had been travelling. They would invite them and feed them hospitably. They had put their belongings into the house where they were going to be staying.

Among these belongings was a *pənskiẏa*, a special box in which they used to keep their weapons. I also have seen such a box. The Bəlx̌ʷalla had left this small box among their belongings at the house of our aunt, Kʷənx̌ʷaloğʷa's mother, while they were being fed at their host's place.

They say that our aunt decided to see what was in the box, and there she found a *mad̓is* – a *haṁaċa* whistle. You have to know how sacred that was in the early days. I always insist on telling that. This *mad̓is* was a bellows whistle, the type that you bind under your armpit.

I am going to tell you exactly what was told to me. I have never talked about it before because I was ashamed of it – if that really is what caused the massacre.

Kʷənx̌ʷaloğʷa's mother stole the *haṁaċa* whistle. She took it or stole it, they said. This is the only reason given for the massacre. ʔAṅica [Mary Dick] and I are probably the only ones alive now who know the facts. Some people among the younger generation have heard a few things about it. They have heard mainly that our people were massacred by the Bəlx̌ʷalla because of a stolen *haṁaċa* whistle; but they have heard very few details.

After they had been fed, the Bəlx̌ʷalla left the house of their host and went back to the house where they had left their belongings. They did not notice right away that the whistle was missing; it was only the next day that they noticed it. They never caused any disturbance or mentioned anything about it. They just quickly left and did not even bother getting what they had come for – clover roots. They just went quickly home and told the others what had happened. This was the reason our people were massacred by those terrible people. We think they hired others[9] to join them in the raid against the Qʷiqʷasuṫinux̌ʷ.

They returned to Ǧʷayasdəms [Gilford Island] much later. They did not return for quite some time; they went around and called others to join them. With them were the Haida. They reached Ǧʷayasdəms and sneaked up on the Qʷiqʷasuṫinux̌ʷ. They did not retaliate right away.

Ǧʷayasdəms was spread out. One end of the village had been extended and some of the houses had been built along this extension. At the end of the village was a little stream where the people of Ǧʷayasdəms got their water. I saw all this because I stayed there with my grandmother, Max̌ʷaloğʷa.

One of the Bəlx̌ʷalla tied a *kad̓əkw*, a cedar-bark ribbon, on one of the branches near the stream in the hope that someone would notice it while fetching water. That person, it seems, wanted to warn the Qʷiqʷasuṫinux̌ʷ that some danger was about them. When that warning failed, the Bəlx̌ʷalla person then tried to use *qəmx̌a* [eagle down], but the Qʷiqʷasuṫinux̌ʷ took no notice of that warning either. My mother always said later that the Q'iq'asutinux̱' were foolish not to have seen these warnings while the Bəlx'əlla were sneaking up on them. For some reason, one of the Bəlx'əlla must have cared about the Q'iq'asutinux̱'.[10]

It was dawn when the Bəlx'əlla attacked. They massacred the Q'iq'asutinux̱' at dawn. It was just horrible what they did to them. It was my mother who told me this. Her father's name was Ẏaquʌas. They stabbed the people right in their beds. They killed them, beheading the men in their sleep. It was at dawn when they attacked.

One man was sleeping with his son, who had no mother. He was what you now call a "single parent" [said in English]. They beheaded the man, who was lying beside the boy, but did not notice the child. The boy woke up, lying in a pool of blood. He sat up, turned to look at his father, and, to his horror, saw that his father no longer had a head. That was when he became aware that the Q'iq'asutinux̱' were being slaughtered by the Bəlx'əlla.

It was now getting light, and the Q'iq'asutinux̱' were running around in a panic. The survivors managed to drag a canoe into the water. Because they were all in a panic, they tried to scramble into the canoe all at the same time, and it capsized and sank. The rest of the canoes were on the other side of the village.

Our mother's father was there. His name was Ẏaquʌas and he had his two children with him. He was holding the hand of one and carrying the other on his shoulders. He was thinking of escaping with them in one of the canoes. There were several canoes still left on the beach, but, in their panic to get away, people overloaded the canoes, which then capsized in the surf. When he saw what was happening, Ẏaquʌas lost all hope. "I better just sacrifice my children and try to save myself," he thought. He lifted the child he was carrying from his shoulders, put it down on the beach, ran swiftly to the water's edge, dove in, and swam away as fast as he could. This happened on the other side of Ǧ'ayasdəms.[11]

As much as possible he made his way under water, coming up for air only when it was absolutely necessary. He came up for air only when he could no longer hold his breath, and then he dove again, swimming under water. He stayed under water as much as possible so that those who were killing his people would not see him. He was trying to reach the small island at the end of Ǧ'ayasdəms.

He dragged himself out of the water on the beach and just lay there because his body was paralyzed from cold and exhaustion. He found that some of his people were also hiding there. He came across ʔOlsiwidi [James Sewid's father's father] and Cux'ĉaʔesa. Cux'ĉaʔesa was Able's [Able Dick's] grandfather and ʔOlsiwidi's brother [cousin]. They had seen their brother [cousin] Ẏaquʌas [ʔAx̱uẇ's mother's father] swimming towards the shore. ʔOlsiwidi and

Cuxʷčaʔesa had also swum to the island to hide. They stayed hidden, watching helplessly as their people were being slaughtered. The Bəlxʷəlla could not see them because they were concealed in the deep woods at the edge of the shore. It was just horrible what was happening. It was my mother who told me these things, just as her father told them to her.

Then the Bəlxʷəlla went into the house of Kʷənxʷaloǧʷa's father, who was going to have a potlatch. He had a huge pile of Hudson's Bay blankets stored in several cedar chests in the corner of the house. The Bəlxʷəlla grabbed Kʷənxʷaloǧʷa. She was Daca's [Billie Sunday Willie's] mother [Wayoł; see Plate 5]. She was just a little girl then.[12] She started screaming and struggling. The Bəlxʷəlla seemed to understand her when she said, "Do not take me. Take those." She was pointing at the cedar boxes in the corner of the room. To examine the cedar boxes, the Bəlxʷəlla had to release the child, and, in so doing, they gave her the chance to run away and hide. These blankets were going to be given away at the potlatch of Kʷənxʷaloǧʷa's father. The Bəlxʷəlla took the blankets with them, meanwhile allowing her to escape.

Then daylight came. I suppose that is when ʔOlsiwidi went to Village Island to ask for help, because my grandfather and he had been separated. I guess that was when, as they say, "ʔOlsiwidi made a run for it," because the Bəlxʷəlla could not catch up to him during the raid against our people. This was when he went to ask for the help of the three tribes, the Mamaliliqəlla, the λawičis, and the Danaxdaxʷ. With the desire for revenge in mind, they assembled a war party against the Bəlxʷəlla. That was when ʔOlsiwidi went to them and informed them about the massacre at Ǧʷayasdəms. The Bəlxʷəlla did not catch up to him.

Everything I am relating is what was told to me by my mother and grandmother. They said that one of our women was barbecuing clams with her husband just before the massacre. He died in the raid but she survived. The Bəlxʷəlla were beheading our people. There were headless bodies everywhere, lying on the beach. They said that all of Ǧʷayasdəms was red with blood at high tide. My mother told me that their bodies looked like those of fish after they had been cut; they had shrunk. They said the men were just stumps because they had shrunk after their heads had been cut off and were left lying all over the beach. The Bəlxʷəlla had cut their throats and beheaded them.

About the woman I mentioned earlier, the one who was barbecuing clams with her husband before the massacre; her husband had accidentally stepped on hot rocks as they were barbecuing the clams and this left a burn mark on his foot. You could not recognize the men because they no longer had heads; the only way she could recognize her husband was by the mark of a burn on his foot. All she could do was to sit by what remained of his body and wail. This is what was told to me. You could not recognize any of the men anymore. The lagoon behind G̱ʷayasdəms was red with blood. By this time the Bəlxʷəlla had left, and the news of the massacre had reached the Maṁaliliqəlla not too long after because they were able to catch up to the Bəlxʷəlla before they got away.

They said that Ẏaquʌas, the father of our mother, was a very good canoe maker. He had just finished building a canoe. Apparently it was different from the regular canoe, xʷakʷəṅa, and was called a məṅga xʷakʷəṅa.[13] It was finished and sitting along the side of his house at G̱ʷaẏasdəms. The Bəlxʷəlla unloaded the things that were in that canoe and pushed it into the water. They abandoned their own canoe in exchange for this one. They loaded the məṅga xʷakʷəṅa that Ẏaquʌas had just completed and paddled away in it. This is what I was told.

My grandmother got shot in the lower corner of one eye, and she is the one who told me this story that I am relating to you. She was Caribou Jack's sister. They shot her in the corner of the eye, just below the tear duct, and it left a scar. I used to sleep with her, and I used to see this scar. This is when she would tell me all the horrible things the Bəlxʷəlla did to our people.

They took many men, women, and children, including my aunt Q̓iqəxʌalla, Caribou Jack, and Jackson, who was half Kʷaguł and half Qʷiqʷasutinuxʷ. These are the people they took away. Those who were part Qʷiqʷasutinuxʷ used to come to G̱ʷayasdəms, and some were still there at the time of the massacre. That is why Jackson was captured also. His mother was Qʷiqʷasutinuxʷ but he was a Kʷaguł, and they had brought him along to dig for clover roots.

The Bəlxʷəlla had loaded the canoes with Qʷiqʷasutinuxʷ captives and had left G̱ʷayasdəms. Prisoners who were strong enough jumped overboard, but the Bəlxʷəlla shot at them even when they were under water.

Finally, the three tribes caught up to the Bəlxʷəlla. The ƛawiċis, Danaxdaxʷ, and Maṁaliliqəlla were the three tribes that pursued the Bəlxʷəlla right after the massacre, pursuing them on their journey home. The men who had been taken as captives and who were strong enough plunged into the sea. The Maṁaliliqəlla yelled at them to swim to one of the nearby islands. "We will pick you up on the way back!" they shouted. They were trying to catch up to the Bəlxʷəlla, who, by this time, were shooting at them. The Maṁaliliqəlla were very concerned about the survivors who were swimming to the nearby islands.

The Bəlxʷəlla saw what the captives were doing, so they covered one really strong man with a cedar mat in the centre of the canoe and stepped on each corner of the mat so that he could not move. This, however, did not hold the man, for he jumped up and dove into the sea. Those who were standing on the corners of the mat fell as he yanked it from under their feet. In his mighty effort to free himself he dove over the side and swam to a nearby island. My aunt Q̓iqəxʌalla, who was sitting in the bow of the canoe, saw it happen and later told me all about it.

The Ṁaṁaliliqəlla came paddling very hard, and they caught up to the Bəlxʷəlla. But they could not draw even with their enemies because of the gunfire from the fleeing canoes. As it happened, they could have overtaken them at any time with no danger for, later on, they learned that the Bəlxʷəlla were out of musket balls and had reverted to firing harmless beads.

My grandmother, Max̌ʷaloǧʷa, was in terrible pain because of the wound in her eye. She was sitting in the bow of the canoe guarded by a Bəlxʷəlla. He felt sorry for her, so he tried to convince her to dive into the sea like the others. But she felt that she would never survive because of her injury, so she stayed on board.

The Bəlxʷəlla stopped somewhere, but I do not know where. They had managed to elude the Ṁaṁaliliqəlla and the other two tribes. The Ṁaṁaliliqəlla turned back. They were afraid to get too close to the Bəlxʷəlla and were very cautious. They were cautious for no reason for, as has been said, the Bəlxʷəlla were using harmless beads rather than musket balls. The beads were powerless, but the Ṁaṁaliliqəlla did not know that. The Ṁaṁaliliqəlla gathered the survivors who had managed to swim to the nearby islands.

At night the Bəlxʷəlla halted at an island, and they all went ashore. They had taken many women and children as captives. The Bəlxʷəlla slept in a circle around the prisoners. One of the women captives had a child, a little baby. The baby slept in a cradle, the kind they used to have in the early days. This woman whispered to the woman next to her, "Do not give up hope; let us see if we can find a way to escape when these butchers are asleep. I am going to make my baby cry so that they will not be able to sleep for a long time. I will pinch the baby," she said to her companion. And this is what she did; she pinched her child and the baby started crying. She did this deliberately to distract the Bəlxʷəlla so they could not sleep and would become very tired.

At dawn she woke up her companion. They swiftly snuck out of the circle of sleeping Bəlxʷəlla. Very quietly they went out and hid in the forest. They did not go very far before reaching a tree covered with many dense branches. Both the women climbed to the top of the tree and, from there, watched the Bəlxʷəlla. In the meantime, the Bəlxʷəlla had awakened and found the women missing but did not want to waste their time looking for them. They did not bother to search seriously for them.

They broke camp, and the mother of the child saw the Bəlxʷəlla seize her baby and toss it into the sea. She turned her head quickly and said to herself, "Well, it was your decision to leave your child behind." The little cradle was floating around upside down in the water. With great effort the woman managed to control her sorrow as she had no other choice but to leave her child behind. The Bəlxʷəlla left this island, setting their course for Cax̌is [Fort Rupert].

The two women who had fled found a flat board that they used as a raft, and on it they paddled back to G̱ʷayasdəms. I guess they were not too far from the village when they managed to escape.

The Bəlxʷəlla stopped at Cax̌is, probably because the Kʷaguł had many relatives among the captives, who were going to be offered for ransom. Indeed, the Kʷaguł paid the ransom to the Bəlxʷəlla for their Qʷiqʷasuṫinux̌ʷ relatives. I do not know all the names of those who were ransomed. All I know is what concerns the members of our own family, what my mother and grandmother told me. The Kʷaguł paid the ransom for their relatives to the Bəlxʷəlla. My grandmother, Max̌ʷalog̱ʷa, was one of those ransomed. She was Caribou Jack's sister, and she was ransomed by the Kʷaguł from the Bəlxʷəlla. That is the reason she never went to Bəlxʷəlla; because she came back right away. The Kʷaguł ransomed her and the other captives with mountain goat furs so that they would not leave Caxis and not be taken as slaves.[14]

My aunt Q̓iqəx̌ƛalla was there also. She was the eldest daughter in my mother's family. Q̓iqəx̌ƛalla was Ẏaquʌas's daughter. She was ʔOlsiwidi's sister [cousin]. The Bəlxʷəlla did not allow her to be ransomed back. Apparently she was an extremely beautiful young girl, just in her teens when she was captured. She had very long hair and a very fair complexion. She was one of the captives taken as a slave by the Bəlxʷəlla. The Kʷaguł were unable to get our aunt back, and so she was taken to Bəlxʷəlla country. She was the eldest in my mother's family. She was older than Wikəlalisəmēẏg̱a. Q̓iqəx̌ƛalla was the eldest child in the family. She was taken to Bəlxʷəlla and was kept there for a long time. She was totally distraught because the Bəlxʷəlla would not release her. They ransomed Max̌ʷalog̱ʷa and, as a result, she did not go to Bəlxʷəlla. She came back to the Qʷiqʷasuṫinux̌ʷ. They took Caribou Jack and Jackson and sold them to the Haida. They took Q̓iqəx̌ƛalla, my aunt, to Bəlxʷəlla. She was there for a long time, many years. This was before my mother and her sister were born.

Q̓iqəx̌ƛalla's Grief

The following event happened during the moons of seaweed [ƚəq̓astən] gathering [April-May]. My aunt Q̓iqəx̌ƛalla was brought to an island by these brutes [ƚiƚał: the dead ones; or, having no feelings]. These brutes were foreigners [gʷitala]. I guess they were the Haida.[15] They had her drying [ləmxʷa] seaweed on this island that was far out in the open sea. This was Q̓iqəx̌ƛalla, the woman who later cared for Nulag̱a.[16] Q̓iqəx̌ƛalla married into the Maṁaliliqəlla [Village Island] after she came back from her captivity. Q̓iqəx̌ƛalla was so unhappy [ẃos] when they put her on this island. They put her on this island to dry [laləmxʷila] the seaweed these brutes had harvested. There was only one house on this island, and this is where she stayed. She was left there alone to dry seaweed for the people who had taken her as a slave. They did not check on her for four days. There was only one house on the island, and it was for those who went there to dry seaweed.

She was so broken-hearted over her situation that she could not help crying and doing what they used to do in the early days. Q̓iqəxx̌alla started scratching [x̌alsa] her cheeks. She could not help herself [k̓is dadəʔeᵐaᵐa] because she was so broken-hearted over her situation. She thought about her brothers [ẁiẁaq̓ʷa][17] [cousins]. "If only there were some way my brothers [ʔOlsiwidi and Cuxʷćaʔesa] could come and rescue me," she said to herself as she was crying. The brutes came back. They had not checked on her for four days. Apparently the Haida who took her really did like her. When they saw the condition she was in they all cried out, "What have you done to your face [g̓ug̓umeȳ]?" Blood was dripping down Q̓iqəxx̌alla's face. "We will never do this to you again," they said to her. They immediately took her home with them.

After her return, my aunt took take care of Nulag̓a and Daduẃ [Dan Cranmer]. She looked after both of them. This was my aunt Q̓iqəxx̌alla, who was taken up north, the one who came back home. She was the one they took as captive. She was the eldest of my mother's sisters. She was taken to the Bəlxʷəlla but she returned home. She was there for many years. I have heard people making remarks about us. Some have said that we were slaves. Among those who said that was Maduwił, wife of ʔAwadˀuẁ, when she was having a quarrel [x̌umaƚala] with my aunt one day. This was when we were trying to stop them from demolishing the house. She said that we were descendants of slaves. That is what she said to our mothers [her aunt and her mother]. But my aunt was not a slave. She came back to us.

They say that they [she hesitates], Jimmy brought a book,[18] one day, and it was quite different from what I know. I don't think it is true. [She refers to the massacre of the Q̓ʷiqʷasuƚinux̌ʷ by the Bella Coola.] Jimmy seemed to believe it. I know what actually happened. I told what happened in the tape we did previously. I said that K̓ugʷidˀiỷ[19] was there when the massacre happened. This is what I know. We have recorded it before and you will add it to this book. They took Q̓iqəxx̌alla because she was a very beautiful woman. They took her as a slave [q̓akuẃ],[20] and these butchers left her on an island. They were gʷitəla, ignorant of our customs. They took her to dry seaweed on this remote island. She was mortified.[21] She used to look after Nulag̓a after her return from captivity, and she married among the Maᵐaliliqəlla.

Note: This section, which deals with slaves and slavery, is out of sequence and follows a question we had asked her on that very subject.

Everybody took slaves; this was the practice in the past. I do not know how many slaves there were in any given household. All I remember is the slave from Ṅaṅimukʷ [Nanaimo]. Jimmy [Sewid] knows about that. They say she was killed at Mimkʷəmlis. There were many slaves. Yes, there were many. The tribes always had war with one another in the early days. They were always prepared for war [wiṅapa]. Take Mimkʷəmlis, for example. It was fortified. They were always expecting to be attacked. Mimkʷəmlis was completely fortified. The walls in the fort had holes for shooting. This was at Mimkʷəmlis. Hada was like that too. I am referring to the little Hada. They say vestiges of the fort can still be seen today. Hada is at Bond Sound. This is where the incident concerning the haṁaċa whistle took place. The haṁaċa whistle, they say, that caused the massacre. Tax̌ʷsus [clover roots] are plentiful in Hada. The Bəlxʷəlla often came there to buy tax̌ʷsus. Apparently there were several houses there. The Bəlxʷəlla were invited by the last house at the far end. Wayoł's mother [ʔAbayoł or Ḱugʷidʐiẏ] was in the house. She apparently searched [xoxʷʔid] this box. They call this box a pənskiẏa. She found a haṁaċa whistle. They say that this haṁaċa whistle is the type that fits under the armpit, and it makes a sound as you apply pressure to it [bellows whistle]. They say this is the type of whistle that Wayoł's mother took from this box. The Bəlxʷəlla never mentioned the whistle. They just packed their belongings and left Hada. They think that that was why the Bəlxʷəlla called their people together for war [hawinalaxʔid] – because of the whistle. The Bəlxʷəlla took captives. They ransomed Ǧaǧasa²² right away. The book that Jimmy [Sewid] has does not say they stopped at Cax̌is [Fort Rupert]. They did stop there. My grandmother [ǧaǧasa], whom we called Max̌ʷaloǧʷa, was ransomed right away. She was ransomed by her Ḱʷaguł relatives [from Fort Rupert].

They did ask for Q̓iqəx̌ałla but they would not ransom her. Those brutes wanted her right from the beginning. The Bəlxʷəlla refused to ransom her. All those who had relatives [in Fort Rupert] were ransomed, and these captives returned immediately. Ǧaǧasa was among them. This happened in Cax̌is when the Bəlxʷəlla stopped there. The book that Jimmy has does not mention that they stopped at Fort Rupert. That book is not true but I did not want to argue [q̓aq̓adʐax̌stēẏ] about it. Jimmy seemed to want to believe it. Ḱugʷidʐiẏ was one of those captives. They took Jackson to the Haida. This is where they took him. He was a slave there.

Jackson was always selling huckleberries. Grandpa [said in English; Moses Alfred] was related to him. They called him Jackson. They brought him to the Haida. His mother was Qʷiqʷasutinux̌ʷ. His mother owned the song we use when we are dancing. It was a *mux̌ʷċalaẏuw̓*, an appreciation song[23] for his mother.

Jackson's mother was a noblewoman [*noxsola*: nobility] of the Qʷiqʷasutinux̌ʷ. They took Jackson directly [*hetusəlaẏuw̓*] to the Haida. Apparently he was there for years. He returned home not too long ago. They took him to the Haida, not to the Bəlxʷəlla. The Kʷaguł ransomed many at Cax̌is, and those captives returned right away.

This is when our tribe, the Qʷiqʷasutinux̌ʷ, scattered. Some people have considered the scattering of our people as a disgrace [*q̓əmudayuw̓*: to talk about something disgraceful]. They just went to their relatives. Many went to the Mam̓aliliqəlla; others scattered among other tribes. They were the survivors of the massacre at Ḡʷayasdəms. They were really devastated [*yax̌ʔid*]. The bodies of the dead were just like stumps [*ċaċax̌ʷsəmala*: cut in short pieces] after they had been mutilated [*qaka*]. Bodies were scattered all over the beach. It was high tide [*ẏax̌ʷa*]. The ocean was red with blood [*ʔəlkʷaxseẏ*]. Both sides of the village [*w̓aw̓axsadʔelis*] were red with blood. Before the massacre this woman was barbecuing clams [*kuċa*] with her husband. Her husband had stepped on hot rocks [*ł̓ipalud*] where the fire was set on this rocky area [*ləq̓ʷa*], and he had scorched his foot. This single mark enabled his wife to identify him. He had been decapitated [*q̓əkʷəmlis*: without head]. This poor woman was sitting beside his body crying [*q̓ʷasalagəlis*]. They had mutilated them all. That is the reason why these butchers were so proud of what they had done [*q̓ʷaq̓ʷaʔelaxila*: to show with pride at a ceremony]. I suppose they were told about the massacre. They showed this ceremony in public; I saw it and I recognized it. The dancers were displaying large hands dripping with blood. They carried these as they danced. I thought this was done with bad taste. The people who performed the dance probably did not know the significance of it. It seems that they lost their dances until these elderly women taught them. They had to have been told about the massacre. They are such good dancers now; and really good singers.[24]

Q̓iqəx̌ƛalla and ʔOlsiwidi

This happened quite a few years after the Bəlxʷəlla raid against the Qʷiqʷasutinux̌ʷ. Everyone on the coast involved in fishing would often go to Steveston. They would all travel by boat [*ẏaẏasəla*: travelling by boat]. I often did this too. My father had a gillnetter [*k̓ʷəmsała*], and we would also travel by boat to Vancouver.

The Haida travelled to Steveston. Everyone from the coast was there. ꝋOlsiwidi was still alive. This was when he was still a young man. He was Jimmy's [Jimmy Sewid's] father's father. ꝋOlsiwidi was Q̓iqəxҡalla's brother [hereafter, brother = cousin]. Cuxʷċaꝋesa [Able Dick's grandfather] and K̓ugʷidʸiy̓ were also her brothers.[25] The Haida people who were guarding Q̓iqəxҡalla went to Steveston, and they took her along. Q̓iqəxҡalla was seated at the stern of the canoe. They were heading up the Fraser River to Steveston when ꝋOlsiwidi and Cuxʷċaꝋesa saw her. Apparently Q̓iqəxҡalla had seen her brothers before they saw her as she was travelling up the Fraser River. But she did not show any sign of recognizing ꝋOlsiwidi and Cuxʷċaꝋesa when she saw them. When they saw her, ꝋOlsiwidi started calling [*laqʷəla*]. "It surely looks like you, my dear" [*ꝋadey:* beloved one]. This is what ꝋOlsiwidi said when he called out to Q̓iqəxҡalla from his the canoe. Q̓iqəxҡala refused to look at him.

ꝋOlsiwidi and Cuxʷċaꝋesa immediately made plans to rescue her. The Haida had made camp at Steveston. Q̓iqəxҡalla would not show any sign of recognizing her brothers. Her brothers understood why she was ignoring them; so they did not bother approaching her. They were afraid that the Haida would find out that they had recognized her. One of Q̓iqəxҡalla's sisters [throughout, sisters = cousins] was married to a White man [*mamaҡna*]. She was one of the first women among us to marry a White man. Q̓iqəxҡalla's sister and her husband lived at Steveston. Her name was W̓iqumax̌uday̓ugʷa. Gertie [Gertie Martin-Hanuse] was named after her. W̓iqumax̌uday̓ugʷa's dance was passed on [*lodʸəm:* to pass on; to transfer] to Flora [Sewid]. W̓iqumax̌uday̓ugʷa was her name. She was a sister to ꝋOlsiwidi and Cuxʷċaꝋesa. She was married to this White man and lived at Steveston. W̓iqumax̌uday̓ugʷa recognized Q̓iqəxҡalla when she came down to where she was selling soapberries [*nəx̌ʷəskən*]. She would not approach Q̓iqəxҡalla nor would she show [*ꝋawilxəs:* make apparent] that she had recognized her. Q̓iqəxҡalla was selling soapberries.

W̓iqumax̌uday̓ugʷa decided it was now time to rescue her. She went to Q̓iqəxҡalla and whispered to her to have a good look at her husband and to remember him. At an opportune time he would rescue her and take her to his house. No one took notice of W̓iqumax̌uday̓ugʷa whispering to Q̓iqəxҡalla because they thought she was just a customer buying soapberries from these brutes. The opportune time to rescue her was at sunset a few days later, when this White man quickly put his arm under Q̓iqəxҡalla's arm and walked away with her. No one took any notice. It was during sunset and the streets were empty. It was getting dark [*p̓ədəkstuxʷꝋid*]. This White man took her straight upstairs [*hedʸəndala*]. This was at Steveston, at W̓iqumax̌uday̓ugʷa's house. Q̓iqəxҡalla returned home, where she married a man by the name of Q̓əlapa. He lived in the Seal house [x̌ix̌x̌əx̌iɬ] at Mim̓k̓ʷəmlis. Q̓iqəx̌alla married a Mam̓aliliqəlla man by the name of Q̓əlapa when she returned home.

The book that Jimmy Sewid has says that Q̓iqəx̌alla had a child with a White man. My mother never said that Q̓iqəx̌alla had a child. My mother knew the truth because she always talked with Q̓iqəx̌alla.

The reason I know the truth, and I am probably the only one now who *does* know all the facts about what happened to our people, is because it was told to me by my mother. She got her facts from my aunt after she escaped; it was at Steveston. She escaped with the help of Ẁiqumax̌udayug̓ʷa. By this time she was a grown woman and went to live at Mim̓k̓ʷəmlis. Ẁiqumax̌udayug̓ʷa stole her from the Bəlx̌ʷəlla and she later went to live with the Mam̓aliliqəlla [Village Island].

After the massacre the Q̓ʷiq̓ʷasutinux̌ʷ scattered. Many joined the Mam̓aliliqəlla, some joined the Dᶻawadaʔēnux̌ʷ, some went to stay with their relatives among the Kʷaguɬ, the Danaxdax̌ʷ, and the x̌awičis. Our people scattered. Later, ʔOlsiwidi moved to Victoria and stayed there for a long time, and this is where he met his wife, Ɬaxʷaɬa [Lucy Sewid].

Shortly after Q̓iqəx̌alla came back to us she married a Mam̓aliliqəlla man by the name of Q̓əlapa. This was after she had escaped with Ẁiqumax̌udayug̓ʷa's help. She went to Mim̓k̓ʷəmlis where most of our people, the Q̓ʷiq̓ʷasutinux̌ʷ, had moved after the massacre. They joined a large number of Q̓ʷiq̓ʷasutinux̌ʷ who had remained at their summer camps for quite some time before the raid. All the members of ʔOlsiwidi's family went to Village Island and built new houses there. Many of them lived in the house of x̌ax̌axʷas, Billy. His other Indian name was X̌ix̌anyus.

This was the house where Mungo's [Mungo Martin] family lived. Mungo's father died in that house. Mič̓a [Herbert Martin] was just a little boy at that time. He was the youngest child of ʔIwanukʷ. My mother was related to him because, when ʔIwanukʷ was dying, he told my mother to take care of Mič̓a. He said Mič̓a was the only one he was worried about because Spruce and Mungo were old enough to look after themselves. This is what happened.

Ḡʷayasdəms was abandoned for a long time after the raid. Two groups, the Q̓ʷiq̓ʷasutinux̌ʷ and the Mam̓aliliqəlla, lived together at Mim̓k̓ʷəmlis. Sometime later, the Dᶻawadaʔēnux̌ʷ began to occupy Ḡʷayasdəms. They were joined by the Həxʷaməs, the Gʷawaʔēnux̌ʷ, and some Q̓ʷiq̓ʷasutinux̌ʷ. The Q̓ʷiq̓ʷasutinux̌ʷ, the Həxʷaməs, and the Gʷawaʔēnux̌ʷ joined the Dᶻawadaʔēnux̌ʷ and are now called the "Mugəmək̓ʷ Dᶻawadaʔēnux̌ʷ": the four Dᶻawadaʔēnux̌ʷ tribes.[26] That is what they are called now because all four of them lived together. They went back to Ḡʷayasdəms and built new houses there. A few of our people who could overcome their sorrow went back to Ḡʷayasdəms, while the others scattered. The

Bəlxʷəlla really hurt the Qʷiqʷasutinux̌ʷ greatly. They did some atrocious things to them at Ǧʷayasdəms.

Caribou Jack came home also, but he did not escape. He became rich working at a place where many caribou could be found. That is why they called him "Caribou." He paid his own way back home after he had become rich. He came to Yəlis [Alert Bay] and Mrs. Jane [Stephen] Cook looked after him. She really took good care of him and they built him a house. He also worked at a sawmill for a long time. Some Christians built a house for Caribou Jack when, as an old man, he retired. He was Max̌ʷaloǧʷa's brother. When he died at Yəlis they dismantled his little house. This is what I know about our people.

I want you to really understand. Y̓aquλas's daughter was Q̓iqəx̌alla, the one who was taken as captive. My mother and Q̓iqəx̌ala had the same father. Y̓aquλas was also Wikəlalisəmēẏǧa's father. Q̓iqəx̌alla's mother was not Q̓ʷalaxəloǧʷa, my mother's mother. Y̓aquλas's first wife was Qʷiqʷasutinux̌ʷ, and she was Q̓iqəx̌ala's mother. My mother and she had the same father. She was the eldest but Q̓ʷalaxəloǧʷa was not her mother. Q̓ʷalaxəloǧʷa was Nəmǧis and Y̓aquλas married her after he lost his wife in the massacre. Do you understand?

(See Appendix E, kinship diagram 3.)

Names and Places

Note: This passage was not told in sequence but was part of her general comments on slavery. As ʔAx̌uw̓ realized her omission during the course of the narratives, we have included it here. It shows the complexity and the importance of genealogy and how it is intertwined with the acquisition of tangible and non-tangible privileges [λugʷēẏ] such as names and rights to winter ritual dances and masks, family crests, and re-enactments of family myths, which come with rights to the territory. What follows is an incredibly vivid picture of a people. The cross-weaving of family ties with their λugʷēẏ emphasizes the richness and the depth of the relationship between Kʷak̓ʷakəwak̓ʷ cultural and artistic expressions, whether at the individual or the group level.[27]

As I said before, our people, the Qʷiqʷasutinux̌ʷ, scattered after the massacre. These are the names of the people who are part Qʷiqʷasutinux̌ʷ: Ǧʷix̌sisəlas, Harry Brown's mother, and Monak̓ʷəla, the Danaxdax̌ʷ. They are part Qʷiqʷasutinux̌ʷ. Monak̓ʷəla's aunt was also called Ǧʷix̌sisəlas, and her mother's name was M̓axm̓əw̓id̓əmǧa. It has the same origin as my grandmother's [throughout, grandmother = great-aunt] name. M̓axm̓əw̓id̓əmǧa is a

Qʷiqʷasuṫinux̣ʷ name, and this was Monakʷəla's mother's name. x̣ałilix̣a is
another Qʷiqʷasuṫinux̣ʷ name used by some x̣awiċis. It is because some of the
x̣awiċis are part Qʷiqʷasuṫinux̣ʷ. They also adopted in their rituals the ʔAləmḵala,
the Cradle Dance,[28] because they are part Qʷiqʷasuṫinux̣ʷ. They performed this
dance, or "cradled Ẏeqawilas's child," as they say. This child's name was Puλidiẏ,
"Satiated." This was the name of the child whom Chief x̣aλilix̣a [John Clark],[29]
the chief of the x̣awiċis, put in the cradle. He performed this particular dance
because he was part Qʷiqʷasuṫinux̣ʷ. The people whom I mentioned earlier,
Harry Brown and Jackson, they were both part Qʷiqʷasuṫinux̣ʷ.

I have forgotten to mention something about Caribou Jack after he came
back from his long captivity. He had quite a temper. He was always irritating my
grandmother with his remarks. He would always say, "Max̣ʷaloḡʷa, you are such
an old-fashioned Indian, always following the Indian ways." After his return he
would only eat strange food. He always had to have coffee, for example, and
would have to cook for himself as he ate nothing but strange food. He completely
adopted the White man's ways and had no desire for Indian ways anymore. This
is how Caribou Jack became after he returned from his long stay among the
Haida.[30] It must have been the Haida who owned the land where he worked.
That is why they called him Caribou Jack, because he worked in the country
where many caribou could be found; that is what my mother and aunt told me.
His names were Yeẏaqux̣alas, ʔAλudalalis, and Ṅuɫilakʷ. These were his names.
They call Jack Henry Yeẏaqux̣alas also, because he was related to Caribou Jack.

My grandmother, Max̣ʷaloḡʷa, lived in a house on the beach across from
Ḵʷamax̣əlas, who was a Həx̣ʷaməs man [from Wakeman Sound]. It was
just a cabin. She lived there after the four groups merged. As I have said, the
Qʷiqʷasuṫinux̣ʷ, Gʷawaʔēnux̣ʷ, Həx̣ʷaməs, and Dᶻawadaʔēnux̣ʷ lived together at
Ḡʷayasdəms. Ḡʷayasdəms came to be known as "the Four Tribes." Max̣ʷaloḡʷa
əmḡa lived in Caribou Jack's cabin on the beach across from the house of
Ḵʷamax̣əlas, a Həx̣ʷaməs man, and that is also where I stayed when I went
to Ḡʷayasdəms.

There is another thing that was told to me. It took place at Sawigax̣tuwēẏ
[on an island near Gilford Island].[31] I guess this site is high up on a hill. ʔOlsiwidi
had a brother by the name of Lalakənis and a sister by the name of Hahikənis.
They both were Ṅəṅalalał, Weather dancers [or the embodiment of the Weather].
People were amazed at their strength because they could perform this dance up
the hill. They performed the Weather Dance at Sawigax̣tuwēẏ because this is
one of the lands that belongs to the Qʷiqʷasuṫinux̣ʷ. This is something related to
ʔOlsiwidi that I had forgotten to mention.

My mother knew her father's side of the family extremely well, and she knew
all that belonged to them. Whenever I went clam digging with my grandmother

and Qʷayugʷiɫilakw, my grandmother would point out to me all the lands and rivers that belong to the Qʷiqʷasutinux̌ʷ and tell me their names. The town of Ǧʷayasdəms and the rivers, the fishing grounds where people got their fish, and the sites where they processed and preserved them; the berry fields and the hunting sites, Hada³² and also Ǧʷaʔi, belong to the Qʷiqʷasutinux̌ʷ. Ǧʷaʔi, or the head of Hada [head of Bond Sound], is where they later built a sawmill. Also a place called Waqʼanakʷ [Wa-ka-no Bay on Tribune Channel]. These are the lands of the Qʷiqʷasutinux̌ʷ. Also ʔəpsaguw̓ [Shoal Harbour on Gilford Island]³³ and Mitəp [at the head of Viner Sound, Gilford Island]. She said this was all Qʷiqʷasutinux̌ʷ land, as was this place called Wotuw̓ [Thompson Sound]. I have never been to Wotuw̓, but they told me this is where the Qʷiqʷasutinux̌ʷ had their great feasts. It is called Wotuw̓, and it is somewhere in the inlet near Ǧʷayasdəms. This is what they said belonged to the Qʷiqʷasutinux̌ʷ. My mother named all the sites to me: Gəpgəpe, Yuxbuxdala at the mouth of the river, and Gʷaligina at the headwater where they stayed when they prepared the fish for later use. Also the sites called Nugani, ƛusƛuxsayuɫ, and also what I have already mentioned – Gʷaligina. A particular gathering place near Hada is called ʔəmdigalis [Bonwick Island]. There were many other sites, such as Ǧʷamula, Tetagis, and Yukakaliɫ.³⁴

Yukakaliɫ and Gegulsala are places where, they say, sea monsters dwell. We were not allowed to make any noise there because there were sea monsters all around. This is what they told me when I was a child. At Ǧʷamula I used to see these things, whatever they were, floating and sticking out of the water, travelling across to the other side and disappearing beside or across Yukakaliɫ. These are all the things my mother told me and these are the things I saw.

She named all our lands and rivers. I know many of the names around Hada, like Tetagis and others. ƛux̌alanukʷ is the name of a mountain just across from Hada. They say that each time they went up there, they could feel the mountain shaking. Another mountain is called Qʷinwadʔaqʼaweẏ because it makes such an incredible sound when the wind is blowing. It is up from ƛusƛuxsayuɫ. There is a lake up the mountain called Q̓aluqsəm. There is a beautiful land called Nahnahlus. This is where the Gʷaligina River runs and becomes a waterfall. I guess a White man tried to do some farming there, but he left because the wolves ate all his cows. Nahnahlus is a place with many wolves. You could see the fields that this White man had worked out there. He just ended up leaving that place. My mother and my grandmother always talked about this White man who had to leave his farm because of the wolves.

There is another thing they told me. Gʷaligina is also a place where they used to dig clover roots. It is a vast meadow. Each dʼuyas [digging garden] had its own name. The only names I can remember right now are Waxʷbàʔas and Hixsolisəlaɫ.

These digging gardens were made into ditches. People would dig long ditches in the ground where the Qʷiqʷasuṫinux̌ʷ dug for clover roots at Hada. They even ran along the side of our house. They told us that someone there would throw frogs at you. We were so afraid when we were there. This place is called Q̓ʷagəm. They said that if you ate outside, something would happen to you. Someone would throw frogs at you. They told me this when I was a child. I used to be so afraid of this happening to me.

This is another thing that I forgot to mention. Gʷaligina Lake is a place where qiqəlis, wild cranberries, grow in profusion. We went there also. One cranberry site is called Maxʷayoliɬ, and another one, located on a little island, is called Məlgʷa. Another one is named Q̓ʷumdigilis. These are the names of the places at the head of Hada, where we gathered wild cranberries. This is what I remember. There is another one called Q̓akʷekən [at the head of Thompson Sound]. My mother and grandmother named all the Qʷiqʷasuṫinux̌ʷ lands to me.

Hada is Qʷiqʷasuṫinux̌ʷ land. We decided to build a house there. We got lumber from a sawmill at Ḡʷaʔi. Wakəs, who was part Qʷiqʷasuṫinux̌ʷ, used to go there to gather sea grass. He built a house there. He was Abbey's grandfather [on his mother's side]. Maxʷaquɬəla [John Scow] and Xanasugwilakʷ [Peter Scow] built a smokehouse at Hada. The smokehouses collapsed after the White man came to Hada. Arthur Bondsound, whose Indian name was Yaquλasəme, had a smokehouse there too. At the end he was the only one living at Hada. This is why he took the name Bondsound. Everyone left but he stayed. That is it.

My husband [ɬaẁənəm], Moses, went to a lake called Q̓aluq̓səm. Yaquλasəme also used to talk about this site. They said they found the remnants of a settlement there, at Q̓aluq̓səm. There were q̓əbilis [crushed clamshells, indication of a midden] on the ground of this settlement. They could not believe that anyone would pack clams that far up the mountain. He said that from there the river runs north. Her father [i.e., Moses Alfred. Here, ʔAx̌uẁ was pointing at her daughter, Flora Sewid] went there. Yaquλasəme wanted to show it to him. It is at this place called Qʷinwadᶻaq̓aweẏ. That is where it is. It is near a lake. They say the lake looks just like a round bowl and that the mountain is called Qʷinwadᶻaq̓aweẏ. The river is running north from this mountain. There was a settlement there at one time, he said. There was no doubt that someone was living there as it looked just like one of our earlier settlements except that it was high up the mountain. This is what was amazing to them – that someone could pack clams that far up.

So many people followed ʔOlsiwidi to Ṁimkʷəmlis after the massacre. Others went to stay with the Gʷawaʔēnux̌ʷ. Many went to Village Island. Some people merged with other tribes. As I said, our people scattered after the Bəlxʷəlla massacre.

A short while after the Bəlx^wəlla raid against the Q^wiq^wasuṫinux̄^w, a ṗəsa [potlatch] was given at Mimk^wəmlis. As I mentioned earlier, ˀOlsiwidi was one of the survivors of this raid. He had built a house at Mimk^wəmlis with his uncle Ẏaq̓aɬˀənala. During the ṗəsa, ˀOlsiwidi made a mistake while he was conducting the singers. You know how strict they were about this during the dances. The singers made a mistake as ˀOlsiwidi was conducting them. Ẏaq̓aɬˀənala threw a ṗəsa on account of this mistake. ˀOlsiwidi got up, rolled up his sleeves, exposed his naked arms, and told the haṁaċa to come and bite him. This is what happened. Then he went into the forest for purification. Everybody was waiting to see what he would be transformed into. This happened during a ṗəsa at Mimk^wəmlis some time after the Bəlx^wəlla raid. He received a magic weapon, a large club with a round head, and with it he smashed all the canoes on the beach. His uncle Ẏaq̓aɬˀənala paid for the damage that ˀOlsiwidi caused by smashing the canoes. Daduẇ [Charlie Dick's father] told me this when he later married my mother. Ẏaq̓aɬˀənala paid them with mountain goat furs to compensate for ˀOlsiwidi's smashing of their canoes. This happened when ˀOlsiwidi reappeared transformed as a *Miɬa* dancer,[35] a Prankster. Ẏaq̓aɬˀənala was ˀOlsiwidi's uncle. It cost him a huge amount for this dance.

It breaks my heart when I hear this new generation of youngsters saying that the Q^wiq^wasuṫinux̄^w survivors who moved to Mimk^wəmlis do not own Ǧ^wayasdəms. This is where they went after the Bəlx^wəlla massacred them. This is where they settled after the massacre, and some of them went to other tribes. Some joined Dᶻawadaˀēnux̄^w country and many went to Mimk^wəmlis. ˀOlsiwidi's family lived for many years at Mimk^wəmlis. Other tribes decided to amalgamate: the Həx^waməs, Dᶻawadaˀēnux̄^w, and G^wawaˀēnux̄^w amalgamated and lived together, and that is why they are called the Mugəmək^w Dᶻawadaˀēnux̄^w – the four Dᶻawadaˀēnux̄^w tribes.

Hanuse married my grandmother Max̄^waloǧ^wa. I used to call her ǧaǧasa [grandma]. She was an old woman and Hanuse was an old man when they married. They were married for a number of years. I used to live with them in Nulaǧa's house. Max̄^waloǧ^wa lived with Hanuse at the house with the Loon on top. When Hanuse died, all the Dᶻawadaˀēnux̄^w chiefs living at Ǧ^wayasdəms came to Mimk^wəmlis to get my grandmother and brought her back to Ǧ^wayasdəms.

The land where Allan James built his house belonged to ˀOlsiwidi. My mother showed me where he lived. Jimmy Sewid mentioned at one time that this was where his grandfather's house was, and he was pleased that Allan James had built there.

Again I hear the new generation talking about what has happened. They do not know anything. Jimmy Sewid and I were educated in the Indian ways. We were informed and we knew. This is what I would like to say: Jimmy Sewid was educated by the old people, in the ways of our people. He visited them one by one, the old people of the Maṁaliliqəlla. He questioned them about many things. He asked them about the geography and the history of our people. That is why he knows so much. I remember Simon Beans being so annoyed with his mother. Jimmy tried to convince Simon to stay and to question his mother, Qʷaqa, also known as Məmxuyog̱ʷa. He was so annoyed that he left, and Jimmy was the only one listening to the old woman. She taught him about the Maṁaliliqəlla and many other things about our people. That is the reason why he is so knowledgeable about the Maṁaliliqəlla. He also knows many things about the Qʷiqʷasutinux̱ʷ. These are the things that were taught to us because we are Qʷiqʷasutinux̱ʷ, because of my mother and ꞋOlsiwidi. Jimmy knows about our past because he was taught everything that happened to the Qʷiqʷasutinux̱ʷ.

As I said, our people scattered; some joined the Maṁaliliqəlla, some the Nəmg̱is, some the Danaxdax̱ʷ, and some the D̉awadaꞋēnux̱ʷ. These were the survivors of the Bəlx̱ʷəlla raid that occurred at G̱ʷayasdəms. The Qʷiqʷasutinux̱ʷ are not slaves. They did not become slaves of the tribes they went to. They went to stay with their relatives. Sometimes you hear people saying that the Qʷiqʷasutinux̱ʷ were slaves. This is not true. They were not slaves in the tribes they went to because they were only living with their relatives. I guess after the massacre no one lived at G̱ʷayasdəms for quite a while. This is what my uncle Ḵugʷid̉iy̓[36] told me; he really knew the truth. Also, my mother told me the same, and she got her facts from her father, who was one of the survivors. I think my account of the story is more accurate than those that have been written before because I got it from the old people who were there when it happened.

Slavery

I would like to bring up something that my daughter Flora asked me to talk about. It is about a song. It is said that a boy had a father by the name of Ǧusdid̉as. He was the eldest of his family. They owned a feast bowl in the shape of a bear, and it was named N̉əniy̓. During a feast, Ǧusdid̉as took a male slave and sat him inside this feast bowl and handed him over to the Kʷaguɫ, who started singing this song.

> We sat the slave in our feast bowl.
> He had big staring eyes.

His big eyes were blinking.
He was whimpering.
He was peeking out of the feast bowl of the chiefs.

These are the words of the song. I know the song. [ʔAx̌uw̓ sings the song.]
That is the song. That is where we will stop. I was anxious to record the song
about the Big Blinking Eyes. They took the slave and sat him in the feast bowl
and served him to the Kʷaguł. He was a slave.

Why did they serve him to the Kʷaguł? This was part of their rivalry [ʔaʔy̓ut:
to compete, to fight, to rival]. They used to always have contests between rivals.
Rivalry. All the tribes picked on the Kʷaguł. "Rivalry," they would say. I have no
idea who exactly was involved. I've tried to ask Mungo Martin to record it. "That
would be going too far," he said to me. Of course I understood why he did not
want to reveal what he knew because this was a Kʷaguł who received (or was
served) the bear dish with the slave in it – the whimpering slave with the big
blinking eyes. As a Kʷaguł, he wanted to protect the Kʷaguł. That is it. "That
would be going too far," he said. That is all I want to say.

Flora asked me to tape this song. She was always teasing me. "We should
give it to Billy Cook [Dora Sewid's husband] as part of Dora's dowry to him,"
Jimmy said. "We should give him the Big Blinking Eyes." [Much laughter.]

Do I remember seeing a slave at Mim̓kʷəmlis? No, I don't. I have only heard
about them. One was called Gʷadił. Kʷənx̌w̓aloǧʷa's cow was named Gʷadił, after
this slave.

There is another terrible thing I would like to mention. Jimmy [Sewid] is the
one who really knows this story. It concerns a terrible thing the Mam̓aliliqəlla
did; it concerns the Mam̓aliliqəlla's wrong-doing. They said that they dressed up
this slave girl in full regalia and walked her to the end of Mim̓kʷəmlis. Then they
killed her. That is what they say. I don't know if that really happened. Daduw̓ told
me about it. They say that this beautiful young girl's face was lying on the ground
after they clubbed her to death. Gʷadił was her name. I think they say she was a
Coast Salish girl from Nanaimo. Her body was floating around at the waterline
of Mim̓kʷəmlis. This is what Daduw̓ told me. They clubbed her to death. And
then they later saw her walking on the surface of the water, chanting at the end
of the village. I know her chant. [ʔAx̌uw̓ concentrates, trying to remember the
words and the tune of the song.]

The chant went like this: "I was standing on the back of N̓əmkalaga, supernatural gigantic halibut." These are the words of the chant she was singing as
she was walking on the surface of the water at the end of Mim̓kʷəmlis. She came
back to life after everybody saw her dead body floating around on the surface of

the water. She had been supernaturally revived. They say she was clubbed to death at Mimk̓ʷəmlis. She came back to life and was walking on the surface of the ocean singing this chant. This chant has more to it, and it has a really good "tune" ["tune" said in English], and I used to know all of it. Daduẇ used to sing it for me. She came back to life. That was a terrible thing the Maṁaliliqəlla did. They killed her. Jimmy really knows about it.

This must have happened long ago. They used to always have wars in the early days and enslave their captives. We are so fortunate to be a peaceful people now. *Ayoho!* Peace, is good.[37]

3
Childhood

Introduction

ʔAx̌uw̓'s childhood recollections emphasized her daily activities, which consisted mainly of learning the traditional ways of Kʷakʷakəwakʷ women which have been passed to young girls for thousands of years. Following her female relatives around, she observed and copied them, developing her skills in a variety of domains, such as food gathering, preparing, and preserving. We sense that at an early age ʔAx̌uw̓ was very proud of the fact that she was able to be of some help while discovering and learning to cope with her environment, all the while enjoying the normal activities of childhood. This training, combined with a strong sense of who she was in relationship to her nuclear family and descent group, gave her the basic knowledge essential for her future life.

Where Do I Come From?

I come from many places. My father was M̓am̓aliliqəlla and my mother was Nəmg̱is [Yəlis: Alert Bay]. My mother's father was Qʷiqʷasutinux̌ʷ [Gilford Island]. I come from three places. And it became four when I married a Kʷaguł. That is the way it is.

I was born in my father's house, at M̓im̓kʷəmlis, Village Island. My problem is that I do not know the moon [month] of my birth. All I know is that I was born during the winter. That is what I always say when you give a birthday party for me. We are just guessing the moon of my birthday. It was during winter that I was born. I do not know the moon I was born. It did not matter at that time. But I was born in our home. It was not too long ago that my birth home was dismantled.

My father [ʔump] was a full-blooded Maṁaliliqəlla, and his Indian name was Ǧʷutəlas. It is a name that was given to your[1] grandfather, Moses, as part of my dowry when I married him. ƛasutiẇalis was my father's position name in what they call the p̓əsa [investing potlatch]. It was his p̓əsa position among the Maṁaliliqəlla. Ǧʷutəlas was his everyday name. His English name was Joe. "Joe Glenglen is my name," he would say. He was trying to say "Glendale." Whenever he had to pronounce his English name, or after he had a few drinks, he would say that his name was Glenglen. [Laughter.]

My father's father's name was Ẏax̌ƛən. This is now your mother's [Flora] p̓əsa [potlatch] position name within the Maṁaliliqəlla. Ẏax̌ƛən was my father's father's name. He had several children. Ẏax̌ƛən was one of them, and his name within our descent group [ṅəmayəm] was Ǧusdidᶻas. Another was called Q̓ix̌ƛaladᶻiẏ. And of course there was Məllidiẏ. And then there was my father. The youngest was Xaxəlquća, and he used to own the apron that was given to your mother, Flora. He was the youngest, and he belonged to the haṁaća society.[2] The apron that was given to Flora is very old. Make sure that it is well looked after. He used to wear it while he was dancing the haṁaća dance. He gave me a small brooch shaped like a miniature gun, the handle of which was inlaid with abalone shell. He gave it to me when I was a baby. I was still a child when he died. I lost my brooch at Gəldala, at the cannery near Rivers Inlet. [See Appendix E, kinship diagram 2.]

My mother's name was Puƛas [Place Where You Are Satiated]. The White people called her Puƛas too. In Indian and in English her name was Puƛas. She was part Nəmǧis on her mother's side [Alert Bay] and part Qʷiqʷasutinux̌ʷ on her father's side. Q̓ʷalaxəloǧʷa was the name of my grandmother on my mother's side. She was my mother's mother. I did not get to know her, but Nulaǧa [ʔAx̌uẇ's half-sister] did for a short time. Ẏaquƛas was the name of my mother's father. They say Ẏaquƛas was a really good canoe maker. Q̓ʷalaxəloǧʷa married Ẏaquƛas, and my mother Puƛas was born from this union. The other children, in order of their birth, were two girls, Wikəlalisəmēẏǧa and Ǧaʔəx̌talas; a boy named X̌aneyus; then Puƛas, my mother; and finally Məllidᶻas, who was the youngest. When Ẏaquƛas died, Q̓ʷalaxəloǧʷa remarried a man from the ʔAwik̓inux̌ʷ. He became my mother's stepfather. She had two boys with him, Q̓ʷəmxuduẇ, also known as Ṅumas, or Wakəs, and Hemaskən. They became my uncles. My mother and Q̓ʷəmxuduẇ had the same mother but different fathers. My uncle [stepfather], Q̓ʷəmxuduẇ's father, was ʔAwik̓inux̌ʷ [Rivers Inlet] and my mother's mother was Nəmǧis. Do you understand? Q̓ʷəmxuduẇ's father was not Ẏakuƛas; his father was ʔAwik̓inux̌ʷ. He was my mother's half-brother, but they had the same mother. That is the way it is. [See kinship diagram 3.]

My mother never told me the names of the midwives who attended my birth. All my mother ever told me was that I was the same age as the first-born son of Q̓ʷəq̓əs [Mable Stanley's mother]. I was born on the same day as this boy, who was taken away by his White father. His White father owned a store on Quadra Island, Quathiaski Cove. There was a pole outside his store, on which he wrote his son's birthdate. He took him away from his mother and she never saw him again. The male child was G̱iwiləmɡ̱a's [Mable Stanley's] brother, and I was born the same day.[3] When I was born my father named me Laq̓ʷaloḡʷa [Inviting Woman]. ꞌOlsiwidi [James Sewid's father's father] and Cuxʷc̓aꞌesa [his brother, i.e., cousin] did not like the name my father had given me; he held a meeting about what my name should be. Cuxʷc̓aꞌesa wanted to name me Q̓iqəxˑalla, after our aunt, whom the Bəlxʷəlla took as a slave. ꞌOlsiwidi, my mother's brother [cousin], said, "I do not think we should name our sweetheart [ɡ̱əna] Q̓iqəxˑalla." Regardless, Cuxʷc̓aꞌesa wanted to name me Q̓iqəxˑalla. But Q̓iqəxˑalla was a skinny, short Maˑmaliliqəlla woman. They used to call her "petite Q̓iqəxˑalla." That is why ꞌOlsiwidi did not want me to be named after her. He did not want me to be confused with the petite Q̓iqəxˑalla. Because, he said, I was obviously going to be petite too [*bidu*: small; petite; little]. He told them that he wanted my name to be Yakoyoḡʷa.

So it was ꞌOlsiwidi who named me Yakoyoḡʷa. Woꞌca [James Knox] named me ꞌAx̱uẃ. He was trying to say Hadawabidu [petite Hadawa], and, because he could not say it properly, he called me ꞌAx̱uẃabidu. That is all he ever called me. Hadawabidu is a nickname for a mother or an auntie [ʔənis]. It is similar to the name ꞌAnita or Hadawa. They were trying to teach James Knox how to call me Hadawa but he could not pronounce it properly and always called me ꞌAx̱uẃa. This is the only name people refer to me by today – even the White man.

I remember all my Qʷiqʷasutinux̱ʷ names. My father named me Laq̓ʷaloḡʷa [Inviting Woman]. The name of ƛalaꞌēgalis [Leaping Whale with Dorsal Fin Visible] was given to me by Yaqalənala of the Maˑmaliliqəlla. Nəmnasolaga was the name given to me by Tiqwa, also of the Maˑmaliliqəlla. They also called him Jim Sapəlis.

The old people would frequently give you names. The name given to me by Mumuta was Ǧaꞌəx̱talas [A Place to Have a Mourning Feast]. Mumuta was Ǧayuˑx̱əlas [From Whom You Receive]. He was Joseph Wallace, a Maˑmaliliqəlla.

We are closely related to the man named Wohu from Qaluḡʷis [Turnour Island]. My father was related to him. Wohu obtained the name Kʷənxʷaloḡʷa from his wife as part of her dowry. And this is the very same name he gave me as part of my dowry, along with the Weather Dance [Ṅəɬalalaɬ].[4] He also gave me this dance. The name of this particular Weather Dance is Pəɬəla [Flapping].

I received the name Kʷənxʷalog̱ʷa when I was initiated [*sinadəm*] during a big ṗəsa Wohu gave at Qalug̱ʷis. He was a x̱awiċis, and they also say that he was half Comox [Coast Salish]. He was the father of Wadəma, and Wadəma was the mother of James Wadhams.

The old people would frequently call me by all these names. They also called me x̱aɫaʔegalis [Finning Whale] because we are named after the Whale [g̱ʷəýəm]. The Whale story is ours, among the Maṁaliliqəlla. For example, they called Yux̱əs Charlie, G̱ʷəýəm. My brother [cousin] used to tell me that many names derive from the Whale. Indeed, we received many names from the Whale. Did you know this? Names like x̱aɫaʔēgalis, x̱aɫbē, x̱aɫonəm, x̱aɫəmax̱udayug̱ʷa, and G̱ʷika. I really think that people should study and learn the origin of their names.

Some of our names also derive from the Eulachon, [dˀax̱ʷən]. Many names also derive from the Copper [ƛaqʷa], and the Abalone Shell [ʔix̱ċəm]. Some foolish people were named after the clouds [ʔənwēý]. There were two people I knew who were called by the name of ʔənxʷʔidiẏ. They were named after the clouds. ʔənʔənwidˀəmg̱a was a female name deriving from the clouds. They were really foolish at times. [Big laughter.]

The meaning of Sewidi is not seaweed, ɫəq̓astən. It means people are paddling towards your village by sea. Six̱ʷalas has the same meaning. This is Jimmy Sewid's name. Sewidi does not mean seaweed but "People Are Paddling towards You." It also implies that the bearer of that name is always giving potlatches to those who are coming to visit him. That is why those travelling by sea go there. This is the meaning of Sewidi. This is also what one of my favourite names, Six̱ʷasuẇ, means: "Paddling towards You." I love that name so much that I named my favourite cat Six̱ʷasuẇ.

My mother gave me names from the Qʷiqʷasutinux̱ʷ. The names from my mother's side are: Pux̱as, Pux̱idiẏ; female names are: Max̱ṁəẇidˀəmg̱a, Məmxuyog̱ʷa, Wikəlalisəmēýg̱a, and Yakoyog̱ʷa.

Now I will give you some other male names. The name for the chief of the Qʷiqʷasutinux̱ʷ is x̱alilix̱a. The other names are: ʔAwilg̱ʷolas, Pux̱as, Q̓osalas, Nəmogʷis, and Waxilicuẇ. These are the names my mother told me we own, and they are from the Qʷiqʷasutinux̱ʷ. These are the names acquired by x̱ax̱axʷas [Stone Body Man][5] when he went around marrying women of different tribes. That is the reason why we have so many names. He went around marrying women of different tribes.

He went around marrying the princesses[6] [ḵidiɫ; plural: ḵisḵadiɫ] of the different groups of the coast, and he would receive names and dowries along with his wives. This is what they call *winistala*, going around declaring war on the tribes. This is not the same as x̱umaɫa and wina.[7] All they are saying is g̱ag̱agistalisala. What they are really saying is "obtaining brides all around." This is exactly what I told Peter MacNair[8] when he gave me a ride not too long ago. He asked me several questions on the very same subject. I told him that *winistala* meant obtaining wives from neighbouring northern or southern tribes. The groom would obtain the princesses and their dowries. This is not the real killing war. A groom would say "*wəngəlis*" when the time came for him to marry someone's daughter. The marriage was called "*wina.*" We refer to the bride's dowries as "*winanəm,*" acquired after peace is established. This is why the White people always confused our marriage practices with those of war. This was one of the mistakes of George Hunt; but Cuxʷċaʔesa[9] was just as much to blame. When referring to *winistala*, he translated it too literally. All x̣ax̣axʷas [Stone Body Man] did was to go around and marry all the women of all the neighbouring tribes and acquire their dowries. x̣ax̣axʷas would threaten to attack or declare war on a tribe, and the tribe would avoid the conflict by offering a bride and a dowry.

My relatives named me by a male name when they gave me a ṗəsa position. My male position name is Homiskənis. My father had already died and the naming was done by my mother. No, my father was still alive when the naming of the position took place. This is what we call ʎax̣ʷʔid [fulfilling your standing position]. I could then attend feasts [ƙʷilas].[10]

This did not mean that I could attend all inter-tribal feasts, but I could at least attend all the feasts at Mimkʷəmlis. My relatives would come and invite me to attend the feasts being held there. Not very many women had this right and this privilege. When my father and my mother gave a potlatch or a feast, they would ask me to attend. This is called ʎax̣ʷʔid. They would refer to it as ʔicistasuw̓ [called for the second time]. Our people would hold a feast for those who were being bestowed with this new position. If you did not have a male position you could not attend these feasts. They would give a feast in your honour to show that you could now attend them. This is what my relatives did. And only a few women held these privileges. The father of Qaqasolas did it for her, so she was able to attend the feast. She would sit among the men and that is what I did. I was able to sit among the men. This is what you call ʎax̣ʷʔid, ƙʷilasiɫ [feast; having a feast for a newly introduced member] and ʔicistasuw̓.

Nulag̱a was my only sister [half-sister]. I had a brother [half-brother], but his father was White.[11] He died from injuries. He would have been between myself and Nulag̱a. He was just a baby when he died. My mother put him in a "hammock." It broke and fell on the floor, and he hit his head. He developed meningitis and died. His father was a White man.

I do not know whether or not I am the reincarnation of someone [x̣ʷilaqa: to come right back]. The only thing that I have heard concerns my grandmother [hereafter, grandmother = great-aunt], Max̣ʷalog̱ʷa. They used to say that Gaguw̓ [ʔAx̣uw̓'s granddaughter, Louise Assu, one of Daisy's older sisters] was her reincarnation. They used to say that some babies were born with pierced ears. These babies, they would say, had been born many times over. x̣apa was one of those. They would say that these people have come back. Max̄ʷaloḡʷa had a pellet wound in the corner of her eye. She was Caribou Jack's sister [cousin]. She was injured when the Qʷiqʷasutinux̄ʷ were massacred by the Bəlx̣ʷəlla. Louise happened to be born with a hole near her eye-duct, like Max̄ʷaloḡʷa. We always said she was the reincarnation of my grandmother. They used to believe that people were reincarnations of others. I used to hear them talk like this. They never said anything like that about me. But people with many birthmarks, scars, and so on were those who were thought to be reincarnated.

I had a dream about Lena. I sensed she was the reincarnation of someone. In my dream I saw this whale [ḡʷəẏəm] lying on the bottom of the ocean, and then it suddenly turned into a baby. A person brought it to me and it just disappeared. A few days later, I found out that I was pregnant with Lena. I dreamt she was Edna, the daughter of Babasa, and I sensed she was Edna's reincarnation. The baby looked like Edna when it was brought to me. Ọacuḡow's mother was Jerry May's [Ḡix̄kən's] sister [cousin], and Edna was his daughter. We were really closely related to Edna.

I do not know whether reincarnation can occur outside the family, but the dream I just told you involved only people who were closely related. I do not really think that a person from one tribe can be reincarnated in a person from a different tribe. Look at the ńuẏəm [myth] in which a son is the reincarnation of his father.

There was a really gentle man who had a son. This man was a great carver. The little boy would always bother him. He would bring pieces of wood to his father and ask him to make him a toy boat. This was when his father was in the middle of carving. But he would always stop and make the thing that his son had asked for. The boy would also ask him to make him bows and arrows, and again his father would interrupt his work to make him what he wanted. So he was never angry with his son. He never ever wanted to get upset with his son.

One day the father died, but somehow he was aware of his surroundings and he knew what was happening. When he was reborn, he became the son of his son. This is a ńuẏəm. This man died but he was still conscious of his surroundings. He knew when he had died. Someone told him that he was going to become the son of his son. He was aware when his son's wife became pregnant with him. This was the son who used to interrupt him during his work, asking him to make all these toys for him. He became the baby of his son. His son grew up, and he also became a carver. When the father became older, during his reincarnated state, he decided to imitate what his son did to him. When his son started carving he went over and asked him to do things, as his son used to do to him. He did not do it too often because his son got so upset that he beat him. This was the reincarnated child who was his father in a former life. The father said to the son, "Well, now you see what I went through with you. When you used to bother me, I never minded. You see, I am your late father." This is what the ńuy̓əm says. This is what I know about reincarnation, about this man who became the reincarnation of his own child.

I forgot to mention one thing. During his lifetime, the father used to hide some ṗəsa [potlatch] material, like baskets and woven garments, in a cave. He used to hide these with the help of his mother. After his reincarnation, he asked his son if he ever checked on these things. The son said he did not know what he was talking about. They both went to the cave to check on these things. When they got there, these things were so old that they had rotted away. These things were garments to wear for dancing and things for giving away. They did not look like anything anymore. They were so rotten. These are the things they had hidden in the cave.

Learning Our Ways

I will begin with when I was a child. Since my early childhood I wanted to learn everything. I wanted to learn all the ways of preparing food. But, with other children, I also played the games of the early days, such as ṁaṁax̌ʷsəma, a rock game.[12] The game I liked the most was k̓ʷəmła, the feather game. This game made use of something resembling your shuttlecock. We had a feather ball that we would hit and bat back and forth and score according to how many times we hit the ball. The idea was to get the highest score. We were counting and keeping track of the score. This game we called k̓ʷəmła.

We also went swimming. We were told to immerse ourselves quickly. If we were not fast enough, our skin would become like a toad's back.[13] That is what we were told.

I used to always follow my grandmother around. I called her ğağasa [grandma]. She was Caribou Jack's sister [cousin], and she was at Ğʷayasdəms during the Bəlx̌ʷəlla massacre. She was hit and wounded by a pellet just below her right eye. They captured her, but she was immediately ransomed back by her Kʷaguł relatives at Cax̌is. That is why those killers did not take her up north with the rest. Her name was Max̌ʷaloğʷa. I used to sleep with her, and I followed her around wherever she went.

For now, I want to talk only about the things I know personally, the things I saw while I was growing up. I watched my grandmother in all her daily activities, whether cooking, preparing fish, digging roots or clams, weaving baskets, or making rope.

My mother would make cedar strips out of split red cedar[14] withes. She would break them into strands [*d̕ax̌a*] and twist [*m̓ala*] them together, and she would make beautiful ropes. She started twisting with two strands. This is what we used to tie up our canoes [*mug̱ʷan̓awēy̓*] and our anchors [*q̓əlcəm*]. Our anchors were made out of an elongated [*sax̌ʷsəm*] rock tied with cedar rope. The cedar rope was the rope of earlier times. When my mother twisted the cedar she would start with two strands. Then she would add another strand, which they call *məlikəla* [twisted in the back]. "It is not twisted in the back," they would say while adding a third strand. The cedar rope would then be thicker [*ƛax̌ʷʔid*]. This is what I saw my mother doing. She made very long cedar-bark ropes. This was for tying the canoes up when we moored them.

We went digging for clams and put them in special baskets. We poured them on the beach because they were muddy, and then we put them in an openwork basket and washed them with salt water. Clam baskets [*d̕igaciy̓*] were woven out of split cedar withes and split cedar root. The weaving consisted of loose, open work, which allowed the sand to wash away easily. We loaded our canoe with our harvest of clams and went home to prepare them. We heated some rocks in the fire until they became red hot, and then we put them into a cooking box full of water. When the water was boiling, the clams were put into an openwork basket and lowered into it. This way of cooking clams or anything that had to be boiled, like fish soup, is called *q̓uła* [to boil]. That is why they call these small cooking boxes *q̓ulaciy̓*. Another way of cooking was *n̓əka*, steaming. They would dig a hole and heat stones in the fire. When the stones were red hot they would put them into the hole that had been dug. I saw Łax̌ʷała [Lucy Sewid] do this with a plant called *łəx̌ʷsus* [clover roots]. She would steam them. They would take *kiḵaʔokʷ* [skunk cabbage leaves][15] and cover the stones so the food would not get dirty. Then they would put the *łəx̌ʷsus* on top and cover it with a mat. They would pour water over it and steam it. They call this *n̓əka* [steaming]. This is how steamed food was prepared. They do not add water to the food. They pour the water over it, and it steams when the water is in contact with the hot rocks. In the early days they covered the food with *ḵaḵubana* [old red cedar-bark mats] to contain the steam, but now we just use *ćex̌sǝm* [sacks]. When the food was ready, they uncovered it. We would not uncover the food for a long time. We would wait until the food was cooked. They call this *n̓əka*.

They call the really old red cedar mats *ḵaḵubana*. These are the discarded red cedar mats. This is also what they used when they steamed clams. They call the old discarded red cedar mats *ḵaḵubana*. Do not confuse them with *ḵubaẃas*, which is the name for the red cedar-bark blanket. *Ḵaḵubana* is the old discarded red cedar mat. There is a story about a man being covered with it to hold him down, they say. These are the old, spoiled, discarded red cedar mats. This is what they call *ƙaƙubaṅa*. This is what I saw as a child.

There are many steps to preparing smoked barbecued clams [*ƙumaciẏ*]. Clams were washed in salt water and the flesh taken out of the shell. I watched and learned because this is what my grandmother told me to do. She said to me one day, "I will not always be around to do these things for you." This is the reason I had to follow her around, so I could learn as I was growing up. She barbecued clams until they turned brown. We used some sticks that we had gathered in the forest as barbecue skewers. These sticks were made of thimbleberry [*caǧaɬ*][16] and salmonberry shoots [*ƙʷaɬəm*][17] that were gathered in the spring, while soft, before the berries were ripe. Rows of clams were skewered on these sticks and arranged on split cedar racks over the fire. The *ǧaluk*ʷ [clam "buttons"][18] were pierced with a stick and placed in neat, even rows on the racks. We removed the clam muscles when they were semi-dry. We also smoked them [*xəɬa:* to smoke fish]. Then we put them into red cedar containers. They were a real delicacy and very tasty. So, as you see, I learned how to smoke barbecued clams. We also dried them. We put them down and stepped on them because they bulged out too much. We flattened them so they would not take very long to dry. Each rack was about two feet [said in English] long. We broke the racks in half and folded them. We stored them in a cedar box called *xaċəm*. This box was the kind of storage container they used in the early days. We filled many of these containers whenever food was to be stored for any length of time. Steaming [*ṅaka*] was another way of cooking. Before barbecuing clams on a stick we would first steam them, as I said.[19]

These are some of the daily activities I carried out. I also followed my grandmother around when she was stripping bark off the trees so I would know how to do it myself. But I never did see how they prepared what we call *sagʷəm* [bracken fern rhizome].[20] For that reason I do not know how to prepare it. It is a root that I think was roasted in the fire. However, I saw *cakus* [sword fern rhizome][21] being prepared by Tumido. She was Moses's grandmother [ʔAx̌uẇ's husband's grandmother]. They were first roasted and then steamed. Oh, they were a real delicacy too! We could also boil them in a container called *ɋulaciẏ*. We used many types of containers in the old days. One of them was called *ƙəmẏax̌ɬa*. It was a bentwood box used to store *ɬina*, eulachon grease. The seams of this steamed box were pegged with wooden pegs made of *ɬəmɋa* [yew wood]. I guess they used it because it is hard wood. Clay [*ɬiɋa*] was rubbed on the inside of its seams to prevent leaking. Then uncut eulachon [*dʼax̌ʷən*] were laid in a box. You could see all the boxes loaded in the canoe for they made a great quantity of eulachon grease in the old days. They always tried to produce and preserve as much eulachon grease as they could. These boxes would never leak because they rubbed clay into their corners. That is what I have seen them do.

K̓əmy̓ax̌ƛa were big grease containers [vats], while ʠulaćiy̓ were small cooking boxes. Rocks were put in the fire until they became red hot, and then they were thrown into the cooking box, which was full of water. When the water came in contact with the hot rocks, it was brought to a boil. Then, whatever had to be cooked, ƙutəla [fish] or meat [said in English], would be added. This is what we did in the early days as we had neither pots nor pans. We could also put a mat over these containers, which would function as a lid. That was our way of doing things in the early days.

We gathered as much wood as possible for everyday use. We gathered firewood, cut it into kindling, and tied it up into bundles. I saw my grandfather [great-uncle], Ẏaqaƛ̓ənala, doing it. He was Jimmy Sewid's great-great-grandfather [great-great-uncle]. This is what we used to do even when we just went for a walk, for a torch was our only night-light in the early days. We always had it ready. A torch was also used while digging for clams if low tide happened to occur at night. The torch was made of a cedar stick that was split at one end so that it could hold cedar bark or kindling mixed with spruce pitch. Kindling was used that way. I have seen it. This is what we used to do in the early days. We never did what they do today. Today we are always buying fuel for our fire. We used to gather driftwood on the beach. We loaded our canoe and took it home. Wood was our fuel; it never cost us anything. We used to sit on the floor of the big house and put driftwood on the open fire to keep it going.

We also gathered as much ƙupəlx̌ [dry, dead cedar] as possible in order to make ƙupsayu, cedar tongs for barbecuing fish [ƙupak̓ʷ: barbecued salmon]. Cedar braces spread salmon to keep the fish flat and open for roasting. Split cedar tongs held fish over the fire. Of course, I was shown how to x̌ʷaƙa, to prepare and to filet fish, during our food harvesting for the winter [wiwamis: to harvest food for winter use].

What I really liked was being at Hada. I was still a small child then. But when I grew a little older, I gaffed for fish. There were many pink salmon [hańun] in this small stream during the salmon run. They were so many that their backs protruded out of the water. I would be running among them and they would scatter. Some of them would jump out of the water onto the shore. I would also gaff some of them. I would cut, clean, and prepare the fish all by myself when I was at Hada.

My grandmother used to dig for ƚax̌ʷsus, clover roots,[22] as well as λaxsəm: cinquefoil.[23] We ate them in the early days. They are white and stringy. They were dug out of the ground. We would go to Hada to get ƚax̌ʷsus. Women had their own digging gardens. They all had their own ancestral digging gardens at Hada.

These gardens had names that referred to their specific locations where *ƚəх̌ʷsus* and *λəхsəm* were found.[24]

Near D̓aẃadiẏ [Knight Inlet], we would gather *muƚexsdi*, wild blue camas,[25] which grew in profusion in the large meadows. We could eat the bulbs raw or cooked; they were really delicious either way. We gathered them at D̓aẃadiẏ and also at Gʷaiẏ [Hada].

We also picked berries to make cakes. We crushed and dried them on split cedar racks over the fire and shaped them into flat squares so that they could be stored. We made a lot of those cakes because we served them at feasts. We had so many kind of berries – huckleberries[26] [*ǧʷadəm*], salmonberries[27] [*q̓əmd̓ək̓ʷ*], red elderberries[28] [*ćixina*], and salal berries[29] [*ńak̓ʷət; ńak̓ʷad̓u:* dried salal berry cakes]. Another thing we ate was *ƚals* [cranberries].[30] We used them all and dried them. That was the jam of the early days. We could eat them all winter long. We also stored them in cedar boxes and preserved them for a long time. The same was also true for *ćalх̌ʷ* [wild crabapples].[31]

Stinging nettle[32] plants [*d̓ənd̓ənx̌ƚəm*] were also gathered. One day I went to the house of a Mamaliliqəla woman named λix̌ʌalix̌ćəmǧa [Always Inviting]. I could see these very long stinging nettles hanging over the hearth to dry. Stinging hairs were removed to obtain a smooth stem. She would weave them to make nets [*kiλəm*] and snares for small animals. Nettle fibres are very strong. A *kiλəm* was also used for catching eulachon. Nettle fibres [*ǧʷən*] were split and dried over the fire in the same way as were red cedar-bark strips. They made nets of different sizes: small, medium, and large.

I used to travel with the old people, following them when they were gathering our winter food at Yəlis and in the Nəmǧis River. That was such a good river. They would catch from 1,000 to 2,000 [said in English] fish. That was a lot of fish to dry. The men would gaff the fish. My mother would cut, clean, and prepare them. When I was not old enough to do it myself, I just watched. She would pack them up and put them in cedar baskets. She would bring them to the house at night. There she would make *kawas* – thin, sliced, sun-dried salmon belly – a real delicacy.

It was also at that time that we started using an oil lamp for light. By the light of the oil lamp my mother would filet the fish the same night they were caught. Before, of course, we just used our torch. The fire was put out and, with a ladder, she would hang the fish on a platform [*saʔoq̓ʷ*] over the fire to smoke. Each board could hold four fish. The Nəmǧis did it in a rather different way: they smoked the fish with the *kawas* still attached on either side of the fish. This way is called *təlukʷ*.

There was also an unusual way of gathering cockles [*d̓oliẏ*] that I learned at Hada. I stepped on them. We call this *ƚipo* [to step on]. We walked over the

Chapter Three

cockles but only with our heels. We did what they called *łəmgilisəla* [archaic word meaning to walk on the beach with your heels]; we walked on the beach with our heels. This was at night, when the tide was out. We stepped on cockles with our heels, and we could feel them. And then we would dig them up with our toes without seeing them. We just felt them with our heels. This is what I used to do when we were at Hada and also at Dᶻaẃadiẏ.

There was another unusual thing that I used to do. We ate *laʔēs*, mussels, not cooked but raw [*kəlxʷ*]. I ate them raw too. We had to swallow them whole when we ate them raw. We could not chew them. If you chewed them they would irritate your throat, they say. When we ate raw mussels, we had to swallow them whole; if we didn't, our throats would hurt. This is what they said.

I used to be really scared when we went down the rapids on the Nəmǧis River. The river is so large. Some men knew how to approach the rapids. Of course they were not using engines yet, but they kept their canoes on course with the aid of a *dᶻuxʷəms*, a pole. I must have been a brave girl because I soon overcame my fear as we came down the rapids with the rest of our party. Although I was still a child, I was already married to Moses Alfred. He was with my mother and my uncle Q̓ʷəmxuduẃ [or Wakəs, Dan Cranmer's uncle][33] in this great big canoe ahead of us. I was following them in another canoe. With me was the younger brother of Yeᴋala, whose name was Gʷimolas. We had our own little canoe called Yakənudᶻeẏ, and we were at the rear, following them. I was brave to come down, drifting along the rapids. Now that I am wise, I would never do it again. I must have been quite childish to drift down the river like that, just the two of us. Oh! It was really rough! [Big laughter.]

No matter what the old people were doing I was never left behind. I was always there, watching and learning. I used to go with them trapping animals, like the *məća*, the mink. They used a *k̓ʷəλayu*, a trap, to catch mink.

The roots [*λuṗək*] of the spruce tree were used to make big traps for big animals. Some of these traps were huge. The rope leading to the trap was also made from this root. A heavy weight was put on top of the trap. When the animal tripped over the rope, the trap collapsed and the heavy weight would fall on it.[34] These types of traps were used for bears and deer and were called *ṁaṁaćayuẃ*. I used to travel with the trappers and learned all kinds of things when I was young.

I really liked catching birds. I used to trap them. I caught many different kinds of birds. The *k̓ʷəλayu* was one of the traps I used for them, and I used a stick of some sort to brace the trap. I was sitting at some distance, and when the bird entered the trap, I pulled the rope and the bird was caught. I once caught a blue jay, *k̓ʷəsk̓ʷəs*. Oh! I was speechless! I used salmon eggs, *ǧineẏ*, as bait. The trap had a hole in it, which was covered with a cedar bark mat so I

1 TOP LEFT Ḡʷuɫəlas: ʔAx̄uw̓'s father, Joe Joseph. *Charcoal drawing, c. 1880.*

2 TOP RIGHT Puλas: ʔAx̄uw̓'s mother. *Charcoal drawing, c. 1880.*

3 BOTTOM Yəlis (Alert Bay). The house adorned with the Raven frontal pole was owned by ʔAx̄uw̓'s uncle Q̓ʷəmxəduw̓ (N̓umas, or Wakəs) and was passed on to Moses Alfred when he married ʔAx̄uw̓ as part of her dowry. *Photograph by H.I. Smith, 1898; American Museum of Natural History Library 411790.*

4 TOP LEFT Ǧaʔəxtalas: Wife of ʔAx̌uw̓'s uncle, Q̓ʷəmxuduw̓ (N̓umas, or Chief Wakəs), holding baby ʔAx̌uw̓, c. 1894.

5 TOP RIGHT Wayoɫ or Kʷənxʷəlaʔoǧʷa: The mother of Billie Sunday Willie (also called Daca), who, then a child, was grabbed by a Bella Coola warrior during the massacre that took place at Ǧʷayasdəms, around 1855. She pointed at the valuable Hudson's Bay blankets that were piled up in one corner of the house and managed to escape and survive the deadly raid. She was also one of ʔAx̌uw̓'s midwives.

6 BOTTOM Daisy Roberts (left) with her aunt Margaret (Q̓acuǧow), the mother of Moses Alfred. Margaret holds her granddaughter, Flora Alfred, c. 1913.

7 TOP Qʷiqʷasuṫinux̌ʷ village of Ǧʷayasdəms. Vestiges of a traditional house with carved house-posts depicting human ancestors. *Photograph by C.F. Newcombe 1900; RBCM collection PN241.*

8 BOTTOM Hudson's Bay blankets piled up in house, in preparation for a potlatch. *AMNH 22861.*

9   Mamaliliqəlla village of Mimkʷəmlis. House front decorated with a three-dimensional painted carving of Sisayuɬ, the Double-Headed Serpent. The painted house frontal pole represents the Grizzly Bear surmounting a partially hidden base figure, a land animal, a bird, a killer whale, and the Thunderbird as finial. *Photograph by C. F. Newcombe c. 1917; collection* RBCM PN1067.

o TOP LEFT ʔAx̌uẃ and daughter Flora (b. 1911).

1 TOP RIGHT *From left to right:* Arthur Alfred (b. 1915), Flora Alfred (b. 1911), and George Alfred (b. 1914).

2 RIGHT Mam̓aliliqəlla village of Mim̓k̓ʷəmlis. Between two house posts with the representations of a Grizzly Bear at their base (one with an articulated arm), four people are seated *(from left to right):* Emma Sewid's youngest sister, in European dress, Emma Sewid (James Sewid's mother), Henry Bell (his uncle), and James Sewid (his father). The adults wear Chilkat blankets and headdresses. Several carved wooden feast dishes can be seen in the foreground. A traditional Kʷakʷakəẃakʷ house was "regarded as the sacred container of the lineage," its very structure a crest. It was decorated with a crest painting on its front, was given a crest name, and was itself an entity within the social organization (Goldman 1975: 47, 63). *Photograph by C.F. Newcombe c. 1917; collection* RBCM PN1063.

13 TOP ʔAx̌uw̓ with her children, c. 1920. *From l. to r.:* Emma Beans (ʔIlag̱a, ʔAx̌uw̓'s sister-in-law), Alvin (b. 1910), George (b. 1914), Flora (b. 1911), Arthur (b. 1915), and Lily (b. 1916).

14 BOTTOM LEFT ʔAx̌uw̓ (left) with Nuladiy̓, Ben Alfred's wife (right).

15 BOTTOM RIGHT James Roberts (N̓umas) or Cultus Jim, and wife Daisy Roberts.

16 ʔAx̱uw̓'s home in Alert Bay, c. 1918, before Moses Alfred built their modern,
three-storey house. The frontal pole depicts the following crests, from top to
bottom: Thunderbird; Double-Headed Serpent with human inside; Killer Whale;
Wolf and human; and Dᶻunuq̌ʷa with child.

17 TOP Indian Agent William Halliday described the potlatch as "evil." In 1914, he wrote: "The law against the potlatch has been passed because it has been seen that where the potlatch exists there has been no progress and the Government wants to see the Indians advance so that they are on the same footing as the white men, and this can not be as long as the potlatch continues" (Sewid Smith 1979: 16). PABC 95771.

18 MIDDLE The Anglican Reverend and Mrs. A.J. Hall. The resistance of the Kʷakʷakəwakʷ people to the colonial authorities, who wanted to abolish the potlatch and other potlatch-related customs, led the missionaries to regard them as the most "incorrigible" of all British Columbia ethnic groups, having an "almost intractable character." ʔAx̌uw̓ was baptized by Rev. Hall and went to school under the tutelage of Mrs. Hall. PABC 89312.

19 BOTTOM Credit note from Cultus & Cranmer, General Merchants, to Bob Harris; Alert Bay, 2 April 1923

OPPOSITE PAGE

20 TOP LEFT Top row, second from left, ʔAx̌uw̓ at the cannery.

21 TOP RIGHT ʔAx̌uw̓'s children raising money for the Red Cross.

22 BOTTOM ʔAx̌uw̓ (middle, second row from bottom) with members of the Anglican Church Women's Auxiliary group, Alert Bay, c. 1930

23 OPPOSITE Potlatch at Alert Bay, before 1914. Among the items to be distributed were dressers, sewing machines, mirrors, and other pieces of furniture. *RBCM 1887*.

24 ABOVE LEFT ʔAx̌uẃ (left) and her daughter Flora Sewid, holding confiscated paraphernalia during a visit at Ottawa's National Museum of Man in the 1970s.

25 ABOVE RIGHT Billie Sunday Willie holding a mask, following the return of the confiscated paraphernalia.

6 OPPOSITE The Alfreds' new three-storey big house at the centre of Alert Bay, c. 1975.

7 TOP Agnes (ʔAx̱uw̓) and Moses Alfred with their great-grandchildren, during their 50th wedding anniversary, 1959.

8 MIDDLE Lorne Smith wearing the Chilkat blanket that Daisy passed on to him as a dowry. The abalone shells and other huge pieces of abalone shell ornaments decorating her noble's hat were distributed by ʔAx̱uw̓ to certain women at the end of the wedding ceremony. *Photograph by Martine Reid, October 1978.*

29 TOP LEFT Chief Jimmy Sewid holding his Copper during Daisy Sewid and Lorne Smith's traditional wedding, Alert Bay, 7 October 1978.

30 TOP RIGHT Women with new ceremonial outfits surrounding Daisy at her wedding.

31 BOTTOM ʔАx̌uw̓ singing and drumming at the peace treaty potlatch, Campbell River, 1987. *Photograph by Martine Reid.*

32 TOP Chiefs of the Northwest Coast First Nations
witnessing the signing of the peace treaty
between the Kʷakʷakəẃakʷ and the Bella Coola
at a potlatch hosted by Chief James Sewid, at
Campbell River, 1987. *Photograph by Martine Reid.*

33 BOTTOM Chief James Sewid and Daisy Sewid-
Smith at the peace treaty potlatch in Campbell
River, 1987. *Photograph by Martine Reid.*

34 TOP Angie, one of ʔAx̱uw̓'s great-great-granddaughters, dancing with her baby girl Amilia, during ʔAx̱uw̓'s memoria potlatch, Alert Bay, 1996. *Photograph by Martine Reid.*

35 MIDDLE ʔAx̱uw̓ participates in a potlatch, Alert Bay, c. 1978. *Photograph by Martine Reid.*

36 BOTTOM ʔAx̱uw̓'s descendants, following her memorial potlatch at Alert Bay, 1996. *Photograph by Martine Reid.*

could put my hand through to get the bird. The blue jay was caught in my trap when I was young. I ran really fast to ask someone to get it out for me. This is the bird we call *ƙʷəskʷəs*. This is what I used to do when I was young.

I kept the bird as a pet. I made a cage, *kəlxáči*, by overlapping pieces of wood. When it was completed, the little bird was sitting in it. I would get worms from a piece of rotten wood. The bird would peck worms out of it. Worms [*ǧalayuẃ*] were its food. I had many birds as pets.

I used to do all kinds of things. I watched them catch *ṗoʔiẏ* [halibut]. In the early days branches of a spruce tree [*ʔaliwas*] were broken to make a fire, over which they would put their halibut hooks [*yəkuẃ*].[35] Jimmy Sewid's grandmother, Nukʷənidᶻəmgilakʷ, used to do this. The hooks were put over the fire under a mat to be smoked. The halibut fishermen would smoke their hooks to cleanse them. This was what they did to catch halibut. They would smoke the hooks with smoke from some spruce tree kindling. In order to smoke the halibut hooks, they would cover themselves with a mat, holding their halibut hooks in their hands. This is what they used to do in the old days. They used to believe that this would ensure a successful catch. *Ṗaṗəẃa*, "catching a halibut," was what they called such a procedure. After they had caught a halibut, they filleted [*ƚəlsa*] it to make *kawas* – sun-cured filet of fish.

I want to talk more about things I saw while I was a little girl. I spent most of my childhood at Mirhkʷəmlis [Village Island], where I was born. In the old days the shampoo that they used – perhaps I should not talk about it. I have not seen it; I have just heard about it: is it all right for me to continue? The shampoo in the early days was not very nice. [Much laughter.] Are we going to talk about it? So we are. At Mirhkʷəmlis they told me that these short little old women who were sitting by the seashore were washing their dirty hair. They were using this "stuff" that is not very nice. They would gather it in a watertight container as it was their shampoo. And they would rinse their hair in salt water to remove it. It was – urine, *kʷeéiẏ* [literally room box; i.e., chamber pot]. This was our shampoo in the early days. My grandmother told me what they were using it for. I also saw Ẏaǧaƚʔənala saving the contents of his chamber pot. Later on I found out that it was his shampoo. That was the way it was.

It happened also that I had to fetch water [*ẃap*] in the dark. We would *məlista*, stir the water and shine light on it with a torch in order to bring to the surface whatever crawling things were in it so that we would avoid catching them.

When someone died, relatives had to take the water out of the house of the deceased person. The water in a house would be changed after someone died. Furthermore, the relatives of the deceased would not be allowed to speak for four days; but today no one has any respect for the four days of mourning. In the old days, they would not speak but just whisper. This was after someone had died. They would mourn for four days. This is what I personally experienced when I grew a little older.

I wonder if I missed anything about the ways our people prepared their food. I will talk now about the uses of wood. They used it for everything. The most important was the red cedar [*wilkʷ*]. Red cedar was used for everything in the early days, even for toilet paper. We used to see hundreds of toilet sticks floating around Yəlis before the tide carried them out. We also saw them around the houses built on piles at Ṁiṁkʷəmlis, where a little stream called *dᶻadᶻawaxsila* runs into the sea.

Red cedar was, of course, essential for making our canoes. There were two types of canoe, the regular type *xʷakʷəṅa* and the type called *məṅga* [war canoe]. The latter is slightly different at the bow [*ʔugiwēý*]; this feature is called *q̓iq̓agola səlačiý* [gatherers]. My father and grandfather owned the second type. We used to sail to Vancouver in our canoe to attend marriages such as McDougall's father's wedding, when he was married to Habədən.

I also saw my grandfather sail his canoes. He took two canoes and a *saʔoq̓ʷ*. A *saʔoq̓ʷ* is a board from the roof of a house. This is part of the roof of a house. He laid the plank down and tied it to the canoes. This brings two canoes together and makes a platform.[36] We sat on this platform and went to Ṁiṁkʷəmlis. I was with Ýaq̓ał̓ʔənala, my grandfather, and my mother. Oh! I was scared when we went through strong tidal currents! The canoe made such a noise when the tide ran strong. I am telling you about my personal experience. I did not just hear about things. I really rode on a platform between two canoes, or, as we say it, I *hawanaqəla* my way to Ṁiṁkʷəmlis from Yəlis. That is what I did.

Oh! I forgot something. I just remembered something else. We would go looking for pitch gum [*ǧʷəlik*], the Indian chewing gum. It bleeds from the *ʔaliwas* [spruce tree]. The spruce is the only tree from which we collected pitch gum. It drips down the bark. We would carry a wooden drip bowl. People would chop the spruce and set fire to it so that it would burn. This caused the gum to melt down and drip so that we could gather it in our dripping bowl. Then we would squeeze and work it in our hands; it would harden like candy. We would take a bite out of it and go home. It is called *gʷakʷəlna ǧʷəlik*, to gather pitch gum. If the Indian chewing gum got hard – and sometimes it really got too hard – we would take a pinch of *yasək̓ʷ* [mountain goat fat] and mix it with it. Then it would soften. We call this *ṁalixʷʔid* [to chew]. If it was no longer any good, we spat it out. This is what would occur when the pitch would dissolve and break apart. We would spit [*kʷisʔid*] the pitch gum ball out and take another bite. The women kept supplies of pitch gum. I used to do this when I followed my grandmother around.

There is something else I just remembered because of the gum. This is ǧʷəmǧʷəmyuw̓ [sun cream]. My aunt, ʔAnita, used to make it when we were at Dᶻaw̓adiy̓. She used to melt the pitch gum, mix it with oil, and then used it as a facial cream to soften her skin and to protect it from sunburns. She would put some on her face every day. This was the x̌ums [makeup] of our early days. Our people call it ǧʷəmǧʷəmyuw̓. She would mix it with oil and anoint her face, and it would last for several days. She would not wash her face for several days so that it would stay on. This cream was also used during the dancing, but in this context we called it ǧʷəmǧʷəmslelas. This was when we were at Dᶻaw̓adiy̓.

4

Becoming a Woman

Introduction

The onset of a Kʷakʷakəwakʷ girl's puberty was the first major transitional phase through which she would pass and was celebrated in a ritualistic manner. It marked a very important turning point in her life because, upon her emergence from this ritual, she was recognized as a woman and was eligible to marry. A pubescent girl was secluded and could not see other people nor be seen by them, except by the elderly female relatives who attended her. The duration of seclusion varied according to the girl's rank but it was usually lengthy, up to seventeen days, comprising a period of preparation of four days followed by a period of purification (Boas 1966: 368-70). It is said that the seclusion of girls of high rank was used to prevent premarital sexual relations, which were considered disgraceful to the girl and the entire group (Drucker 1965: 100). In spite of the fact that ʔAx̌uẇ was married before she had reached puberty, she went through her puberty ritual as the traditional cultural custom and her standing required. ʔAx̌uẇ did not volunteer information on the personal and intimate consequences of that particular situation nor its sexual implications.

When the seclusion and symbolic cleansing rituals were completed, the father of the girl would give a potlatch in her honour to mark her entry into womanhood, at which time her new name was made public. At each subsequent menstrual period a Kʷakʷakəwakʷ woman went into a brief seclusion.[1] The duration of these seclusions diminished after contact, and the seclusion itself is no longer observed. Today adolescent girls of noble descent who have reached puberty are sometimes recognized at potlatches, at which point they receive a new name. Toys are sometimes distributed to mark the end of childhood, and soaps and combs are handed out to symbolize purification after the onset of menses (Cranmer-Webster 1990: 388).

The topic of menstruation has long been the subject of extraordinary symbolic elaboration, in a wide variety of cultures. For a critique of the literature and new analyses of the subject, see Buckley and Gottlieb (1988) and Héritier (2002).

Growing Up

I was not a child any more. I had grown a little older. When I was the age of my great-granddaughter Gloria,[2] a teenager [said in English], I was not allowed to go for a walk on my own. I was always told to stay home. The old people lectured me regularly. When we ate fish, for example, I was always told not to eat the rear end part of the fish just before the tail, otherwise my future husband would be *dəmp̓ax̌stēy̓:* he would have a salty backside. [Much laughter.] That means that he would be a commoner. This is what the elders told me, not to eat this part of the fish. I was told to be careful about what I ate to ensure that my future husband would be a *giǧaméy̓*, of noble descent and from a high-ranking tribe. Noble parents would always try to arrange for their children's spouses to come from the higher-ranking tribes such as the Kʷaguł, the Maṁaliliqəlla, and the Nəmǧis. They would also tell the same thing to the young men. They would be reminded not to eat that part of the fish in order to ensure that their future wives would not be coming from lower-ranking tribes. This is what they used to say to us.

Our home on Ṁimkʷəmlis [Village Island] was never completed. We just partitioned it with curtains. We lived there with Məllidiy̓, my father's older brother. Y̓aq̓ałʔənala was our relative, and Waċaʔow̓ lived in a small cabin on the beach. During this period Mr. Hall built a sawmill for the Nəmǧis at Alert Bay.[3] My father used to get logs and ask him to cut them. His original big house had burnt down during the Village Island fire. He asked Mr. Hall to cut the lumber for him at his Alert Bay sawmill. And this is what we used to build our house.

For the inside Məllidiy̓ used *saʔoq̓ʷ* [planks]. He worked with Y̓aq̓ałʔənala [ʔOlsiwidi]. He was my grandfather [great-uncle]; he was Łaxʷała's [Lucy Sewid's] husband. *Saʔoq̓ʷ* is the Indian lumber of the old days. My father built the structure himself, but the lumber came from the White man. That became our home. It was a big house, *gokʷəm*. With what was left over he built a small cabin.

We lived in the big house, and we used the cabin as a bedroom. This was when my father was still alive. He died shortly after the house was completed. He gave whatever lumber was left over to Alec. Alec was his nephew. Alec built a house with it, which was later bought by ʔAssuw̓. Three houses were built with that lumber: the big house, the cabin, and Alec's house.

My father, my mother, and myself, three of us were living in the cabin. We just used it as one room. We lived in the big house. This is what we did in the old days. Q̓acuw̓ did the same thing at M̓im̓k̓ʷəmlis.

We used to sit on the floor of the big house. We had no chairs. During our meals we sat in a squatting position,[4] wearing blankets[5] over our shoulders. During meals we were not allowed to stretch our legs.[5] We would become lazy if we stretched our legs,[6] they used to say to us. The elders always told us to q̓ap̓ix̌ała, to have our blanket wrapped around and folded in front of us, and that meant that we could not play anymore. I had to pin up my blanket very tightly. I was pinned in my blanket, sitting there stiffly without moving. I hated it.

Before I reached puberty I was trained how to sit properly; I was never allowed to stretch my legs. The boys were told the same. Their hands also had to be kept behind their backs. We had to sit very stiff and straight to avoid becoming lazy, which is what would happen if we were to stretch our legs or to hunch our backs.

If I wanted to visit someone I had to be chaperoned. I was taught how to wrap my blanket around me. I was even chaperoned when I visited my relatives. When I became a little bit older, elders would come and ask me to accompany them. I was not allowed to acknowledge any of the boys. We were not permitted to look around when we went for a walk. We were always being lectured about how we should behave.

Well, the day came when I had my first menses, ʔix̌anta.[7] I was already married to Moses Alfred. I guess I must have been around thirteen when I got married. I was married before I had my first menses. It was a long time, perhaps three years, before I could get pregnant. Yes, I think I had been married for three years before I could have my first child.

My mother prepared me for my first menstruation. Young girls were told that one day they would get their period, so it was not a surprise when it happened to me. However, I did not have my period until after I was married. My grandmother, Max̌ʷalog̓ʷa [great-aunt], and my mother's mother told me I would have to go through a ritual when it happened.

I was being prepared for womanhood. The elders surrounded me and performed the necessary rituals. I was secluded from the rest of the household; I had to sit in a corner of the room in our house at Yəlis concealed by a curtain. This is where I stayed during the total length of my period – twelve days. Women decorated the room, putting many button blankets all over the walls, surrounding me with them. They also surrounded me with all the goods they were going to p̓əsa with – including bracelets [k̓uk̓ʷəla] – after the end of my seclusion so that I would be wealthy. That was the symbolic meaning[8] of all the things that were surrounding me. I sat there day after day, the entire length of my period. I was wearing the hat [*giqəmɬ*] reserved for nobility, the same type of hat that Daisy wore at her wedding. It was adorned with strips of white mountain goat pelts. I was wearing strips of mountain goat wool made into rings on some parts of my body. They say mountain goat wool is good [*lamaduw̓*] because the goats are gentle animals. Mountain goat pelts were covering all the important parts of my body – my head, my wrists, and my ankles – so that I would not have a bad temper.

I was not permitted to stretch my legs. They made me sleep in a very short bed. I really do not know why they did that to newly menstruating girls. I was sleeping on a bed of *k̓ak̓iƛama*, bulrushes. I was really petite in stature. While I was wearing my noble hat, they fed me very little. They would not allow me to drink any water; this was so I would not become a glutton. Being a glutton is improper. They also bathed me. They hired three old women to bathe me. Oh! My poor mother, she was really following the traditional ways. I did not always like it either. She sewed strips of black wool cloth around my ankles to guarantee that I would have beautiful legs. All the girls in the same situation wore it around their ankles. Only recently did they stop making young girls wear black cloth around their legs so that they would not have wrinkled legs. Oh! Our old people, they were really something!

During my pubescent isolation, they took really good care of me. Q̓ag̓ʷoɬ's mother [Johnson Cook's mother], whose name was ʔIx̣ćəmg̓a, was hired to pluck my eyebrows. Qʷaxilog̓wa and a third woman, G̓ana, who was a *pəx̣ala* [shaman], were hired to bathe me. The female shaman chanted. The three women were always around me, looking after me. They woke me up early every morning and sat me up with my back straight and wearing my noble hat. Thus I would sit rigid and motionless. Every day, at dawn, they ritually bathed me. They performed exactly the same things as they used to during the four phases of an initiation ritual.[9] They heated four rocks in the fire, which they then threw into my bathwater. They did not really bathe me. They sprinkled water over me, like during baptism [ʔAx̣uw̓ says "baptism" in English]. They would do it four times, sprinkling warm water over me four times. The last day of my purification they brought a large red cedar-bark [kəlxsəm] neck-ring [ƛag̓ək̓ʷ]. They held it above my head and sprinkled white eagle down all around it. Then they lowered it down and put me through the hoop [kəlxsəm]. I went through the red cedar-bark neck-ring.

G̓ana was chanting. She put me through the red cedar-bark ring the first time. This is what we call *qəxa*,[10] the first step of the *weliqa* [the first of the four steps performed during a purification ritual]. Then I went through the hoop the second, third, and fourth time. Then, at dawn of the final day of my seclusion, the shaman woman took the ring, rubbed it all over my body, and then threw it in the fire [*lax̌ʷ ƛənd*]. The ceremony of my puberty ritual was then complete; it happened at dawn.

When my period was over, the mother of Johnson Cook plucked my eyebrows. This was to make me beautiful. It was really painful. This was when my period was over. They cut my very long hair short. I really did not like to have my hair cut. All this meant was that my first period was now over, and I could resume my normal social life.

As soon as my puberty ritual was finished, my mother took my mattress and soaked it in a puddle outside Nuḷaga's house [ʔAx̌uw̓'s half-sister, Florence Knox]. This was done so that it would put some weight on me.[11] [Laughter from Daisy, Flora, and ʔAx̌uw̓.] That was my purification ritual; our way of acknowledging the passage of girls of noble descent from childhood into womanhood.

I Give Birth to My Children

ƛalis [Alvin] was born first[12] [*mayuƛa:* to give birth]. I delivered him at the house of Q̓ʷəmxuduw̓. Many people had gone to a feast at Campbell River, so we were all alone here, at Yəlis. It was New Year's time [ʔAx̌uw̓ says "New Year's" in English] when I gave birth to ƛalis. My mother was really following the Indian way. During the delivery, she and the other women bathed me by sprinkling warm water all over me. The women were upset because they wanted your grandfather to walk very fast up and down the village during my labour pains, and he really did not want to do that. It was thought that if he would do so, it would help me give birth quickly. So the poor man did what he was told. This was the custom in the old days [laughter], to have the husband run back and forth in the village to ensure his pregnant wife a fast delivery. The women sprinkled warm water all over me and put *cixməs* [mountain ash bark],[13] and *ƛəq̓ax̌uliy̓* and *q̓ax̌amin* [other barks] in the water. They rubbed water and bark all over my body. This was done three days after the birth of ƛalis. They sat me in warm bathwater to melt the milk in my breasts. Then they took the *cixməs* again, cut them up, and put them in a pail of water. They heated a rock, and I held it against my breast to melt my milk. The milk then thawed and began to drip. It seems that women were stronger in the early days than they are now.

When a woman had no breast milk, they used *maƛənēy̓*, horse clams, as a soother [*ƛig̓ʷax̌stēy̓*]. The siphon of the clam was sucked by the baby whose mother had no milk. I also ate *k̓umaċiy*, Indian celery. Eating Indian celery helps you to have more milk [*d̓am̓a:* breast-feeding]. My midwife always prepared it for me hot and with some rice ["rice" is said in English]. Only during my first pregnancy did I have a lot of milk; it just slowly diminished as I gave birth to more children. I eventually had to give my babies a bottle when I could not breast-feed them anymore.

During my pregnancies I went through rituals but they did not consist of eating birds' eggs, as you said Boas mentioned. My mother was a real tradition-alist: she used to do all kinds of things following the Indian ways. She would catch these little birds called *ćax̌uw*, which existed in great numbers on the beach, and fed me with their breasts so that I would have many children. She used to make me swallow the breasts of these little birds that lived on the beach. She probably did this in the hope that she would see many of my children. But she only saw three of them. My mother lived to see x̌alis [Alvin], ʔAda [Flora], and Ḱʷamax̌əllas [Georgie]. She saw three of my children before she died. She did not live long enough to see all her other [ten] grandchildren. [See Appendix E, kinship diagram 4.]

She also performed the ritual of the seal on me. After someone had shot a pregnant seal, she would remove the fetus and come with it towards my back. She did this four times in order to make my delivery easier. And surprisingly, it did. I always had an easy time during delivery. Oh! My mother was a real traditionalist. She always used many Indian medicines. She oiled my stomach with *dᶻiḱʷis*, ratfish oil, when I was pregnant. She rubbed my stomach to prevent me from having a difficult labour.

Two midwives attended me. Their names were Ćiḱʷa [Seagull Woman] and Wayoł [Old Dog]. These women were our doctors for pregnant women. These two women were able to handle successfully the highly feared breech birth. There were only a few midwives who knew what to do in this situation. They could feel your belly and tell if the baby was in the wrong position. They would manipulate your belly in order to put the baby in the right position. Yakoyog̈ʷa was also a midwife, and she was also capable of handling a breech birth. She was a *pax̌əla*, a shaman. These midwives were called *pax̌əla*, medicine women. Ćiḱʷa was the wife of x̌ax̌ʷsəm [Red Cod]. She was a Nəmǧis woman. They used to call her Ǧana. Wayoł was Daca's [Billie Sunday Willie's] mother. She was one of the last midwives who attended me.[14]

I went through another set of practices. My mother used to stir up *nax̌ʷəskən* [soapberries][15] and pour them down my throat when I was overdue. The worst medicine of all consisted of *q̓ʷalobəs* [ashes] mixed in my drink. This was supposed to help me have a swift delivery. The midwives asked Moses to walk back and forth really fast, up and down the street; this was also to help me have a quick delivery.

My mother used to unravel all my knitting and crocheting, and she would take the thread out of my sewing machine. She used to say, "If you do not do this, the child will be born with the cord around its neck." She used to unravel all my unfinished works. [Big laughter.]

They used to do some really peculiar things in the old days. When men went out halibut fishing [*luqʷa*], their wives were told to eat a lot while they were out so that the fish would take their bait. Stephen Cook's mother was somewhat excessive with regard to this custom. When her husband Qʷaxila went halibut fishing, she took pilot biscuits, tied a rope to them, and hung them up. Then she would bite at them, just like she wanted the halibut to bite at her husband's bait. Johnson Cook sure laughed at her when he heard that! She was told later that it would have been enough just to eat the biscuits.

When a child was ten months old, its hair was cut off. This is called *hiłogʷila* [out of danger]. They say they used to singe the hair of the child as well, but I never saw it. And they would give gifts to the guests in honour of the child. This is called *hiłogʷila*. Not everybody would do that, only the high-ranking people. Tom Alfred [Moses's younger brother] did it for my daughter Flora. He gave a feast [*kʷilas*] in her honour at our house at Yəlis. He gave away butter[16] when Flora was *hiłogʷila* – ten months old.

Flora, my second child, was not born at our house but at a fish camp. We were harvesting fish at Ḱaǧis.[17] I remember that Josephine Cook's younger sibling was born three days earlier, and she was also a baby girl. We went across to the Nemǧis while I was carrying Flora. We had just arrived, and it was getting dark when I started having my labour pains. And then Flora was born; she was born at Ḱaǧis. I had to improvise for diapers. I used a red blanket we had, so all her diapers were red.

Q̇acuǧow, my mother-in-law, was with us when I gave birth to Flora at Ḱaǧis. My mother-in-law was very upset because Ẇaćaʔoẇ [Q̇acuǧow's brother] was very sick. They carried me to a nearby smokehouse. This was so that I would not ... They used to be so afraid in the early days, afraid that menstrual blood might harm you. They believed that menstrual blood could *ḱaxʔid* you. *Ḱaxʔid* means that someone who is not well and who is exposed to menstrual blood could become worse and could even die. That is why females were secluded when they had their period. That was our custom in the early days, and that is why they moved me to the smokehouse. I delivered Flora in the smokehouse at Ḱaǧis. [Happy laughter.]

I absolutely refused to see a doctor when I delivered my babies. Q̇acuǧow was my midwife. She was Moses's mother. It was only when the old woman was no longer strong enough to help me that I went to see a doctor. I was scared at the idea of seeing a doctor because Q̇acuǧow had been my midwife all that time. I was petrified of doctors. I agreed to see a doctor for the first time when Jackie was born. I went to the hospital for the first time for Jackie and then for Clarence. The last child delivered by the old woman was little Jimmy.

How I Got a New House

I was alone in the big house with my children. I think Pənuẇ [Arthur Alfred] was my baby when Moses's father died [1915]. I really went through a bad time. Ẇaċaʔoẇ [Q̇acuǧow's brother] had built himself a new house in the style of the White man, and Q̇acuǧow had moved in with him. She had been living with us at the big house. She moved out but kept a room at our big home and came to sleep there once in a while. Nuladiẏ, my sister-in-law [see Plate 14], was staying with me too, but her mother bought her a little house, a modern, White-man's style home. She also left me. That is why I was totally alone in the big house. Occasionally, Q̇acuǧow would come and sleep there, but she would return to Ẇaċaʔoẇ's place. I was heartbroken because I was so afraid to live alone. I got driftwood for firewood so that we would always have a fire. There used to be four fires in the big house, one at each of its four corners. It used to be really smoky in there. There were always four fires in the big houses. That was the way the houses were at Ǧʷayasdəms too. Moses installed some partitions in the house by curtaining off each area. And he put a big stove in it; this is the stove we still use now. My cooking-stove chimney was connected to the chimney of the heating stove. We were no longer using the open fire. The stove was curtained off in the front of the house, near the door. It had a long chimney. Oh! I was old-fashioned for such a long time.

When I became pregnant with Puλas [Lily Dorothy] I told Moses to do what Dəndas did: to build a modern house on the beach. Right away he went to buy lumber at Wastal [Telegraph Cove]. We were going to build a modern house so we could leave this big house because I was living there all by myself. By this time, Nuladiẏ and all of them lived in modern homes. On the other hand, Q̇acuǧow used to visit her brother and stay with him. She really respected her brother. He was an invalid. They all had left, and I was alone in this big house.

Shaughnessy started to build our house. This is the house we tried to give to Flora. We lived in it for a long time. This is where I gave birth to little Jimmy, and that was the last time that Q̇acuǧow performed as a midwife.

How I and My Children Received Christian Names

I was named Agnes Bertha when I was baptized at Yəlis. This was very late in life. I never came to my senses early [concerning her Christian beliefs]. It was much later in life. I was already married to Moses when I was baptized. This was when the bishop came. x̱aliⱡila [Mrs. Joe Harris][18] named me Agnes Bertha. My Christian name is Agnes Bertha. They just looked in this book with Christian names in it. I did the same thing later when I had my children baptized. I looked into this book. Mrs. Cook and x̱aliⱡila used to bring this book to me. Nearly all my children were named after someone from this book. My son George was named after x̱aⱡalis [George Luther]; Jackie was named after Caribou Jack; Arthur was named after Bondsound; and Alvin was named after Dan Cranmer. He is the one who said he should be called Alvin. And he also gave Alvin his middle name, Edgar. Dan's name was Dan Edgar. Dan was the one who named Alvin. I found the name Flora [Daisy's mother] in this book. No. She was named after my sister, Florence [Nulaǧa]. Violette is the one I must have got from the book. George was named after George Luther. His name was George William. He was named after a Kʷaguł man named William. He was Wadəma's father and Neda's husband [William Brotchie]. Pənuẁ was named after Bondsound. We gave him the name Eugene, from this man who was Kʷaguł. We named him Arthur Eugene. He was named after Jane Hunt's son. He was Harry's son. He just died not too long ago. His name was Eugene, from the Kʷaguł. Jane Hunt was ʔAnisəlaǧa's daughter [Mrs. Bob Hunt]. They had a son named Eugene.

I must have got Dorothy's name from the book. Yes. We got Lily Dorothy from the book.

I had a really good friend among the Heiltsuk [Bella Bella] called Nora Sarah. She was the sister of George Wilson. She attended school at Alert Bay and asked me to name my daughter Nora Sarah. Jimmy was named after Woʔca [James Knox]. His name was James Daniel. He was also named after Dan Cranmer. Lena was named after a friend from the Squamish called Lena, Lena Mary. Lena was named after Giga [Mary Hanuse].

Phillip was the name of the youngest boy of Q̓acuǧow [Moses's mother]. We named our son Phillip Witcliff. Moses's brother's name was John Witcliff. Remember I gave you [Daisy] a picture of a man holding a child? That was him. His name was John Witcliff, the youngest of the boys of Q̓acuǧow.

Allan was named after a fish commissioner. He was in the air force. His name was Allan Cameron, and his mother was a good friend of mine. Joseph [Allan] was named after my father. My father used to always say to me – the poor thing, he was such a drinker – he used to say crazy things about his name.

He used to tell me his name was Joe Glenglen. Apparently that was the other name [Glendale]. Your [Daisy's] husband [Lorne Smith] teased me and said he was probably named after the White man who used to come to Dˀaẃadiẏ. His name was Glendale. Because Gəyux̌ʷ [Glendale Cove] was named after him. This is why my father used to say his last name was Glenglen [Glendale].

Elizabeth Margaret [Libby] was named after my mother-in-law, Q̓acuǧow. Her name was Margaret. She was named Bessie, after ˀAnita. That is why she is called Elizabeth. It used to be so difficult to find names and godparents for my children.

5

Marrying Moses Alfred

Introduction

Anthropologists who have studied marriage as a cultural institution have pointed out that "more often than not, when marriage is viewed in cross-cultural perspective, it turns out to be a relationship between groups rather than just a relationship between individuals. A marriage system that at first seems odd to us will often make more sense if we view it as a contract between corporate groups" (Vivelo 1978: 170). A traditional Kʷakʷakəwakʷ marriage is more than the establishment of a family; it is a form of exchange involving a transfer of rights and obligations between contracting parties.[1]

Daisy Sewid-Smith (1979: 10-12) reported some interviews she had conducted with her late grandmother (great-aunt), Daisy Roberts,[2] in 1964. One aspect of these interviews dealt with Kʷakʷakəwakʷ marriage. Because this is an institution that was deeply misunderstood by the nineteenth-century White authorities, we thought it would be appropriate to include a brief discussion of marriage practices. The following comments are offered as a preamble to ʔAx̌uw̓'s account.

First, we should say that, in accordance with the social mores of the Kʷakʷakəwakʷ, matrimonial rituals were practised only by the nobility.[3] When a girl came of age, after completion of her puberty ritual, she was eligible for marriage. The father of an eligible boy would look for the right bride for his son. He would send an emissary or a messenger to the girl's father to inform him of his wish for his son to marry his daughter. He would announce a marriage proposal, and the father of the girl would think it over. As a noble father, he had to consider several matters, such as rank, privileges, and wealth. He would not give his consent right away. He would want to observe the character of the young man, so the pair would be "betrothed" for quite some time. If he concluded that the boy would be a suitable husband for his daughter, he would then consent to the marriage, q̓ad̕iƛa, "a journey through life." Only the parents were involved in pre-marriage procedures such as these, and they never asked for their children's opinion. When the future spouses became husband and wife, they did their best to make it a satisfying union, abiding by the choice of their respective fathers.

The Kʷakʷakəwakʷ did not have a strict rule regarding postmarital residence; however, in the majority of cases, women went to live with their husbands regardless of the village to which they belonged (Boas 1920: 368; 1966: 52).

Traditional Kʷakʷakəwakʷ marriages between people of noble birth were complex and involved a series of events that could go on for years. Here, we merely summarize the fundamental three-step procedure. The first step, as we have mentioned, was the initiating of negotiations between the fathers of the prospective bride and groom, at which time the marriage proposal was offered and the sum of the marriage payment, or bridewealth (sometimes also called bride-price), was agreed upon. Bridewealth (q̓ad̕iƛam) is a marriage payment made by the husband and the husband's group to the wife's group. On this occasion, chiefs of both sides display privileges and make speeches.

If a marriage were arranged when the children were not yet eligible, the father of the boy would give only a portion of the marriage payment to the girl's parents. The "downpayment" would be invested at a potlatch given by the girl's father as security for his daughter and any children that she might bear. Paying the "security investment" gave the boy's parents first choice when the girl became eligible to marry, for there were always many suitors for a girl of noble descent. If for some reason the girl's father decided that the boy was not suitable for her, the marriage payment would be returned (without interest) to the boy's father. This payment was called q̓ʷəlaƛa (in secret; i.e., secretly paid); however, this non-public secret transaction, which terminated the alliance, seldom occurred.

The second step was the formal wooing that followed the acceptance of the suit, and the transfer of the bridewealth payment from the groom's family to the bride's family at a potlatch. No one was actually "buying" a wife. Through the payment of goods, the husband and his group were securing, in a socially recognized way, his rights regarding his new wife and any children they might have. Bridewealth, therefore, should not be thought of as a one-sided transaction going from the husband's group to the wife's group; it should be seen as a mutual exchange, with value flowing both ways.

After the formal acceptance of the suit, the bridewealth payment was given to the father of the bride. Daisy Sewid-Smith refers to this payment as the "marriage security investment" because, as soon as the goods were given at a potlatch, they began circulating within the potlatch network. In traditional times this payment was always in the form of mountain goat furs, which, during post-contact times, were replaced by Hudson's Bay Company blankets (see Plate 8). In return the bride's family promised both material and immaterial wealth, such as offices in secret societies, songs, dances, masks, and other paraphernalia. These were only brought out during the third step of the marriage procedure.

When a traditional wedding was performed among the Kʷakʷakəwakʷ people, each tribe attending it would re-enact the very first marriage – the one that took place after the Great Flood, as is stated in the origin myths. The members of the groom's family would hire all the tribes (except the bride's) to accompany them in requesting (or compelling) the father-in-law to yield his daughter and her associated privileges. They would do this by displaying their own powers and treasures (Boas 1925: 237ff). This was all a staged performance as the bride's parents had already agreed to the union. The groom's family and confederates would pretend to "make war" on the bride's tribe, and peace would finally be established when the chief offered to have his daughter marry the invader's son.[4]

Kʷakʷakəwakʷ wedding ceremonies were performed this way because it is said that the very first brides within the highest ranked descent groups were obtained by conquest. Each tribal chief would be called by the groom's family to come forward to recite the traditions of his noble lineage and to re-enact his part in the myth relating to how the Kʷakʷakəwakʷ obtained their first brides. After all the tribes had re-enacted the traditional bridal capture, the bride's tribe would re-enact its own sequence of the myth, establishing peace between the two tribes through marriage. They would, at this time, announce the dowry that would accompany the bride. The groom's family would then symbolically carry the bride off to its village, thereby completing its sequence of the marriage myth. The war-like symbolism of the matrimonial rites is further conveyed by the Kʷak̓ʷala expression *winanəm*, obtained through war.[5]

The third and final step is the marriage repurchase, when goods, names, and privileges go from the bride's family to the groom's family. It took place several years later, usually after the birth of the first child. In the ethnographic literature, this last step is referred to as the "return of the marriage payment" or the "return of the marriage debt." Since the wife's group had been the recipient of the marriage potlatch given by the groom's group, it was in debt until it could return payment in kind. The repurchase took place at another potlatch and constituted a return that consisted of such things as Coppers, titles of nobility, ranked positions within the potlatch network, and ceremonial prerogatives, all of which were handed down in the "privilege box" or "container of dowries" (ƙawaćiy̓).

The marriage repurchase differed from bridewealth and could also be referred to as a dowry. Though some anthropologists (e.g., Taylor 1976: 157) have equated dowry with property given to the husband's group by the wife's group, most seem to consider it the woman's inheritance from her natal group – an inheritance she took with her upon marriage. Of course the size of a woman's dowry could play a significant role with regard to planning marital alliances. Among the Kʷakʷakəwakʷ, the dowry was moderate and not given all at once. Each time the groom gave a potlatch, the bride's family would pass on more dowry items to him, especially if they had children, as this would guarantee offices in secret societies and ranked potlatch positions for the bride's parents' grandchildren.

The Kʷakʷakəwakʷ (and their northern Northwest Coast neighbours) held as their most precious possessions large flat sheets of beaten copper cut in the shape of shields with T-shaped ridges. They were called Coppers, ƛaqʷa. Coppers varied greatly in size, being anywhere from six inches to two-and-a-half feet high. They were blackened, and their upper portions were often painted or incised with the representations of animals, probably the clan crests or ancestral symbols of their first owners, which in turn conferred the name to the Copper (Lévi-Strauss 1975: 135; de Widerspach-Thor 1981: 157-74). Each Copper had its own identity, which was expressed in its name.

Toward the end of the nineteenth century, they [Coppers] could attain a value of several thousand contemporary dollars, and their owners enjoyed a corresponding amount of public credit. The owners could keep them, but, in general, they were destined to change hands in the course of potlatches, sold or given away whole or in fragments. Sometimes the owner would even throw them into the sea, to prove his wealth by sacrificing such a treasure for his personal glory and that of his lineage. (Lévi-Strauss 1982: 135)

ʔAx̌uw̓'s father performed just such a great deed, as we shall see later.

Coppers were particularly associated with the transfer of privileges from the wife's group to the husband's group upon marriage. The value of a Copper depended upon the amount of property that had been paid for it and then given away at the potlatch at which it last changed hands. If the Copper were given outright, (ʔoʔdexʔid), then the giver and his family no longer had any right or claim to it.[6] But if the Copper were given in trust to the groom's family (səp̓id),[7] then the owner maintained his right or share to it, and the name of the Copper and its associated value could still be used as a security investment in the investing potlatch network referred to as p̓əsa. Sometimes at the beginning of the transaction the bride's family would səp̓id or səp̓idayuw̓, but, at the end of the transaction, they would decide to *ʔoʔdexʔid* it, to give it outright to the groom and his family. This would result in immediately raising the value of the Copper for the bride and the groom.

The ranked nobility of each tribe and of each *n̓əmay̓əm* (anglicized by Boas as "*numaym*"; i.e., corporate descent group) had its own investing network or *p̓əsa*,[8] and, in order to become a member, an individual had to inherit a name that stood for a title of nobility, a "seat," "standing place," or "position" (*ƛax̌ʷēy̓*) in the *p̓əsa*. There were a limited number of seats, and these were highly sought after. The system was competitive. If the groom had no position in the bride's father's group, the bride would bestow one on him, as a dower. However, he was not allowed to use it for himself – only for his children. If no children were born from the union, if the married couple separated, or if the wife died, then the position would be returned to the bride's family. The new bride could also receive a name or a position from her relatives; that would enable her to partici-pate in the *p̓əsa* in her husband's network. This would also secure her position in her husband's tribe. Men held most of these positions, and when women held them, they had to use the male names that went along with the positions.[9] A bride could also receive a seat from her kin, as was the case for ʔAx̌uw̓'s daughter, Flora, when she married James Sewid. Her name was Yaxƛən among the M̓am̓aliliqəlla.

The marriage repurchase could occur only when the bride's family was in the position to return the marriage payment to that of the groom and his family, for what was returned was far in excess of what the bride's father and his *n̓əmay̓əm* had received. Among the Kʷakʷakəwakʷ, the marriage repurchase also signified the formal ending of the marriage; that is, the formal ending of the contract in the *p̓əsa*. Such ending was called *ḡʷaɬ* (finished) and the spouse was free to return to her own *n̓əmay̓əm* if she so wished (or if there was a good reason, such as violence or adultery). What was actually "finished" was the assistance the bride's family had given to the groom in establishing his position in the *p̓əsa*. When this assistance was returned in kind, the bride's family was no longer obliged to invest for the son-in-law. (Of course, if the son-in-law gave a potlatch, then the bride's family would assist him by giving him cash, goods, or both; but the son-in-law and his family could do their own investing independently as well.) When the payment was returned, the son-in-law and his family could invest what they had received from the father-in-law during the time of marriage. The groom's father-in-law (*negʷəmp:* in-law) would also pay the interest that he and his family had accrued while investing in the marriage payment. The purpose of this transaction was to help the couple establish themselves in the *p̓əsa*.

Under traditional Kʷakʷakəwakʷ custom, following the completion of the repurchase of the marriage payment, the wife was free to remarry if her family so wished. As Boas (1966: 55) pointed out: "Often, after the annulment of a marriage through repayment of the marriage debt, the woman is married to another man. After four marriages, her high rank is established, and it seems to be assumed that after this she should stay with her last husband."

Marriage Practices (in presence of Flora Sewid)

We are now going to talk about the marriage practices of the Kʷakʷakəwakʷ people. When they verbally announce a dowry, it is called *hanəmsx̌ʔa*. My uncle Q̓ʷəmxuduw̓ [Ṅumas or Wakəs] *hanəmsx̌ʔad* Moses Alfred and Legix̌; he gave a verbal dowry to both of them. Peter Knox married Florence [ʔAx̌uw̓'s half-sister] at Q̓agʷoł's house.[10] Q̓ʷəmxuduw̓ announced the dowry verbally and, later, started thinking about actually fulfilling the marriage agreement.

We went to Fort Rupert. One of my children, Jackie, had died, so we had a *ẏaqʷa* at Fort Rupert. We took some of our furniture and all the things we had put away for Q̓ʷəmxuduw̓ to *hanəmsx̌ʔa* in order to fulfill my marriage agreement. The *ƛasəla* [Peace Dance] and his house, the facade of which was adorned by a Raven pole, were to come to Moses as part of my dowry. We went to Fort Rupert to attend a *p̓əsa*, but our uncle died before he could fulfill all his intentions. Dan Cranmer ended up looking after things after our uncle's death. So it was Dan Cranmer who officially gave my dowry to Moses. It consisted of the *kik̓əsʔuw̓* [treasures, privileges, ritual paraphernalia], like the house and the *ƛasəla*. The dowry of my older sister [Florence Knox] was given at the same time. To Legix̌, Dan gave a *ćeqa* dance [a cedar-bark dance] called the *ʔAⱡlaqima*.[11] As far as my dowry was concerned, Q̓ʷəmxuduw̓ had specified that I should be the recipient of those dowry items that were to be given to Moses.[12] That was what he received.

We really had a difficult time in those days because the authorities just wanted to arrest us whenever we gave things away. We wandered around in the big house. We never danced because we were trying to abide by the law, which stated we were not permitted to do anything pertaining to our *p̓əsa*. This is why Moses never danced the *ƛasəla*, which had been given to him. We were trying to abide by the law, which stated we were not permitted to dance. Later, Moses gave the *ƛasəla* to our daughter Flora's husband, Jimmy Sewid; it was much later. When Jimmy Sewid's grandfather, Max̌ʷalagəlis, came to ask for Flora's hand, the *ƛasəla* was verbally promised to Jimmy.

Jimmy Sewid asked for Flora's hand, and she was married to him. She was supposed to have married Gəlidiẏ [Henry Speck]. The arrangement had already been made. Gəlidiẏ had helped build the new house we were living in as we were going to leave the big traditional house. Gəlidiẏ and his father came to work on the chimney of the house. They were trying to please us because they had asked for Flora's hand in secret. All the arrangements had already been made. But Gəlidiẏ went crazy over Qixƛalaǧa; she was Charlie Wilson's mother. They ended up living together. Flora's father was very angry because Gəlidiẏ was living with Qixƛalaǧa. However, Gəlidiẏ's father was still asking for Flora's hand. Moses did not want to let him know of his disapproval at that particular time; however, he did not like what was going on.

One day, Watəs and Jim Bell came to our house and formally asked for the hand of Flora on behalf of Jimmy Sewid. I told them that it was very difficult for me to answer because her father was not at home. Henry Speck's sister was staying at our home at the time. She was using my sewing machine. She was Gəlidiẏ's sister, and they did not understand why she was there. I asked them to wait for Moses to return from Vancouver. I guess they must have been waiting for him because they came as soon as he returned home. He said to them: "I think it is better that we marry Flora to Jimmy right away." We returned the q̓ʷəlaƛayuⱡ [secret bride-price] as well as all the other presents Gəlidiẏ and his family had bought for her. I returned it and asked Adax̌ʷəlis to bring all the other things to them. That is what we did. And Flora and Jimmy were married. ʔɪlaǧa [Emma Beans] was married at the same time.

They ćewid for Flora; this is when they announce from whom the dowry is coming and of what it is comprised. They gave Ǧamadʔiẏ $500 [əkas gəmgustu]. Ǧamadʔiẏ just returned it to them. They also gave a Copper. And they returned the Copper to the groom. Her father returned the money and səṗid the Copper. I told Moses we should give them our little cabin as a wedding present. This was actually the little house that rolled down the cliff some time later when they tried to pull it up from the beach at Ṁɪṁkʷəmlis. This cabin was part of Flora's dowry when she was married to Jimmy Sewid, and he tried to move it to Ṁɪṁkʷəmlis.

We lived in that cabin for quite a while when we stayed in Yəlis. This was the house we gave Flora as a wedding present. Our big modern house was already built then. That was the house which Gəlidiẏ helped build in order to gain our esteem. He also built Flora's bedroom. As the future groom, he worked on it as a way of impressing us. At that time, he had asked for her hand in marriage. Moses changed his mind quickly because he did not like the fact that Gəlidiẏ was living with Qixƛalaǧa. We brought Flora to Ṁɪṁkʷəmlis. I repeated to Flora what they told me at the time of my wedding: "Don't you ever come back to us," we warned Flora. "You don't want to come home. It would cost your father too much money because he would have to fill the canoe with food so that they could give a feast to the husband's people when you returned." This is what we call x̌ʷakʷəna lubəx̌sala, emptying the canoe; they would have to return with an empty canoe. That was the reason parents discouraged their children from coming back to stay with them after they were married. Because that would be very costly to the parents.

This actually happened when Flora tripped and fell. We put food in a canoe to give away. They used to tell us that they would have to put food in a canoe if we were not behaving properly. Oh! My mother was really so old-fashioned! She would forever tell me not to forget to feed my friends when they came to visit.

My mother left by boat to buy x̌əmas [thin, smoked, crisp fish] and łax̌ʷsus [clover roots]. We were going to have a feast at Cape Mudge. The tribes were going to have a feast there. They gave Moses the privilege of having a feast there. He was giving away q̓aluk̓ʷ [smoked clam "buttons"]. It really pleased Q̓acuǧow [ʔAx̌uw̓ laughs in anticipation of what she is to say next] when they gave q̓aluk̓ʷ to those who were there at the feast. She used to talk about this event all the time. She used to go clam digging at Mim̓k̓ʷəmlis, and she would make Moses give a feast with her clams. Grandpa [in English] gave away grease. We used to go to D̓aw̓adiy̓, and he used to come and join us. And that is the reason why he decided to give grease away. He gave the grease to the Nəmǧis people only. The bride was not permitted to go back to the home of her parents because it would be too expensive for them. This is because her parents would have had to buy food for her husband so that he could give a feast upon her return.

That is one of the things we did for Flora. The dowry went all at once. We bought all kinds of dowry items, and they moved that little cabin. We filled the seiner *J14* with things for her dowry, like pots and pans. Her father bought many of these large green pails. He bought them wholesale and packed them on *J14*. We also bought dowry items for ʔllaǧa when she married Sipa [Beans], and we brought the dowry so her husband could have a *p̓əsa*. Moses bought out the store, which had these big pails and pots and pans.

Sometime later, after Flora had been married to Jimmy, they had a *p̓əsa*, and Jimmy was the *hamaċa* for Q̓acuw̓ [Jim Bell]. Ǧamad̓iy̓ [Q̓acuǧow's brother] gave us as a dowry for her – the k̓ik̓əsʔuw̓ [kisu: treasure; k̓ik̓əsʔuw̓: treasures], which consisted of a set of *hamaċa* masks. He gave these as a dowry for her. He gave a *p̓əsa* and Jimmy was the *hamaċa*. We always used to fill *J14* with all kinds of things.

When ʔllaǧa married Sipa, Mrs. [Stephen] Cook referred to *J14* as an evil boat because it was used to transport people who attended feasts. That is what I wanted to say. Mrs. Cook was anti-*p̓əsa*. That is what I wanted to say.[13]

My Future Husband Marries a Dead Girl

Moses Alfred's uncle Kodiy̓ went to the West Coast to *p̓əsa* [potlatch]. He was accompanied by many of his people. Big Sam, or Samd̓iy̓, was among them.

His Indian name was x̌aq̓ʷadˀiy̓, Big Copper, and he was a Kʷaguł from Fort Rupert married to Copper Woman, x̌aq̓ʷagiloğʷa. She was Harry Brown's aunt. She was the wife of this Kʷaguł man called Big Sam. He went along with many others to attend Kodiy̓'s p̓əsa on the West Coast.

When they arrived at Was Lake, they beached their canoe and continued by land. They started walking, following the well-worn trail leading to the West Coast. Kʷak̓ʷabəlas [You Are Always Seating at a Potlatch], Stephen Cook's mother, was among them. She was still a young girl. They had brought with them many Hudson's Bay blankets [p̓əlx̌əlasğəm].[14] It was because Kodiy̓ was going to p̓əsa, and they were going to proceed with what they call x̌ʷisa, a "marriage for property." Kodiy̓ had arranged for Moses to marry the chief's daughter from the West Coast, or, as they say, q̓adˀiƛa. But by the time they arrived at the West Coast, the chief's daughter had taken ill and died. The West Coast chief decided to honour his marriage agreement even though his daughter was dead. Such a marriage between two young children would never be consummated; it was just a "marriage to acquire property," what they call x̌ʷisa.

Moses was only a little boy then, just old enough to remember. He remembered going there with his uncle Kodiy̓, who did q̓adˀiƛa, as they say, and paid the bridewealth with Hudson's Bay blankets to seal the marriage agreement. In return, they received her dowry, which consisted of several dances. The ƛugʷala Dance was among them; it is a dance that is performed on top of a box, and it re-enacts the initiation of novices possessed by a supernatural Wolf. The other dance he received was the Sisayuł, the Double-Headed Serpent Dance. Many more valuable things were transferred to Moses, including the X̌ʷix̌ʷiy̓.[15] They brought over a great big box of dances that we call gəldasix̌ƛala. They gave all these dances to Moses because Kodiy̓ q̓adˀiƛa for him to obtain the chief's daughter, even though she had died, the poor little girl.

As I said, Moses received all these treasures because this transfer of wealth and privileges – the bridewealth and the dowry – was the reason for the pre-arranged union. That is why he owned what we call ƛugʷala,[16] the Wolf Dance and, more precisely, xisiwala, the Wolf headdress that belongs to it. The Wolf Dance is the West Coast (Nuu-chah-nulth) people's most important dance. This is the hamaċa of the West Coast as it ranks first in the hierarchy of all their dances. This is the dance they brought to him. Its name is Daˀəsəm, the Wolf; it was one of two West Coast dances that were brought over: the Wolf and the Sisayuł;[17] there were two dances. That is what they gave to Moses when Kodiy̓ had arranged for his marriage [q̓adˀiƛa] with this young girl, even though she had died.

Names were given also. Hēnagoyuğʷa [a West Coast name] is the name that was given to K̓ʷəlstolił [Daisy Roberts, Moses Alfred's sister]. In our language

this name means *ʔAwilgʷolas*, "You Are Always Inviting Many Tribes." This
name went along with the *Sisayuɫ* Dance. Daʔəsəm was the name given to
Dadax̌alis [Ben Alfred Sr., Moses Alfred's brother]. It went along with the Wolf
Dance, which, at one time, was performed for Waċaʔow̓. Waċaʔow̓ was Moses
Alfred's uncle [Moses Alfred's mother's brother]. [See Appendix E, kinship
diagram 5.]

How old was Moses at that time? Since he could remember most of what
he saw, he must have been around ten years old. He recalled walking along the
well-worn trail leading to the West Coast. He remembered going there with his
uncle Kodiy̓. They said Kodiy̓ took Moses as his heir as soon as he was born and
that Kodiy̓ wanted Moses to become Nəmǧis. Moses became Nəmǧis through
being adopted by Kodiy̓. His uncle did what the Indians used to do in the old
days when they had no children of their own or could not have children any
more – he adopted one. He adopted Moses. Kodiy̓ was married to a woman
named x̌ilasəmeǧa. She was the mother of Wadəma. You know Wadəma? He
was Ben Brotchie Sr.

At the time of his death, Kodiy̓ was married to x̌ilasəmeǧa. He was going
to *p̓əsa*, but he died before he could do it. And his wife took away some of the
Hudson's Bay blankets. This just further motivated Kodiy̓'s sister, Q̓acuǧow̓,
to help her son Moses to fulfill Kodiy̓'s plans by completing all the necessary
preparations for the *p̓əsa* and giving away all the Hudson's Bay blankets. This is
what they used to do with the blankets in the old days; they would *p̓əsa* with
them. And this is what they did.

We have received so many dowries from the West Coast people, all
contained in this big box of treasures that they call *k̓isuwaċiy̓* [*k̓isu:* treasures;
container of treasures]. It was a great big box *k̓isuwaċiy̓*. *ʔUxʷiċa* is the West
Coast name for the big box of dances. The West Coast people always reminded
my eldest son, x̌alis [Alvin Alfred], of all the treasures we had received from
them. As a result the children used to call x̌alis ʔUxʷiċa, when he was a little boy.
This was the dowry received by Moses when his uncle and adopted father, Kodiy̓,
q̓ad̓iλa for the chief's daughter on the West Coast, even though she had died.

Marrying Moses

Then came the time when they decided that I should marry. I was still very
young then, and my real father had died. He died early in life, when I was a child.
Then my mother, Puλas, married a man whom I called Daduw̓, but he was
known as K̓ʷak̓ʷabalas. He was Charlie Dick's [Haʔēλəkʷ] father, and he was from
Mim̓kʷəmlis. He was one of Jimmy Sewid's relatives. Our family and his family

were sharing the same house at M̓irh̓k̬ʷəmlis. Q̓acuw̓ [Jim Bell: Jimmy Sewid's mother's father] was related to him also. Daduw̓ was now my father. Shall I tell all about my suitors? [Big laughter.] Because Moses was the last among my suitors to ask for my hand.

Several men wanted to marry me. I was still a very young girl. These men who were my suitors would come to our house and visit Daduw̓. I remember when this man called Ǧix̌kən came to our house. Also W̓aċaʔow̓. Ǧix̌kən came to visit my father and talked to him. Ǧix̌kən was an emissary who was asking for my hand on behalf of Cipa [Matthew Salmon]. And then Lagix̌ came on behalf of Binats. They came, one after the other, asking for my hand. Then X̌ałalis's father, Billy, came; he was representing his son James Crow, who also wanted to marry me. Lagix̌ came for Binats. All of them came to visit Daduw̓, each one taking his turn. They were all reclining in the main room of our house. Billy and this man called Ǧix̌kən. W̓aċaʔow̓ was the last one to come. He was asking for my hand on behalf of Moses Alfred. But Moses had a younger brother, Dadax̌alis [Ben Alfred Sr.], who was supposed to marry W̓adˀidalaǧa. I guess something happened for the marriage never took place, and she later became the wife of Paul. According to our custom the eldest son should marry first. Daduw̓ wanted Dadax̌alis to marry me, but Ben Alfred did not want to since Moses was the eldest. But Moses was already living with a woman in Vancouver. They finally agreed and decided that Moses should marry me. They told Moses to come home immediately for they were going to ask him to settle down and marry me. Two people objected; one of them was Q̓ʷəmxuduw̓, my uncle. He said that Moses would beat me all the time. While my mother was defending the choice of Moses, Ǧʷułəlas [Jimmy Sewid's grandmother's brother] was objecting to it. Everyone else wanted me to marry Moses and finally everybody agreed. Moses was willing to come home, providing that his future bride would be me.

Q̓ʷəmxuduw̓ surely did not like Moses, who had the reputation of being a very proud man. He said I should not marry him because he would beat me all the time. He was very upset and did not feel it was right to proceed with the marriage agreement. Ǧʷułəlas came to see my mother, and despite pressure from him I was married to Moses.

Poor me; I was being married at such a young age! My poor wedding outfit was red. As you remember, we were not allowed to go without a blanket, a shawl, or a wrap of some sort. We had to wear a big shawl at all times. Even more so after I had reached the age of not playing anymore; I had to wear a tight wrap around me, keeping it close to my body with my hands. And I had to walk slowly. They gave me a red wrap for my wedding dress. They stood me outside the house of Q̓ʷəmxuduw̓ at Yəlis. We stood in front of the house of Q̓ʷəmxuduw̓, me in the middle, tightly holding my new red wrap. Then many Nəmǧis people came. As was the custom, they came in great numbers to attend the wedding ceremony that was going to take place outside; the whole village was the theatre for these occasions. The Nəmǧis were facing us. Daduẃ, my stepfather, was holding a Copper that he was going to give to Moses later on as part of my dowry. He did what they call *sayubala*, or *səṕid*, this Copper. Daduẃ had bought a Copper from a Kʷaguɫ man named x̌aq̓ʷadʔiẏ, Big Sam. He died not too long ago. My dowry to Moses was a Copper, which was *səṕid*. But this happened much later, after I had my children. I will come back to it later.

There was a group of women making many loud noises. I was standing in the middle of them. Q̓acuǧow was among them. They were making many loud noises, the noises they always made during a traditional wedding, when they re-enacted the capture of the first bride. Many Nəmǧis people came and brought me into Moses's big house at Yəlis. I had now left my mother's side.

Living with Moses

I was so young when I got married. I was still quite childish [lit., my heart was still childish]. I was married to Moses. They sailed away with me right away, and they brought me to this logging camp. I was really much too young. I had not even menstruated [ʔix̌ənta] yet. I was perhaps only twelve or thirteen. I was really young. I was married for quite some time before I menstruated. Immediately after the wedding ceremony, Moses took me with him to a logging camp near Ǧʷayasdəms [Gilford Island]; he took me to a place called X̌ux̌p̓a. There was a big logging camp there. We lived in a tent there. With us were N̓umas [James Roberts], Dadax̌alis [Ben Alfred], Dᶻeliẏ [Jerry May], and x̌ex̌aǧəmēẏ. These were the men hired along with Moses by this White man. We lived in a tent and the White man lived in a float house. There were all kinds of booms [said in English, meaning logs] in the water near the beach. K̓ʷəlstoliɫ [Daisy Roberts, ʔAx̌uẃ's sister-in-law] cooked and baked for us. I would go look for sardine cans, and I would get dough from her and bake little breads. [Laughter.] The baking sheet K̓ʷəlstoliɫ used at this logging camp was stored in our modern big house. I was trying to look for it. It went outward from you and it was made out of tin [probably a reflector oven]. She would sit it by the fire and bake the bread. She did not have a stove to bake in. This is how K̓ʷəlstoliɫ baked her bread. I would go down to the beach. I would break long grass and tie a noose on the end of the grass; then I would lie on my stomach on the boom ... I was trying to catch little fish such as kʷəma [bullheads]. K̓ʷəlstoliɫ was watching me, making sure that I would not fall in. [Big laughter.] I was so young when I got married. When I had caught a little fish I would proudly show her my catch. [Laughter.] The men left for Yəlis and we were in the logging camp by ourselves. During this time I started thinking about the stories our people often told us. They would tell us that when you are alone some creature will appear to you. The camp had many wolves. I pleaded with K̓ʷəlstoliɬ to go to the float house where the White wife of the owner was staying. There was a path along the beach, and K̓ʷəlstoliɬ started to walk along the path, so I jumped from a log toward the float house. K̓ʷəlstoliɬ kept calling me to come back and walk with her but I refused to go. The float house was not that far from our tent but I was too afraid to walk along that path that K̓ʷəlstoliɬ was following. This is what happened when I first got married.

My mother heard about my childish behaviour. K̓ʷəlstoliɬ had mentioned it to someone and now everyone was talking about it. They were talking about my catching those little bullheads. My mother came to the camp to pick me up and to bring me home. I had left my mother at the time of my marriage. But someone reported to her that I was trying to catch bullheads off one of the booms at the logging camp. It was true. I guess my mother got angry when she heard people talking about my childish and playful behaviour, in spite of my being married. She did not like it and immediately came to fetch me. Moses followed me. He stopped working at his logging job that day.

When I first married Moses he never kept the money he earned for himself. He always gave it to his mother. He would never keep it for himself. All his earnings went to his mother. That was the custom in the early days, to give one's earnings to his mother; but he did keep a few dollars for our needs. He supported his mother. He did this for a number of years.

Return of the Marriage Payment

The dowry that Daduw̓ gave to Moses was a Copper that he had bought with the payment he received for his fishing season. His payment was in gold coins, and he spent it all to buy a Copper. He used every cent for it and did not keep anything for himself. He spent it all to buy this Copper. The Copper was originally owned by Samd̓iỷ, Big Sam, who was K̓ʷaguɬ. It is too bad that I cannot recall the name of it just now. He bought this Copper from Big Sam. G̓ʷuɬəlas contributed a certain amount to help Daduw̓ acquire my dowry. Q̓ʷəmxuduw̓, k̓iɖag̓améy, N̓umas, and Ẏaɢaɬʔənala [ʔOlsiwidi, husband of Lucy Sewid (Łaxʷaɬa)] also helped, each giving one hundred dollars to Daduw̓. One thousand dollars was what my dowry cost them. Daduw̓ purchased that Copper for one thousand dollars, five hundred of which came from him, my stepfather.

They used to lecture me before and after the marriage. Oh! did my brother [cousin] ever give me lectures! "Never go alone for a walk without your husband," he said to me. If I wanted to go somewhere I had to ask my husband's sister to chaperone me. They also did something to me that they call *haẏaxsǝx̌ʷsila*. It happened at a gathering composed only of women, who assembled for a feast. They used to bring candy, lots of candies. And the women would lecture me, as I was now the new bride. But not just any women would participate, only those who had successful marriages. One after the other they would lecture me, holding their speaker's staff as they spoke. Women from every tribe took turns delivering speeches, lecturing me, and passing the speaker's staff from one to the other. The K̓ʷaguⱡ were first, then the Maṁaliliqǝlla, then the Nǝmǧis, and so forth, according to their tribal rank. They used to do everything according to tribal rank, and the K̓ʷaguⱡ were always first.

They lectured me at length. I was sitting at the front of the room [ʔugʷiwaliⱡ: front of the house]. One of the women was told to give some candies to the bride [gǝlq̓asa: to hand-feed]. It is similar to what they do to the *haṁaċa* during the *haṁaċa* ritual, when they hand-feed him. They hand-fed me, but in this case with candy. Those sweets were coming from the women sitting beside me. Those women had to be from the nobility. They were specially chosen to hand-feed the bride with sweets. They would break a piece of candy and stick it into my mouth. And they would lecture me. That was our custom. That is what we mean by *haẏaxsǝx̌ʷsila*. Poor me, I was married.

Of all the pieces of advice I ever received from these women, one contained a most important truth. Holding her heraldic speaker's staff, Qumaʔēnux̌ʷ [grandmother of Maṁdoẇ/Ethel Alfred] said to the new bride, who happened to be me: "At one time or another you will quarrel with your husband. Don't ever get out of bed and run to your mother. Just go back to bed when you have a quarrel with your husband until the bad feeling towards him has disappeared. Never tell your mother because she will go and quarrel in your defence." That is the most important piece of advice I remember receiving. "Never go to your mother and tell her," they counselled me. It is really true, because a mother would always take the side of her daughter. I took this advice to heart and practised it.

My Dowry

My dowry was given much later, when we *ṗǝsa*. It was when I completed the marriage agreement with Moses. My uncle, Q̓ʷǝmxuduẇ, had said that Nulaǧa [ʔAx̌uẇ's half sister, Florence Knox] should be the first to complete the marriage agreement. But she never did as she was told and did not complete her marriage agreement until very much later. By that time many of our relatives had died.

Q̓ʷəmxuduw̓ proceeded with the repayment of the marriage debt. It took place at Q̓agʷoⱡ's [Johnson Cook's] house. He told the assembly that we were going to complete my marriage agreement and return the marriage payment. It is also called the "repayment of the marriage debt." "We are going to pay back what we p̓əsa with." That is what Q̓ʷəmxuduw̓ said. He had brought with him some cash [dala, Chinook jargon for dollars] because we were going to repay the marriage debt. He split the amount of cash he had in half. Half was for me and half was for my sister Nulag̓a. At the same occasion he also returned the marriage payment for Legix̱ [Peter Knox, Florence Knox's husband, N̓uṅuw̓'s[18] father-in-law]. This is what he said in his speech at the house of Waswasəla. This happened not so long ago. This is the way he did it. Q̓ʷəmxuduw̓ just divided between us. Then, shortly after, he died.

Q̓ʷəmxuduw̓ was not sick for very long. He died of a heart attack. Before he died he had told me to take the ⱡasəla y̓ax̱ʷiw̓ēy̓ [Peace Dance headdress] with me. "The Peace Dance headdress is for you," he said. This is the regalia that has since been passed on to Flora [one of ʔAx̱uw̓'s daughters and Daisy's mother]. "You take this," he said, referring to the Peace Dance headdress.[19] As you know, this y̓ax̱ʷiw̓ēy̓ is a really old piece, and it belonged to him. "You take it with you, for we promised it to your husband during your wedding ceremony." This is what he told me. So I took it to my house and kept it. That was before he died. It was not long after that he passed away.

His plan was that the ⱡasəla, the Peace Dance, should come to me as part of my dowry to Moses, but the actual transfer was delayed because it was during the time the p̓əsa was prohibited. Daduw̓ [Dan Cranmer] announced that the Peace Dance was part of my dowry quite some time later, after the old man passed away, thereby making public the old man's wishes. This happened at Cax̱is [Fort Rupert]. I did not attend the gathering because I was suffering the loss of my child Jackie [around 1936], but ʔAnid̓oⱡ [Daisy Roberts, Moses's sister] went.

About Moses Alfred

First Moses had a tiny little boat that he had built himself. He bought an engine on credit from BC Packers to put on this boat. And then he built himself another boat. He and Dadax̱alis [Ben Alfred Sr.: Moses's brother] went into partnership and bought the boat called Weham. They used to joke about the name. This name itself was a joke. I think it is in the language of Hartley Bay.[20] It is not a very nice name. They always joked about it. Weham was the name of that boat. Q̓iq̓əxsdad̓iy̓ is what Weham means, a person who uses a great quantity of toilet paper. This was the name of the boat that just ended up rotting on the beach at Mimk"əmlis. It is just a wreck now on the beach. x̄ex̄ag̱əmēẏ bought it from them. Then, from the sale of the *Weham*, they bought the seiner *J14*. At that time Moses was the only Indian allowed to seine commercially. No other Indian could fish that way.[21] He bought a commercial fishing licence for $350, and Mr. Beswick helped him out.

Mr. Beswick was building a hotel on the reserve at Yəlis. He had a hotel there on the foreshore of ʔAgadi. He had borrowed $500 from Moses because he did not have enough to complete his hotel. So, in return, Mr. Beswick helped Moses obtain his fishing licence. Yes, I have heard that Mr. Beswick's name was on the licence. He became a very good friend of Moses. No Indian was allowed to seine; Moses was the first Indian to have done what they are all doing today.

Moses just stopped fishing up north, where they were gillnetting, and came down south. He was going to fish with the seiner. He seined for many moons for BC Packers, until his death [1962]. He held meetings with his younger brothers. He always looked after his younger brothers that way, taking care of them after their father died. His brothers were Dadax̄alis [Ben Alfred Sr.] and Ċax̄ċəg̱isa [Tom Alfred]. He employed them so that Q̇acug̱ow [Margaret], their mother, and their sister, ʔIlag̱a [Emma Beans], who was very young when their father died, would have some money to live on. They worked to support their mother and their young sister. They formed a company and bought a boat at Wawal. They bought it from a Japanese fellow.

They created a company and bought the boat. There were three partners: Ċax̄ċəg̱isa, Dadax̄alis, and Moses. Moses was the very first First Nations seiner and he was a successful one. They never made the mistakes that many others did while trying to copy them. Some bought boats and lost them because of bad management. Their boats were repossessed.

As I mentioned, Moses bought *J14* at Wawal, from a Japanese man. ʔIlag̱a often likes to reminisce about when Dadax̄alis used to talk about this heavy investment, which he considered to be a bad risk. He had doubts at times.

They went out fishing, and at the end of the season they divided the cash they had earned. Moses said to his younger brother, Dadax̄alis, "Our investment has been returned. I know you were quite wary when we made this investment; but it worked out fine." ʔIlag̱a said that she used to be with them a lot, and she knew what they used to do. She used to look after the money Ċax̄ċəg̱isa gave to their mother. They fished for one season and got their investment returned. They did not pay much for the boat, maybe $1,000 or $2,000 [said in English].

Fishing became their major occupation, and they worked together all the time. It was only recently that the partnership broke up, after they had founded families of their own. Dadax̱alis then became captain of *J14,* and Moses became captain of a BC Packers boat.

Moses was always looking for new things to do. First, he supported his younger brothers and sister when his father passed away. His sister ʔIlag̱a was always surrounded by a lot of money. They used to make a lot of money that they would share.

That is all. He was really the only one to be employed as an Indian seiner, and many tried to copy him, but they did not succeed. Boats like the *Siwayu* and the *Flora H* were repossessed due to mismanagement. Many people tried to copy Moses's seining activities, but they did not succeed.

Moses and his partners decided to go into another business. They started with a cider store [ʔAx̱uw̓ says "cider" in English, pronounced "sigh-da"]. I really suffered through this business because I never liked drinking. They were running their store in one corner of our big house. This was Dadax̱alis's bedroom. From there they sold what they called cider. People who would buy cider would quarrel after they got intoxicated. That was their first business after fishing.[22]

Then they decided to go into another business. I knew they were up to something. It was a poolroom business. They went to Vancouver. Dadax̱alis, Moses, my brother [cousin] Dan Cranmer, N̓umas [Jim Roberts], and Ambers [Jack Sr.] were partners in the poolroom business. I really did not like it when I found out what their new business was. Moses was afraid to use his name in this affair. The poolroom became known as Cultus [N̓umas] and Cranmer. He did not have his name on it because I would not permit it. Because of the cider store, I did not like it. Only much later did I learn from Moses that he was a silent partner in the poolroom business too.

They added a store at the end of the poolroom. This building, which was situated across from George Alfred's house, recently burned down. That was too much. You know how people ask for credit and never pay their bills? So many did this. They would just buy things on credit. Moses and his partners were in business together for quite a while.

Qaqasolas [Lily Shaughnessy] and Dave Shaughnessy were trying very hard to be good Christians, attending the Anglican Church regularly. They went to church, really trying hard to be good Christians. Dave Shaughnessy and Qaqasolas had a disagreement with the rest of the congregation. They left the Anglican Church. But they met a man called Mr. Howard and asked him to come to Alert Bay. They brought Mr. Howard from Vancouver to set up a new Apostolic Church at Alert Bay. I really did not like this either. I knew that our church would not like representatives of another religion coming to evangelize us. Mr. Howard was from a different religion. But again I lost. He talked Moses into renting them the vacant poolroom; so the poolroom became Mr. Howard's church. The first preacher came with his wife. Qaqasolas attented the church there. I was aware of this, but I continued to go to the Anglican Church with Mrs. Cook [Jane Cook]. Some of these religions can be so different. They told us that some children had fainted in the new church. Wadəma was one of them. They said they really went overboard with wailing. Two children actually fainted. As a result, the Nəmǧis decided at a meeting that the representatives of this new church should leave. They were asked to leave on account of the children who had fainted during the wailing. Our church did not like it.

Jack Ambers Sr. became Moses's partner. He was related to Ṅumas [Cultus, Jim Roberts]. George Luther took the poolroom and converted it into a school. They used it for many years after they demolished the old day school. They fixed up the poolroom, putting the electric wires into conduits. It was still in use when I went to elementary school. The poor store eventually went under because of too much credit. It went bankrupt. [Big laughter.]

Oh! We did some foolish things for our *ṗəsa* [potlatch]. Ṅumas was going to *ṗəsa*. He took some of the pool tables and *ṗəsa* with them. And the radio too. We were also the first ones to have a radio, and they *ṗəsa* with it. The radio from the poolroom went as a *ṗəsa* gift. It was a radio with a big horn [a gramophone].

There were four pool tables in the poolroom; two went to Ṅumas. You see, Ben Alfred Jr. was born at Gəldala [up north]. Dadax̌alis took some of the store supplies and brought them to Gəldala to *ṗəsa* with. This *ṗəsa* was to bestow a name on Ben Jr. They just kept doing this. Taking lots of stuff from the store. Finally, Daduẇ [Dan Cranmer] did it too. He took the two remaining pool tables and *ṗəsa* with them at Ṁimk̓ʷəmlis. Ṅumas and Daduẇ took two pool tables each and *ṗəsa* with them.

They claimed that a Dᶻawadaʔēnux̌ʷ man used to make fun of them by saying: "I can hear too, you know." In response to his mockery, they gave him that "thing" at a *ṗəsa*. They gave this man, who used to make fun of them all the time, the radio with the big ear. Yes, the gramophone. [Big laughter.] They gave it to him. They gave him the radio with the big ear. Ṅumas gave it to this Dᶻawadaʔēnux̌ʷ man who used to make fun of them by saying, "I can hear too." This is what he got.

Moses worked at all kinds of things. He built a little boat by himself and bought an engine for it from the BC Packers. He came to join us at Dᶻaẇadiẏ. He would travel in and out of Dᶻaẇadiẏ. His gas boat would stop because it was sucking up sand. The river was so sandy. I guess the filters used to fill up with sand. His little gas boat would always stop when he was around Dᶻaẇadiẏ. This was around the time that Jimmy Sewid's father x̌aquλas got hurt. He and Q̇acuẇ went for a hike in the mountains, backpacking. An axe was tied to his pack. During the climb the axe fell off, cutting the tendons of his heel.

Yes, x̲aquƛas was your [Daisy's] father's father. Then things started to go wrong. x̲aquƛas always had a difficult time walking after this incident. The tendons on his heel were cut when the axe fell on him. We immediately left the inlet with him. We used Moses's boat, the little boat I mentioned that he built himself, and we brought x̲aquƛas to the hospital. Ḱʷəlstoliɬ ended up coming with us, but my mother did not. We brought him to the hospital. His mother, poor old Gagudiẏ, was out on the boat somewhere with his father Ẏaǵaɬʔənala [ʔOlsiwidi]. We brought him to the hospital, and that was the first sign we had that things were going wrong. He was never able to walk properly again. The large tendon on his heel got severed when the axe fell from his back. That is what happened.

Moses was the first one to build a gas boat by himself. He also bought a big light. It was a really huge light. I think he bought it from a policeman. He made a lamppost for outside our house. The light could be seen for quite a distance. We had a light for outside our house at Yəlis. Then he decided to try something else. He bought an engine, like the one we enjoy now, that could generate electric light. Only two houses were connected to it, ours and Waċaʔow̓'s. The little engine was kept at the door of the big house. It was Pənuw̓ [Arthur] who kept starting it when it stopped. It gave us electricity.

Dadax̲alis [Ben Alfred] built himself a house. Moses bought a bigger generator, bringing to three the number of people who had electricity. This was before Yəlis had any electricity. We were the first ones, along with Dadax̲alis and Waċaʔow̓, to have electricity. The engine was outside our home. The cement block where it was sitting is still there today. The engine that gave us electricity. We did all kinds of things.

When Moses's father died, he gathered up his younger brothers and, with their help, managed to gather some money. They went to work because ʔIlaǧa was just a baby when her father died, and Moses did not want his mother to be poor. He always took his younger brothers wherever he went logging. The three of them created a company and this enabled them to buy Jı4 from a Japanese man. Later, as I have already said, they got a commercial fishing licence.

Moses also got himself a musical instrument. What do you call it now? It is round at one end and you work it like this [ʔAx̲uw̓ makes a strumming motion]. The banjo! Yes.

[ʔAx̲uw̓ is laughing.] x̲alis, our first-born son, was just a young child. He did all kinds of things. [Laughter.] One day, x̲alis decided to tie a rope on the banjo and use it as a toy boat on the beach. Oh! That was terrible. Later, he received a saxophone, but he gave it away at a pəsa. It went to Gəlidiẏ [Henry Speck]. It was huge. Tom bought another musical instrument for ƛalis, a slide trombone. He never learned to play it. It was given away.

We had three musical instruments. They were among the things that were given away at a ṗəsa. There were three of them [*puxʷbe:* any wind instrument]. One ended up with one of Bill Scow's children. It was never paid for. It was just a little horn.

6

...... Ceremonies and Rituals

Introduction

As we have said earlier, nowadays the word "potlatch" means to give – a meaning shared by all Northwest Coast First Nations. Franz Boas (1966: 77; 1897: 341) defined its meaning as "distribution of property" and treated it as "a single named taxonomic category in Kʷakʷakəwakʷ culture" (Berman 1996: 246). However, as others have pointed out, the term "potlatch" is local trade jargon, not a Kʷakʷala word.[1] Used in place of the exact Kʷakʷala words for these diverse public ceremonial and social events, during which property is given away, this term obscures our understanding of what is really happening. ʔAx̌uw̓ very seldom, if ever, used the term "potlatch" in her narratives. It is clear from her stories that what have come to be thought of as "potlatches" were specific ritual occasions "commemorating marriage, death, the construction of a house, the investiture of an heir, the elevation of young people to new positions, the 'sale' of Coppers, the giving of Winter Ceremonial dances, the giving of oil feasts in connection with the Winter Ceremonial, and the display of supernatural properties shortly after they had been received" (Goldman 1975: 131). There are several other occasions upon which the Kʷakʷakəwakʷ would give away property – occasions upon which an immediate and modest distribution of property would be required. One reason for such a spontaneous gift-giving involved wiping away the shame after a child fell on the beach or out of a canoe or whatever. Parents would tell their children to be attentive and to behave or else their careless mistakes would cost them. This cost took the form of a distribution of property (ẏaqʷa) to the witnesses of the appropriate ceremony, who would acknowledge that the shame had been wiped out.

ʔAx̌uw̓'s careful and metaphor-rich vocabulary guides us towards the indigenous meanings of the different occasions upon which property is given.

As we shall see, the Kʷakʷ̓ala language uses at least four terms to describe gift-giving events, and we prefer to use these rather than the monolithic term "potlatch."[2] These terms are: p̓əsa, max̌ʷa, ẏaqʷa, and k̓ʷilas. Although the events these terms describe share many similarities, their differences speak to the contexts within which they occur: why? where? for whom? what types of goods are being given away, and in what quantity? P̓əsa refers to an inter-tribal distribution of property with the expectation of having one's gifts returned with interest. Max̌ʷa (literally, "doing a great thing") also connotes large-scale, inter-tribal ceremonies. Ẏaqʷa connotes an event during which property is distributed without any expectation of having it returned (e.g., naming ceremonies, memorial events, and so on). K̓ʷilas is a feast during which property is distributed.[3]

Besides these serious events during which gift-giving took place, there also existed not-so-serious occasions upon which goods were given away. These occurred in the context of what was called the "play potlatch," which was intended to be amusing and entertaining. People would gather and mock the dignified, grandiloquent, and pompous features of real potlatches, as we shall see in Chapter 7. ʔAx̌uw̓ seemed to delight in recounting an amusing, playful situation, during which a mock naming ceremony between friends and relatives took place. Here everyone named everyone else with totally non-potlatch-related but satirical, irreverent – and, to her – terribly funny names.

Coppers and the Death of ʔAx̌uw̓'s Father

Before I tell you about my father's death I would like to talk about the p̓əsa, which you call "potlatch." P̓əsa means to flatten gift containers.[4] Oh! We sure suffered because of the p̓əsa prohibition. We even did p̓əsa upstairs in our own house! Moses had told his children that he had built an exercise room upstairs for them. It did have some gymnastic equipment, but, as they grew older, they found out that exercise was not the true purpose for this huge room. It was for p̓əsa. We were holding our p̓əsa upstairs, in secret. We would gather p̓əsa gifts and then take them and wrap them with Christmas wrapping. All p̓əsa were planned around Christmas time, for that is the one time of the year when the White people give gifts to each other. That is also the reason why so many couples married at this time of year: so they would not arrest us for giving gifts. One time, my older sister attended a secret p̓əsa, and we were once more raided by the police. Bartley [Jack Bartley] was the name of the policeman. ʔAdəwis [Lucy Brown] was sitting beside the stove with her husband [the late John Speck]. The tub was full of all kinds of p̓əsa gifts. Bartley came in and kicked the tub. They had sent for two Redcoats [Mounties] to spy on us and our p̓əsa activities.[5]

Everyone was so afraid. Bartley kicked the tub and asked what its contents were for. Moses kept answering his questions, telling him that they were our Christmas gifts. Because they could not prove any different, the policemen left.

Note: Here, we have deleted a paragraph and moved it to Appendix C.

My father broke a Copper and held a big *p̓əsa*, during which presents were given away [ẏaqʷa]. He held a big feast [k̓ʷilas]. I attended many types of *p̓əsa*, even those during which button blankets, aprons, and other ritual paraphernalia were given away. My father held many *p̓əsa*, all the types of *p̓əsa* that existed, like k̓ʷilas [feast], q̓əlta [breaking a Copper], and ẏaqʷa [to give away presents].

A short while before his death my father had become involved in a power struggle with a rival from Miṁkʷəmlis. Both were contesting the ownership of a ranked position [ƛaƛax̌ʷaẏap]. Individuals who participated actively in *p̓əsa* held one or more positions [ƛax̌ʷeẏ: position] that were ranked in order of prestige and that determined the order in which guests received property. The inflexible rule was that, at a *p̓əsa*, those highest in rank received property first. My father's rival was trying to challenge that order by outranking him. In a desperate attempt to overthrow his rival, my father called upon every device he knew to bring humiliation and disgrace to this man, even contemplating the ultimate destructive forces that are released when a Copper is broken. This is what happened. My father broke his Copper to destroy his rival. My father's instructions were that the broken Copper should never be revived. Under no circumstances should the broken Copper be pieced back together. He wanted the Copper to remain dead forever. And that is why some people said my father died of witchcraft.

My father broke his Copper, and to symbolize that momentous event he commissioned three pins to be made as silver replicas of the Copper he broke. Today my children Nora and Flora wear the Broken Copper pin. My first pin was a very small one. And the last pin represented a broken Copper that I gave to Nora. I received the last pin when I was much older. He commissioned a replica of the Copper he broke, and that is also why he did not want it to be revived. He passed it on to me. That is what we call ʔomayugʷila ["establishing your rank as a noble-woman"]. Broken Copper pins are signs of prestige and achievement; they are visible proof that he did the right thing in breaking his Copper. His rage was justified; it was a victory over his rival. As I mentioned earlier, he gave orders that under no circumstances was the Copper to be brought back to life. To piece a Copper back together is called ƛapid [nailed back together]. As you know, a Copper could be revived by piecing it back and making it whole again and by reselling it.

My mother and her family arranged to invite the people and provided the goods to be distributed for me to *saligeẏ* [to give a memorial potlatch] at

Mimkʷəmlis. Well, my mother called all the people together in my honour. Everyone gathered at the big traditional house with a loon on the facade [xawigiwala]. I started to dance, holding the broken Copper. Then my father, G̱ʷułəlas, took the broken Copper from me. He went outside the house and cast it into the sea to drown it. The tide was high at Mimkʷəmlis, when it happened, and he cast it as far as he could. The Copper sank into the sea and came back jumping out of the water like a fish; my father started shouting when the Copper jumped out of the water because he had ordered that the Copper should forever be destroyed so that no one could reuse it or resell it.

Later that same night I saw a light on the beach. People were looking for the Copper. x̱aqʷagila [Tom Johnson], who was a young man then, retrieved the broken Copper that my father had destroyed by casting it into the sea. He did exactly what my father ordered everyone not to do. He retrieved the Copper and pieced it back together. Later, his father held a p̓əsa with it. But they were using a worthless Copper. It is q̓əmēẏ, a disgrace and a shame to build up a name with a worthless Copper. It is undignified and shameful. Even if we, the owners of the Copper, had pieced together this valuable object, it still would have been a dishonour to us because this act would have been carried out against my father's instructions. x̱aqʷagila pieced it back together and held a p̓əsa with it. That was really shameful on the part of ꞋOwax̱alagəlis, Tom Johnson's father. To the eyes of the Mamaliliqəlla, the Kʷaguł dishonoured themselves that day. The name of the Copper was Ꞌəng̱ʷala. That was the name of the Copper my father broke to over-throw his rival, who was challenging his ranked position in the p̓əsa. My father mysteriously took ill and died not too long after this event.

I guess I must have been eleven years old when my father died. We were living at Mimkʷəmlis. We took him to Vancouver after he became ill, but his health did not improve, and he died shortly after his arrival. Legix̱, my brother-in-law,[6] brought his body back home immediately after his death. He was buried at Mimkʷəmlis, on the furthest little burial island, where there were several other graves. Some people said that my father died as a result of witchcraft.

Death and Mourning

Whenever I had a baby we would ẏaqʷa and give the child his or her birthplace name. We always did this with Dadax̱alis and Nuladiẏ [Mr. and Mrs. Ben Alfred]. Whenever they had a child, they would also ẏaqʷa to give a name to the newborn. We ẏaqʷa at Yəlis when my newborn children were given their birthplace names.

Following Jackie's [ꞋAx̱uw̓'s eighth child's] death we literally gathered everything in the house and ẏaqʷa with it. The only thing remaining in our house was the piano, because it was too heavy to handle. We gathered everything we could for Moses to give away.

Dorothy [Puʎas] died first, then Jackie. Daduw̓ [Dan Cranmer] ẏaq̌ʷa for Dorothy because he and his first wife, Emma, had adopted her. Dorothy was about ten [ʔAx̌uw̓ says "ten" in English] years old when she died. It was shortly after this picture was taken.[7] She took ill all of a sudden during the night, and by four o'clock in the morning she was dead. She died of meningitis,[8] they told me. That was when she was attending the girls' school. At that time we were at the cannery at Water Lake, up north. That place eventually burned to the ground. I was not aware that she had been put in the school. She had gone to live with Daduw̓ and his second wife, Agnes, and he took her to the girls' school. I guess that, as soon as the school opened, they brought her to it. She was there only for a few months, because she took ill and died shortly after having arrived there.

I wonder how old Jackie was when he died. I do not remember. He came after Jimmy. He was quite young.[9] Lena [born in 1931] was just a baby when he died. I think he also died of meningitis, although he was sick for a very long time. He fell out of Mr. Anfield's[10] automobile. Mr. Anfield was the principal of the residential school. You know the way children behave; they are always climbing on and jumping from cars. He was sick for a long time before he died. He never went to the hospital. He died in one of the rooms upstairs in our big house at Yəlis. We put a stove in the room where he was staying. He died in that room.

I really do not know how old I was when my mother died. But George was my baby when she died [George was born in 1914]. I had three children at the time of her death: ƛalis [Alvin], ʔAda [Flora], and K̓ʷamax̌əlas [George].

With her cannery earnings my mother went to Vancouver. They said she had cancer. She was always losing blood. A big lump appeared here [showing the lower part of her abdomen], and that was the reason she went to the hospital. The doctors removed the lump, but then she contracted pneumonia. We went to Vancouver to visit her, and this was what we were told. George was under a year old and not yet walking because I was carrying him when we went. It was during the fishing season. You could see the smoke coming out of the cannery.

When a parent dies, his or her close relatives are what we call ʔaʔəmsila [potentially dangerous]. After my father died, my mother and I were both ʔaʔəmsila, and had to go through a purification period [ʔaʔēkila]. We were staying at the house of my uncle Q̓ʷəmxuduw̓ during the period of mourning. My mother was curtained off in a small area close to the main entrance of the house. This was ʔaʔəmsila, a time for purification during mourning. To purify herself she would go into the woods and bathe with fresh water for several days. Men did exactly the same thing following the deaths of their wives. They had to purify themselves by going into the woods and bathing with fresh water for several days.

While mother was ʔaʔəmsila, she was not allowed to come among us. She could only sit in her curtained area and go into the woods to bathe. She was really distressed. My older sister, Nulaǧa, and I would follow her and try to comfort her. In the old days, people in mourning would scratch their faces, and often the wounds would become infected. My mother mutilated her face too; the blood was running down her face. We found her in the woods, guided by the sounds of her sobbing, and brought her home. She was really sorrowful over the death of my father. Then we decided to go back to Mimkʷəmlis so that I could give a memorial ẏaqʷa. My mother gathered all her button blankets and silver bracelets for me to give away at my father's memorial ẏaqʷa.

We had another Copper that had been pawned at Lizzy's store at Yəlis. My mother went there and reclaimed it. My uncle, the older brother of my father, came and asked her for that Copper. He wanted to take the Copper away from her. My mother obstinately refused to give it to him. He wanted to break into the chest that was sitting on a ledge because he assumed that this was where the Copper was, inside that chest. He took the chest down and put it on the ground. "Go ahead," said my mother in a threatening voice, for she was now outraged. I think she was just about to beat him. "You go ahead and break into the chest. The Copper is not there. It is still at the store where it was pawned." My mother told him a lie, for the Copper was indeed lying in the chest.

The name of my uncle, who was arguing with my mother, was Məllidiẏ. He was ƛaẋaquɫəmēẏ's father. My uncle lived only one year after this incident. His death was a consequence of how he behaved over the Copper. This is what they say. He died because my mother was so indignant over what he had done that she wished him to die [hənkʷa: to wish death to someone]. And that is really what happened. He survived the death of my father by only about a year.

And this happened when my mother was ʔaʔəmsila. She was not allowed to sit among those who were eating. They say that she was hənkʷa when she chewed her food [malikʷəla: to chew]. She was not permitted to cut with a sharp knife until the end of her period of purification. This was also when she was ʔaʔəmsila.

In the old days they used to say that, during ʔaʔəmsila, those who were using a knife or any sharp utensil were ʔaʔəms [potentially dangerous]. ʔAʔəms means to hənkʷa, to wish death to someone. Those who were ʔaʔəmsila could be wishing the death of someone if they were using a knife. That is why they would not dare use a knife during that period. They carefully followed the rules during the ʔaʔəmsila period. It has not been long since they stopped this practice. Until recently, some were still respecting it. I saw my mother practising it, and that is also what I did for her after she died.

He did a lot of bad things, my uncle, my father's oldest brother, the father of x̌ax̌aqułəmēẏ [McDougall]. His name was Məllidiẏ. The house in which we were living was tiny. It was a small shack left to us by my father. My uncle took this house away from us. He took everything away from my mother. He chased us out of the little house my father had built. He even set fire to it because he did not want my mother or me to have it. So my mother had really good reasons to feel extremely resentful towards him. These were the terrible doings of my uncle towards my mother because she did not want to give him that Copper.

That is what they did.

There are a few more things they used to lecture me about when my father was dying. I was told never to accept chewing gum [ǧ"əlik": pitch gum] when it was offered to me. If anyone wanted to cut my hair, I also had to refuse. If I accepted I could be ʔiqʔidcuʔ [bewitched]. You had to be very cautious of these people because this is what happened to my father. So I was really afraid of sorcerers.

Witchcraft[11] or Sorcery

Ṅəgeẏ Is Bewitched (recorded in 1983)

My aunt [ʔənis], Wikəlalisəmēẏǧa, was married to Ṅəgeẏ [Mountain]. Ṅəgeẏ told me someone once bewitched him. They say that witchcraft actually works. You know Harry Mountain's father, Ṅəgeẏ? Ṅəgeẏ was married to Q̇acuǧow's relative, Ḱesug"ilak". She then married Ǧ"ułəlas. They separated [ḱikəsoʔ]. Ǧ"ułəlas was so angry with her, he told someone that she had cursed [dadala] Ṅəgeẏ. She hired three men to put a curse on Ṅəgeẏ and bewitched him. Ǧ"ułəlas talked about it after he separated from her. That is how everyone found out about it. When they told me about it, they referred to it as ǧəmx̌atola. My aunt's husband [Ṅəgeẏ] told me about this. When Wikəlalisəmēẏǧa was married to Ṅəgeẏ, he told me how she had arranged for someone to bewitch him [ʔiqa: witchcraft; ʔiqʔid: to bewitch]. She paid three men to do this, they said. This is what they mean by ǧəmx̌atola. She gave them money. No! They said it was pəlx̌alasǧəm [Hudson's Bay blankets], not money. And she gave them herself when she took them as lovers [ʔaʌadəxʔid: to take a person as a lover]. Hudson's Bay blankets were added to the price, so it was referred to as ǧəmx̌atola [having a bonus]. This is how they referred to it.

They succeeded in bewitching Ṅəgeẏ. This was unfortunate for Ṅəgeẏ, who took ill. He used to wander around aimlessly, and he lost a lot of weight [ʔəldʔiẏ:

fat]. He was nothing but skin and bones [ƛaÿaka: skinny]. They said that his skin turned black as he got weaker and weaker. It was around that time that Ǧʷuƚalas started talking about witchcraft, when they stuff a corpse [lolinuxʷ: corpse; ghost] with bodily scraps of the person to be bewitched. They call this type of witchcraft labatanuw̓ [to stuff with]. The men left Dᶻaw̓adiy̓ [Knight Inlet] because Ǧʷuƚalas told them where to look for the corpse and the paraphernalia the sorcerer [ʔiʔiq̓ʔinux̌ʷ] had used against N̓əgey̓, who was really in a pathetic state. They say that the corpse was on one of the islands near M̓imk̓ʷəmlis. Many men came from Dᶻaw̓adiy̓ to look for the sorcerer's paraphernalia. The men got off the canoe but N̓əgey̓ stayed behind because he was so weak. The men went into the forest to search for the sorcerer's paraphernalia. Each group consisted of nine men forming a line shoulder-to-shoulder, searching [y̓aʔēpamaƚa: walking abreast]. The men had agreed with one another that whoever would find the sorcerer's paraphernalia would həmc̓igaƚ, utter the "haaap" like a hamac̓a. This is what the men said to N̓əgey̓. N̓əgey̓ remained seated in the canoe in his pathetic state. It was a sunny day. All of a sudden he wanted to have a bowel movement. He crawled out of the canoe and headed towards an area covered with moss [p̓aləms]. They used moss to clean themselves in the early days. He crawled toward this mossy area [p̓ap̓aləkəkʷʷa] located at the base of a spruce tree [ʔaliwas]. He did not take long to get off the canoe and reach the p̓aləms that he was going to use as toilet paper. Suddenly he saw a red cedar rope dangling down from the tree. It was a dənak, a cedar-bark rope. He decided to investigate a little further, pulled at the rope, and found a coffin [dəgac̓iy̓]. That is what he told me, and this was during the time he was married to ʔənis [auntie; Dan Cranmer's mother]. It was sitting on the ledge where the sun would shine on it as soon as it rose in the morning. He found it himself. And the sun would hit this coffin, where a corpse [lolinuxʷ] was lying stuffed with some of his bodily scraps and some of his belongings. He realized immediately that this was the corpse that had been used against him. The rope was used to wrap around the coffin to keep it closed. N̓əgey̓ hamad̓əlaqʷa, uttered the hamac̓a cry. N̓əgey̓ had found the corpse that the sorcerer had used against him.

The men from the search party came running out of the forest. They were searching in vain in the forest. The men took the coffin down, unwrapped it, and pried it open [k̓ʷit̓ʔid]. As soon as the coffin opened all these flies [ǧaǧadina] came swirling out of it. They took down this corpse that had been placed in such a way as to be flooded by the sun's rays the first thing in the morning. Apparently this coincided with the time when N̓əgey̓ was suffering the most – when the sun was hot and shining on the coffin. It was the corpse of a man who had recently died, and there was still some skin attached to its skeleton. They checked the body all over. The men used to wear headbands in earlier times. The sorcerer had carved [ƙuƙ"axʔid] this corpse around the head and stuffed the headband into the wound, under the skin. The sorcerer had pitched [g"əlxʔid] with gum all around the cut to seal it. They had put things in the mouth and pitched it. They would pitch all the openings that they had stuffed things into. The sorcerer had put all Ṅəgeẏ's bodily scraps, or anything else he had used or touched during his daily activities, into these openings. These were scraps gathered from anything he did or left behind. They found a lot of potato peelings in the corpse. Ṅəgeẏ liked potatoes [dᶻəmidᶻəm][12] and he would steam them and throw the peelings beside the stove. Whenever he was invited, he was given a new mat upon which to step and upon which to drip his body sweat. They found all kinds of things, including soil where he had spat or urinated. Also his sharpening stone. Men used a special rock, called ćəlq́"əɬ [a filing stone], to sharpen their tools. It is a very smooth rock, and they spat on it to make it smoother. The sorcerer's helpers who had been hired by Ṅəgeẏ's rival had obviously taken Ṅəgeẏ's stone, which had been rubbed with his saliva, and hid it in the corpse, for they found it in the stomach of the corpse. They found all kinds of things hidden away inside the corpse.

These three men would invite Ṅəgeẏ many times, and each time they would lay a cedar-bark mat for him to sit on. It would be a new mat that had never been used before. After he had left, they would cut the area of the mat where he had been sitting and where he had sweat. It was with these kinds of things that they chose to stuff the corpse. Anything that had touched Ṅəgeẏ's lips, anything that he had breathed on, any hair left after combing, anything upon which he had urinated, or any bodily waste, they had selected. The three men would take all these things that had either belonged to Ṅəgeẏ or been in contact with him, and they would stuff them into a corpse.

Before they baked potatoes, our ancestors used to peel them and throw the peelings beside the fire. This is also what was found beside the corpse. Any type of waste that the victim had touched, breathed upon, or spat upon. The three men used to invite Ṅəgeẏ often, and he found out later that it was mainly to acquire all these things in order to use them against him by means of witchcraft. He was once such a stout man.

Ṅəgeẏ told me Ẏagəx̌salas had been paid to bewitch him. He told me the names of the others who helped him, but I cannot remember them now.

Oh! I forgot to mention something. When they first took the coffin down from the ledge, the men knew they had to treat it not too roughly [ʔiʔoɬcila: rough]. They took the corpse and submerged it in salt water. Oh! Ṅəgeẏ started to shake all over [x̌"ənuɬʔid: the whole body shakes]. This was when they submerged the corpse in salt water. They submerged it so it would be easier for them to detect where the sorcerer's paraphernalia was located.[13] The crown of the head and the eyes had been stuffed and then pitched. After an item had been stuffed [ǧudiƛəm] they would seal the opening with pitch. These openings were pitched. The eyes: they would seal both eyes with pitch. The lips: they would pitch them closed. The same would be done over the entire corpse. This is what they called labəɫanuw̓, to stuff a corpse.

The men from the search party submerged the corpse in water before they dismantled it. The huge corpse was wrapped [ǧənipsəmalad̓iy̓]. N̓əgey̓, who was sitting on the canoe, started to shiver when the corpse was put in the water. He became very cold. They wrapped the corpse up and put the coffin back after they had taken everything out. When they paddled away, N̓əgey̓ fainted on account of the jerking of the canoe, which occurred because the men were paddling so fast. The power of witchcraft was still having an effect on N̓əgey̓ even though the corpse had been dismantled.

N̓əgey̓ told me this story himself when he was married to my aunt Wikəlalisəmēy̓ǧa [Dan Cranmer's mother]. They call this type of witchcraft labəɫanuw̓. N̓əgey̓ lived for a long time. Everyone thought that he was going to die. He told me that he had been bewitched. He came back home and had a long life. He eventually married ʔənis, this man called N̓əgey̓, father of a man called Mountain. N̓əgey̓ was his p̓əsa name, his nobility [gigəx̌ƛēy̓] name. His everyday name was Hemasilak̓ʷ. He was one of the last ones to have been bewitched by K̓esug̓ʷilak̓ʷ.

Oh! They were just terrible, those who used to hate [ƛix̌əsapa] each other to the point of practising witchcraft. They called what happened to N̓əgey̓, ǧəmx̌atola, because ƛaʔēd̓iy̓ paid her three lovers with Hudson's Bay blankets. This is what they told me.

Daisy: Who did you say bewitched N̓əgey̓?

You know her [ʔAx̌uw̓ is speaking very softly, almost whispering]. She was a relative of Q̓acug̓ow. Her name was K̓esug̓ʷilak̓ʷ. Desiy̓ [Dora Speck] was named after her. [Laughter.] It was not too long ago [ʔaɫʔaɫa] they said that she put a curse on Dawson and also on G̓ʷuɫəlas. She bewitched him, I guess, because she and N̓əgey̓ hated each other. But she was married to G̓ʷuɫəlas at that time. And she left him. G̓ʷuɫəlas got angry at her and told everybody she was bewitching N̓əgey̓. That is what she did, and that is the reason why people found out. And she paid these men. This is what they used to do in the old days. They used to pay people to bewitch those they did not like. They used to conduct rivalries through witchcraft. I used to be so afraid when I was listening to N̓əgey̓ telling this story. I used to believe him. They used to lecture me about how to avoid these people.

Winter Ceremonial

In the old days, when our people wanted to invite guests, they used to sing
Ya?alalalo – the invitation song. How does the song go? It seems to have only
one melodic phrase, "*Ya?alalalo.*" This is all there is to this song [ʔAx̌uw̓ is
laughing]. There are no words to it. When our people were inviting other tribes
to attend a ceremony, they would sing this particular song as they gathered where
they would have a feast. Those were some of the events that I saw. *Ya?alalalo.*

Now if our people were going to perform the *ƛasela*,[14] the Peace Dance, with
dancers wearing ermine headdresses, they would sing an inviting song we call
ix̌ʷsala. They would perform the *ƛasela* dance for them. I once saw my uncle
Q̓ʷəmxuduw̓ performing it not too long ago. I went with him. It was around this
time of the year, close to Christmas, when he went around inviting. On several
occasions he danced the *ƛasela* and the *ƛəwəlax̌a*, when he was inviting. They
used to perform these dances to announce to the guests that their hosts were
going to have a *ƛasela*, a Peace Dance. I travelled often with him when they went
from tribe to tribe to invite guests. The other tribes would welcome us canoeing
sea-dwellers. They often gave gifts to those who made the invitation. We would
receive quite a bit from the high-ranking chiefs and their families at each village
we visited. This custom of giving gifts to those who made the invitation was a
matter of individual choice. It is still practised today to some extent; the Kʷaguł
practised it at Fort Rupert. We used to end up with quite a lot of presents at the
end of our inviting trips.

ƛasela: Healing Dance, or Peace Dance
In earlier times, not too many people had the right to use the *ƛasela*. The
first one I saw performing the *ƛasela* was a man named Həmd²idiy̓; he was a
Danaxdax̌ʷ. I do not know how he acquired it. For a long time Qaluǧʷis [Turnour
Island] did not own a *ƛasela*. In earlier times the *ƛasela* was separate from the
Red Cedar-Bark Ceremony. They would never dance the *hamaċa* and the *ƛasela*
during the same ceremony. They would have one or the other but it would never
be performed at the same time.

When they held a *ƛasela* and the guests started to arrive, the host tribe would
come out of the ceremonial house and sing. They would dance the *ƛasela*. The
guests who had the right to dance the *ƛasela* would be dancing in the canoe.
The hosting tribe would cast supernatural power into the canoe. A whistle, called
ƛax̌ax̌s, would sound. This was a large whistle with a deep, melancholic sound.
The dancer in the canoe would catch the supernatural power and cast it back to
those dancing outside the ceremonial house. They called the throwing back and
forth of the supernatural power *maqaþa*. They would do this four times. On the

fourth time the dancer outside the ceremonial house would catch the supernatural power and cast it into the ceremonial house. All the *ƛasela* whistles would
sound in the ceremonial house. This is when all the guests attending the *ƛasela*
ceremony would come ashore and enter the ceremonial house. They called these
large *ƛasela* whistles *ƛaẍaẍs*. They would dance the *ƛasela* for three days before a
ƛugʷéẏ [supernatural gift] appeared. It was on the fourth day that all the *ƛugʷéẏ*
appeared. All the masks appeared on the fourth day. The one who had a *ƛasela*
among the Maṁaliliqəlla [Village Island] was Wallas. Jimmy Sewid's father[15] was
the first one among the Maṁaliliqəlla. Wallas got his *ƛasela* from Ǧamadʑiẏ's
sister [Q̓akʷiẏéẏgilakʷ]. These are the ones I saw having a *ƛasela* ceremony
among the Maṁaliliqəlla. *ƛaqʷáduƛəlas* gave a *ƛasela* to Ṅəgeẏ [Mountain] when
he married Wikəlalisəméẏǧa [ʔAẍuw̓'s aunt]. Now the Maṁaliliqəlla had two
ƛasela. The last one to receive a *ƛasela* was Səmcaliẏ [Sam Charlie] when he
married W̓aʔoćas. He received his *ƛasela* from the Həxʷaməs. Munday of the
Danaxdaẍʷ [Knight Inlet; New Vancouver] had received a *ƛasela* from his wife.
His wife was Kitty Ferry's aunt. When he received it he had a big *p̓əsa* at New
Vancouver. Now the Danaxdaẍʷ had two *ƛasela*, Munday's and Həmdʑidiẏ's, the
uncle of Ẍiẍaṅyus. Ẍiẍaṅyus was Henry Speck's grandfather. These are the ones
I saw who owned a *ƛasela*. The only tribe that did not have a *ƛasela* for a long
time was Qaluǧʷis. Just recently Yakoyoǧʷa brought one to Ẍiẍaṅyus. Kənniẏ
had one because of this mother. This is the one that eventually came to our
family. *ƛasutiwalis* had a *ƛasela*. He was from the same family as Ẏeqəndas and
Q̓ʷəmxuduw̓ [ʔAẍuw̓'s uncle]. His name was *ƛasutiwalis*. He is the one who
committed suicide. These are the ones who had a *ƛasela* among the Nəmǧis:
Ned had a *ƛasela* and his *hilikəla* [lead dancer in the *ƛasela*] was Joey. They were
brothers so they just took turns in performing the *ƛasela*. That is it.

Usually, the oldest son of the owner of the *ƛasela* would be the *hilikəla*.
The *hilikəla* and the *haṁaća* were always reserved for the eldest. The Red Cedar-
Bark Ceremony and the *ƛasela* were never performed together. The *ƛasela* was
considered a very important ceremony too. It was against our ways to perform
them at the same time.[16]

Those who owned a *ƛasela* among the Kʷaguł were George Hunt and
ʔAbusa's [Mrs. Johnathan Hunt] uncle, Hemisaqa. Also Nułbéẏ. His name was
Alec. He was related to Flora.[17] Also Ǧusdidʑas, whom they called Billy McDuff.
These are the ones who had a *ƛasela*. And, of course, Ǧamadʑiẏ [Moses Alfred's
uncle]. Ǧamadʑiẏ was part Hiłdʑuqʷ [Bella Bella]. He was married to Mumuta's
[Joseph Wallas] mother. That foolish man left her. I think I was already married
to Flora's father [Moses Alfred] when he left her. Then he married that woman
who wore the biscuits around her neck. Mumuta was one of the best dancers
of the *ƛasela*. Dadiq̓a had a *ƛasela*. His *hilikəla* was Mungo Martin.

Daisy: Who would be my father's hilikəla, *since the eldest, Bobby, is already a* haṁaċa?

It would be the second eldest son, Ozzie.

Also, during the ċeqa, if someone wanted to *x̌ʷasa* [to take part in the ceremony], then that someone would give gifts to the hosting tribe. Not everyone got something, unlike nowadays. Nowadays we give gifts to everybody; there is no such a thing as *ʔalaʔeł* any more. In the early days you would never give gifts to your own tribe; you would just give gifts to the visiting tribe. For example, if someone from the Maṁaliliqəlla invited several tribes, *haṁaċa* impersonators from a visiting tribe would *x̌ʷasa*. Only the Maṁaliliqəlla would receive gifts from the performing tribe for having given them the privilege of dancing their *haṁaċa* dance at the Maṁaliliqəlla's ceremony. This is called *ʔix̌ʷugiwēẏ*. It means "dancing on the bow of the canoe." The performing visitors would not give gifts to the others at the feast, only to the hosting tribe. That is what they did in the early days. They never gave gifts to everybody. They call this *ʔalaʔeł*. They would say, we are *ʔalaʔeł*. We will not be receiving any gifts, they would say. The members of a family who had performed the *haṁaċa* would *ṗasʔid* [from *ṗasa*: to invest by giving gifts]. But they would give gifts only to the hosting tribe.

One time my uncle Q̓ʷəmxuduẇ invited many people for a *ṗəsa*. His house was adorned with a frontal pole representing the Raven with a movable beak (see Plate 3), a copy of which is now standing at Stanley Park. When the guests arrived the beak of this huge bird would open; they would walk through the mouth of the bird, and the beak would close behind them. This is how people used to enter his big house whenever my uncle held a *ṗəsa*. Then the welcome pole would speak. The carved figure would say "*wigax̌ʷuẇ*," "come in, we are ready." It was ʔAnita who stood behind the speaking pole.

"*Wigax̌ʷuẇ*," the welcome figure would say. We called this talking welcoming pole *yaq̌əntṗiq*. It came to the Liǧiłdax̌ʷ [Cape Mudge people] through Q̓ʷəmxuduẇ by marriage. There is a similar carved welcoming figure in the local museum at Campbell River.[18] *Wigax̌ʷuẇ* means that the people had to be prepared to give gifts, and it also refers to the breaking of a Copper. This is what we say when we are going to give gifts: "*wigax̌ʷuẇ*." We would also say, "*wiq̌ʷa*." Other tribes would say it differently, like: "*qasakas, qasakas* [*qasa*: to walk]." Jimmy used to say, "Go and take a seat." But in the early days they would say: "*wigax̌ʷuẇ, wiq̌ʷa*," "go ahead, boast," with a very deep voice. All the nobility would enter through the large bird's beak and be swallowed by it [*həmsgəm*: to swallow; closing up beak]. And the beak would close behind them. The beak operated through a latch. You only had to push it up; there was a hidden mechanism to make it close and open. In the meantime, the hosts would pile high all the Hudson's Bay blankets.

My uncle gave Hudson's Bay blankets as gifts. Nulaǧa and I stole one blanket each to buy some fabric with it. No one ever noticed that two blankets were missing from this huge pile that my uncle had stored to give away at his *p̓əsa*. We stole a blanket each so that we could buy some fabric to make our own clothing. I guess it was around May the 24th, "Sports Day" in Alert Bay[19] [said in English]. One blanket used to be worth one dollar. We used to get seven yards of fabric for one dollar, in those days. We stole just enough for what we needed. We did it so that we could buy some clothing material. Seven yards for one dollar. Material is so expensive today.

The *Haṁaċa*

You know that in the early days the *haṁaċa* initiates[20] used to disappear in the forest [*xəsala:* to be lost]. I once witnessed the return of a *haṁaċa* novice at Caxis [Fort Rupert]. Caxis was the best place to hold these types of happenings and the subsequent *p̓əsa* and *k̓ʷilas* [feasts]. Guests used to stay there for a long time. People from several tribes would gather there and *p̓əsa*. Some did not practise the return of the *haṁaċa*, along with its subsequent feasts and dances, at their own tribal villages, preferring to perform them at Caxis. The *haṁaċa* used to vanish from sight and stay in the forest for a period of *nəqapənxwas*, ten days. During this time the novice[21] was *xəsała* [missing], because he had disappeared. Ten days. Of course in the days before the Whites, it took much longer. But this is what I saw. The *haṁaċa* novices would *xəsała*, disappear, and come back in, and some of their female relatives would be taken away. Initiates would disappear for a while and would be *kəmyanəm*, gathered up, later on.

The old *haṁaċa* carried off the novices. They entered the house and examined the people who made up the gathering. Then they would select and take away the novices who were going to *xəsała*, disappear into the forest. Later, everyone would go out and search for them. This is what we call *kəmya*, the capture of the initiates. The *Gəla*, the grizzly, would come and carry away a new male novice, and he would also disappear for a while. He would reappear later as some kind of animal; that is what they used to do. And so on. The Nəmǧis had very precise proceedings.

Winalagilis[22] is the spirit of war. He is impersonated in a particular dance that used to be performed during the *kəkənəla* [the gathering of all the initiates who had disappeared]. At that particular time, all the dances would be performed.

This is what we call *kəkənəla*. This ceremony consists of trying to capture the *haḿaċa*. The *Winalagila* wore branches all over their bodies and rolled all over the floor. They used to be dripping wet with water. They also used to carry people away. This was the custom in the early days. Many aspects of these traditional rituals are no longer seen.

There was also the *həmspiq*, the tethering *haḿaċa* pole, that used to stand in the centre of the house and extend through a hole in the roof. There was a group of people called *ṭamemiɬ*, who would never leave the building. They kept singing all the time when the *həmspiq* was standing and the *ḿawiɬ*, the ceremonial screen, was up. Red things would hang down from the pole. Some people would shake the pole and the red objects would sound. Then the *haḿaċa* would climb down the pole because, by now, he had been captured and brought back from the forest where he had disappeared. I saw this at Cax̱is and also at the place where we are living now, Yəlis. This was at the house of Ḿiċa [Herbert Martin]. The pole was extending through a hole in the roof. There was a feast. The *lolinux̌ʷ* [ghosts][23] were singing, and they asked members of the nobility to serve them some food, as they were hungry. Snacks such as candy, apples, and sweets were served. They ate all day. People brought them all kinds of things to eat, apples or anything else good to eat, because those who were *lolinux̌ʷ* would inevitably be hungry.

The *lolinux̌ʷ* sat inside the building and sang *ċeqa* songs. They sang all day and all night. This is what they call *ṭemimiɬa*. Then the *haḿaċa* came out of the forest. The *lolinux̌ʷ* kept singing. That is why we had so many good singers in the old days, because they used to sing all day and all night. When the *haḿaċa* came out of the forest, it was called *ṭamemiɬ*. During the *kəmya*, they stayed there all night, and, slowly, the initiates reappeared in a ritual procedure that we call *kəkənəla*. A *laluɬalaɬ* [ghost dancer] was there to catch them.[24]

The *haḿaċa* first appeared on the roof of the house. Everybody stretched out their arms and looked towards the hole, their hands shaking with tremors. Then the *haḿaċa* climbed down from the roof to the floor. A rope was attached to the roof so that he could climb down, or sometimes it was attached to his ankle. He had now appeared and was eventually captured by the *kəkənəla*. It used to take all night for the *kəkənəla* to capture him.

The women used to hold a blanket by its corners in order to break the *haḿaċa*'s fall as he jumped down through the hole in the roof. It was a very difficult and dangerous thing to do in the old big houses. Then the *haḿaċa* would disappear again. The men from his own family would pretend to grab hold of him when he reappeared. This was when he jumped on the blanket held at the corners by four women. He jumped on the blanket and ran to each corner of the house before disappearing again. The *haṁaċa* wore hemlock branches when he jumped through the hole of the roof.

All the congregations would start to assemble in the morning. The people would just go home to sleep for a short time, wearing their button blankets and having painted or rubbed their faces with *ğʷəms* [red ochre]. They would meet the ritual congregation and dance outside. Then they would encircle the crowd and sing, according to the various secret societies to which they belonged, the *haṁaċa*, the *Nuɫcistalaɫ*,²⁵ the *Quminəwaĝas*,²⁶ the *Tuxʷʔid*, and so on. Each would have its own special group encircling its members, and they would sing the songs to which they were entitled as they proceeded to the ceremonial house. The gathering group was made up of women who were dancing their welcoming dance [*ẏaẏaẃalasuẃ*: to meet someone by dancing]. It used to be so beautiful when they were all dressed up in their button blankets during the *kəmya*, the gathering of initiates.

Various Dances

For each dance only one person at a time would disappear, depending on the dance society they would to be initiated into. Even for the very important dance groups, like the *laluɫalaɫ*, the new initiates had to disappear. The elders would decide who would impersonate which guardian spirit. The elders sometimes argued between themselves because they were not always in agreement over the choice of the impersonators.

This is what I saw at Cax̌is. They had brought Miċa on a barge to Cax̌is because Yəlis did not have the proper terrain for a *kəmya*. They also held a *Tuxʷʔid*²⁷ initiation at the same time. The *Tuxʷʔid* novice was Xixca's daughter, Spruce Martin's daughter. She was the older sister of Jessie [Jessie Dawson, Miċa's niece]. She was the eldest daughter. In one picture taken at Yəlis, the girl was carried on a platform. She was a *Tuxʷʔid*. She was Annie's mother. She is the one walking. I recognized her in this picture as well as poor old Dadawa. From the group that stands on the barge I can identify these two people. The people disembarked from the barge and went to our home when we were still living in the big house. This is where they were having the ceremony. They came from ʾUgʷitəmalis [the non–First Nations section of Alert Bay] because there was no adequate place to have the *kəmya* at Yəlis.

At Miṁkʷəmlis they used to *kəmya* on that end of the island [motioning with her hand], at ƛasudis. This was where they *kəmya* us when ʾIwaqalas initiated us. ƛasudis is the little island across the way from Miṁkʷəmlis. That is where the Gəlaɫatid appeared, the great big carved Bear. It seemed to crawl out of its hiding place. And the initiates kept appearing from behind it. They came to pick us up, because the only way to go to ƛasudis was by water. Mimkʷəmlis did not have an adequate place for kəmya so everybody preferred to go to Caxis. The terrain at Caxis is ideal for kəmya; the beach is huge there, easy to land by canoe, easy to capture and walk the haṁaċa into the big house.

Ǧʷuɫəlas had his marriage contract completed by his wife Qixʎalaǧa at Caxis. I was one of the dancers. I disappeared. They named what I was going to be: ƛagustuyu [lifted up]. Strange things kept appearing. They had long hair hanging over their faces. As the ceremony began, I was xəsaɫa [lost, hidden]. So I never got to see the whole ceremony. My dance was what we call Yeḋentalaɫ. I was just a child at the time. This is what I was for Ǧʷuɫəlas. I was initiated at Caxis. Many people attended the ceremony.

I remember a dance called qəxa suẁ [the Red Cedar-Bark Ring] and a dance called weliqa. Ǧʷuɫəlas initiated several of us into the weliqa. We no longer see this dance performed. ƛaqʷagilogʷa, an aunt of Harry Brown, pretended to have frogs in her stomach [a Tuxʷʔid performance]. She was supposed to walk out very slowly and very gently, and give birth to frogs. Oh! It really irritated us because she was ever so slow, and we could not leave her behind. This type of walking is what nowadays they would call slow marching. We were all in a row, walking around, at Caxis. We were invited into one of the houses we passed. When the ceremony was completed, people invited us and fed us. ʔAnisəlaǧa received so many oranges. People peeled the oranges and squeezed them for us. This was when we were initiates, weliqa, and our initiation was sponsored by Ǧʷuɫəlas.

When evening came, they gave us a bath and purified us in the same way they did when I first menstruated. They took a hoop made out of branches. Before the purification ritual we weliqa,²⁸ and what we did next is called kʷesa [purification by bathing]. It happened late during that same night. Not too many were chosen to be initiated. And we had to carry with us the gifts that were going to be given to those who witnessed the kʷesa. They gave us a bath by ritually sprinkling fresh water over us.

The men were still wearing their red cedar-bark headdresses. They did not remove their red cedar-bark ornaments after the ceremony, although the dancing was all finished at this time. It is visible in one picture, which, I think, was taken at Bond Sound. That is what they call dʲidʲax̌liẏ. This was the way the men were dressed while they were dancing. They wore red cedar-bark headdresses and red cedar-bark rings around their necks. They used to go through purification rituals [ʔaʔēkila: going through purification]. I witnessed the initiation and purification of Bondsound and Gerry. He was initiated as Ṁaṁaqa, the Death Thrower. Another time I saw Bondsound when he became Bəkʷʼəs, the Wild Man of the Woods.

Hawiṅalaɫ: Warrior Hook Dance

The *hawiṅalaɫ*[29] is performed during the Red Cedar-Bark Ceremony *ćeqa*. The initiate must *xəs?id*, disappear into the forest, and he must be *kəmyaṅəm*, pursued and captured. Mungo Martin was Qumēy̓'s *hawiṅalaɫ*. Qumēy̓ was Mungo's grandfather. Mungo danced the *hawiṅalaɫ* for him at Caẍis. Qumēy̓'s *haṁaċa* was Hemadᶻalas. Ẏaq̓aɫ?ənala's [?Olsiwidi's] *hawiṅalaɫ* was Lalakənis [one of the survivors of the Bella Coola massacre] at M̓iṁk̓ʷəmlis. Ẏaq̓aɫ?ənala's son [Jimmy Sewid's father] told me this. Ẏaq̓aɫ?ənala was Gagudiy̓'s [Lucy Sewid's] husband. Ẏaq̓aɫ?ənala had a daughter named Wilk̓ʷilak̓ʷ. Hazel's mother was named after her. She was named after Ẏaq̓aɫ?ənala's daughter. Ẏaq̓aɫ?ənala's son was Lalakənis. Wilk̓ʷilak̓ʷ and Lalakənis were Ẏaq̓aɫ?ənala's children from his first wife.

Daisy: What do they do to the hawiṅalaɫ?

Oh my! They do a terrible thing to them. Billy McDuff's wife was pierced [?utasuẇ].

Daisy: Women could be hawiṅalaɫ *too?*

Yes, I told you. Hawilk̓ʷilak̓ʷ was pierced.[30] They would pierce the shoulder blades [ƛaq̓ʷədanēy̓] and the knees [?uk̓ʷexēy̓] and there would be a rope attached to the hooks. They would pull the person up. The person would be bent over as they are pulling the ropes. It was terrible. Hawilk̓ʷilak̓ʷ was suspended on a mast of a boat and when they got to M̓iṁk̓ʷəmlis they lowered her on the wharf [tix̓ʷwəɫtuẇ]. It had to have taken place at M̓iṁk̓ʷəmlis otherwise why would they have used a boat? The *hawiṅalaɫ* usually just walks. Oh, my! It must have been painful. During the ceremony they would pull the ropes until the flesh [?aldᶻiy̓] breaks. They would pull at the ropes until it breaks. Apparently it was really terrible for Q̓ax̓ʷstuƛēy̓ [Stephen Cook]. He had his flesh pierced as a *hawiṅalaɫ*. He was just a child. He would yell his *hawiṅalaɫ* cry "ay̓ ay̓ ay̓" and end with "son of a bitch G̓ʷik̓ʷiy" [or Ẇasẇas]. [Laughter.] This was addressed to Ẇasẇas, who was initiating him. He would always end his *hawiṅalaɫ* cry with "son of a bitch, G̓ʷik̓ʷiy." [Laughter.] I did not see this, I was just told about it. I guess I was just a child when he was initiated.

Daisy: Do you know of any legend that speaks of the hawiṅalaɫ?

No, I do not know any.

Daisy: Do you know any hawiṅalaɫ *songs?*

No. I do not know any. The songs seem to just say one thing. They would beat the boards with a steady beat and then change to a regular beat. No, I do not know the words of the song. There are some really good *hawiṅałał* songs. ƛ̓itəs [Jack Peters] knows them. We will ask him to record one.

Daisy: Why does the hawiṅałał *point to the corner ceiling of the ceremonial house?*

The cross beam of the ceremonial house. He would yell "aẏ aẏ aẏ" and point at the cross beam. He does this because he wants to be pierced and hung up. He would then be pierced and hung up on the cross beams[31] of the ceremonial house [ʔugʷiwalíł].

Daisy: Would the hawiṅałał *hang there for a long time?*

I doubt it. I was just told that he points to the cross beams of the house to be pierced and hung there. The rope that the *hawiṅałał* is going to be hung with is sometimes wrapped around their waist while they are dancing. The novice would have two initiated *hawiṅałał* following him and holding the rope. I saw ƛ̓iła [Margaret Cook] do this when she was initiated. When the other *hawiṅałał* danced they would wrap the rope around their neck. These are the ones I have seen. They no longer practised the piercing by that time. They would wrap the rope around their neck to symbolize the piercing. The two ends of the rope would drop behind them and it would be held by two initiated *hawiṅałał*. I saw ƛ̓iła when she was initiated and they did this to her. ƛ̓iła was a *hawiṅałał*.

Daisy: When did the practice of piercing end?

A long time ago. I never saw anyone being pierced. I was just told what I know about it. Those who, I was told, did actually get pierced, were Mungo Martin, Q̓axʷstuƛ̓eẏ [Stephen Cook], and Hawilkʷilakʷ, the wife of Billy McDuff.

Miƛa: Prankster Dance

Daisy: Would you sing Dada's [Jimmy Sewid's] Miƛa song?

[ʔAxūẇ sings:]

> *Ho, ... Ho, Miƛa ... gila ... aa*
> Ho, ... Ho, Prank ... ster
>
> *Miƛa ... gila ... aa*
> Prank ... ster
>
> *Ṅaṅəwala ... g̓olic ... cuẇ*
> People are trying to come near me

Miƚa ... gila ... aa
Prank ... ster

N̓ən̓əwala ... ǧolic ... cuẁ
People are coming close to me

Miƚa ... gila ... aa
Prank ... ster

Miƚa ... gila ... aa
Prank ... ster

Q̓iq̓a ... ǧolic ... cuẁ
Many people are gathering around me

Miƚa ... gila
Prank ... ster

Wo ho, wo ho.

These are all the verses I know. It has many verses. Wayoƚ [Billie Sunday Willie's mother and ʔOlsiwidi's sister] would chant it just before the *Miƚa* appeared, and, after she finished chanting, the singers would sing for the *Miƚa*. They call the main song *N̓əqax̌əla*.

[ʔAx̌uẁ sings:]

Hey ... aah, hey ... ah, hey ah hey ah,
Hey ... aye, hey ... aye

Kikaƚəllayuẁ kas
Everyone is afraid of you

M̓am̓iλallaǧʷəm ƚaʔos
When they hear you singing your chant

M̓iƚagila kas ʔu
Prankster

Hey ... aah, hey ... ah, hey ah hey ah,
Hey ... hey

Kikaƚəllayuẁ kas di
Everyone was afraid of you

Kʷix̌ayuw̓ k̓ʷəllis kas di
When they saw you with your club

Miƛagulow kas ʔu
Prankster

Hey ... aah, hey ... ah
Hey ... aah, hey ... ah.

That is all I know. Daca [Billie Sunday Willie] knows it all. Daduw̓ told me many canoes were destroyed by a *Miƛa's* club at Cax̌is.[32]

ƛ̓ina ƙugʷikila: Grease Feast

When they had a grease [*ƛ̓ina*: eulachon grease] feast they would use these huge wooden spoons. They would dip these huge spoons into the vat of grease and yell "*laʔums ƛix̌ʷʔid da ƛē*," "You are going to have a sip"; then they would yell, "*la ʔums x̌ʷəmʔid da ƛē*," "You are going to slurp" as they walked towards the guests with these huge wooden spoons. Each guest would be given a sip of grease from this huge wooden spoon.

> *Daisy: Can you tell me why they poured grease into the fire during these times? I have read in a book that we poured grease into the fire to burn the ceremonial houses of our rituals. Is there any truth to that?*

No, no. I have never heard anyone say this. The people who do such a thing are very proud [*ẏalaqaƛa*] of their grease. They would pour grease in the fire so the flames would shoot up in the air and in some cases almost burn the house. This is my understanding of this practice.

> *Daisy: Someone said that a man kept drinking grease until he just passed out. Do you know of this practice?*

No. During a seal feast they would do what they referred to as "*dukʷasuw̓*," a seal feast during which string blubber was served. Waċaga told me this. She was ƛəlbəsʔalla's wife. She said to me, "*dukʷasuw̓ naxʷ x̌ʷuƛ ƛən nuxʷ*," "they would string us." They would cut seal blubber [*x̌ʷəd̓iy*] into long thin strips and the guests were required to swallow a string of blubber in one piece. It was some form of a contest between the guests. Waċaga would vomit [*hux̌ʷʔid*] because she would not know yet how to do this. They had this type of feast often but only certain individuals were invited. She found out how to swallow the blubber whole, or what appeared to the other guests as swallowing it whole. Waċaga had a small container hidden in her chest. She would quickly bite off pieces of blubber and drop them into the hidden container. The host would have the guests swallow these long thin blubber strips. [Laughter.]

There is another practice called *"xisəłita x̌a mig"ad"* [the serving of a seal head]. I don't think this practice was very nice. They would cook and serve a seal head to a guest who had shamed the host. The guest who received the head would have to give gifts away to the host and other guests to wipe away the dishonour.

Feast Bowl
It was an insult to place the rear end of a feast bowl towards your invited guests. If you did this to a tribe, the chiefs of that particular tribe had to give away gifts to the other guests to wipe out the insult. On account of this, the tribes were very cautious. They were careful to face the rear end of the feast bowl towards the door so that no tribe would be insulted. I guess if you had the rear end of the feast bowl facing you it was an insult in the early days. [Laughter.] They would now put the food in the feast bowl and the men would carry it and serve the guests. When all the guests were served, they would place the feast bowl in the *ʔustolił* [rear of the house] with the rear end facing the door.

Songs

We tried to ask Mungo Martin to record a song for us. He was embarrassed [*pəlsǧəmxʔid*] because he was unable to sing the song. Moses tried to record him. All he was able to sing was the chanting "*Heey Hoe, Hoe, Hoe, Hoe.*" Jimmy [Sewid] and I later sang it for Lalooska. [ʔAx̌uẃ sings the song:]

> *Heey Hoe, Hoe, Hoe, Hoe,*
> *Heey aah, Hoe, Hoe, Heey, Hoe,*
> *Heey Hoe, Hoe, Hoe, Hoe,*
> *Heey eey ẏa*
>
> *Heey Hoe, Hoe, Hoe, Hoe,*
> *Heey aah, Hoe, Hoe, Heey, Hoe,*
>
> *Wənwənǧəmliłala kas ƛis*
> They will hide their faces those
>
> *Ńańaṗayus kas ƛaʔus*
> That you throw stones to

Bak̓ʷəsala dᶻiɏ kas
Great *Bak̓ʷəs*

ƛugʷallow
You have favoured me with good fortune

These are the words [q̓aẏas] of the song.

Daisy: Say the words of the song for me so I can write them down.

[ʔAx̌uẇ repeats the words:]

Ẇanẇanǧəmlit
They will hide their faces

Kikaɫalagila kas ƛis Ṅaṅap̓ayus kas ƛaʔus
They will fear the stones you will throw

That is the line I forgot:
Kikaɫalagila kas ƛis Ṅaṅap̓ayus kas ƛaʔus
They will fear the stones you will throw

Bak̓ʷəsala dᶻiɏ kas
Great *Bak̓ʷəs*

These are the words sung during the *cax̌aɫa* [beating with a fast steady beat]. Then they sing the *ṅəqax̌əla* [dance beat].

Hem, Hem, Hem, Hem,
Ha ma mēɏ, Hum, Hum, Hum,
Hem, Hem, Hem, Hem,
Ha ma mēɏ, Hum, Hum, Hum.

Song 1

ʔa kas nawalakʷ[33]
O Supernatural One

ʔa dᶻiy kas suɫ nawalakʷ
O Great Supernatural One
Hem, Hem, Hem, Hem,
Ha ma mēɏ, Hum, Hum, Hum,

Ya ... gi ... quw dalagəlis kas x̱is
They will all surrender those who

Ṅaṅa ... p̓a ... yuẁ ... kas x̱aʔus
You throw stones to

Ṅəmc̓aq ... qəyalił dᶻiẏ kas
Great Solitary One

ƛugʷala kas ʔuẁ ẁa
How fortunate I am.

Song 2

ʔa kas nawalakʷ
O Supernatural One

ʔa dᶻiy kas suł nawalakʷ
O Great Supernatural One
Hem, Hem, Hem, Hem,
Ha ma mēẏ, Hum, Hum, Hum,
Ya, kikał ... łala gila kas x̱is
They will fear the

Ṅaṅa ... p̓a ... yuẁ ... kas x̱aʔus
Stones you will throw

Ṅəmc̓aq ... qəyalił dᶻiy kas
Great Solitary One
Bak̓ʷəsala dᶻiẏ kas
Great *Bək̓ʷəs*

ƛugʷala kas ʔuẁa
How fortunate I am.

Song 3

ʔa kas nawalakʷ
O Supernatural One

ʔa dᶻiy kas suł nawalakʷ
O Great Supernatural One

Hem, Hem, Hem, Hem,
Ha ma mēẏ, Hum, Hum, Hum,

Ẏa, ẁanẁən ... ğəmliƚila kas ƚis
They will hide their faces those

Ṅaṅa ... ṗa ... yuẁ ... kas ƚaʔus
To whom you throw stones to

Ṅəmċaq ... qəyaliƚ dᶻiẏ kas
Great Solitary One

Bak̓ʷəsala dᶻiẏ kas
Great Bək̓ʷəs

ʌugʷalla kas ʔuẁa
How fortunate I am.

Song 4

ʔa kas nawalakʷ
O Supernatural One

ʔa dᶻiẏ kas suƚ nawalakʷ
O Great Supernatural One
 Hem, Hem, Hem, Hem,
Ha ma mēẏ, Hum, Hum, Hum

Ya ... gi ... quw dalagəlis kas ƚis
They will all surrender those who

Ṅaṅa ... ṗa ... yuẁ ... kas ƚaʔus
You throw stones to

Ṅəmċaq ... qəyaliƚ dᶻiy kas
Great Solitary One

Bak̓ʷəsala dᶻiẏ kas
Great Bək̓ʷəs

ʌugʷala kas ʔuẁa
How fortunate I am.

ʔa kas nawalakʷ
O Supernatural One

ʔa dᶻiy kas suɬ nawalakʷ
O Great Supernatural One.

That is it. This is the song Ṅəqax̌əla [verses to a song]. This is the song
for ƛax̌uɬilakʷ when he danced the Bək̓ʷəs Dance for Ǧʷuɬəlas [Bell] at Cax̌is.
Apparently Yawapsəms [Covered with a Tent] made the song "ʔa kas nawalakʷ."
I don't know if he also made the cax̌aɬa [fast beat] song.

[ʔAx̌uw̓ sings another song, Ẏiẏanḍəntəlaɬ (The Speaker Dance song):]

Waaaa
He yaa ... ḍəntəla kas ʔuwaaa
Oh! Wonderful Speaker

Ẇoxsbəndalayuw̓ gʷila kas ʔuwaaa
Would they potlatch in the morning, then again in the evening for you?
Aaa ... a ... a ... a ... hey ... hey ... he

Waaaa
He yaa ... ḍəntəla kas ʔuwaaa
Oh! Wonderful Speaker

Həẏẏa ... siɬ ... ǧʷiẏala gila kas ʔuwaaa
So this is what they would do for you
Aaa ... a ... a ... hey ... hey ... he

Waaaa
He yaa ... ḍəntəla kas ʔuwaaa
Oh! Wonderful Speaker

A ... maxʷx̌ʷəlanəm gila kas ʔuwaaa
Would they give a potlatch to all the tribes for you?
Aaa ... a ... a ... a ... hey ... hey ... he

Waaaa
He yaa ... ḍəntəla kas ʔuwaaa
Oh! Wonderful Speaker

Həẏẏa ... siɬ ... ǧʷiẏala gila kas ʔuwaaa.
So this is what they would do for you
Aaa ... a ... a ... a ... hey ... hey ... he

Waaaa
He yaa ... q̓əntəla kas ʔuwaaa
Oh! Wonderful Speaker

Həy̓y̓a ... sił ... ǧʷiy̓ala gila kas ʔuwaaa
So this is what they would do for you
Aaa ... a ... a ... a ... hey ... hey ... he

Waaaa
He yaa ... q̓əntəla kas ʔuwaaa
Oh! Wonderful Speaker

T̓eqʷapəlanəm gila kas ʔuwaaa
Would they constantly give feasts for you?
Aaa ... a ... a ... a ... hey ... hey ... he

Waaaa
He yaa ... q̓əntəla kas ʔuwaaa
Oh! Wonderful Speaker

Həy̓y̓a ... sił ... ǧʷiy̓ala gila kas ʔuwaaa
So this is what they would do for you
Aaa ... a ... a ... a ... hey ... hey ... he

Waaaa
He yaa ... q̓əntəla kas ʔuwaaa
Oh! Wonderful Speaker

K̓ugʷikəlanəm gila kas ʔuwaaa
Would they constantly give feasts for you?
Aaa ... a ... a ... a ... hey ... hey ... he

Waaaa
He yaa ... q̓əntəla kas ʔuwaaa
Oh! Wonderful Speaker

Həy̓y̓a ... sił ... ǧʷiy̓ala gila kas ʔuwaaa
So this is what they would do for you
Aaa ... a ... a ... a ... hey ... hey ... he

Waaaa
He yaa ... q̓əntəla kas ʔuwaaa
Oh! Wonderful Speaker

Q̇aq̓əltəlanəm gila kas ʔuwaaa
Would they break Copper on your opponents for you?
Aaa ... a ... a ... a ... hey ... hey ... he

Waaaa
He yaa ... q̓əntəlla kas ʔuwaaa
Oh! Wonderful speaker

Hə yaa ... sił ... ğʷiẏala gila kas ʔuwaaa
So this is what they would do for you
Aaa ... a ... a ... a ... hey ... hey ... he.

That is all.
Ƙugʷigēẏ refers to the backrest of a seat. This song was made by Q̇iqəxƛalla for Sewidi. When Sewidi danced it, his name was Ẏaq̓əntinux̌ʷilakʷ [Expert Speaker].

Daisy: Why do they refer to feasts as kugʷikila?

That is just how they call them. The name *kugʷikila!* It is a very important name. This refers to the backrest of a seat at a feast. Names like *kugʷikila* and *kakugʷikila.* They refer to the backrests at feasts, the boards you rest your back on. This is how we obtained these names. These names originated from the feasts. Also Ƙʷikilağəmēẏ. There are many names that originated from the backrests of the seats at a feast.[34]

The Blinking Slave Song: Ṗəłəla dʼiyuła

Hi ... wo ... oh
Wo ... oh, wo ... oh
Ahhh, Hi wo oh
Wo ... oh

La muł lax xi laƛ,
They went and

Ƙʷaċud di yax̌i,
Sat him

łuʔəlqʷəłił sa,
In a feast bowl

Dixəła dʼiyuła
He who had big wide eyes,

Ṗəƚala dᶻiyuƚa
He who had big blinking eyes.

X̌ʷəmyala dᶻiyuƚa
This big sniffling man

Niƚəmdᶻoy wuƚ lax̌
Peeking out of

Łuʔəlqʷəliƚ sa
The feast bowl

Čiǧəmaẏ ẏa
Of the chief.

Hi ... wo ... oh
Wo ... oh, wo ... oh
Ahhh, Hi wo oh
Wo ... oh.

That is it. Of course it has many more verses. What I find amusing is that they actually put a slave in a feast bowl and served him to this man. This is what the song says, "peeking out of the feast bowl with his big wide eyes, this big sniffling man." This song refers to the slave as having big blinking eyes. They had served this slave to this man. So this is the song. [ʔAx̌uw̓ is laughing.]

Daisy: Why did they serve the slave to this man?

I guess it was the custom.

Daisy: Was he served to this man so he could eat him?

No! They just gave this slave to this man as a gift. [Big laughter.] Whenever Camağa's father got drunk he would sing this song. Other people sang it just recently. Pəlankidᶻiy [Frank Walker] used to sing it often. I tried to ask Mungo Martin to record this song. "Oh! That is going too far," he said to me, motioning for me to stop. So I thought right away that the man who received the slave had to have been a Kʷaguƚ. [Laughter.] "That is going too far," he said, motioning to me to stop. This was when I asked him to record it on Flora's father's[35] tape recorder ["recorder" said in English].

Baxʷiẏala

Daisy: What do you mean by baxʷiẏala

Bax"iy̓ala is a type of dance used when you don't have a *ćeqa* [Red Cedar-Bark Ceremony]. The dancers would fold their arms inside their blankets and hold them in place with their hands [*k̓ip̓ix̌aɫa*] and dance. They do not hold their hands out [*ƛ̓alq̓"aɫa*]. There would be many women dancing. This was during gift-giving [*y̓aq̓"a*]. The songs do not have words, but just melodies. When the song is sung, people would clap their hands to the beat. This is what is called *bax"iy̓ala*. The women would dance, folding their arms inside their blankets and holding them in place with their hands. They would not wear the cedar-bark headring. All they would wear is their button blankets. Nor would they wear ermine frontlet headdresses. Only certain people could do the *bax"iy̓ala*.

Daisy: Is this during a feast?

No! This is when they give money away. This is when the singers sing when the money is being given away. Then the women, whom the chief wants to honour, dance. This is during the *bax"iy̓ala*. This is what they call *bax"iy̓ala*. The dance for the *m̓ulúlǝm* is similar to the *bax"iy̓ala*. There are three events during which this type of dance is performed. It usually happens when someone has received a gift. The other two events occur when someone *sǝp̓id* [gives a Copper away and then buys it back] and *ẁaẁaɫx̌ilasuẁ*. They would sing to show their appreciation of the dowry being given to the groom by the bride. His relatives would sing. This is what they call *m̓ulúlǝm*.

N̓ǝn̓alalaɫ Song[36]

> *Lax dǝn q̓uq̓ǝma?ēy̓d²ǝms si y̓a,*
> They potlatched for me y̓a
>
> *Ha, y̓a, lax dǝn q̓uq̓ǝma?ēy̓d²ǝms si y̓a,*
> Ha, y̓a, they potlatched for me y̓a,
>
> *Lax dǝn lasta?ēy̓d²ǝms si y̓a,*
> They travelled around the world with me y̓a,
>
> *Ha, y̓a, lax dǝn q̓uq̓ǝma?ēy̓d²ǝms si y̓a,*
> Ha, y̓a, they potlatched for me y̓a,
>
> *Lax dǝn lasta?ēy̓d²ǝms si y̓a,*
> They brought me around the world y̓a,
>
> *Lax dǝn q̓uq̓ǝma?ēy̓d²ǝms si y̓a,*
> They potlatched for me y̓a.

This is the song they sing for the *n̓an̓alalał*. They would just sing short songs for them. This is the song I know that is sung for the *n̓an̓alalał*. Everyone had his own songs. My mother talked about it often. This is our *n̓an̓alalał* among the Q̌ʷiq̌ʷasut̓inux̌ʷ. This dance was once performed by two brothers, Lalakǝnis and Hahikǝńis. I guess Sawigax̌tuw̓ēy̓ is located on a slope. People were absolutely amazed at them when they were dancing on this slope [*xǝkustolayuw̓:* to dance on a slanted hill or board]. My mother often talked about how strong they had to be to perform on a slope [*xǝkustola*] at Sawigax̌tuw̓ēy̓. They were performing on this slanted hill. I guess Sawigax̌tuw̓ēy̓ was a fort [*x̌ʷǝsǝla*].

When a Man Inherits His Father's Position[37]

The son of a chief, who is about to succeed his father, will inform his people when he *saligēy̓* his father, gives a memorial *p̓asa* [potlatch] to honour his father. If the chief had no son, he will take one of his closest relatives to be his heir. They call this *λax̌ʷstud*, to stand in someone's position or *ƛ̓ay̓ud* [to replace someone]. The female [first child if a daughter] will hold the position until a male child is born. Or a male child of one of the chief's female children. If he already has a male grandchild, the grandson will take the position. They always take the eldest son or the eldest grandson. They call this *n̓ulaw̓ēlił* [holding the eldest position]. They would not take the younger son. He is the *n̓ulaw̓ēlił*. This is what they would say when talking about these positions. They would take the eldest son to be chief, *n̓ulasƛ̓aǧamēy̓*.

Ǧǝmy̓asap̓a: Nickname Playing or Play Potlatch

Ǧǝmy̓asap̓a is like a game. We sure had fun playing it. That is why people today have funny names. It is because of the *ǧǝmy̓asap̓a*. Vera [Newman] played it recently. She gave candy away. I guess she really wanted to play it so she came and asked me to help her. She gave candy away. [ʔAx̌uw̓ laughs.]

Daisy: What names did you use during the ǧǝmy̓asap̓a? Name them for me.

We named the singers when we played the *ǧǝmy̓asap̓a*. We sang a song. Mǝmdow̓ [Ethel Alfred] was with us. I announced that Vera was doing this on behalf of all her brothers [*w̓iw̓aq̓ʷa:* cousins]. Bill [Cranmer] announced all the names of the singers. There was a man visiting from ʔAwik̓inux̌ʷ [Rivers Inlet]. We named him Guda [goldeneye duck]. You know that is what the little ducks are called. It comes from one of the legends. This name belongs to the Rivers Inlet people. I named Jim King Sisax̌olas's name, K̓ʷǝm̓a [bullhead]. We named ʔIlaǧa [Emma Beans] W̓ǝnd̓ʸisbalis [deadhead log that floats under water].

[Laughter.] This was her uncle's name. I gave Bobby Joseph Ẏeẏaqux̌alas's name, Hadaṅiẏ. Bobby wanted to know the meaning of Hadaṅiẏ [ʔAx̌uẃ is laughing]. Hadaṅiẏ means *bag"aṅiẏ* [skate]. We named Harry Joseph, Ċasq"aṅa [bird]. It was his father's name. We named him "Bird." [Laughter.] We named Henry George Qəmx̌"aċiẏ [eagle down container]. This was the name of a man among the Nak"axdax̌" who was related to Kitty Ferry. I do not remember who gave Ben Alfred his name. They called him Dəbaqa [tobacco]. [Laughter.] There was a Danaxdax̌" man named X̌"aλaẏuẃ [fish filleting knife]. We gave this name to Jack Peters's son, Giẏaqa. Johnny Moon was named Bək̇"əs. That was his name during the *ğəmẏasaṗa*. You could name someone Qəmdˀək̇" [salmonberry] or Ẏəsxən [plant]. We named Ernest Willie Məssiq" [sea egg]. Məssiq" was a Dˀawadaʔēnux̌" name. This is the name that Vera gave to Ernest Willie. [Laughter.]

My name in the *ğəmẏasaṗa* was Ċax̌ēẏ. This refers to the riptide. I gave it to Lorne [Smith] and he named someone else with it. I think he gave one of his White friends this name. [Laughter.] Ċax̌ēẏ was my name. You can use all kinds of names at the *ğəmẏasaṗa*. Qiqəxƛalla's name was Q̇"əṅiẏ [lupine]. Someone else was called x̌amax̌"əla [large barnacle]. That is it. ƛax̌ƛidˀəmğa's name was Ṁallis, Dˀəṅiẏ's daughter. Ṁallis means salmon weir. It has a really good song and that is what we sang. Her name was Ṁallis.

Daisy: Do they use ṁusṁus [cow] as a name for the ğəmẏasaṗa?

I do not know if they used that name. Millow used to tease the first Nəmğis by calling them that name. He called them *ṁusṁus*.

Daisy: It is written somewhere in Boas's book that some of our people used the name ṁusṁus.

Yes, Ẁataẃ was called Ṁusṁus Tom. He was registered at the Indian office with this name. They used all kinds of names, like Təğ"aċiẏ [octopus container]. Another was called Ġak̇əs [?]. A Nəmğis woman was named x̌osğas [flirt]. [Laughter.] She had a really nice song also. They all had all kinds of different names. Ẏəsxən is a part of the plant ṅək̇"əł [salal berry]. You know they have tiny leaves [ṁaṁaṁa]. This is what you call ẏəsxən. I believe Ṁəmdoẃ's [Ethel Alfred] name is Qəmdˀək̇" [salmonberry].

Daisy: Did the ancient people do this also?

The old people [galuł] did this also. I was part of this as I was growing up. When they were going to have a *ğəmẏasaṗa* [an ochre potlatch] they would instantly *k̇"adək̇"a* – make a song for those who were going to receive a name. ʔOṅat often helped those of us at Ṁiṁk̇"əmlis when we had a ochre potlatch there. Qiqəxƛalla's name was Q̇"əṅiẏ [lupine]. We were having a hard time making her song; then I thought of this visitor who went to Dᶻaẃadiẏ [Knight Inlet] from the Liǧiⱡdax̌ʷ [Cape Mudge and Campbell River]. They fed him q̓ʷəṅiẏ.³⁸ This was at Knight Inlet. He apparently liked it very much. When you eat q̓ʷəṅiẏ, you eat it raw. It has little bumps [ⱡəms?ənala] and you shave them off. This Liǧiⱡdax̌ʷ man really liked it. So I decided to make a song telling this story. I made a song for Q̇iqəxⱡalla.

> *Ya! Gʷaⱡ dᶻos səns sax̌ x̌əns gagelasaⱡ ⱡix̌*
> Hey! Let us stop what we are doing before it kills us

> *La dᶻow ?um məns hiⱡ?aḱəsa*
> We have had enough

This is what this man said that he liked the q̓ʷəṅiẏ so much.

> *"Gagela kas ?uⱡ ⱡax̌ x̌ən,"* he said. [Laughter.]
> The wonderful thing that is going to kill me.

These became the words of the song because Q̇iqəxⱡalla's name was Q̓ʷəṅiẏ. She was Nuladiẏ's [Mrs. Ben Alfred's] aunt. We often listened to the West Coast people sing. I remembered one of their songs so I took the melody for Q̇iqəxⱡalla's song. [?Ax̌uẃ sings:]

Ho	ha	eee	ẏaẏəṅ	ṅa	ah
Ho	eee	ẏaẏən	na	ah	
Ho	eee	ẏaẏən	na	ah	
Ho	eee	ẏaẏən	na	ah	
Gʷaⱡ	dᶻos	səns	ẏaẏən	na	
Let	us	stop	ẏaẏən	na	

x̌əns gagelas kas ?uⱡ ⱡax̌ x̌əns
This wonderful thing that is going to kill us

x̌ux̌ q̓ʷəṅiẏ   dᶻiẏ ẏix̌
This great lupine plant

These became the words to the melody because Q̇iqəxⱡalla's name was Q̓ʷəṅiẏ. I had heard the West Coast people sing this melody. I took it and made a song for Q̇iqəxⱡalla.

Daisy: What does ǧəmẏasapa mean?

It means to give away gifts. People would say, ǧəmẏas?idas suw̓ w̓ən [they gave me a gift]. That is what it means. That is what ǧəmẏasapá means, to give gifts to one another.

About Nobility

There were quite a few noble people in the early days, but I cannot list all their names. I am just going to mention those who were highly respected among the Maṁaliliqəlla. They really respected chiefs Qumalagəlis, Q̓ad̓u, and Hix̌ʷagalas. Hewalakas was highly respected within his own family. I used to hear them talk about their respect for him. G̓ʷułəlas was another one who was very much respected by his people. And also the ancestors of Mənx̌idas [Chief Dawson]. Head chiefs are called ?ug̓ʷəmēẏ, and the highest ranked among them owned the privilege of beginning the Red Cedar-Bark Ceremony [ćeqa] by going through the red cedar-bark ring [qəxa] during the ćeqa. ?Ug̓ʷəmēẏ [meaning up front, head of the descent group] is λax̌ʷəmēẏ, the head chief; xax̌ʷəmēẏ is the family head; and giǧamēẏ is a noble person owning one or more pəsa positions or seats. Not very many people among the Liq̓ʷala tribes[39] had this privilege. Mənx̌idas was the only one at Miṁk̓ʷəmlis. They passed the red cedar-bark ring over Mənx̌idas during the ćeqa. His family then had to pay the witnesses. It was very expensive to hold a ćeqa because the hosts always had to give gifts to their numerous guests.

I recall another important chief among the Nəmǧis. He was Ǧusdid̓as's brother. His name was Ǧa?əx̌talas. I am certain that this was he who brought out the qəxa. Wadəs was another Nəmǧis chief who was respected.

Mud̓ił and K̓idił

K̓idił refers to the daughter of ?ug̓ʷəmēẏ [the chief of the ńəmaẏəm, or descent group]. When she marries an ?ug̓ʷəmēẏ of another ńəmaẏəm, she is to be called mud̓ił, chieftainess. They call those women who are married to ?ug̓ʷəmēẏ, mud̓ił [plural: ṁusṁad̓ił]. They call the eldest daughter of a chief k̓idił [plural: k̓isk̓idił].

Lecturing the Brides

When they held bride lectures[40] they would ask the ṁusṁad̓ił to speak. They would choose one chieftainess from each tribe to speak. They would feed us candy during the haẏaxsəx̌ʷsila [bride lectures]. They would take the ćisk̓ala [tongs] and give them to the K̓ʷaguł first. They would go by their tribal ranking order as they lectured the bride. They would not select those who had troubled marriages. They would select chiefs' wives who had successful marriages. They would lecture the bride on how to achieve a successful marriage. This is what they did.

They would hand-feed the bride in the same way they hand-fed the haṁaċa. They call this hand-feeding gʷaẋstēy̓, or hamanudʔaẋstēy̓. This is what they call it. They would feed the bride with candy. It would be the person sitting beside her that would feed her. I saw this when they did this to Fred Williams's sister when she married Alec. They fed her syrup. This happened when Kʷənxʷaloğʷa gave a bride-lecture gathering for her. Kʷənxʷaloğʷa dipped the biscuit into the syrup as she tried to hand-feed ẋaɬamaẋday̓ugʷa but she turned her head. The syrup dripped down her mouth. She was so young and very shy when she married Alec. [Laughter.]

Why do they feed the brides? They call this practice "gəlq̓asa, the first meal of married life." They are fed first just like the haṁaċa. They would feed the wives candy when they gəlq̓asa [feeding in small quantity]. They call hand-feeding gʷaẋstēy̓. Hay̓axsəxʷsila is to lecture the bride.

The houses of ʔugʷəmēy̓ [head chiefs] were always right at the centre of the village. The people would build on either side of the chief's house. This is where Ḵʷamaẋəlas's house was located, right at the centre. That was the position of the houses in the early days, with the chief's house in the centre. Look at that humiliating song from the Nəmğis, for example. It says: "You live right at the edge of the village." We had really awful songs. "X̌əmbala," the song says: "Clam feeders." People at the edge had only clams to eat. "You live at the edge of the village"; this is what that awful song says.

7

Fragments of Recollections

ʔAx̌uw̓'s long life spans a period of great social and cultural change since the arrival of the first Europeans. This is made more personal through the recollections of her first encounter with some aspects of Western culture. These recollections came in direct response to a series of questions asked by Daisy. They bring to a personal level what it might have been like for a First Nations woman to be introduced to electricity, or to use a washing machine for the first time. We see that some aspects of culture, such as material culture and technology, are somewhat less resistant to change than non-material aspects such as attitudes and beliefs. We hear about conservative and progressive Kʷakʷakəwakʷ attitudes towards potlatching, the Church, and other issues. By talking about things that are gone perhaps forever, such as specific rituals or food ingredients, she also brings into focus how she experienced a sense of loss that is common to the continuing human experience.

Note: What follows is told in the presence of ʔAx̌uw̓'s daughter, Flora, and her husband, James Sewid.

Missionaries
Mr. Hall was a wonderful man [see Plate 18]. You have heard what ʔAnid̓oɫ [Daisy Roberts] used to say about him. He really just became part of the Nəmǧis people. He would go from house to house having meals with the people. It is said that he first went to Cax̌is [Fort Rupert].[1] I do not know too much about it, but I guess he went way up north first and then he came to Fort Rupert. I was told that he was treated very badly at Cax̌is. The Cax̌is people tried to beat him up, and he fled to Alert Bay.

They said that ʔAdag̱amēy̓ tried to use an axe on him. This was Peter Edward. This is how the Reverend Hall came to Alert Bay. Mr. Hall composed a song "*ƛina ʌuv̓x̌əmasa*" [eulachon oil and brittle, dried fish song]. The people would sing it at feasts (*k̓ʷilas*) even if there were only six people. I guess he attended these feasts often. He always mingled with the Nəmǧis people.

[ʔAx̌uw̓ sings a song to the tune of "Are You Sleeping Brother John?":][2]

> *Ǧila ga həmx̌ʔid, Ǧila ga həmx̌ʔid*
> Do come and eat, do come and eat
>
> *ƛina ʌuv̓x̌əmasa, ƛina ʌuv̓x̌əmasa*
> Grease and dried fish, grease and dried fish
>
> *Ǧila ga, Ǧila ga,*
> Do come, do come,
>
> *La mi ƛəmsʔid, La mi ƛəmsʔid*
> It is ringing, it is ringing
>
> *ƛina ʌuv̓x̌əmasa, ƛina ʌuv̓x̌əmasa*
> Grease and dried fish, grease and dried fish

"Bacon and potatoes" [said in English], he would say. [Laughter.] This is what he would sing.

You know how the Church is always looking for converts. That is why he used "*ǧila ga*" [do come]. Then you have "*La mi ƛəmsʔid*" [it is ringing]. The church rings its bell to call us. That is the meaning of that song. That is why Mr. Hall sang "*ƛina ʌuv̓x̌əma*sa." He was a wonderful man. They say that the smoke in the big traditional houses really bothered him. All the big traditional houses were very smoky.

I saw him when he left Alert Bay. Alvin was my baby. He came to our house at Yəlis to say goodbye to us. This was at the house of Q̓ʷəmxuduw̓. He came to say goodbye before he sailed away. His wife was our teacher when we went to school. That is, when I attempted to go to school.

He went back to England. He came and sat by our fire [*k̓ʷabix̌ʌala*]. Tears were running down his face because the smoke really bothered him. Some of the houses were really smoky, and that bothered him a lot. He always went visiting from house to house. You know already the story of his building a sawmill at Alert Bay.[3] He built a sawmill so the Nəmǧis people would have employment.

Yes, he was in Alert Bay for a long time. During that time the Nəmǧis were really united [*ṅəmak̓ała*]. The Nəmǧis would fill the church. They would attend church wrapped in their blankets. The whole Nəmǧis village would go to church, as well as the visitors who came to town. The church was always filled to capacity. It has been only recently since the people stopped going to church, because they have turned away from the church's teachings. The Nəmǧis never ever missed going to church. Mr. Corker [Norman Corker's father] had a movie projector to show movies. He would go from house to house with his projector. He often showed movies at the big traditional house that stood where we later built our big modern house. He had a projector and he would show movies in the big community houses, going from house to house. It was Mr. Corker I saw doing this, not Mr. Hall.

Yes, Mr. Corker came after Mr. Hall. Many missionaries came after Mr. Hall. I just remember MacCumlliy. He was a minister who came later. Many ministers came later.

Daisy: Did you get converted to Christianity right away?

Yes. You just reminded me of something. I had a cape, that kind of garment that you call a cape. It was lined with this red material. Ćaćabalagilak͆ʷ made it for me. She was a big woman. She was married to a White man. Her name was Ćaćabalagilak͆ʷ. My mother had bought the material so she could make a cape for me to go to church. This was when I was a child. I would attend church regularly. I was converted to Christianity when I was very young but I did not get baptized until after I was married. I was married to grandpa⁴ when I was baptized. It was my sister [Florence Knox] who wanted me to get baptized. She arranged it with Mr. Hall.

Hawkins Sells ʔUg͆ʷitəmalis, the Land at Alert Bay

On Sundays we would go for a walk to ʔUg͆ʷitəmalis, what is now the European end of Alert Bay. They called our Sunday walks *sasəndiẏaxsa* [walking around on Sunday]. There was a man by the name of Hawkins who lived on the beach at ʔUg͆ʷitəmalis. They said that he put a fence around that area of Alert Bay and he apparently sold all this land. The whole foreshore of this area of Alert Bay was fenced [q̓əlax̌ək͆ʷ]. It had been fenced by this man who was named Hawkins.

Daisy: Why was it fenced?

He was claiming it as his own [ǧuɬʔid]. He was the only one living there other than the man they called Spencer.

Daisy: Are you talking about where the Europeans live now?

It was right at the end of the island [*makitəmalis*]. This was where Hawkins lived, and he fenced that area along the foreshore. It was fenced. The fence that Hawkins put up was horizontal [ǧiǧəẏaɬa]. Hawkins was a White man married to a First Nations woman by the name of Ċiⱡwalağa. She was a devout Christian. Whenever she went to church she would travel by canoe because she lived at the other end of the island with this White man by the name of Hawkins. They had a child, but he died. There was a graveyard behind their house and a totem pole was standing in that graveyard. This is where she buried their child. This woman went by the name of Ċiⱡwalağa.

I Dye My Hair

When I first started to turn grey I heard about this solution that turns your hair dark again. ʔⱡlağa [Emma Beans] ordered it for me. ʔⱡlağa ordered two bottles. When it arrived she put it on my hair. She used a toothbrush to apply the colour to my hair. She would grasp locks of my hair and brush them with the solution. I became irritated because the process was too slow. I took the bottle away from her and decided to apply it to my hair as you would hair oil. When we applied hair oil we would pour it in the palms of our hands, rub our hands together, and then apply it to our hair. I took the hair dye and poured it in the palm of my hand, rubbed my hands together, and applied it to my hair. Nothing happened to my hand. So I took the other bottle and poured it on my hand. My hand turned black. I did not know that the contents of two bottles were supposed to be poured together to make the hair dye. The palms of my hands were black. I guess this is what was supposed to happen when you poured the two solutions together. For days I kept my palms down trying to conceal their blackness. This is what happened when I tried to dye my hair black. This is what ʔⱡlağa and I did.

I Curl My Hair

When I was a little girl I was watching some of the women curling their hair. We decided to copy them. We would take the thimbleberry [cəğaⱡ] sticks that they used for barbecuing clams, and we would use them to curl our hair. We would stick the thimbleberry sticks in the dirt floor beside the fire to heat them. When they were hot we would use them to curl our hair. Our hair did curl a little. That is what we did.

When I got older I actually got myself a metal curling iron. I saw curling irons plugged into electrical outlets attached to the electric ceiling lights and they would get hot. I plugged my curling iron into the electric outlet. I reached for the curling iron to curl my hair. The curling iron swung and hit me on the forehead. A whitish scorch mark [ƙaməlxʔid məlkatała] appeared on my forehead. It took months to heal. That is what happened when I decided to copy those who curled their hair.

I Fear Inoculation
I did so many foolish things. I always had a fear of doctors. They came to Yəlis to *kusa* [to scrape; to inoculate] the people. I had children then. I did not like the idea of my children and myself being scraped. I packed my things together [x̌ʷanałʔid] and went across to the Nimpkish River to hide. I took my clothes to wash them in the Nimpkish River, but in reality I was hiding from those who were scraping the people. At that time I was so ignorant[5] about scraping. I did not realize then that it was a good thing. Flora and her younger siblings [ćaćiẏa] were just small children. We went to the Nimpkish River to hide because I did not want to be scraped.

My First Baby Buggy
Oh! I was ever so foolish [nułəmała]! Flora's father tried to buy me a baby buggy. It was for one of Flora's younger siblings. It was high off the ground [ʔik̓agəlsəla]. Apparently this type of baby buggy was very expensive. It had large wheels and it stood high off the ground. Oh! I did not like it [ẏaxmuta] either. I stored it at the empty big house because by this time we were living in our cabin. I did not like it because it looked so dreadful [ẇənẇənxəs]. It had very large wheels and it was so high off the ground. Ẏeqawilas ended up buying it from us. I did not like it. Again it was because I was so ignorant about such matters. I never used it once.

Daisy: When you took your baby for a walk, what did you use?

We would have our shawls on. We would wrap and tie the baby against our bosoms. Now you have reminded me of something else. When Nuladiẏ [Mrs. Ben Alfred] and I went to church we would pack our babies in this manner. She had a baby the same time as I did. We wore our shawls. We would never think of leaving our babies at home [ʔəmlixʷ] the way they do today. Our children went along everywhere with us.

One day we were in church. I was so afraid of cows [mimusmus]. I was so foolish. [Laughter.] There were many cows in Yəlis. There were trees growing around the church [k̓ʷax̌əlg̓ʷis]. There was a cluster of alder trees [ƛaq̓ʷməs d̓ək̓əlla] in front of the church. Nuladiẏ and I came out of the church. We saw a cow among the alder trees. George was my baby, and I was packing him. ʔAd̓zidiẏ was Nuladiẏ's baby at the time. By that time we had small baby buggies that we pushed. I had seen the cow when we came out of the church, so all my attention [nəmig̓amała] was on this cow. I did not realize one of my breasts was hanging out of my dress. [Laughter.] "Hey! Your breast," Nuladiẏ yelled at me. Oh, my! How we laughed! My breast must have been exposed [d̓amasəla] in church. This is what happened to us. This was because I was frightened to death [kałkən] over that cow and my attention was not on anything else [n̓amip̓a̓ła] but the cow among the alder trees. [Laughter.] This is what happened.

My Washing Machine

I was using one of the modern washing machines. Modiẏ [Moses Alfred's sister, Maud] was visiting me. She was changing my baby's diapers [k̓əlgax̌stəndala]. I must have put too many clothes in the washing machine because it started shaking violently. It was swaying back and forth [łelela]. I ran over to the washing machine to pull the plug out of the electrical outlet. I never thought of just turning the washing machine switch off. Before I could reach the electrical outlet my washing machine toppled over. The wringer rollers were scattered all over the floor. [Laughter.] I heard someone running towards the house. "Lock the door," I yelled at Modiẏ. I knew someone was going to come and see what had happened [ʔołcəmēẏ]. All the children came in, including Dadax̌alis [Ben Alfred]. So we reluctantly opened the door for them. Dadax̌alis picked up the wringer rollers that were scattered around the floor and put them back together again [ʔaẏatux̌ʷʔid]. That was one of the foolish things I did.

My Mother and My Aunt (Mother's Sister) Wash at the River

We used to wash our clothes in the river. I watched Wikəlalisəmēẏǧa and my mother beat their clothes with a stick when they washed their clothes. They would sit beside the river and beat their clothes with a stick. I guess it did actually remove the dirt. We would sit by the river and wash our clothes. When she checked the clothes she found many holes all over them. [Laughter.] Rocks are not good to use against clothes. When ꞌAnita used a rock it caused holes in the clothes. [Laughter.] That is what happened.

They did not have soap [ćuǧʷaẏuẇ] to wash their clothes with. They used to use urine to wash their hair. You must remember that in earlier times they did not use European clothing. Of course, when I was a child, European soap was in use.

Urine Shampoo

The old people told me about these shrivelled up, very old people at Mimk̓ʷəmlis who washed their hair with urine [depending on the context, k̓əlgʷa: male urine; ʔəssa: female urine].They would sit in the ocean and rinse themselves off with ocean water. They would sit in the ocean up to their necks at dᶻaqʷstuẇ [evening]. Urine must have actually worked to take all the dirt out of their hair. [Laughter.] I heard this from the old people. They would have boxes outside the front door to store urine. I saw Ẏaq̓ałꞋənala do this. Later they cut European barrels in half to store their urine. When they came out they would urinate in these barrels.

[Laughter.] I suppose they poured it out when the barrels got full. Our house had one of these urine barrels. It belonged to Ýaq̓at̓ənala. This is what I saw at Mim̓k̫əmlis.

Names of the Waters of the Mam̓aliliqəlla

There was our stream near Dᶻad̓ᶻawaxsila [a place to set fish traps]. My father made the pond. We had a boardwalk [paɫa] from the back of our house to the pond. The pond had a little roof covering [sisǧəms]. The pond was called *Sisayuɫ* [double-headed serpent]. That is what our water pond was called.

Behind the house Hanuse had built was a well called ƛ̓ug̫éy̓ [Fortunate]. I guess they dug a well behind their house.

Beside Sam's [Sam Charlie's] house was a stream called ƛaq̓ʷaq̓ʷaxstəls [Copper Stream]. It was a stream. I guess it started somewhere in the forest and it flowed down beside Sam's house. ƛaƛ̓utilak̫ dug a well near where Miss O'Brian's house was built. It was really good water. It was so clear. This was the well that they called ƛ̓ug̫éy̓. There was ƛaq̓ʷaq̓ʷaxstəls, *Sisayuɫ*, and ƛ̓ug̫éy̓. These were the waters of the Mam̓aliliqəlla.

Things I Ate

There was a place at one end of Mim̓k̫əmlis called Q̓ʷisbala [On the Far End] where the men used to play. There was a field [ʔigamənk̫ᶻəs] at this end of the village. We called it Q̓ʷisbala. It was a clearing away from the village near where Miss O'Brian built her house. We would go there to pick wild strawberries. There were many strawberries to find and pick [lita]. That was the reason we went there. That is where the men played baseball, men like Haʔēλek̫ [Charlie Dick], ƛaƛ̓əɫawis, and an older man by the name of ƛaquλəlas. They were playing there. I guess this was their playground [ʔəmlid̓əs]. It was a field. I suppose it is all overgrown now. It was covered with plenty of strawberries and that was the reason we went there. We played there. It was covered with moss [p̓əliẍəlk̫ᶻəs].

Daisy: When did you put grease in syrup?

Yes, that is what we did. We would take eulachon grease [ƛ̓ina] and pour it into the syrup [salap] and stir it together. It was ʔAdəwis [Lucy Brown] who really enjoyed it [ʔiʔatənx̫ᶻaɫa]. We would mix the syrup with the grease and dip [ćapa] into it. It really tasted good. We would stir the grease and the syrup together. This is what we did.

I also ate ćićadanuʎ⁶ [barley]. I just loved it. I have been trying to get some but I still have not got anyone to get it for me. I guess they feed it to the chickens. It is really good but you have to cook it for a long time [ǧixƛala]. I always ate it at the home of Ǧaʔəẍtalas [Jane Cook]. Łax̫ᶻaɫa [Lucy Sewid] always fed it to me also. It is like beans; it takes a long time to cook. The foodstuff that they call *ćićədanuu̓* is really tiny.

When it snowed, we ate snow. I saw our grandfather Ẏaq̓aⱡʔənala [ʔOlsiwidi] do this.[7] We call it *ńax̌stənd*. We would get snow for Ẏaq̓aⱡʔənala and he would pour eulachon grease in it. He would mix the grease into the snow with his hands. The snow would harden. That is what they ate. They would add sugar to the mixture. They would have feasts and they would serve it to their guests. They would refer to this kind of feast *ńińax̌staʔak̓ʷ*. This was the ice-cream of the early days. They would also use this to oil the inside of a feast bowl.

Widows Marrying Their Brothers-in-Law[8]

When a man dies his brother will marry his widow. We call this *k̓ʷalus*. I just found out that this is what happened to ⱡilinux̌ʷ. She has now passed away. Her brother-in-law was called ⱡaquⱡas. He was a huge man. I always thought that the children belonged to her husband but apparently the father was the brother-in-law. I just learned of this recently.

Pole Used for Insulting Someone

"Ḱeẏuw̓eẏ gən," "They made a pole for me," they would say. This was done when a person had insulted another person. I saw this happen once but I am not going to mention any names. This happened at Yəlis. I guess his wife did something to him. It was the custom that the wife and the children of the host of a feast eat last, after everyone else has eaten. The husband would then feed his wife and children. This is what you call *w̓aw̓aqilayuu̓*. I guess this man had fed his wife and children with biscuits after his feast. When his wife left him he commissioned a pole and tied a biscuit around the pole's neck, and he pulled the pole up and down the streets of Yəlis. As he was pulling the pole he was hurling insults at it. The reason he was doing this was because his wife had left him. He commissioned the carving of this pole and he dragged it up and down the streets of Yəlis.

Daisy: Who was represented by the figure on the pole? Himself, or his wife?

The carved pole enables people to work out their frustrations by talking to it [*nixdəmanuk̓ʷ*]. The pole with the biscuit hanging around its neck represented his wife and he was hurling insults at it to work out his frustration and anger towards his wife. This is what they did in earlier times if they wanted to hurl insults at someone.

Daisy: Do they always drag the pole up and down the street?

No. That was the only time I saw this. They usually just stand in front of the carved pole and hurl insults at it. They call these poles k̓ik̓ēy̓ [carved poles]. They are small poles. We had one of these poles in our house. You would use it to work out your frustrations. I saw people do this.

More about Potlatches and Feasts
We are going to talk about the names of the p̓asap̓a [potlatches]. Max̌ʷa is when you have a big potlatch. All the tribes of the nation are involved. This is when you can say "c̓ex̌ʷʔid dən, Lix̌c̓oy̓ gən ƛ̓aǧəkʷix," "I had a Red Cedar-Bark Ceremony. My red cedar-bark ring is wide." This is what the chief says as he speaks. If you have not potlatched to all the tribes at the same time you cannot refer to your cedar-bark ring as being wide. You cannot say Lix̌c̓oy̓ gən ƛ̓aǧəkʷix if you have potlatched to only a few tribes.

Then there is the expression "ʔusǧəm dən ƛax̌ x̌a Dᶻawadaʔēnux̌ʷ," "I pot-latched only to the Dᶻawadaʔēnux̌ʷ." This is what they call ʔusǧəm.

When you p̓asa only to your own tribe, ƛ̓ənsila [exclusively] and ʔussila [solely] are the two words they use. Another term is ʔalaʔēɫ, "you do not receive a gift[9] because your tribe is giving the gifts." If the Mam̓aliliqəlla are the hosting tribe and they give gifts away, then you do not receive a gift. You do not receive a gift if your tribe is the one giving the gifts away. They would give to all the other tribes. Because you belong to the hosting tribe and you are not going to receive a gift, you are referred to as ʔalaʔēɫ. Sometimes arguments broke out during a p̓asa. K̓ʷənx̌stuw̓ [wet eyes] one would say to the other. This is during a p̓asa, and this is when two chiefs are arguing. One of them would say, "ʔo ʔum meɫ gən k̓ʷənx̌stuw ƛa," "I shall have wet eyes."

When a tribe invites another tribe and the guest tribe leaves the same day to go back to its village, then the guest tribe would say, "ʔo ʔum ƛal ləns sisay̓uw̓atəla," "we are going to hold on to our paddles." The feast is referred to as sisay̓uw̓atəla [holding paddles]. This is because they are not going to stay very long. Həmdᶻidiy̓ [Rachel Bell Whonnock] mentioned this one time. She was talking about the first ancestral chief [giqagiw̓ēy̓] in her family, Max̌ʷayalisdᶻiy̓. He had invited the tribes. All his guests [ƛitəlakʷ] had rifles propped up behind their chairs. They call this gulala. It means that they were afraid of one another. Max̌ʷayalisdᶻiy̓ invited the tribes so that they would get to know one another. He wanted them to make peace with one another.

Daisy: Where did this happen?

His name was Max̌ʷayalisdᶻiy̓ at Mim̓kʷəmlis. I heard Həmdᶻidiy̓ [Rachel Bell Whonnock] when she spoke at Haʔeλəkʷ's p̓asa.[10] They had guns behind their chairs. He wanted everyone to make peace with one another. They often had wars [*wiwanapa*] with one another. He invited them so they would get to know one another.

This incident occurred quite recently. The father of Ǧamadˀiẏ [Moses Alfred's mother's half-brother] invited the Maṁaliliqəlla to Cax̌is. He used the feast to conceal his true intentions because he had plotted [kʷix̌eẏ] against the Maṁaliliqəlla. The Maṁaliliqəlla went to Cax̌is to attend the feast.

Daisy: Who plotted against the Maṁaliliqəlla?

He was apparently the father of Ǧamadˀiẏ. He was Hiłdˀuqʷ [Bella Bella].[11] Miṁkʷəmlis was fortified. They just had holes in the walls for shooting. It was completely fortified, and all of Miṁkʷəmlis was covered with crushed clamshells *q̓əbilis* so that they could see anyone waking around at night. When the men left for the feast in Cax̌is the Hiłdˀuqʷ warriors tried a sneak attack [*wənigeẏ*] on Miṁkʷəmlis. Only one man remained in Miṁkʷəmlis. The rest were women.

Daisy: The people who tried to attack us were Hiłdˀuqʷ.

Yes, they were Hiłdˀuqʷ. The peoples from Miṁkʷəmlis found out that these warriors were sneaking in to kill them. All of those who remained in the fortified Miṁkʷəmlis were the women, because the men had left for Cax̌is to attend the feast. The women quickly dressed themselves up as men. They tied their hair in ponytails [*ċiċidˀəx̌ƛela*]. I guess the men wore ponytails in the earlier days. They tied their hair in a knot at the back of their head, and they let their hair hang down. This must have happened at night because the women had fire tongs [*ċisƛala*] over their shoulders so that the enemy would think they had guns. They would show themselves every now and then to the enemy. The enemy thought that there were many men inside the fort. One of the women managed to sneak away and paddled to Cax̌is to tell the Maṁaliliqəlla what was happening, to tell them that the Hiłdˀuqʷ were sneaking their way to Miṁkʷəmlis with the intention of attacking them. Apparently it was not that long ago. ˀAssuẇ always talked about it. The Maṁaliliqəlla left Cax̌is, and they were in a rage when they heard the news. The men arrived at Miṁkʷəmlis before the Hiłdˀuqʷ were able to attack. The men came home immediately after hearing the news. I never did find out why the father of Ǧamadˀiẏ did this. He was the one who invited all the men to Cax̌is so that the Hiłdˀuqʷ could slaughter the Maṁaliliqəlla women. I suppose he had a reason, but I never did find out. All the tribes had wars with one another in the early days.

Pəx̌əla: Shamans

Daisy: Do shamans disappear into the forest like other initiates?

No. Those who disappear [xəs?id] into the forest are the dancers of the ċeqa [Red Cedar-Bark Ceremony]. They do call some people pəx̌əla.[12] Our language is so confusing sometimes. There are some people called ǧix̌sigēy. They have not been initiated into the ċeqa. They just sat outside the big house because they have not yet become shamans. They say that they wore kadᵊək̓ʷ [undyed cedar bark]. I guess this was a long time ago. They had not become shamans yet. Then, when they are initiated they are referred to as pəx̌əla. Is this what you were asking about? The real shamans had a supernatural encounter – the real shamans. Also people who had experienced a miraculous healing [?ikilak̓ʷ] could become shamans. K̓emmax̌əllas, the wife of Monak̓ʷəla was a shaman. They always sang for her. By this time I had left Mimk̓ʷəmlis. She had a very good song. x̓iłəs [Jack Peters] knows it. She is one person I know who became a shaman because she was miraculously healed. Also Wex̓a's [Mrs. Alfred Dawson's] mother. She was also miraculously healed. She was just skin and bones before she was miraculously healed.

Daisy: What does the pəx̌əla *do?*

Well, I know the men do a lot of chanting. I do not know if the women do this. Wex̓a's mother lived for many years after her miraculous healing. I saw her when she was so sick.

Daisy: Do shamans work on the sick?

They are usually summoned. These are the male shamans. I know of the men but don't know about the women. They call the men to suck [k̓əx̌ʷa] their sickness away. I really believed in this at one time. I was so afraid of the shamans. They would bring a round bowl into the big house. This was the shaman's k̓awaċiy̓ [container] where he would spit what he sucked out of the person, who was ill. We would all sit around him [k̓ʷᵊsimił].

He would suck certain parts of the body, blow at it, and chant. Then he would make a noise as though he were about to vomit. He would quickly cover his mouth with his hands. He would make a loud vomiting sound and grasp something in his hands from his mouth. The shaman we were watching was a man. We would sit there in silence, watching him. I just forgot his name. Mr. Hunt did this too. He would suck the bodies of sick people. He would chant, grasp the sickness, and cast it out to get rid of it. He would shake the sickness into the tub of water [max̌ʷᵊltən] with his hands after he vomited it. The k̓awaċiy̓ was like a basin. It was filled with water. He would grasp the sickness in his hands and shake it into the water. He could chant for a long time, then he would cast the sickness out to get rid of it. I truly believed it in those days. [Laughter.]

He would just blow on the body with his mouth [*hamax̌stala*]. They call this blowing. If someone fainted he would blow on the person's head [*pux̌ʷəx̌ƛela*]. They actually started to breathe again. He would blow on top of the head or the area of the heart. This is what I saw. I saw medicine women do this; they were not shamans. If someone fainted these women would blow on that person.

We had women shamans, but all they did was chant. Qəlx̌ʷʔaneẏ was a woman shaman. Some shamans knew how to attend a breech birth [*hiƛalisəla*]. They would examine the baby's position [*p̓ix̌ʷa*]. There was a woman by the name of Ċik̓ʷa [Seagull]. She chanted when she was attending a breech birth. They must have had knowledge of our inside organs. This is what I know. The Ligiłdax̌ʷ had many of these shamans. They were women. All their chants talked about God. I once knew my girlfriend's [ʔeǧas] chant. She was the granddaughter of ƛənak̓ʷəla. We would watch and listen to her grandmother chanting. We would sit there very quietly.

> *Sisababuẇ lisəla yuwwax dən*
> He brought me into this great light

They are talking about our God [*Giǧameẏ*], who brought them into this great light. This is what my girlfriend's grandmother sang. I knew it at one time but now I have forgotten it. X̌ʷabeẏ was one of them. She was the mother of Ṅuṅuẇ [Mrs. James Knox]. She always chanted. They said she was a shaman. *Sisababuẇ lisəla yuwwax dən* means he brought me into this great light. They are talking about God. All the chants of the Lig̓ʷiłdax̌ʷ women talked about God. Many of them were shamans. I don't remember anyone from Miṁk̓ʷəmlis.

Daisy: Did the shamans also practise witchcraft?

Oh, no! Witchcraft was practised by ordinary men.

Daisy: That is what I wanted to know.

Oh, no! Not at all. People always gave us the sorcerers' names so we would know who they were. I heard people talking about them when I was a child. It was such a horrible practice. This practice was carried on until recently. They said that is how ƛaləbəx̌ʷʔalagəlis killed my father.

They found whatever he was using on my father at G̓ʷax̌ƛalla. He was killed because of the p̓əsa rankings. He died. They said they found the witchcraft bundle where my father harvested fish at G̓ʷax̌ƛalla. It has not been long since my father died.

Daisy: Do you know anything about grandpa Moses's mother being a victim of witchcraft?

Yes. She was married to a much older man [q̓əýanas].¹³ Nulaǧa [ʔAx̌uw̓'s half-sister, Florence Knox] was related to him.¹⁴ He was ʔAǧadiẏ's brother. Q̓acuǧow [Margaret Alfred] married him when she was just a young girl. They bewitched her when she was married to this old man. This old man's sister, ʔAǧadiẏ, would ask her if she could come over for a visit to sew with her, and to comb her hair. ʔAǧadiẏ had been instructed to do this to Q̓acuǧow. Q̓acuǧow took ill. She was dying. When it was windy she would toss and turn with pain. This was when it was windy because they found out later that the witchcraft bundle was hanging from a tree. A little spruce tree at the far end of Yəlis at the ʔUx̌ʷλalis.¹⁵ When it was windy, the tree would toss back and forth. Q̓acuǧow would get very sick when the skull inside the witchcraft bundle was swinging back and forth. This was what the sorcerer Łaqanuw̓ used against her. People were talking about Q̓acuǧow. They sensed her sickness was related to witchcraft. Q̓acuǧow's uncle, ʔAmawiyus, stood up and spoke to the people outside. He told the people that at the very moment his niece would close her eyes in death he would avenge her death by taking someone's life for her life [həǧʷəmgila].¹⁶ He said this as he was talking to the people. When the people dispersed, this man came back and said he had found the witchcraft bundle. The people suspected that he was involved with those who were bewitching Q̓acuǧow. They said that this man became frightened when Q̓acuǧow's uncle ʔAmawiyus threatened that someone would die the moment Q̓acuǧow died. They found the witchcraft bundle hanging from a tree with a skull dangling from it. It was a small spruce tree close to the beach. Q̓acuǧow took really ill when the wind blew. They unravelled the bundle. When they showed it to Q̓acuǧow, she recognized the pieces of material that she used during her sewing. These were taken when ʔAǧadiẏ was sewing with her. They found her chewing gum inside the skull. They had put the witchcraft bundle inside the skull. This is what was causing her illness. She was just a young girl when this happened.

Daisy: Was it her husband who did that?

It was this old man to whom she was married who did that to her. My mother was also a victim of witchcraft by a man by the name of Ǧaduw̓. She was apparently married to him when she was a young girl. My mother told me about it. Ǧaduw̓ was the father of λeλagəmēẏ. Ǧaduw̓ was an old man and my mother did not like him. When they found the witchcraft bundle they discovered her menstruating pad wrapped around a stick with a snake wrapped around them. The snake was dead when they found it. She left this man right away, this old man to whom she was married. Perhaps he was not that old because I have seen this man called Ǧaduw̓. I think this is when she left and went to Vancouver.

Daisy: Do you know anyone else who was victim of witchcraft?

No. Just N̓əgéy̓ [Mountain]. He told me someone did that to him.

There is another type of witchcraft. It is called witchcraft by heat [ćalq̌ʷasuw̓]. They would take a steel rod [dᶻəxʔən] and heat it. They would get the victim to take this rod out of the fire and throw it with great force into a corner of the big house. Whoever would throw it would drop dead. I heard Qumey̓ talking about this. A woman was barbecuing fish across from Yəlis. She was barbecuing sockeye [m̓əɬik]. There were several old men watching her, and they really wanted some of that fish. They sent some of the men to ask her for a feed of sockeye. The woman refused to give them any of the fish. The old men got very angry and sent still another man to get one of the bracing sticks she used on the fish. Women had the habit of biting pieces from their bracing stick if it was too thick. The men were really angry with her. Waća?ow̓ told me this story. She fell dead right beside her barbecued fish. The men practised witchcraft on this woman. She fell dead right beside her barbecued fish. The men bewitched her because she refused to feed them. It happened across from Yəlis at the Nimpkish River. I guess it was at ʔUdᶻolas.[17]

?Iməs: Symbolic Representation of a High-Rank Deceased Person[18]

This is during a memorial p̓əsa that you would see an ?iməs. Not everyone would have the privilege of using an ?iməs. Only certain people. I saw it when they did it for K̓ʷamax̌əlas. It was at G̓ʷayasdəms. A Killer Whale came into the big house. An Eagle came down and grasped the Killer Whale and took it out through the smoke-hole.

Daisy: What other type of ?iməs is there?

Sometimes the ?iməs is a mask of the deceased person. If he was a hamaća in his lifetime, he would come back as a hamaća. The speaker announces that he is the same in death as he was in life. If he was a hamaća, they announce that he is returning as a hamaća.

Another type of ?iməs that is used is Qumug̓ʷēy̓ [Lord of the Sea]. This is what I saw as I was growing up. The ?iməs wear masks including the hamaća ?iməs. When they come into the big house the attendants would spread mountain goat fur on the floor for the ?iməs to step on. The ?iməs would dance as the singers sing softly. When the ?iməs comes in they spread mountain goat fur on the ground for the ?iməs to step on. Just like what they do for the queen.[19] Then they would give the mountain goat furs away, one pelt to each chief. The ?iməs who appears is the being who appeared to his ancestor after the Flood [Nuy̓əmagiwēy̓]. The ?iməs always wear a mask. When the ?iməs came in, the family members always broke down in tears. I saw the ?iməs many times.

Daisy: What do the attendants say when the ?iməs first appear?

The attendants would announce that the person has come back just to see his family one more time [*duq̌ʷğuⅈⅉuⅈ*] – that he is the same during death as he was in life. I suppose they are referring to the supernatural side of him. This is what they say when the *ʔimǝs* comes in. I saw an *ʔimǝs* using the mask of Q̇umugʷēy̓. They would use whatever being that appeared to them after the Flood. The *ʔiƙǝxsoⅈ*, the Eagle coming down to grasp the Killer Whale, must have been the symbolic representation of the deceased's ancestral story of his origin.

I Lived in a Tent and Dried Fish

The people who went to Vancouver stayed in tents. They did not go to hotels as we do now. They would live in tents at the far end of Vancouver at a place called "Union." The people would live in tents at the foot of Union Street ["Union Street" said in English]. Above them the trains would be travelling. The people would live in tents when they went to Vancouver. They did not go to hotels then. We also lived in tents when we went to D̓aⅈadiy̓ [Knight Inlet]. We lived in a tent. There were not that many people who lived in houses. A few people did have houses. They were like smokehouses with a shelter covering them. We would go there to dry *ćǝmdaq* [dried, hard eulachon] and we lived in a tent. These are the things I have seen. I was only told about how they made grease in the very early times; I did not experience it myself. They used what they call *ƙǝmy̓aх̌ƛa* [a large grease container]. They would toss [*haх̌ʷƛala*] rocks into the fire and pour water into the grease containers; then they would pour the eulachon into the water. This is what they call *sǝmka* [boiling out the grease]. They used these huge containers called *ƙǝmy̓aх̌ƛa* after the Europeans came. This was when they could obtain what they call *d̓ǝgad̓uⅈ* [tin].

Working at the Cannery

We would hear the Chinese working all night. They had a machine that made lids and they had to peddle it. They had to peddle it, and we heard that noise all night. They would make lids all night long. They were making lids for the fish that were going to be canned. They would throw the rejected lids off the wharf in Alert Bay. These were the rejected lids. There were many of these rejected lids under the cannery in Alert Bay. This is what they did in the early days. It was so different in those days. Now everything is so easy. [See Plate 20.]

There were many Chinese people working in the canneries. I was filleting fish. We would bring our baskets, so they would put the fish heads in them for us to take home. Also fish tails. I started working when I was still a child. They paid me ten cents an hour. I put cans out for filling and then put them into boxes after they were filled. They paid me ten cents an hour when I worked at the cannery. I received a raise every year as I was growing up. I was washing fish, and they raised my wages to twenty cents an hour. I was transferred to a person named MacTavis. We weighed the fish, and I was now paid twenty-five cents an hour. We had scales to weigh the fish. We set aside the small fish. This is what we did at the cannery. When they were canning fish, I was making twenty-five cents an hour. My wages were a little more than before. That was when I was a child. We put tin lids on the cans; we would cover the cans with tin lids. The Chinese painted the cans. I don't know why they did this. They would paint them after they had been sealed. The can sealers did not come until later. We could hear the Chinese working all night. There was a machine that made lids and they had to peddle it. And this is the noise we would hear all night long.

Food Is Expensive

I am going to talk about all the things I have seen in my lifetime. I was born at M̓irhk̓ʷəmlis. They say this is where I was born. When I was younger we did not eat the food we eat now. This was during the earlier days. The only new things we ate were rice, also flour balls [*məx̌ʷstaʔakʷ*] and beans. They added sugar to the beans. We did not know that we were not supposed to do this. We did not know that we were supposed to add bacon [she says "bacon" in English]. In spite of all this, we liked the beans with the sugar in it. At first I did not eat the food we eat now. I ate the food of the old days, like *ƚəx̌ʷsus* [clover root], *ƛaxsəm* [cinquefoil root], *cakus* [fern root]. The only thing I did not eat was what they call *sag̓ʷəm* [bracken fern root]. I never saw it. I knew how to prepare these foods – the old foods that we no longer eat, such as *loq* [hemlock sap] and *xuk̓ʷəm* [lily bulbs]. These are the foods I ate as a child. Food was not as expensive then; it costs so much today. The pilot biscuits used to cost only two dollars a box when they first came out. It cost only two dollars for a large box. It is extremely expensive now. We would eat pilot biscuits, and we would bake bread. They would build up the fire and the bread would look so nice when you *kanolisa* [put beside the fire] the pans. You would put the bread in the pans and put it beside the fire. We would take it out and keep turning it, browning it on each side. The women of the early days were good bakers in spite of the fact that baking bread was a newly acquired practice.

The period we are living in is so hard. Food is so expensive now. At one time we had enough money for everything. In the early days the men who went fishing up north made only one hundred dollars. It was not very much. This fish camp paid them only ten cents a pound but it was enough to carry us through until the following fishing season. This was when I was a child. Food is now so expensive. That is why I mentioned the boxes of pilot biscuits. I had saved one

of these boxes. They were large boxes that cost only two dollars to purchase.
They were so good.

Automobiles
The first vehicle I saw was the horse-drawn carriage. This is the vehicle I went
on. I saw automobiles but they looked different from what we see today; but
they were cars nevertheless. You know the cars they have today, but their style
was different. This is the first automobile I saw, but the vehicle we used was the
horse-drawn carriage. This was when I went hop picking. We would transfer
onto the carriage from the train, and they would transport us to where we were
going to pick hops. It was drawn by horses. There were two horses pulling the
carriage, and we would sit in the buggy with our luggage when we went hop
picking. This is what I did in my childhood.

Trams, Buses, and Trains
I saw the *q̓ʷəligəlsəla* [going by itself; self-moving]. They call the tram *q̓ʷəligəlsəla*.
Q̓ʷəligəlsəla is the vehicle that pulls carts behind it. I went on it also. We would
travel into tunnels [*ƛəmcəwakʷ*]. This was during the time we went hop picking.
This is when we would travel by train. It would get dark when we went through
the tunnel. It would take a long time for the train to get through the tunnel. This
is what I did as a child.

Airplane
I also saw the airplane [*p̓əʎa; p̓ətʔid:* to fly]. It has not been long since it came.
Jimmy [Sewid] mentioned it. The children were fascinated [*ʔawilpəʎa*][20] by it
when it first came. It was not very big, the airplane that came to Yəlis. It was a
tiny thing – not like the huge airplanes you see now.

Steamships and Paddlewheels
Of course, we had the small steamships, these tiny little things. There was a
little steamship named *ƛaᵂḣis* at Yəlis. It had an Indian name. This little steamship was named *ƛaᵂḣis*. Billy worked on it. It belonged to the cannery. This is
what I saw, along with what I have already told you. I also saw a vessel named
Gʔosgʔica. It had paddlewheels on both sides of it. It was round with paddlewheels on both sides of it. They referred to it as *ƛaƛəlakiẏa* [having spirits on
top]. They apparently named it *Gʔosgʔica*. This is a different steamship than the
one that hit a rock. It went right by Yəlis and never stopped. We saw only it when
it went by. It had a thing on top of the ship that tilted back and forth, and they
had these big round things spinning on either side of it. They called it *sisonus*
[paddlewheel]. I saw two of them, including the one they called *hilagəlis* where

we went to pick hops. This was when we travelled on the river. The local Indians [bibax"ƙəm] called it hilagəlis. It was not very big. It had paddlewheels.

Steamship Passengers Toss Money to Children

Daisy: Do you remember when they used to toss money off the steamships?

Oh! Yes, do I ever! We shall talk about that. They tossed money off the steamship. Everyone would rush down to the dock. WaċaɁow [Moses Alfred's uncle] would go. The old people would go down to the dock and sit, watching the children who came rushing down to catch the money that was tossed to them by the steamship's passengers. They were tossing money to the children. The children were just like chickens, running back and forth. Cəx"əltola, "they are going to toss money," they would say as they came rushing down the dock. The passengers would all gather off the ship.

I was sitting at home. ƛalis [Alvin Alfred] was a little boy. He was just starting to walk. He had a little ƛabat [basket]. The passengers of the ship would be crowded around the street. They gathered in great numbers into the big, traditional house we were staying in. They say ƛalis was carrying this little basket. [Laughter.] He would shout, "Hey!" as he pushed the people coming through the door and lifted his little basket towards them. They say that they tossed money into it. [Laughter.] Nuladiy's [Mrs. Ben Alfred's] mother was standing beside him, and she said they actually put money in his little basket. [Laughter.] ƛalis would shout "Hey!" and he would not let the people enter the house until they put something in his little basket. [Long laughter.] It was quite an event, the coin tossing from the steamships [xiqayala]. Even older people went, like Wadᶻidalaɣa. This is what ƛalis did, when he pushed the passengers out until they put something in his little basket. [Long laughter.]

Red Cross

So many things happened, like the time I was hired by Halliday [Indian Agent William Halliday; see Plate 17]. He was the first one to ask me to do this. He asked me to look after the Red Cross when they were soliciting funds [see Plate 21]. That was one of the good things he did. He gave me boxes filled with kikəloses [crosses]. This is what the girls would carry. Among them were G"ag"adax̌əlla [Dorothy Alfred], ƛalis's daughter, and Gədiy [Kitty Beans's and ɁAx̌uw's niece], Puλas [Dora Sewid], Ɂənispalla's [Mrs. Gideon Whonnock's] daughter, and Elsie Abraham. These are the girls I used. I would dress them up in button blankets and ermine frontlet headdresses, and we would go down to the dock and meet the tolisda [tourists]. The tourists would toss money in the Red Cross boxes the girls were carrying. We were soliciting for the Red Cross, dressed in our button blankets [ƛ̕iq̓əngax̌tola]. We did not dance, we just stood on the dock. They took pictures. They just stood on the dock. When I heard the steamship blow its whistle, I would get ready, put on a button blanket, and chase the girls down the dock to stand there. That was the end of my soliciting for the year. The following year Mrs. Cameron asked me to do it again. Mrs. Cameron's husband was the local fish commissioner. She hired me again. Bessie [Elizabeth Alfred, ʔAx̌uw̓'s youngest child] has a picture of it. Have you seen it? It is a picture of Bessie and Sam Scow's daughter. Sam Scow's daughter was younger than Bessie. They were wearing their ceremonial aprons and their button blankets. Their pictures were taken beside the cannery at Alert Bay. This was when Mrs. Cameron asked me to solicit for the Red Cross. I used Puλas when Mr. Halliday asked me to do this. This is what happened.

Europeans

I saw my first European when I went to Vancouver.

Daisy: Why were you so afraid of them?

It was because of my sister. Although G̱ʷix̌sisəlas [Florence Knox] was educated, she was still afraid of the Europeans.[21]

Daisy: She was educated?

She attended the first girls' home school. We would always travel to Vancouver in my father's gillnet boat. We would travel to Vancouver many times. That is where I saw the Europeans [Mam̓aɫn̓a].

Shoes

It took me a long time before I liked wearing shoes. I used to go around with bare feet. I remember when we went to Vancouver to keep Bondsound company. He was twelve years old and in prison; he had been charged with murder. They took him to the Supreme Court and he was in prison for such a long time. My mother would send me to buy candles. I went to town barefoot. I noticed that the White people were staring at me. I went to town barefoot to buy candles to take back home. This was when they forbade us to put up tents like we used to. This was when that picture was taken, the one you have in your book. This was the time when they put Bondsound in Oakalla.

I Hated Drinking

Early in my life, I hated drinking. My parents always used to drink. We were docked in one of the Vancouver docks. Ýux̌əs came down the dock. You know how people disapprove [waniqǧəm] of drunks. He knew people disapproved of his drinking. I guess he decided to come down and see us. He looked down and shouted at us, "What would my beloved ones like to eat?" he said. Someone yelled back, "Peanuts." The poor old man, he was drunk. He just shouted down at us. We were already in bed in my father's gillnet boat. We heard him saying, "Peanuts, peanuts, peanuts," as he was going towards the town. [Laughter.] I guess he did this so he would not forget the name of what he was going to buy. [Laughter.] He bought me peanuts when I was a child. [Laughter.]

My Father Abducted Me

I got lost once. Is it all right to talk about this? They say that my parents separated [ƙiƙəsoʷ]. They drank so much during that time. My father fished with Ẏux̌əs Charlie at Steveston. There were just two of them on the boat. They say my father abducted me when I was a very young child. I do not remember the incident. They say my father abducted me and took me out on the boat with him when he was fishing with Ẏux̌əs Charlie at Steveston. They say everyone was searching for me. The weather was terrible, they say. It was raining so hard, and the wind was blowing. My father and Ẏux̌əs Charlie were gillnetting, but because of the terrible weather they had to return to Steveston. My father decided to go for a walk so he left the boat, and Ẏux̌əs Charlie started drinking; however, as the storm got worse he sobered up enough to realize he had to move the boat to a safer, protected anchorage. He moved the boat under the wharf. There was such a downpour. They continued searching for me. They thought I was dead, they say.

They questioned my father but he would not tell them anything. They asked him what he had done with me. He just stared into space and would not answer them. They all thought I was dead. That same night Gʷagʷadax̌əlla decided to check behind the cannery. It was pouring with rain. All of a sudden Gʷagʷadax̌əlla saw Ẏux̌əs Charlie pulling himself up the dock [ǧənǧənbēy] and he had me in his arms. This was poor Ẏux̌əs Charlie pulling himself up the dock, and he had me in his arms. This was poor old Ẏux̌əs Charlie. He was my father's uncle. When Gʷagʷadax̌əlla saw him, he tried to beat him up. "Please do not do this to my dear ƙugʷēẏ [treasure] he said. "I am just trying to save the life of ćaẏa [younger sister or brother]. Her father must have just left us." Gʷagʷadax̌əlla came to his senses [yoɬʔid] and released the old man. He grabbed me, and they say I was frozen stiff [qəkaɬa]. The streets of Steveston were flooded. When they brought me back to my mother she heated a tin sheet [dˀagadˀuʷ] and laid me on it. They were warming my body [pixa] and forcing my limbs to move. I guess this is what happens when people freeze. This is what happened to Emma Gəlis [Emma Brown] one time. They were warming my body to bring my body temperature up. This was at Steveston. This is what happened.

My English Name

Daisy: When did you get the name Agnes Bertha?

When I was baptized. It is not long ago that I was baptized. I grew up without an English name. I went to school for a very short time. Mrs. Cook [Jane Cook] hated my Indian name, Ẏakoyoǧ"a, Woman Lost to Gambling.[22] She hated it. [Laughter.] I did not get baptized until after I was married. It was x̓aliⱡilaʔoǧ"a [Mrs. Joe Harris] who gave it to me. She got the names out of a book. My name is Agnes Bertha.

Daisy: When did grandpa get the name Moses Alfred?

They gave him these names when he went to school. The boys who went to school got their names from the Bible. He got it from his father Qumayuẁ, and the Reverend Alfred Hall gave it to Qumayuẁ. Qumayuẁ was Flora's [her daughter's] father's father. That is why the family has the name Alfred. The school gave him the name Moses and he took his father's first name for a last name. Paul and Legix̌ [Peter Knox] got their names from the school. The boys who attended the school were named after the disciples of Jesus.

I Went to School

I tried [*wanuⱡa*] to receive an education. All I learned was the A, B, C's. Mrs. Alfred Hall taught me. They made us say a prayer as soon as we went to class. We would all stand and say a prayer before classes started. We would all have to stand again and say a prayer when classes were over. I got cheated when I was a little girl. This girl by the name of ʔAʔumuⱡ was chewing gum. ʔAbusa [Mrs. Johnny Hunt] was in her teens. Mrs. Hall took ʔAʔumuⱡ's gum out of her mouth. She did not allow chewing gum in class. Mrs. Hall put the gum on her organ [*dənx̌aẏuẁ*]. When Mrs. Hall played on her organ she would close her eyes. She would play for us when we sang. She asked us to pray, and she closed her eyes while we were praying. The girls told me to go and get the gum. Mrs. Hall opened her eyes and found the gum missing. We found out later she had intended to give the gum back to ʔAʔumuⱡ after class was dismissed. Those brutes [*ⱡiⱡəⱡ*] denounced me right on the spot. They told Mrs. Hall that I took it. She sent me out of the class and strapped me. I was strapped because of the gum of ʔAʔumuⱡ, Ẏeqawilas's younger sister. ʔAʔumuⱡ was ʔAdoloⱡ.

Daisy: How old were you when you went to school?

I was older. I was maybe ten years old. I was quite a bit older than the others.

Daisy: Did you attend it for very long?

I attended it just for a short time, and my family would come and get me, and take me back to Mi̓mk̓ʷəmlis. My mother did not want me to attend. They tried to tell her that they wanted me to attend school. She told me that the school was a bad place to go. My mother said that the girls of the first school ended up being pregnant. That was the reason she would not let me go to school. I wanted to go. Nuladiẏ [Mrs. Ben Alfred] went. She lasted two days. They brought her to the girls' school. I was younger than Nuladiẏ. Her grandfather, x̌ax̌ʷsəm, came to school. He sat outside on the porch all day, crying. He wanted his grand-daughter released from the school. [Laughter.] Nuladiẏ was x̌ax̌ʷsəm's grand-daughter. [Laughter.] They took pity on x̌ax̌ʷsəm and discharged Nuladiẏ from the school. That was the reason she did not know how to write.

All I learned was A, B, C and C-A-T: cat; and R-A-T: rat; and H-A-T: hat. [Laughter.] That is what I have learned to spell. [ʔAx̌uw̓ is laughing so hard that she can hardly talk.]

My First Washing Machine

Well, my goodness, my mother was so old-fashioned. I was the same. I never liked anything my husband did. He bought a washing machine. This was when the first electric washing machines came out. I sure did not like it. I hired my sister [cousin] G̓ʷixsisala, to come and help me wash clothes. They delivered the washing machine but I just kept pushing it back outside. I was thinking about how expensive our electricity bill was going to be. I just kept pushing it out, and that is where it sat. My sister and I were washing our clothes. I was washing the clothes by hand, and my sister was helping me. I finally said to her, "Why don't we try the new washing machine?" This was the washing machine I just had pushed out of the house, and it was sitting outside our cabin at Yəlis. So, we pushed it in and washed our clothes with it. To my amazement, it was wonderful. I thought it would never get the clothes clean. Nuladiẏ [Mrs. Ben Alfred] had one of those spin washers and it never got the clothes clean. It would spin. The first washing machine I saw was the spin washer. You would spin the handle on the side of it. It was a European washing machine, and it never got the clothes clean. That is what I was thinking about. I thought that the washing machine that her [Flora Sewid's] father bought me was not going to get the clothes clean. So we started washing clothes with my new washing machine.

Radio

Another thing he [Moses] wanted to do was to buy a radio for her [Flora's] brother. I sure did not like this either. I was always careful with money. I was always taught never to spend money foolishly. That was the reason I did not like it. I felt we were going to spend a lot of money on this radio, because it was

Fragments of Recollections

electric. I sure did not like it either when he bought the radio. That was my experience with all these new gadgets when they first came, the gadgets we now own.

My First Bathroom
I never liked anything he [Moses] wanted to do that was European. He decided that we should have a bathroom. I would not allow him to do this. "You want us to defecate on the floor?" I said. [Big laughter.] I was really old-fashioned.

My First Telephone
He [Moses] decided to install a telephone in our house. I did not try to stop him; I just avoided the telephone. I felt that it would be too complicated for me to understand. I refused to touch the telephone. This was when all the telephones were installed in Alert Bay. I was really amused at one time when I went to Vancouver with Puλas [her granddaughter, Dora]. I don't remember why we went down to Vancouver. She went with me when she was a child. Someone phoned us at the hotel. She was just a little girl. We were staying at this hotel. What was the name now? I knew the name at one time. I was with her. Our hotel room telephone rang. "This is the first time I am ever going to touch a telephone," she said to me. [Laughter.] Puλas was just a little girl. She probably still remembers it. [Laughter.] She answered. It was the clerk telling us that checkout time was at noon the next day. If we did not check out by that time we would have to pay for another day. They telephoned us to let us know that we would have to pay for another day if we did not check out at noon. "This is the first time I am ever going to touch this," she said. [Laughter.] She was just a little girl. She went to stay with me at Steveston.

The First Peanut Butter I Saw
Another thing I did. Oh! I was really old-fashioned. I never knew that peanut butter was good to eat. I was with Ḵʷəlstoliɫ [Daisy Roberts]. We travelled to Namu. This is where we were. We saw these pails. Pails were a big thing in those days. Usually they contained lard. We saw these cute little pails [qusqaḵʷa]. They contained, we learned later, peanut butter. Ḵʷəlstoliɫ and I bought some. [Laughter.] We went down to the wharf of Namu and dumped the contents into the water. We just bought it for the little pails. We did not know that peanut butter was good to eat. [Laughter.]

The First and Second World Wars
That was the first time we went to Steveston. Oh! The poor Japanese suffered! Flora's father [Moses] was hiring cannery workers for BC Packers. He was the boss. He was hiring the people. We were going to look at where the workers

would stay. They were really treating the Japanese very badly. All their possessions were piled up outside the houses. The poor Japanese people. They were trying to sell their possessions to us. One Japanese man tried to sell a bed to her [pointing at Flora] father. I think he bought a watch from him. They were being thrown out and ordered out of their houses. We happened to be there when this happened as we were looking for housing for the workers. This was when we first went to Steveston. He was hiring workers for BC Packers with Yequx̱alas [Chief Billy Assu] and ʔAdaliẏ [Mrs. Billy Assu]. They also saw the Japanese being thrown out of their houses.

The company threw them out. They told them to get out and leave. They were all being asked to get out and leave. Their poor possessions were scattered all over the ground. We were with ʔAdaliẏ. She also saw this. Billy Assu was also hiring workers for the cannery. This is the person with whom grandpa [she says "grandpa" in English] was working. They hired workers. That is why they went there. They looked for houses for the workers. That is why we happened to be there when they did this to the Japanese. This was during the war.

Daisy: What do you remember about the First World War?

Mrs. Cook's son was killed. There were two of them. K̕ʷəlstoliɫ's [Daisy Roberts's] son was killed, the one she had adopted. You know – Edwin.

Daisy: He did not join the army until the Second World War.

Yes, the Second World War. Both of them were killed. One was in the First World War. They drafted many men. Charlie was drafted during the Second World War. Also little Frank. He went. Also Godfrey Hunt and x̱aquʎas. They all went, when the draft was announced. They drafted Sam Hunt and Arthur Dick. Arthur had a weak heart, so they sent him home. They apparently would not take anyone who was not physically fit. Sam and Arthur were gone for a long time. They were wearing their uniforms when they returned home. I had pictures of them. These are the pictures Vera took; the pictures of her dad and Sam.

Daisy: Do you remember when you received news that Edwin had been killed?

That was a terrible time. He was such a fine young man. His girlfriend, whom he was going to marry, told K̕ʷəlstoliɫ and me that there were some blossoms [q̓ʷasama] on an apple tree in Port Alberni. It was so beautiful that year, the woman told us. "Remember me whenever the apple blossoms are in bloom, if I don't return from the war," Edwin had said to his girlfriend, Pearl. She was carrying his child. They say she was pregnant with his child. She came to us. "Remember me whenever the apple blossoms are in bloom," Edwin said. Edwin was referring to the blossoms of the apple tree. You know that the apple tree must blossom before it bears fruits. That is what he told this woman. That is what that poor creature told us. She said every time trees bloomed, she would think of him, just as he told her to do. Her heart was aching thinking of him when the apple trees blossomed [*bulix̌ʷid*]. She did this because Edwin told her to remember him if he did not return home. [At this point, ʔАx̌uw̓ becomes very quiet and sad.]

Eulogy for Granny ʔAx̌uw̓

We are laying to rest a very special lady today. The name ʔAx̌uw̓ will long be remembered not only by her family but also by every person who has come in contact with her. She touched the lives of many, and I am sure that, as we sit here today, we have our own very special memories of how she touched our lives.

It is said that God has a plan for every soul. He sent us to earth, and no birth is an accident. In Granny ʔAx̌uw̓'s case, this is so true.

There would have been no Granny ʔAx̌uw̓ had her grandfather, Ẏaquʎas, not survived the Gilford Island massacre. It was part of God's plan that Ẏaquʎas would survive and have two daughters, Betsy and Puʎas. Betsy was Dan Cranmer's mother and Puʎas was the mother of Granny ʔAx̌uw̓.

Granny ʔAx̌uw̓'s mother was to marry several times. Her first marriage produced a daughter, Nulaga, who was later to be known as Florence May Knox. Her second marriage produced Granny ʔAx̌uw̓, who was later to be known as Agnes Bertha Alfred. A third child came from a third union, and his name was Məllidʔas but he passed away before he reached his teens.

Puʎas married Granny ʔAx̌uw̓'s father, Joe Joseph of Village Island, and this is where she was born. According to Grandpa Moses's old records, she was born January 26, 1889, so she would have been 104 this January.[1]

She lived at Village Island until the death of her father, Joe, and then they moved to Alert Bay to be near her mother's uncle.

When she was fourteen years old, an arranged marriage was made between her and Grandpa Moses. They were married in the traditional custom. She always laughed when she talked about her "little red wedding gown." On December 26th, 1933, they renewed their wedding vows at the Anglican Church.

This union produced thirteen children: Alvin, Flora, George, Arthur, Dorothy, Nora, James, John (Jackie), Clarence, Lena, Phillip, Allan, and Elizabeth, whom we know as Libby. Only seven of her thirteen children survive her today.

Whenever she lost one of her children, it broke her heart. When she lost Alvin, her eldest, only a month ago, it was too much for her to bear.

Granny and Grandpa were to renew their vows again at the Anglican Church when they celebrated their golden wedding anniversary [see Plate 27]. I am sure many of you will remember what a wonderful ceremony that was. I remember trying to find an old record that Grandpa used to dedicate to Granny ʔAx̌uw̓. It was called, "You Can't Break the Chain of Love."

They had a happy marriage, but they also had many trials, such as when Grandpa was put in prison for two months in Oakalla for giving away apples at a wedding ceremony, and when Granny ʔAx̌uw̓ was arrested a few years later for attending her cousin Dan Cranmer's potlatch at Village Island. She was not sent to prison, but her sister Florence, whom she adored, was sent away to Oakalla prison for dancing at this potlatch.

Granny ʔAx̌uw̓ saw many changes in her 103 years, some good and some very bad, she would say. She grew up in the traditional big house, and later Grandpa built her a modern house that we all nicknamed "the big house" (see Plate 26). He also put all the modern appliances in this house. At first she refused to use them, but later on she got use to them. We have many funny memories of how she adjusted to each one.

Granny was a very devoted Christian. I am sure many of the children and grandchildren will remember how Granny insisted that we attend Sunday school and church regularly. From the time she became a Christian she devoted her time and energy to the Anglican Church. She belonged to the first Kʷakʷala choir, and she encouraged us to do the same. She was a lifetime member of the Women's Auxiliary of that church, and she used her many talents to help raise money for the missions [see Plate 22].

She also worked in several canneries. In Alert Bay she supervised a group of Native women who worked at the Alert Bay plant. She also worked unceasingly for the Native Sisterhood of British Columbia, again using her many talents to raise money for both the Sisterhood and the Native Brotherhood of British Columbia. She was a multi-talented lady, and when you think of it, that is quite an accomplishment for someone who spoke very little English.

She was very talented and knowledgeable in all things. She loved her own culture and traditions. She encouraged us to use our own Native language when we spoke to her because she did not want our language to disappear. My father always referred to her as our dictionary and thesaurus. She was also our history book and book of knowledge. Family unity was very important to her. She preferred to use the traditional relationship system rather than the European; consequently every first cousin was a brother or a sister. She believed that family members should look after each other. Whenever there was a family breakdown, she never took sides or fuelled the situation. She was always fair because she always said the greatest rule taught by God was to love one another.

I once asked Granny why she thought she had been given a long life. She said one of the regrets she had was that her mother Puλas did not see the rest of her children. She only saw the three eldest, so when ʔAx̌uẇ became a Christian, she asked God to grant her a long life so that she could see her grandchildren. She not only saw her grandchildren but she was to see four generations of her grandchildren, a total of six generations altogether. She was always so happy when a new baby was born because it was an extension of her and Grandpa. All her descendants were special to her, and she seemed to draw energy from us. She could be very sick, but when we gathered around her she would become strong again.

She was a wonderful storyteller. We would gather around her, and she would tell us many stories for hours, and we loved it. She also loved to teach us to dance and sing our traditional songs and dances. With Granny ʔAx̌uẇ there was no such thing as a generation gap. We once took her to Disneyland, and we went to a New Year's Eve dance. My brother Bobby had asked her to dance a rock-and-roll dance. She got on the floor and everyone stopped dancing and formed a circle around them. They could not believe that someone her age could dance like that, but that was Granny. She loved life and life loved her. She was always smiling or laughing.

She loved to be around children, especially around Christmas time. Both she and Grandpa loved Christmas because they loved to give presents. They had a special bedroom where they would have all the gifts. Grandpa had the list, and Granny picked out the gift and handed it to Grandpa to wrap. The list included every relative and friend that they had, which meant the whole village.

Granny ʔAx̌uẇ cared for many people in her big house. The four who were especially dear to her heart were her own grandchildren Clarence, David, Bruce, and Harold. Harold was just a baby when she took them, so he was more than a grandchild to her. So it was not surprising that his name would be the last name she would call.

When it came to her children, grandchildren, and great-grandchildren Granny ʔAx̌uẇ had what is called "*agape* love": unconditional love. She did not just voice it, she showed it. Some of us did things that did not please her, but she loved us anyway. She had so much love in her that it overflowed to other relatives and even to strangers whom she met, and it changed their lives forever. She taught this *agape* love to Aunt Libby, who cared for her for many years. We talked about it often, and Aunt Libby said she would never think of putting Granny in a home. She kept that promise right up to the time she lost her own health and had to put ʔAx̌uẇ in the hospital.

Granny ʔAx̌uw̓ would ask me many times about things written in the Bible. She loved to hear about the prophecies and about heaven. During one of our talks not too long ago she told me how much she missed Grandpa and longed to see him again. She has now been granted that wish, and I want to thank God for allowing us to have had her for so long.

Granny ʔAx̌uw̓ was an extraordinary woman who lived an extraordinary life. She was not only our grandmother, she was our best friend. She leaves behind a great legacy and example for us to follow. It is up to each and every one of us to choose how we will use this gift.

Daisy Sewid-Smith
December 1992

Epilogue

ʔAx̱uw̓ died on 11 December 1992. Several years later, in 1996, a memorial pot-latch was given in honour of "Granny ʔAx̱uw̓" at Alert Bay. Several hundreds of her immediate descendants, relatives, and friends were present. (See Plates 34 and 36.)

Today, ʔAx̱uw̓ is remembered not only as everybody's favourite granny but also as a pillar of Kʷakʷakəwakʷ culture and society. She certainly would be pleased to know that the U'mista Cultural Centre has chosen to quote her words on the potlatch for their website:[1]

> When one's heart is glad, he gives away gifts. It was given to us by our Creator, to be our way of doing things, to be our way of rejoicing, we who are Indian. The potlatch was given to us to be our way of expressing joy.
> – Agnes Alfred, Alert Bay, 1980

Ten years after her death, on September 28th, 2002, ʔAx̱uw̓ was acknowledged publicly at a memorial potlatch given for Chief Don Assu of Cape Mudge. She was acknowledged for having instructed the present generations on proper ritual and protocol, for being the keeper of traditional knowledge, and for seeing that it was passed on to her family and friends. Jean Pouillon (1997: 18) has defined tradition "as the part of the past that persists in the present to which it has been transmitted and where it remains active for those who have received and accepted it and, in turn, pass it down through speech, education or writing." We can surely say, therefore, that ʔAx̱uw̓ remains very much a part of contem-porary traditional Kʷakʷakəwakʷ cultural life.

As we stated in the Introduction, it has not been our intention to produce another comprehensive survey of Kʷakʷakəwakʷ culture; rather, we have attempted to give an accurate translation and transcription of the self-selected reminiscences of one vibrant female Kʷakʷakəwakʷ elder – a woman who could serve as a bridge between nineteenth-century Kʷakʷakəwakʷ traditional knowledge and history, and present and future generations. Had she lived another eight years, ʔAx̌uẇ would have lived in three centuries. Surely she witnessed the period of greatest cultural, social, and technological change for her people since their first contact with Europeans.

In retrospect, we realize that we could have asked more questions about several other features of ʔAx̌uẇ's history, daily life, and culture; instead, we honoured our initial decision to allow ʔAx̌uẇ free access to her memory, to explore and to reveal those episodes of her and her people's history that she chose to reveal. Although we anticipate criticism for having left several gaps in ʔAx̌uẇ's personal history, we hope that the clarity and immediacy of her memories have provided unprecedented insight into her personality and inner landscape. It is obvious that what she most wanted to talk about involved relationships, genealogy, myth, and ceremonial protocol. If these recollections preserve and perpetuate her legacy for her immediate relatives and other Kʷakʷakəwakʷ people, and if they prove valuable to the anthropological and general understanding of these "much-studied" Northwest Coast people, then we will have fulfilled ʔAx̌uẇ's objectives.

Linguistic Key to the Kʷak̓ʷala Alphabet, Spelling, and Pronunciation[1]

Kʷak̓ʷala Alphabet:

b, d, dᶻ, λ, g, gʷ, ǧ, ǧʷ, ʔ	(unaspirated stops and affricates)
p, t, c, ƛ, k, kʷ, q, qʷ	(aspirated stops and affricates)
p̓, t̓, c̓, ƛ̓, k̓, k̓ʷ, q̓, q̓ʷ	(glottalized stops and affricates)
s, ł, x, xʷ, x̌, x̌ʷ, h	(voiceless continuants)
m, n, l, y, w	(plain resonants)
m̓, n̓, l̓, y̓, w̓	(glottalized resonants)
a, e, i, o, u, ə, ē	(vowels)

This appendix offers a brief description of the allophonic distribution of the phonemes of Kʷak̓ʷala. However, the allophony of the vowels is general since much depends on both preceding and following consonants. At the same time we have attempted an approximate description of some of the sounds of Kʷak̓ʷala in order to help those who do not know or speak this language.

a   low mid-central unrounded vowel; pronounced like the *a* in cat (*ʔayasuw̓*: hand); after sounds in the back of the throat (ǧ, k̓, x̌), like father (*ʔeǧas*: girl)

b   voiced bilabial stop; pronounced similarly to the same phoneme in English (*bak̓ʷəm*: Indian person)

d   voiced alveolar stop; pronounced similarly to the same phoneme in English (*dəntalla*: disagreeing)

dᶻ   voiced affricated alveolar stop; pronounced as in English "*adze*" (*dᶻoliy̓*: cockle) ə   the shwa; mid-central unrounded vowel; pronounced as in English "about," or "gallop" (*Nəmğis: Nimpkish; ʔən:* I/me)

e   lower mid-front unrounded vowel; in most cases, it is pronounced either like the *u* in "b*u*t" or like the *a* in "sof*a*." However, after "palatalized" consonants (i.e., those that have a y sound with them, such as k, g, x, etc.) the vowel sounds more like the *i* in "p*i*t"and after "labialized" consonants (gʷ, kʷ, etc.) its sound is more like the *u* in "p*u*t" (*ʔeğas:* girl)

ē   lower mid-front unrounded vowel; pronounced similarly to the *a* in "potato" (*həmaʔēlas:* store)

g   voiced palatalized velar stop; pronounced similarly to English gy but with a slight y sound (palatalization) after, much like "egg yolk" (*gukʷ:* house)

gʷ   voiced labial velar stop; pronounced similarly to the elided sound in "big one" (*gʷəsuẃ:* pig)

ğ   voiced uvular stop; pronounced like g above but without the palatalization and much farther back in the throat, where the *ch* in German "Bach" occurs (*ğila kasla!:* greetings)

ğʷ   voiced labialized uvular stop; pronounced like ğ above but with rounded lips, as in gʷ (*ğʷəẏəm:* whale)

h   voiceless laryngeal fricative; pronounced similarly to the same phoneme in English (*humowilas:* museum/place for viewing)

i   high front unrounded vowel; there is considerable latitude in the pronunciation of this vowel determined by dialect, but most often speakers use it like the *i* in "*i*magine" (*ʔigis:* sand)

k   voiceless palatalized velar stop (kʸ); pronounced similarly to the same phoneme in English but with a y sound (palatalization) following, much like the second *c* in "ac*c*use" (*kəx̌əlağa:* crow)

kʷ   voiceless labialized velar stop; pronounced similarly to the *qu* in "*qu*een" (*kʷikʷ:* eagle)

ḱ   voiceless glottalized palatalized velar stop (kʷ); there is no sound like this in English; pronounced exactly like Kʷaḱʷalak (including palatalization) but is accompanied by a very strong "exploded" quality caused by building up air behind the tongue before its release (*ḱattaẏuẃ:* pencil, pen; *ḱatta:* to write, writing; *ḱat:* write)

ḱʷ   voiceless glottalized labialized velar stop; pronounced like ḱʷ but with the same exploded quality described under ḱ (*ḱʷisa:* snow)

q   voiceless uvular stop; pronounced somewhat like k but without the palatalization and much farther back in the throat, where the *ch* in German "Ba*ch*," or in Scottish "lo*ch*," is pronounced; (*qasa:* walking)

qʷ   voiceless labialized uvular stop; pronounced like q above, but with rounded lips, as in qʷ (*qʷəx:* flour) q̓   voiceless glottalized uvular stop; similar to *q* above, but with the strongly "exploded" quality described above (*q̓asʔanēy̓:* shirt)

q̓ʷ   voiceless glottalized labialized uvular stop; similar to q̓ above, but with a strongly "exploded" quality (*q̓ʷasa:* crying)

l   voiced lateral alveolar resonant; similar to English (*lastuẁ:* ten)

i̓   voiced glottalized lateral alveolar resonant similar to *l* but with a weakly "exploded" quality at the beginning, much like "bott*le*" pronounced with a Cockney accent (*l̓aqʷa:* log)

ł   voiceless lateral alveolar fricative; a friction sound similar in quality to *sh* or *th*, but the tongue tip is kept in the position for pronouncing *l*, and the air is released silently between the sides of the tongue and the sides of the upper back teeth; the closest approximation is the *thl* in "a*thl*ete" (*łanx̌a:* green)

m   voiced bilabial nasal resonant; similar to English (*may̓us:* raccoon)

m̓   voiced glottalized bilabial nasal resonant like *m* but with a weakly "exploded" quality, or catch in the throat, at the beginning (*m̓akʷala:* moon)

n   voiced alveolar nasal resonant; similar to English (*nax̌aq:* goose)

n̓   voiced glottalized alveolar nasal resonant; like *n* but with a weakly "exploded" quality, or catch in the throat, at the beginning (*n̓əm:* one)

o   low back rounded vowel; similar to the English pronunciation of the *o* in "c*o*d," or "g*o*d" (*ʔogiwēy̓:* boat)

p   voiceless aspirated bilabial stop; similar to English (*puxʷans:* balloon)

p̓   voiceless glottalized aspirated bilabial stop. There is no equivalent sound in English. It is pronounced like *p* but with a strongly exploded quality caused by building up air behind the lips just prior to release (*p̓əsp̓ay̓uẁ:* ear)

s   voiceless alveolar slit fricative; similar to English (*siłəm:* snake)

t   voiceless aspirated alveolar stop; similar to English (*təminas:* squirrel)

t̓   voiceless glottalized aspirated alveolar stop; similar to English *t* but with the strongly exploded quality described above (*t̓ibayuẁ:* show)

λ   voiced laterally affricated stop; similar to English "mau*dl*in" but never as in "mi*ddl*e" (*λabəm:* nail)

ƛ   voiceless glottalized laterally affricated alveolar stop; similar to the sound in English "righ*tl*y" but never as in "bo*ttl*e" (*ƛaqəla:* clapping)

ƛ̓   voiceless glottalized laterally affricated alveolar stop; similar to ƛ but with the strongly exploded quality described above (*ƛ̓isəla:* the sun)

c   voiceless affricated alveolar stop; similar to the sound in English *ts* as in "ca*ts*" (*cup̓aliy̓:* bird)

c̓   voiceless glottalized affricated alveolar stop; similar to the sound in English *ts* but with the strongly exploded quality described above (*c̓amac̓iy̓:* church) u   high back rounded vowel; there is considerable latitude around this vowel sound, but most often speakers use it like the *oo* in "mood" or the English *o* in "mode" (*ʔup̓igēy̓:* knee)

w   voiced bilabial semi-vowel; similar to English (*waq̓es:* frog)

ẇ   voiced glottalized bilabial semi-vowel; similar to w but with a weakly exploded quality, or catch in the throat, at the beginning (*ẇaċiy:* dog)

x   voiceless palatalized velar fricative; a friction sound, pronounced like *s*, but made with the tongue in the position for pronouncing *k*; similar to the *ch* sound in German "*ich*" but accompanied by a y sound after it (palatalization) (*xəltta:* a cutting instrument; *xəlt:* to cut)

xʷ   voiceless palatalized velar fricative; similar to *x* but pronounced with rounded lips (*xʷeyuw:* club, bat)

x̄   voiceless uvular fricative; a friction sound like *x* but pronounced farther back in the throat; very similar to the *ch* in German "Ba*ch*" or Scottish "*loch*" (*x̄aq:* bone)

x̄ʷ   voiceless labialized uvular fricative; similar to x̄ but pronounced with rounded lips (*x̄ʷənukʷ:* child)

y   voiced palatalized semi-vowel; similar to English (*yawapsəms:* tent)

y̓   voiced glottalized palatalized semi-vowel; similar to y but with a weakly exploded quality, or catch in the throat, at the beginning (*y̓ugʷa:* rain)

ʔ   the "glottal stop," or catch in the throat; very similar to English Cockney pronunciation of "butter" (buʔer), or to the pronunciation of "Hawaii" (Hawaiʔi) (*ʔayasuẇ:* hand; *q̓əsʔanēy̓:* shirt)

Myth 9 – The Animal Kingdom

There is a place named ꞋƏpsaguẃ [Shoal Harbour], a place that belongs to the Qʷiqʷasuṫinux̌ʷ. Here Ꞌanus lived with his wife and his children. One beautiful sunny day the tide was very low. You could see the lowest point of the tide at the place they call ꞋƏpsaguẃ. ꞋAnus saw a beautiful house glittering at the lowest point of the tide. The roof was completely covered with abalone shells that were shimmering in the sunlight. This was Q̇umugʷēẏ's house, rising out of the water. ꞋAnus started to beat rapidly on a log. Meanwhile, one of his children was pacing back and forth at the entrance of the house, preparing to enter it. He ran into the house and was fortunate [ƛugʷala] to receive it with all its abalone shells [Ꞌix̌ċam].¹ He received many other treasures, including the names ꞋIxċamalagəlis, ꞋIxċəmǧa, ꞋIxċəmǧaṫilakʷ, and ꞋIxċəmxəmliɬ. These are all abalone-shell names. These names that he received refer to the abalone shell and its radiant beauty. He was really fortunate to find this house.

One day ꞋAnus and his wife had a misunderstanding. To comfort himself ꞋAnus went into the forest. He walked and walked until he came to a beach at the edge of the woods where he could dig for cockles. He started to dig, as he was now very hungry. Little did he know that someone was lurking in the darkness, watching him digging for cockles. The unseen visitor crept closer and closer. ꞋAnus did not take any notice, for he was too busy digging. Closer and closer the creature came. ꞋAnus thought he heard a strange noise, so he stopped digging. "What was that? Did I hear something? Oh! It must have been the wind." He continued to dig. Suddenly he heard the noise again and dropped his stick as he was very scared when he saw what it was. It was the Wild Man of the Woods, Bəǩʷəs. "I wonder what he wants," thought ꞋAnus. Bəǩʷəs slowly approached him. He lifted his hand, motioning to the man to give him some cockles. ꞋAnus shook his head defiantly. Bəǩʷəs then told him his story, hoping that he would give him some cockles. "The animals are having a what? A dance, you say? A Cedar-Bark Ceremony? Ridiculous! Animals are animals! They cannot dance," replied ʔAnus. Bək̓ʷəs bowed his head, hurt that ʔAnus did not believe him. ʔAnus knew that he was telling the truth when he saw that he was hurt. ʔAnus gave him some cockles to get him talking again. "You are being initiated into the Cedar-Bark Dances and you only came down to eat when you saw me digging. But where are the animals holding their ceremony? Where? In a cave up there?" ʔAnus pointed towards a nearby cave, and Bək̓ʷəs nodded his head in reply. He motioned to ʔAnus to show him that he had to leave. "You what? You must go now?" he said.

ʔAnus was very interested in what he had learned and wanted to see the ceremony for himself, so he cleansed himself to ensure that the animals would not smell him. First he bathed, and then he rubbed himself down with hemlock branches. He approached the cave ever so slowly, crawling as he went. In the distance he could hear singing. He crawled closer and closer. He looked into the cave and watched. What a sight he saw! Who would have thought that the animals could shed their animal forms and become like human beings! Suddenly the singing stopped. ʔAnus crouched down quickly, for he knew something was very wrong. What if they saw him? What would he do? Suddenly he heard a rustling noise. "Oh! Someone is coming!" he said. The rustling noise got louder and louder. He lifted his head slowly and saw the Mouse Woman standing beside him. The Mouse Woman seemed friendly enough. Suddenly his fright changed into excitement. "Can I go and watch?" The Mouse Woman shook her head in reply. Disappointed, ʔAnus installed himself comfortably. He took from his belt a pouch that held his *yasək̓ʷ* [facial cream], which was made from mountain goat tallow. He started rubbing his face with this ointment. To his surprise, Heḷaḿolaǧa [Mouse Woman] smelled the *yasək̓ʷ* and motioned to him for some. "Ah! If I give her some maybe she will let me watch," he thought. So ʔAnus gave it to the Mouse Woman, who ate it. She then left ʔAnus and went back into the cave. ʔAnus peeked into the cave again and saw the Mouse Woman approaching the Wolf. He could not hear what was being said, but the dancing continued. For a second time the Wolf stopped the dancing, and again the Mouse Woman was sent out to check for a human being, as the Wolf could sense that one was near. The Mouse Woman, of course, knew that the man wanted to see more of the dancing. She also really liked the taste of *yasək̓ʷ* and wanted just a little bit more. "Our leader feels a human presence. He sends me, Heḷaḿolaǧa,[2] because I am swift, just as my name states. Of course, if you give me more *yasək̓ʷ*, I will go back in and tell the Wolf again that there is no one here." ʔAnus gave her more *yasək̓ʷ* and she returned to the cave. Four times Mouse Woman was told to check for a human being, and four times ʔAnus gave her more *yasək̓ʷ* so that she would not tell the Wolf who was watching. ʔAnus, overcome now with excitement, stood up suddenly and jumped into the cave. The animals, being caught out of their animal skins by a human being, were very embarrassed. They hung their heads in shame and no one said a word. "There is no need to be embarrassed. We have been caught by a human being, but it is his good fortune and not our shame. He wants to see our ceremony, so let us show him. Let him now see what no human being has ever seen before, the ceremony of the Animal Kingdom Dance!" The leader of the animals, the Wolf, called out to the leader of the dancers, the Grouse.

The leader of the dancers called out for his assistant, the Kingfisher. The dance leader and the assistant always waited for the final approval of their leader, the Wolf. He called the Owl, the Wise One; he called Bək̓ʷəs, the Wild Man of the Woods; he called the Mouse Woman, the Messenger of the Animal Kingdom; he called the Deer, the Curious One; he called the Raccoon, the Fire Keeper;[3] he called the Marten, the beautiful weasel and the Composer of the Animal Kingdom Songs; he called the Beaver, the Builder; and he called the Raven, the Messenger of the Air. In order to prove to ʔAnus that he was not hallucinating, the animals shed their animal forms and danced for him in their human form.

When the dancing was finished, the Wolf faced ʔAnus, who by then knew that this great, dignified creature was truly the leader of the animals. He motioned to ʔAnus to walk towards the entrance of the cave. Pointing towards the mouth of the cave, the Wolf said: "Go, man. Go back to your people. To them we make this great gift. Learn it well and use it when you have your ceremonies. Tell them it was a gift from the Animal Kingdom."

To this day, this great *ńuýəm* has been told and retold among the Mírhawiǧəm or Wiʔumasǧəm of the Qʷiqʷasutinux̌ʷ tribe on whom this supernatural gift has been bestowed.

APPENDIX C
Prohibition of the Potlatch[1]

Following European contact and its aftermath, the colonial administration made concerted efforts to abolish important Kʷakʷakəwakʷ practices that were thought to violate the moral code of the colonizers. Canadian authorities considered cultural practices that emphasized Kʷakʷakəwakʷ autonomy to be a threat.

Some hundred years after the first contact, the Canadian Act, 1876, prohibited all Northwest Coast First Nations, the Kʷakʷakəwakʷ included, from potlatching or carrying out the winter ceremonial.[2] Anglican (and Methodist) missionaries saw the potlatch as a heathen custom impeding their efforts to "civilize" and convert First Nations peoples to Christianity.[3] Furthermore, people involved in potlatching would leave their home villages, sometimes for long periods of time. It was difficult for federal authorities to understand and to justify these absences, which were perceived as posing obstacles to education, employment, and so on. While the amassing of material property was seen as a good thing by the White authorities, the Native practice of inviting guests and giving that property to them at a potlatch violated Western ideas of rational economic behaviour.

The two ethics – Protestant and Kʷakʷakəwakʷ – were in direct conflict. The potlatch reinforced the Kʷakʷakəwakʷ's sense of identity, their status system, and, indeed, their entire social structure. It had to be eliminated if these people were to be turned into "useful" Canadian wage earners and citizens.

One of the largest potlatches ever given among the Kʷakʷakəwakʷ was held in December 1921 by Nəmǧis Dan Cranmer, who had married Emma Bell, a noblewoman from the Ṁaṁaliliqəlla. Dan Cranmer's potlatch marked the finalization of his marriage contract, or the return of the bride-price, an event that calls for the display of many privileges and winter ceremonial dances. This potlatch took place at his bride's family's place – Ṁiṁkʷəmlis (Village Island), and it is said that more than 300 people attended, among them Moses and Agnes (ʔAx̌uẇ) Alfred. Dan Cranmer added a feast to his potlatch, which in the past would have taken place at a separate event. Holding them together around Christmas time, a time for feasting, was a way of avoiding Indian Agents. The potlatch lasted six days, after which time Dan Cranmer claimed he "could call anyone down" (Codere in McFeat 1966: 117). Goods worth about 30,000 Hudson's Bay blankets were given away. The kinds of goods distributed at this potlatch, in addition to blankets, reveal the kind of changes that were taking place in this ceremony as it adapted to changing times.[4]

Hovering in the background of these events, however, were spies who recorded the proceedings in some detail.[5] For the first time the law was enforced to the extent that many people who participated in this memorable potlatch were arrested by the Royal Canadian Mounted Police. They were prosecuted and brought to trial. However, sentencing was delayed a month due to a suggestion that the defendants could buy their freedom if their tribes would surrender their potlatch regalia.[6] Several chiefs agreed[7] to surrender ceremonial gear and did not go to jail, while others refused to cooperate and were sent to prison. Carved masks, paraphernalia, and other regalia were confiscated, eventually (and ironically) ending up in the National Museum of Man in Ottawa,[8] while other ritual objects (around thirty-five) were sold to George Heye for the Museum of the American Indian in New York. (For more details on the potlatch collection, see Sanders 1995: 57, n. 34.)

However, the Kʷakʷakəwakʷ potlatch was not going to be abolished by decree. In fact, it continued to flourish through the first two decades of the twentieth century, despite the Indian Act. Because they had entered into commercial fishing and wage work, the Kʷakʷakəwakʷ had the financial means to accumulate ever larger amounts of goods. However, their potlatches had to be held secretly, away from the government agency and missionary station at Alert Bay. It continued secretly until, finally, the Canadian government, in the Revised Indian Act, 1951, lifted the prohibition on potlatching and winter dances. However, outraged and filled with resentment, Kʷakʷakəwakʷ people intensified their effort to repatriate their confiscated paraphernalia (see Sanders 1995: 59, n. 45). James Sewid – who was the first to go to the National Museum in Ottawa in 1963 (he went at least four times) along with his wife, Flora, Billie Sunday Willie, and ʔAx̌uw̌ (see Plates 24 and 25) – opened negotiations[9] with the museum people there. It is said that he galvanized the media and publicized what was felt to be the museum's illegal confiscation of Kʷakʷakəwakʷ regalia. A new museum act (which had been in the making since 1921) was finalized and implemented so as to allow the National Museum to repatriate the confiscated material. Their efforts paid off, and on June 29th, 1979, the Kʷakʷakəwakʷ Museum and Cultural Centre opened at Cape Mudge. And on November 1st, 1980, the U'mista Cultural Centre opened at Alert Bay (see Carpenter 1981; Greenfield 1986, 1989; Woodstock 1980).

During one of my visits to ʔAx̌uw̓ and Daisy, I brought with me a copy of the official crime report document pertaining to the arrests of the people who attended and played a part in the potlatch held at Village Island. I reproduce this copy below. ʔAx̌uw̓ and Daisy had never seen this official document. Daisy translated it and read it to ʔAx̌uw̓. ʔAx̌uw̓ was in a serious and somber mood. Her tone of voice was deep, soft, and grave as she heard, and commented upon, this report.

Royal Canadian Mounted Police Division
Vancouver, BC   Alert Bay Detachment

March 1st 1922
Crime Report

Re – Billy Assu, Harry Hanus, Johny Drable, Komkute, Amos Dawson, Dan Craemer, Mrs. Dan Craemer, Abraham, Sam Scow, **Moses Alfred, Mrs. Moses Alfred**, Jim Hall, Sam Charlie, Jumbo, Sam Pouglass, Billy Highakus, Herbert Martin, Jas. Knox, Joe Hadone, Nakek, Mrs. Nahok, Kenneth Hunt, Johnson Cook, Mrs. Johnny Warnock, Betty, Mrs. Peter Knox, Kweemolas, and Spruce Martin. (Indians).

Charge-Infraction of Section 149 Indian Act

At the beginning of January I learnt that a large "Potlach" had taken place at Village Island on Christmas day and the three days preceeding that day.

I at once commenced investigations, but for some time could not obtain any definite information as to who had taken part in the "Potlach."

On Jan 5th I obtained the services of one DAVID SHAUGHNESSY an Indian to act as interpreter, and from then till the end of January interviewed a large number of Indians throughout the district, by that time I had obtained sufficient evidence to prove that the following facts took place.

During December one Dan Craemer, Indian of Alert Bay, sent off word to the Indians throughout the Kwawkewlth Agency to gather together at Village Island a few days before Christmas, that he was going to give a "Potlach." A large number of the Indians from the district gathered at Village Island, and on the 22nd December the proceedings started. On that day JIM HALL paid back canoes, and KOMKUTE spoke thanking HALL. (The first proceedings of a "Potlach" is usually the paying back of old "Potlach" debts to the man giving the "Potlach," and the speaker for the tribe to which the man giving the "Potlach" belongs then makes a speech of thanks to the man who has paid back). No more was done that day as some of the tribes had not yet arrived. On the 23rd Dec. BILLY ASSU paid back $2000.00 in blankets. SAM CHARLIE paid back canoes, ABRAHAM spoke for SAM CHARLIE. HARRY HANUS paid a copper back. This copper was then sold back to HANUS by CRAEMER for $3000.00. HANUS then paid CRAEMER furniture, canoes, blankets etc. In this transaction HANUS was acting for MRS. DAN CRAEMER who was paying back to her husband, as a woman cannot speak at a "Potlatch" a man has to transact the business for her. At the time HANUS paid the copper to CRAEMER, SPRUCE MARTIN spoke thanking HANUS. JUMBO paid back sewing machines. SAM POUGLASS paid back bracelets and jewelery. BILLY HIGHAKUS paid back money. At all the different paying back either KOMKUTE or ABRAHAM spoke. After the paying back was completed HERBERT MARTIN danced the "Hamitsa" (Commonly known as the "Wild man dance") and JAS KNOX danced the "Komonogis." The giving away then commenced, the canoes and some gas boats were given away that evening. SAM SCOW was the caller. (The caller is the man who announces to whom the various articles are to be given.) After this the "Galoklalath" dance was given by AMOS DAWSON to CRAEMER, this was danced by **MRS MOSES ALFRED**. (These dances are personal property, and what might be termed the copyright is given away by one person to another.) On the following day the furniture was given away. SAM SCOW was the caller, and PETER KNOX, KENNETH HUNT, **MOSES ALFRED**, & JOHNSON COOK carried the various articles to the recipients. Later pool tables were given away. JOHNNY DRABBLE was caller and KENNETH HUNT carried a cue to each of the recipients to signify that they had received a pool table. Then the jewellery was given away. SAM SCOW was caller, the jewellery was tied on sticks and NAHOK cut them off as they were given away, and they were carried to the recipients by JOHNSON COOK. The "Quiaque" dance was then given by BILLY ASSU to CRAEMER. This is a masked dance, danced by four men but I was unable to learn who they were. Three women, MRS. PETER KNOX, MRS. JOHNNY WARNOCK & MRS. NAHOK also danced at the same time. This finished the proceedings on the 24th December. On Christmas day the flour was given away, MONAQUILLA was caller, PETER KNOX, JAS. KNOX, KENNETH HUNT & JOHNSON COOK carried it to the recipients. **MOSES ALFRED** was on the pile of flour (about 400 sacks) handing it down to the aforementionned carriers. Money was then given away, SAM SCOW was caller, and the same carriers acted for this as did for the flour. A "Feast Song" was then sung; this was conducted by JOE HADONE. The Potlatch was then concluded by KWEEMOLAS bringing out a wooden image supposed to represent the enemy, which he knocked down, and jumped on as if he was the winner of a fight. BETTY [KWEEMOLAS' wife danced during this procedure].

On the 1st February I laid informations before W.H. Halliday, Indian Agent under section 149 Indian Act against all of the aforementioned (twenty-nine) active participants of this "Potlatch," and summonses were issued. Summonses were also issued for the following witnesses, OWAWHALAGALUS, KING TOM, IAKALALAS, WOYALA, ALEC SEE, GIAKALAS, JIM PATCH, & LOUISE. The case was set for hearing on the 16th February. The summonses for JAS KNOX & PETER KNOX were forwarded to Vancouver for service, these two defendants being in Vancouver. The summons for BILLY ASSU was forwarded to the Provincial Police at Quathiaski Cove for service, this defendant being at Cape Mudge. The remainder of the summonses I served myself between the 1st and 15th February.

The case was called on the 16th inst. Mr. W. Murry of Mr. Joe Martins staff appeared for DAN CREAMER AND HIS WIFE and for KWEEMOLAS & BETTY, and Mr. Ellis appeared for the remainder. Pleas of "Not GUILTY" were entered for all defendants.

Three of my witnesses, KING TOM, IAKALALS & ALEC SEE had not arrived on account of the stormy weather, and I therefore asked for an adjournment until the 18th inst, which was granted. I then left with the launch Gikumi II to fetch these witnesses, as I knew that they would not be able to come in their small gasboats on account of the storm, and I was unable to get back myself, being stormbound and the Provincial Police therefore appeared for me on the 18th inst and asked for a further remand, which was granted till the 25th inst. On the 25th inst. Mr. Murry appeared for all the defendants, Mr. Ellis being confined to his bed. Mr. Murry applied for the separate trial of the three defendants **MOSES ALFRED**, NAHOK & JOHNNY DRABBLE, these three men have previous convictions against them. He also applied for these three to be tried first. As I would not agree to have these three tried first, court was then adjourned until the 27th inst. In order to prove my case against these three, it would have been necessary to expose all my evidence against the remaining defendants. During the adjournment Mr. Murry and myself reached an agreement whereby he admitted that this "Potlatch" had been a meeting contrary to Sec. 149, and I then agreed to proceed against these three first, it being only necessary then for me to prove that they took part in the said meeting. On the opening of court on the 27th inst I called four witnesses OWAWHALAGALUSE, IAKALALAS, WOYALA & JIM PATCH and showed what part these three defendants had taken in the meeting. TWO of the defendants JOHNNY DRABBLE & **MOSES ALFRED** gave evidence in their own defence, but their evidence consisted of an admission of having taken the parts which I had proven.

One of the defendants PETER KNOX is still in hospital in Vancouver and I did not therefore proceed with the charge against him.

Mr. Murry then changed his plea on behalf of the remaining 25 defendants to "Guilty" and asked for suspended sentence on the strength of an agreement which he produced, signed by all the defendants and about 50 other Indians in the district, promising to give up "Potlatching." I objected to suspended sentence on the strength of this agreement on the following grounds.

About three years ago, in March 1919, several Indians were charged with a similar offence. Both the Crown and the Indians were represented by counsel. The charges against these Indians were withdrawn on the strength of an agreement signed by the defendants and by a large number of other Indians (A number of the present defendants had signed that agreement) in which they agreed to give up "Potlatching" as long as Sec. 149 of the Indian Act remained on the Statutes. Within two months after the agreement was signed, they were as busy potlatching as ever, and have been continuing it ever since. I asked that before the agreement be accepted that the Indians must give some tangible evidence of good faith, and I suggested that the only evidence that I could see that they could give was that the whole Kwawkewlth Agency make a voluntary surrender of all "Potlatch" coppers, masks, head dresses, Potlatch blankets and boxes and all other paraphernalia used solely for Potlatch purposes. The presiding Justices Mr. W.M. Halliday and Mr. A.M. Wastell accepted my proposal in toto, and remanded the whole of the defendants for sentence until the 31st March 1922 in order to give them an opportunity to either accept or reject the terms offered.

An agreement was then drawn up by Mr. Halliday and myself, on the lines of the proposal submitted by me, and copies distributed among all the bands of Indians in the Agency. A meeting was then held during which both Mr. Halliday and myself explained the matter very fully to them and they were given till the 25th March to turn in all the Potlatch material.

From conversations I have today had with several of the chiefs they do not appear to be willing to accept the terms offered.

Sgd. D. Angermann, Sergt.
In charge of Detachment

THE COMMISSIONER:
    Ottawa.
    Sir: Forwarded.
        I am satisfied that these cases could
    not be in better hands than Indian Agent
    Halliday. He appears to have a thorough

knowledge of the Indians of this district,
and, no doubt, his Department has had the
full facts already placed before them.

(T.A. Wroughton) Asst. Commissioner
Commanding B.C. District.
Vancouver: 13-3-22

Note: Daisy read over the list of people and what they were accused of,
and ʔAx̌uẃ commented on the contents of the report as follows:

Why is Kenneth Hunt on the list? He was there at the time, with us. He was
related to us. He was dancing the haṁaċa with Miċa [Herbert Martin]. It was
him, that silly man, who was spying on us, writing down everything about us in
secret.

In Ǧʷayasdəms [Gilford Island], much later, they were having a feast. The
police came after the potlatch and questioned them about what happened at
Miṁkʷəmlis. They picked up ʔOwax̌alagəlis and Woyala, and brought them to a
boat anchored in front of Ǧʷayasdəms, and questioned them. That was much
later. They did not arrest us for quite a long time after the p̓əsa.

Dowries: Harry Hanuse gave a Copper. It was səp̓id. Harry Hanuse, Henry
Bell, and x̌aqʷagiloǧʷa gave dowries for Emma Cranmer [and Dawson] to Dan
Cranmer. Harry Hanuse was spokesman for Ċolaⱡililakʷ [Emma Cranmer]. Emma
Cranmer was completing her marriage contract [hawanax̌ʔid: completing
marriage agreement; paying the marriage debt].

Harry Hanuse gave a Copper to Dan Cranmer, it was səp̓id. Spruce Martin
was a spokesman for Dan Cranmer. The report says that Jumbo [Henry Bell]
gave a sewing machine, but that is wrong. It was Qʷəmkənis. He was
Maʔəmtagila; his everyday name was ʔUmbalis. Ċolaⱡililakʷ gave ʔUmbalis the
sewing machine. He was paying back his debt to her. And it became part of the
marriage settlement payment. Abraham was the spokesman for those who
would pay their debts and return presents [investments].

James Knox danced Quminəwaǧa because Quminəwaǧa was his dance. This
dance position went to Dora Sewid-Cook [Puλas]. That was the dance of
Hemaskən, the brother of Q̓ʷəmxuduẃ, the dance Waċaʔoẃ used to dance.

Sam Scow was dagəme, the potlatch recorder. No. That is not right. It was
Flora's father [Moses Alfred] who was dagəme for the Nəmǧis. Sam Scow was
the yaqʷala, the gift announcer.

Amos Dawson gave the dance *Galu la* to Dan Cranmer as part of the dowry for Ċolałililakʷ. The report says that I performed this dance. But this was not my dance. It was my daughter Nora's dance [Nora Dick]; I danced it as a substitute for her.

Billy Assu gave four X̌ʷix̌ʷiẏ as a dowry to Dan Cranmer for Emma. Billy Assu was related to Emma. Ǧʷəmolas was Dan Cranmer's father; his name was Jackson.

According to this report, Betty danced along with her husband, Ǧʷəmolas [Jackson] when he performed on the totem pole. Betty was Wikəlalisəmeẏǧa [ʔAx̌uẇ's aunt]. She was no longer married to Jackson at that time. Betty was Dan Cranmer's mother. Her real name was Bessie, but they used to call her Betty. She was married to Chief Ṅageẏ [Mountain] at that time. Therefore she was no longer married to Ǧʷəmolas. The report saying that she was dancing when Ǧʷəmolas was stomping on this image is a lie. I wonder who on earth they questioned to get that information. Who did they question? Lots of it is untrue.

Twenty-nine people were arrested at that time. The witnesses were King Tom or a x̌ax̌asiqʷəlla; Woyala, who was a Dᶻawadaʔēnux̌ʷ and Camaǧa's [Dorothy Hawkins's] brother; Alexsi, who was Nulbayuẇ, a Kʷaguł and Kəʔas's father; Giqalas, who was Dᶻawadaʔēnux̌ʷ; and Jim Patch and Louise. Louise was a Dᶻawadaʔēnux̌ʷ, but I don't want to talk about her because she was a prostitute at the logging camp. We were related to her. Jim Patch was also a Dᶻawadaʔēnux̌ʷ, another relative of ours who died not too long ago.

Peter Knox was a very sick man, and he was not in Vancouver, as the report says. He got really sick when Nulaǧa, my sister, went to prison; she was forced to leave him behind in his bed in Alert Bay when they arrested her.

Nulaǧa was never the same after her release from prison in 1922. She developed a nervous condition and had a bad heart. The same thing happened to Mrs. John Whonnock and many others. They often talked about how fire hoses had been turned on them while they were in prison. Some received injuries from the prison guards and were never the same afterwards. Nulaǧa was upstairs with Kʷənxʷaloǧʷa [Mrs. Harry Hanuse], mother of Ṁəmdoẇ [Ethel Alfred]. When someone told them that the police were downstairs, they ran and hid in the bedroom upstairs. They crawled under the bed where some of our ṗəsa goods were secretly stored. We sure suffered. Moses and other guests saw Nulaǧa and Kʷənxʷaloǧʷa hiding under the bed [laughter] because the police were raiding us. That is what we, all of us, went through.

The way I understood it was that we were to have a rest from the ṗəsa, from potlatching. I would have never thought that this rest was forever. But all our ritual objects were taken away from us. Only one apron came back to Dan Cranmer. A huge chest containing some of our paraphernalia was taken down.

They brought all the masks to the parish hall. ʔOdən [John Drabble] started to speak: "Our names are now going," he said, standing beside these masks from the Nəmǧis. He was saying goodbye to all his names. Perhaps Bill Scow denounced us because he was standing with the authorities.

My sister, Florence Knox, was arrested because she danced. It really took a long time before they settled this case. They even had another winter feast at Gilford the next winter. It took them a long time to settle this affair. My husband Moses spent two weeks in prison.

They always tried to stop us from potlatching. There was an Indian Agent we called Dˣubəxstēẏ. We used to shout at him, "Too bad, Dˣubəxstēẏ!" This name refers to something stuck in your mouth. "Too bad, Dˣubəxstēẏ"; we used to say this to him as we were going up and down Mimk̓ʷəmlis. We were informed about Indian Agent Dˣubəxstēẏ. He was stationed at Cax̌is. He was probably Agent Blenkinsop, but we called him Dˣubəxstēẏ. He was the first Indian Agent that I can remember.

All my life I heard about the controversy over our *p̓əsa*, about White people complaining about our custom. I remember that a man called ʔOʔcana, from the Nəmǧis, grabbed the missionary Mr. Hall by the beard, and it was all due to the controversy over the *p̓əsa*. He was angry with him because he was in favour of interfering with our *p̓əsa*. I once heard a Danaxdax̌ʷ talking to ʔOʔcana, saying "I wish someone by the name of Ottawa would come and we would punch his nose." They all burst into laughter.

Note: The following is based on a section of Daisy Sewid-Smith's (1979: 47-53) Prosecution or Persecution, *with minor editorial changes.*

[ʔAx̌uw̓'s voice:]

We sure suffered when we were all arrested for what Daduw̓ [Dan Cranmer] did. We were all arrested. The old man, Q̓ʷəmxuduw̓, was still alive. The day-school bell rang and we all lined up. We held the hands of N̓umas because he was blind. They made us sit down on chairs and they called out our names. We answered, "Yo! Hello." That is all we did, and they made us go. At one time they brought us to the jail at the other end of the island at Alert Bay, and we went through the same thing all over again. It took them forever. They did not do anything right away. They just kept us really worried. I guess it was now time for them to decide to send them to Oakalla [a prison farm in Burnaby, in the Lower Mainland]. They brought us back to the day school. They stood us all up; Nulaǧa and I were there. They made one go left and the other go right. They put those who were not going to prison on one side; they put those who were going to prison on the other side. Nulaǧa was among the group to go to jail. They put the Kʷaguł in the corner with those going to prison. They arrested Nulaǧa because she danced. That was the only reason they arrested her. She just danced for our brother [cousin] Daduẇ. They arrested the other woman because she was a potlatch recorder and, as such, recorded the things that were being given out. She was also recording the names of those who went around inviting people to the potlatch. They were fed after they had gone around by boat inviting the tribes. Ǧusdidʔas [Billy McDuff] was Kʷaguł. Billy McDuff was put in prison because he went around inviting people and because he also fed those who went by boat inviting people to Fort Rupert. That is what happened. I really was heartbroken. My older sister was arrested, and I was not. They say that a police officer called Angermann went to Mrs. Cook. Nora was just a small child; she was my baby then. Angermann wanted Mrs. Cook to look after Nora during my time in jail. Mrs. Cook told him that she could not handle any more children because she already had a handful of them to look after. I guess they were worrying about me because I had Nora, and she was still a baby. They said the plan was to put us all in prison. They said the reason we did not go to prison was because they took our masks. This is what I heard. They said that they would eventually be returned. They just wanted the potlatch to stop. Just to let us have a pause, they said.

They gathered all the masks of the Nəmǧis. Those that belonged to Q̓ʷəmxuduẇ, my uncle, went. Also those belonging to Ǩugʷikila [Chief Joe Harris]. Those I am absolutely certain of, and they had many. Also ʔOdən, he also had a lot. They took the masks to Ottawa, and they say that is the reason we were not put in prison. It was because the Nəmǧis did this. Neither the Maṁaliliqəlla nor the Liǧiłdax̌ʷ people went to jail because they gave up their masks. That is why no one got arrested there. I guess it was like paying a fine so that they would not go to prison. They paid with their masks.

The people going down to Oakalla prison just ended up sleeping on the floor of the day school. They were not permitted to leave. They were going to stay there until the steamship came to pick them up. All were heartbroken because there was no reason for such treatment. They had not done anything really bad, they thought.

My sister Nulaǧa went on the steamship. I was just heartbroken when she went. Ċolałililakʷ [the late Emma Cranmer, Dan Cranmer's first wife] offered to take her place in jail. She did not want Nulaǧa, my older sister, to go. The authorities did not let her do that. Nulaǧa was forced to leave her very sick husband Legix̌ [Peter Knox] at home. He was supposed to go to prison too, but he was seriously ill. I think it just about killed the old man when they took her away to jail in Vancouver.

Everyone really suffered when they first arrived at the prison. They were told to take off all their clothes. The prison guards examined their whole bodies. Poor Nulaǧa really cried because we don't do such things; we never, ever examine each other's bodies. That is what they did to whoever was put in prison. That is what Nulaǧa went through.

I was looking after my niece ƛapasugʷilakʷ [Jennie McDougall]. They called her ƛapa. She was young and stayed at our house. Her parents had arranged for her to marry an old man called Munday. When they came to fetch her so that she could be married, she refused to go; she was heartbroken. Jennie had attended the residential school, where she had been taught that everything about our customs was heathen and that we were the only people practising prearranged marriages. Her parents were upset by her refusal. They told her to go because her father would be heartbroken if she did not. So she went, and they performed the wedding ceremony.

Many people were arrested around that time. Wilǧaméy̓ [Bob Harris from New Vancouver] and Jennie, his wife, were arrested because she was very young and had married an old man, the one they call Munday. They came and arrested them at Alert Bay. The police investigated us because we had been looking after her. The police had questioned Flora's father [Moses Alfred], who was blamed. People were saying we had told the police about ƛapasugʷilakʷ getting married. People thought I did not like the idea of her marrying such an old man.

Several men came and entered the home of Q̓ag̓oł [Johnson Cook]. Along with them came that awful police officer they called Angermann. He came and asked for Moses Alfred. He did not know any of those he was supposed to arrest because during that time everybody used Kʷakʷala names. He came in and asked Moses to help point out those he was to arrest. Moses refused to help. He just sat there, saying nothing when the police officer called him. I was cooking. I was stirring my cooking on the stove. That dreadful police officer kept coming back. I started yelling at him in Kʷakʷala. "Why do you keep bothering us," I said to him. I grabbed him and shoved him out of our house, but that did not stop him from coming. He did not know who he was supposed to arrest. That is why he asked for Moses. He wanted him to point out those he was supposed to arrest on account of Munday marrying ƛapasugʷilakʷ. Well, the next day I was at home, when along came the mother of ƛapasugʷilakʷ [Jennie]. "It is obvious to everyone now, about your husband. So it really was him who had us arrested," Ganaʔo [Mrs. McDougall] said. "The police just picked him up. The police have him in tow," she said. I just snatched my shawl and ran out. They had brought him to Indian Agent Halliday's office. I did not bother to knock. I just walked into Halliday's office and there stood Moses, at the front. They were questioning him. "What are you doing here?" I said. "We are accused by Ganaʔo.

She said you are responsible for all the arrests," I said. I grabbed him and dragged him out. They said it really shocked Dave Shaughnessy [a police officer]. He was standing by the door when I dragged Moses out. He did not try to stop me. I brought Moses home. I literally dragged him out when they were questioning him at the Indian Agent's office. That is what I went through for x̌apa. We were always having a bad time on account of our traditional doings.

At one time Moses was arrested on the occasion of Dita's [Kitty Silas's] wedding, which took place at Johnson Cook's traditional big house. We held a feast, as was the custom. We always held a feast at a wedding. Moses was holding one side of an apple box and my brother [cousin] Daduw̓ was holding the other. They were passing it around to all the guests. A couple of police officers came and stood by the doorway. People were pouring grease into the fire to make the flames light up so that they could see better. People would never know when or if they were actually going to be arrested, for sometimes a police officer would just come and watch and then leave. Little did we know that they were getting prepared to make arrests. They arrested Moses simply because he was getting apples out of the box and giving them to the guests. On that account, he was taken to prison. He was kept in prison for two months.

That is what we went through; all these arrests on account of our p̓əsa [potlatch]. Dan Cranmer did not go to prison because the informant, Dave Shaughnessy, did not put his name on the list. Dan Cranmer's mother, Yotu, my aunt, was married to Dave Shaughnessy's father.

APPENDIX D

Traditional Kʷakʷakəwakʷ Wedding between Daisy Sewid (Qʷiqʷasuṫinux̌ʷ: Gilford Island) and Lorne Smith (ƛawiċis: Turnour Island)

Most of the potlatches that have been accounted for in ʔAx̌uw̓'s narratives were "illegal" potlatches, as they were taking place in violation of the Indian Act, which prohibited potlatching.

In 1951 the Indian Act was revised and the section prohibiting the potlatch was removed, not repealed as the Kʷakʷakəwakʷ had hoped (Cranmer-Webster 1991: 227). Two years later, in 1953, the first "legal" Kʷakʷakəwakʷ potlatch took place. It was in Victoria, in Salish territory. Master carver Mungo Martin, who had been hired by the British Columbia Provincial Museum to teach totem pole carving and build a traditional big house, hosted the ceremony upon completion of the project. Since then several traditional big houses have been built in the culture area in which potlatches are taking place (in some cases gymnasiums are also used).

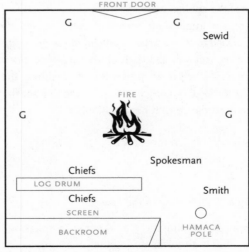

G: guests.

The circumstances for potlatching remain the same as in the past: mourning the dead, naming children, transferring rights and privileges, and less frequently, marriages or the raising of memorial totem poles (Cranmer-Webster 1991: 229).

We are presenting here a translation of the traditional Kʷakʷakəwakʷ wedding ceremony between Daisy Sewid-Smith and Lorne Smith for the following reasons:

To our knowledge no such ceremony has been published in the anthropological literature since the writings on the subject by Franz Boas. As we have seen, there is a plethora of interpretations based on earlier accounts and descriptions, but no such fresh, first-hand material. This is an opportunity for those interested in continuity and change in Northwest Coast ceremonialism to compare this material with earlier ones.

Marriage and the link between marriage and the potlatch are a major topics of ʔAx̌uw̓'s narratives, and it was a marriage-related potlatch that led to the dramatic arrest and imprisonment of some forty-five Kʷakʷakəwakʷ people in 1922.

Until the early 2000s, the married couples within the nobility did not choose their spouses, the arrangements having been made according to rank, privileges, and wealth. Bill Holm remarked that even in the late 1970s, although truly arranged marriages were few, high-ranking and conservative families were still exerting great pressure on their young people to marry properly (1977: 7). Today many Kʷakʷakəwakʷ people marry in the Christian Church without observing traditional Kʷakʷakəwakʷ marriage customs and ceremonies.

It is also in this very context that we have the chance to witness and experience Kʷakʷakəwakʷ oratory at its best. Many speakers involved here are no longer alive. We are given the opportunity to hear those who lived their rituals and their lives by the power of the spoken word.

ʔAx̌uw̓ played several implicit and explicit roles during and after the ceremony. She infused her knowledge to the active participants in guiding the sequence of events and in assuring accuracy in a multitude of significant details. In a later phase of the ceremony (which is not presented here), during the potlatch ceremony itself, she danced, holding in her arms the Copper that was about to change sides, in accordance with her position.

∽

7 October 1978

Tommy Hunt (Kʷaguł; spokesman for the x̌awič̓is)

[Tommy Hunt is not representing the Kʷaguł nor is he speaking for them; rather, he is acting on behalf of the x̌awič̓is during the ceremony, as Lorne's uncle is no longer alive. Tommy Hunt's mother and Lorne's father were half-sister and -brother].

Give me your full attention, Chiefs.
You will now see why we are here attending this gathering of all the tribes of the Kʷaguł. I am summoning you in order to proceed with the wedding ceremony. This is why we are all here, x̌awiċis, all the tribes together. As I already told you last night, we would go all out for our son. [There was a previous potlatch on 6 October, the night before, at which time this announcement was made.]

Come forward, Kʷaguł. Come forward, Kʷaguł.
You will now go forth to ask for the hand of the princess [k̓idił: chief's daughter]. Hawəlkʷalał [Bill Hunt], and Hayałkən,
Come forward, my tribesmen.
I have summoned all of you, Chiefs, so you will go forward in an impressive and majestic manner. I am going to call the tribes according to their rank. I will call you Nəm̓ğis. I will call you according to your rank, tribesmen [nałnamut]. I will go as far as the rank of Q̓umugʷēy̓, Nak̓ʷax̌dax̌ʷ. You will come forward and take your turn, tribesmen. You are still the ones entitled to use the position that you held in ancient times. We are going to try to imitate our ancestors, whom we have replaced. You are still the ones I am depending on. You are still the ones I am depending on. Come now, tribesmen. You will now proceed with the preliminaries, the calling out of all the tribesmen. You will now k̓atid! [k̓atid: the beating of the log drum with a fast beat].

Hawəlkʷalał [Bill Hunt], and Hayałkən [standing by the front door, representing the Kʷaguł, and walking around the fire counter-clockwise, passing the two Smith and Sewid families].

We are now in the house of the chief.
Chiefs, I think we have now received what we wanted, Kʷaguł.

Tommy Hunt (spokesman)
Thank you. Thank you.
We have succeeded!
Endeavour to do your best.

Tommy Hunt (spokesman)
Come forth, Chief ʔUd̓istalis [Alvin Alfred] of the Nəm̓ğis.
Come forth and show them the ways of your grandfather, kinsman [nəmyut].
Come forth.

[The singers beat the log with a fast beat *(k̓atid)*.]

Thank you, Nəmg̱is.

Why should you not be proud of your past, tribesmen?

Our days are so bewildering.

I am referring to the Head Chief of the house of the Kʷaguł, ʔUdˀistalis.

We have endeavoured to choose him to go in his ceremonial finery to woo the future bride.

You will now come forward, Weƛax̌as [Jack Peters]. How could I think of bypassing you, tribesman?

Choose carefully the way of the old people, our people, the Danaxdax̌ʷ.

Come forth, Chief. Go and impress the future bride.

[During the fast beat, Tommy Hunt is shouting:] "Try! Try! Try to lift the bride! Lift her up!"

Jack Peters [Danaxdax̌ʷ]

[Makes one circuit around the fire, symbolizing Dˀuna, the bird that appeared to the Danaxdax̌ʷ after the Flood. After the drumming has stopped, Weƛax̌as shouts: "Try to lift her, my people! Try!"**]**

Tommy Hunt

That is correct, tribesmen. That is correct. Thank you.

We will now ask the Ǧusgimux̌ʷ to come forward.

Come forth, Chief ƛaqʷagila [Jimmy Wallace]. Come forth, Chief ƛaqʷagila. We need your assistance in order to woo the future bride.

Jimmy Wallace [Ǧusgimux̌ʷ] ƛaqʷagila [His father was Ǧusgimux̌ʷ and his mother Nəwidiy̓ (ƛaƛasiqʷəlla)]

We are now going to proceed according to the word. To give a dowry for my child, I am going to choose a custom that my ancestors used for such a ceremony. I am going to start by saying that I belong to the other side called X̌uyalas. You will now beat the log [k̓aƛid].

Beating of the log. Song.

Sisayuł, Sisayuł ...

Jimmy Wallace

Yes, this is a chant from my own ancestral tradition at X̌uyalas. My first ancestors appeared as the Sisayuł [Double-Headed Serpent] in the ancient times. We came to Cax̌is to acquire a bride. This took place in ancient times. The road that the White man has built is the same road that my ancestor made at the very beginning of time. He came as a Double-Headed Serpent to make an offer at Cax̌is for which he received a wife.

I will now select a chant from the other side of my ancestral tradition [origin].

[In the background, Tommy Hunt says,] "This is correct."

Now I will begin with the traditional chant of my ancestors from my mother's side; the courtship song of the ƛaƛasiqʷəlla. This song originated from the beginning of time and was still sung during my youth.

[Chant 1 and chant 2 are sung in ƛaƛasiqʷəlla dialect.]

Jimmy Wallace
This is the chant of my people.
It is a courtship song. This is how they wooed the brides they wanted. What can I do, Chiefs? I can never forget it, for they trained me as a child. They educated me so that I would know the customs of my people, so that I would not be bewildered. I have taken the ancestral traditions of the ƛaƛasiqʷəlla. It does not matter if I am singing alone, but let us just pretend that my people the ƛaƛasiqʷəlla are singing with me.

This is the courtship song of the ƛaƛasiqʷəlla.

[In the background, Tommy Hunt says,] "This is correct."

Tommy Hunt
Thank you!
That is all I ask, Chiefs. That is all I ask.
We are now giving our full attention, ʔOyalał.
We will now leave the ƛaƛasiqʷəlla and give our attention to the Nakʷaxdaxʷ.
We are now impressed.

[In the background someone says,] "That is correct."

We are really impressed.
Come forward Nakʷaxdaxʷ. You will now take something from the customs of your ancestors, tribesmen. Why should you be shy?
We never abandoned our ancestors' ways. So, do not be shy.
Go ahead, Chief!

Charlie George [Nakʷaxdaxʷ]
Yes, Chiefs, yes. Why should I not give my best, my best. I will tell you about the Siwayuẃ, the paddle, the ƛugʷēẏ [supernatural gift] of Gamaligilakʷ. This is how they courted the first princess.

[In the background Tommy Hunt says,] "That is correct."

Charlie George
I am going to tell you the story. Why should I not say this?
Listen to me.

I have now arrived, Chiefs. [Allusion is made to their arrival to attend the ceremonial following the journey from their homeland.]

I have now arrived. So now listen. Listen to me. My ancestors' Siwayuẃnever cease to acquire brides, the *hilba*.

The *ƛugʷēy̓* [the supernatural gift] of Gamilagilakʷ.

That is it.

Tommy Hunt

Thank you!

Thank you, Chief. It is he, whom I have hired in order to be more impressive.

Legends of our ancestral tradition have now been recollected.

We have heard what the Chiefs have to say.

It would not have been right if I did not call you up.

[Long pause.]

We have invited you so that we might be more impressive.

It is good that you came, sister.

Come forth. Come forth.

[Long pause.]

Ḱaƚid! [Drumming on the log with a fast beat.]

Kathy Ferry

[She makes one circuit around the fire, holding two sticks in her hands, miming the holding of a bow and arrow.]

I have tried my best in what I have performed.

This is the legend that was told to me.

This is the legend of my uncles and my grandfathers, the Nakʷaxdax̌ʷ people.

[In the background Tommy Hunt says,] "That is correct, my dear [ʔade]."

I am so fortunate to have remained close to the traditions of my ancestors, even up to this day.

This is how it was performed in the time of my ancestors.

The only thing missing is the feather down. The eagle down flew when they performed the courtship song of the bride.

Now I can say that I have passed on a little of my knowledge of our ancestral ways.

[In the background Tommy Hunt says,] "That is correct, tribesman, thank you."

Tommy Hunt

That is what I have said, so that you could come forward, Chiefs.

It does not matter.

[Reply to comment from audience:]
I think I have made a slight mistake by forgetting one tribesman.
Come forth, ƛaqʷagila [Arthur Dick].
I am so fortunate to have you, tribesman, so that you could join us and be
impressive.

Arthur Dick

Chiefs, and my fellow tribesmen, we do not do this often.
The day has arrived when our search is close to fulfillment.
We are going to, we are going to, we are going to court the bride.
Let us begin. Let us begin. It is now time.
The ways of our old people. My heart feels good.
You will give me the answer: "Yes or no?" [In English. People laughing.]

Tommy Hunt

Thank you ƛaqʷagila! Thank you!
The words spoken by my tribesman are different. Did you hear what he said? Yes
or no? It is all right. It is all right.
You will now take from the tradition of your old people, your ancestors.
Go ahead, Chief. Start beating!

Fred Williams [Gʷawaʔēnux̌ʷ]
[Makes one circuit around the fire, making paddling motions.]

I have taken the canoe that Winagila used, when he paddled back and forth as he
did in the ancient days.
That is all I have to say.

Tommy Hunt

Thank you, tribesman! Thank you!
Come forth Nenakʷulagəlis Ċəndigən [Peter Smith, Ǧʷayasdəms].
Come forth, Chief, so that we may receive what we are looking for at this gathering.
I think you are going to be successful. I would be really embarrassed if the bride
was not passed on to us, because once in a while proceedings such as this one fail
to succeed.
Sometimes they refuse.
Is there any reason for us not to receive her?

Peter Smith

I will try. I will take from our ancestral tradition of the courtship of the bride. I will
take the legend of the bride's arm.
I will take the instrument used by our chiefs during the courtship.
You will now beat the log.

Appendix D

[The beating of the log starts. Motion of the arm suggesting the bringing of the bride.]

Peter Smith [went to the Sewid-Qʷiqʷasuṫinux̃ʷ corner].
I have picked her up, the Chief's princess.
I have now succeeded.

Tommy Hunt
That is correct, Chiefs.
Come forth, Chief Həmdᶻidiẏ [Billie Sunday Willie: Dᶻawadaʔēnux̃ʷ].
Take up the traditions of your ancestors for courting the bride.

Billie Sunday Willie
We are going to succeed, Chiefs.
We are going to succeed.
My child [Lorne, the groom] is now in a good position.
I am going to use the ƛugʷēẏ [supernatural gift] of ƛawidᶻuẇ.
They chanted it for him. We will now sing the courting song.

[The song is sung by fourteen Qʷiqʷasuṫinux̃ʷ and Dᶻawadaʔēnux̃ʷ people.]

We have reached our goal.
It feels good to see the customs of our ancestors.
Our courting song is quite good.
That is it, Chiefs.
That is it.

Tommy Hunt
They will accept our offer soon, ƛawiċis.
We will give our attention. I do not want to contradict my sister, but some people feel I should not be talking for my people the ƛawiċis.
That is what the Kʷaguɫ say.
But that suits me fine.

[The Kʷaguɫ make one circuit around the fire; they include Chris Cook, Mrs. Helen Knox, George Hunt, and Arthur Dick, and are all paddling in line. Tommy Hunt is drumming, Mrs. Agnes Cranmer is singing.]

Tommy Hunt
That is the courting song of the Kʷaguɫ.
My sister is giving me a bad time because I am speaking for my people, the ƛawiċis.

[Drumming.]

Tommy Hunt
Thank you!
We have now obtained her.
Listen to me, tribesmen. Listen to the things I have to say about my sister.
Ǧʷəntilakʷ [Agnes Cranmer] does not think I should speak for the ƛawiċis, but I will, now and forever.

Agnes Cranmer
We will now assemble the noble women to bring the bride over.

[Someone in the background says, "No!"]

Agnes Cranmer
No? OK. Later. I guess they are going to refuse us.
Let's sit down for a while.

Tommy Hunt
How presumptuous of us! [ʔawila wisɬəns: overconfident]:
They refused us, tribesmen.

Henry Bell
[Holding his Copper in the Sewids' corner.]
It is finished.
You have succeeded, Nəmǧis.
You have just obtained the princess [ƙidiɬ]. I was worried that you were never going to succeed. I was just about to have a change of heart.[1]
You have succeeded now. Give me your full attention while I tell you what dowry I will give you.
We will start with this [showing his Copper].
It will be given to you, ƛawiċis.
You will come forward.

[In the background Jimmy Sewid asks Daisy to come beside Henry Bell; she is holding the Copper Lubiɬila.]
You can all see. You can all see.
I received this Copper outright when Norman, my son, took a bride.
X̌ix̌aṅyus, I am so glad he is here.
Listen, my child. I will choose this particular one so that it will be known. You saw it when it was given to me as a dowry. It comes from the Danaxdax̌ʷ, tribesmen. This is what I have chosen, so that you will know how I feel about my children, when they take a husband.

Three Coppers are going to be given. [Only two names are given.]
ʔOgʷumalaxʷ, Lubiɫila. The highest of these is Lubiɫila.

Listen! I will not give Lubiɫila outright [ʔoʔdexʔid].
I will keep it because my older brother Ǧʷəyəmdᶻiẏ [Tom Dawson] and I shared ownership of it.
This was the last Copper bought.
They bought it at Mirhkʷəmlis, my home. There was a large group of people there. Many people know about this transaction. The price paid for it was very high. This occurred when we, First Nations, were still living according to our traditional ways. I shared the ownership of Lubiɫila with my kin.

[Henry Bell holds and displays the Copper, Lubiɫila.]

This is the reason why I want to keep it.
When I will no longer be able to carry on my duties, my son [Jim Sewid, his nephew] will look after it. So pay attention, because you have all heard what I have said.
I have chosen this particular Copper. This is how it was in the beginning of time.

[Referring to Daisy's ceremonial outfit.]

This is how my sister ƛiɫʔəlḵalağa [James Sewid's mother] was outfitted, when she married into the ƛawiċis.
Give me your attention, ƛawiċis.
When Ċəndigən ʔOwadiẏ [Chief John Clark: Lorne's great-uncle][2] took her for his bride, ƛawiċis, she was dressed up exactly in the way my child is dressed today, my child, Mayaniɫ, my Precious One. That is why I named her Mayaniɫ [Precious One] as I mentioned it again at my last p̓əsa [potlatch]. I am proud of her. You can all see her now, the way she is dressed in her finest, Mayaniɫ.
I am going to ... This is why I am asking you to pay attention.
I am going to repeat the transaction that took place for my sister, the one who married into the ƛawiċis, to the chief of the ƛawiċis. Along with this transaction went a house with a Loon on the roof. That was his house. You must have all seen it, those of you who were living at the time, before they destroyed it. Along with the house went this Chilkat blanket. So I am going to renew that transaction and repeat it.
Pay attention, so that you will revive these treasures through their use and not just store them away.
The house was built with a Loon on the roof, our k̓isʔuw̓ [crest].

This name will also be passed along with it. I do not just choose anything, whenever I do this. This is going to be done according to my word; you all know this.
I am going to take the name ʔIwanukʷ. This is one of the ancient names of my

grandfather, ꞋIwanukᵂ.³ I have never used it. This will be passed on to you.
I have never given it to anyone. All this time it has been stored.
He was one of the chiefs of the Maṁaliliqəlla, ꞋIwanukᵂ. This is a name from the
other side of our family. He was our ancestral chief. This name is from my house,
the house I inherited from Lagəyus, the huge house. I am doing this in order for
you to know the position of my child.

This is how princesses [ƙisƙadiɫ] were dressed during their weddings. Let me name
one, ƛaqᵂagiloǧᵂa [Copper Woman]. This is how she was dressed when she got
married. ƛaƛaguɫ, my mother, was also dressed this way. So was Max̌ᵂaloǧᵂa, the
mother of Ǧᵂəyəmdᶻiẏ [Tom Dawson]. This is the way she was dressed at my
house. In my father's house there were Ḱesugᵂilakᵂ, ƛaꞋēdᶻiẏ.
That is how far I will go. These are noble women. In the early days the women just
did not take any position that they wanted. The positions had to be given to them,
officially. They were held with great respect. This is why I have honoured her in this way.
I have disclosed the position of my child. I honour my children.
You have all heard what I had to say.
I have left one more thing, for the end. I will take from the ƙisꞋuẁ [crest], the great
ƙisꞋuẁ from the early days, the HamamaɫꞋa [White Man Dance].
All of you know that my grandfather was always potlatching, my grandfather
Gordon. You all know that. You all knew him. This is the HamamaɫꞋa of Gordon.
It will go to you as well as the name of Gordon. The name of Hamalagəyudᶻiẏ. It
was Gordon's chieftain's name. Also, you will call the companion of the Maṁaɫṅa
[White Man], Hiləmgəƛēẏ.
Listen!
Pay attention! I also gave a Maṁaɫṅa to my brother-in-law Kᵂuliẏ, Dan Cranmer,
when he had that big ṗəsa at my big house at Miṁkᵂəmlis. It came from me also.
My share of the dowry is now complete.
Come forth. Come forth and get the Copper. Come forth.

Billie Sunday Willie
Do not take what has been said lightly.
My chiefs have preceded me.
You have not announced my dowry as you have preceded me.
He is truly a chief.
Come forward. Come forward, Chiefs [referring to the Smiths].
Do not just take it lightly.

Tommy Hunt
This is the reason for the gathering. This is the reason for the gathering. Come and
take it. Come and take it.

Adam Dick
You will now hear what I have to say.
[The tape recorder stopped. Adam Dick said he brought over many things, one of which was a *haṁaċa* mask with copper eyes.]

Billie Sunday Willie
This is what I have said, Chiefs. Come forward now. This is a Copper we greatly value. This is Ẁayatən. Come forth and receive it, Chiefs. Come forth and receive it.

Tommy Hunt
Come forward, ƛaqʷagila [Jimmy Wallace]. We will take them at their words. Come forth.

Billie Sunday Willie
I wish to take one of the Coppers of my ancestors. I would like to give one of the *haṁaċa* that belongs to our grandfather, Həyugʷis. This will go to you. I am going to take a Copper from my child [Jimmy Sewid]. They have all come to him, including the *haṁaċa* of our ancestors.

[The tape is unclear at that moment; Sunday Willie was listing some of his *kikəsʔuẁ*:
A *Nuɫcistalaɫ* dance named *Bubaqolayuẁ* (He Who Scares); *Qominigas; Hawiṅalaɫ; Ṅəṅalalaɫ; Ċiƙʷa*.]

Billie Sunday Willie
Chiefs, for those who would say, "He has no *kikəsʔuẁ*," because many would say this. My *gəlgalis* [first ancestor] is the *Ċiƙʷa* [the Seagull]. As a chief I could wear the Seagull headdress from my ancestral tradition among the Dᶻawadaʔēnux̌ʷ; this was when we wore our ceremonial costume.
This is it, Chiefs.

Jimmy Wallace
I am going to disclose how I am related to him [James Sewid], to make known that he is from our land, the ƛaƛasiqʷəlla tribe.
My mother definitely told it to me. She always told us to take care of each other because we are of the same blood.[4] My heart feels good. I am so happy that he asked me to be part of the bridal party for our child. We are truly of one kin, according to our relationships among the ƛaƛasiqʷəlla.

I will give a small dowry for my tribesman's daughter. From what I know, from my ƛaƛasiqʷəlla side, what will be given will be Dᶻunuq̓ʷa. It is the *ƛugʷēγ* [supernatural treasure] from the Nəwidiγ. It is the Dᶻunuq̓ʷa. I have decided on the Dᶻunuq̓ʷa. Listen to me. The name of this Dᶻunuq̓ʷa is Dᶻunuq̓ʷəmalis.

Now, I will also give as a dowry a dance that belonged to my late aunt, older sister of my mother Yəqukʷala. The k̓ik̓əsʔuẁ [crests] are so numerous.
The Ṁaṁaq̓a [Death Thrower][5] will also go to you.
Go ahead. Take it with you when you go, x̌awic̓is. In doing so, I am showing that I am of the same blood as my fellow tribesmen. I am also showing my appreciation for having been asked to be part of the bridal party, to show we are of one blood. This is where I will end, Chiefs. This is where I will end. This is where I will end.

Jimmy Sewid

Yes, ʔUd̓z istalis [Henry Bell]. Yes. Pay attention people.
You have often heard me say that I will never push my uncles out of their positions. I am a fortunate man. Look at all my younger brothers.
I will not take a dowry from my Maʔəmtagila side. You have heard the speech of my chief ʔUd̓z istalis [Henry Bell]. He was taking dowries from my huge house, as I belong to every ṅamay̓əm [descent group] of the Ṁaṁaliliqella through my grandfather Max̌ʷalagəlis, also called Max̌ʷa. You have heard all my kinsmen.
One thing was forgotten when Max̌mewisa [Jimmy Dick] or Kʷaxsistala [sacred or p̓əsa potlatch name] was speaking. My kinsman also gave $200.
I am referring to x̌aqʷagila [Adam Dick], x̌aqagila for his niece.
Chiefs, you have now succeeded in your wooing. I would like to say to our child, my sister [May Smith, Lorne's mother][6] G̱ʷəntilakʷ and I will not bother to take a dowry from our k̓ik̓esos, as we are of one blood [nəmukʷ ʔum bəgʷanəm].
You will take from our k̓ik̓əsʔuẁ, G̱ʷəntilakʷ, whenever you want. We are of one kin according to our genealogy, children of Ċeqaméẏ, from whom we are the descendants. We are of one blood. I would be very wrong if I used any of this to give to you as a dowry. You are the descendant of the firstborn of Ċeqaméẏ.

Jimmy Sewid [holding a broken Copper]

Look at this, Chiefs. What I am holding is the Copper called Wanəmgila. This is what I have acquired from your dowries, Kʷaguɫ, from the late chief ʔUd̓z istalis.

[Someone in the background says,] "This is correct."

It was given to me outright [ʔoʔdexʔid].
So, this will go to you, chiefs [referring to the Smiths] as a result of the union between my cousin [Lorne] who has ɫanɫaǧoʔ with my child X̌ʷənukʷ. You have challenged me, Ċeqaméẏ. I have great wealth. Look to the south, look to the north. Think of the dowries you have acquired from me for your tribe; I am referring to myself as a Qʷiqʷasuɫinux̌ʷ. The legends of my houses are manifold. Look in this house that I have built, this is my ɫamilas, my painted ceremonial screen. This is where I go in and out [as a haṁaċa] and it is a dowry that I received from you

Kʷaguɫ. It comes from the Hiɫdʐuqʷ [Heiltsuk or Bella Bella]. That is why I have songs that are in the Hiɫdʐuqʷ language. It came from you, Chief ʔUdʐistalis. [Alvin Alfred is James Sewid's brother-in-law and Flora (Alfred) Sewid's brother.]

[Someone in the background says,] "That is correct."

We are supposed to remind you of the dowries so that you will know. Therefore, it is on display in this house that we have built. Take care of my house. I will now review the women of my family. From these women you have received dowries. First of all, I will say to you, Chiefs, come forth and get my Copper. Come and take it.

Tommy Hunt[8]
[Addressing Bert Smith, Lorne Smith's older brother.]

Go forward, Sewidanakʷəla [name of the Smiths before they used their Christian name]. Go and get what we have acquired.

[Bert Smith brought the broken Copper to Tommy Hunt.][9]

Jimmy Sewid
Pay attention, tribesmen!
I am not just going to take an ordinary dowry for my child. You are going to call her ƛaqʷagiloḡʷa. This is a name from my huge house, the house of ʔUdʐistalis [Henry Bell] here. I also have this name on my Maʔəmtagila side from the mother of my grandmother Həxhakʷaʔēdʐəmḡa. We also knew her as ƛaxʷaɫa [Having Many Relations].
I am going to take from my grandfather's side the name of the child of Max̌ʷayalisdʐiẏ. You are going to call my child ƛaqʷagiloḡʷa, when she goes home to Q̓aluḡʷis [Turnour Island, the home of the ƛawiċis]. That is how they are going to call you, child [Daisy]. We shall proceed. Come forward.

[Addressing the women.]

All of you come forward, so that they can look at you. You are all dressed up in your finest.

[Twenty-three women put on their ceremonial outfits.]

This is the ceremonial outfit from the Head Chief of the Qʷiqʷasuɫinux̌ʷ. This is the way Max̌ʷa was dressed, uncle of my father.
It has been given as a dowry to the tribes. My uncle Ḡʷəyəmdʐiẏ [Tom Dawson] was dressed in such a manner. He was from Dʐawadaʔēnux̌ʷ [Kingcome Inlet]. It went to you Həxʷaməs [Wakeman Sound] when my kinsman married the one we refer to as Habadən. This is the way they were dressed.
We are outfitted in our ceremonial clothing, Chiefs. So look on.

[Singing of the song that refers to Daisy's "heaviness."][10]

Billie Sunday Willie:
I am going to sing the song of [incomprehensible].[11]
[Billie Sunday Willie is singing and drumming.]

This is the wedding song of [incomprehensible].
From long time ago [incomprehensible], child of [incomprehensible].

Jimmy Sewid
You have heard, x̌awiċis.
Look at all of them. [He motions to all the women.] They are from my
Mamaliliqəlla [Village Island] side and my Q̌ʷiqʷasutinux̌ʷ side [Gilford Island]. This
is from where you are acquiring your dowries, Chiefs.
I am going to use as an example, ʾUd̓istalis.
This is what we are supposed to do during a gathering such as this one. I will just
take examples from the big house, the huge house from the Mamaliliqəlla. The
house of Max̌ʷa and Hanyus [Ethel Alfred's father from Village Island].
The first one was x̌aqʷagiloğʷa. Pay attention, Weλax̌as [Jack Peters]. This has to do
with the Danaxdax̌ʷ, when the late chief ʾIwasuw̓ asked for the hand of the chief's
daughter. We gave as a dowry to you, Ċad̓inukʷəmēẏ [New Vancouver], Chiefs. We
gave it to you outright [ʔoʔdexʔid]. We went as far as asking the White man not to
list it among the territories of the Mamaliliqəlla. That is the reason why you own it
today. Who else has ever done it? Who, but my people?
The Maʾəmtagila obtained X̌ax̌əm [Port Neville] from the Walacəm.
It went to you outright, Chiefs. It was repeated for Max̌ʷaloğʷa, to you
D̓awadaʾēnux̌ʷ [Kingcome Inlet], mother of my uncle X̌aneyus, also known as
Č̓ʷəyəmd̓iẏ [Tom Dawson]. They also took dowries from the huge house. They
also repeated this for my grandmother x̌ax̌aqlʾos. Pay attention, Maʾəmtagila.
They took the dowry from my grandfather, Max̌ʷalagəlis. We emptied the house
at that time too.

We will now talk about my mothers. You again acquired dowries from us, Kʷaguł.
When my uncle [Ed Whonnock] married my aunt Həmd̓idiẏ, you also benefited,
Nəmğis. He was known as Məkʷəla among the Nəmğis. We gave away all my songs,
the songs of the present chief, ʾUd̓istalis [Henry Bell; Henry Bell and Həmd̓idiẏ
were brother and sister] from our huge house. The dowries were disappearing.
Among these were also feast bowls. Also feast songs. Then they repeated this for
my mother when she married into your tribe, Chiefs of the x̌awiċis, to the chief
Ċəndigən ʾOwadiẏ [John Clark].

[Someone in the background says,] "This is correct."

They were not married long when the chief died. I remember it. She then married Chief Mək̓ʷəla [David Matilpi, Gus's father], father of my younger brother [David Matilpi Jr.]. [Motions to him.] We gave away again dowries from the big house, the huge house. Then they repeated this for my other aunt, Ǧʷixsisəlas to you, Nəmǧis and Qʷiqʷasuṫinux̌ʷ. They again emptied the house for her, our huge house.

That was the way it was also for the sisters of my uncle Hek̓ʷagilaʔog̓ʷa, to you, Dᶻawadaʔēnux̌ʷ. The dowry also came from the house of ʔUdᶻistalis [Henry Bell]. Also the woman you are boasting, Nəmǧis. I am referring to Ċolaliⱡilakʷ [Emma Cranmer]. You have never forgotten her. They flattened our big house for her. Nothing was held back for her. It was just recently [1921]. Pay attention! People! You wanted to hear this, otherwise, why would you have asked for the hand of my daughter, knowing this would be revealed to you? The dowry of my aunt, ƛilinux̌ʷ, went to you also, Kʷaguⱡ, when she first married the son of ʔOwadiy̓. Then, she married ʔUdᶻistalis. Also the dowry of Həmdᶻis [Annie Hanyus-Ambers]. That dowry went to you, ƛawiċis, to the late chief Sewidanak̓ʷəla, Peter Smith. They also flattened the house of Hanyus from our other side. Then they repeated this again for Məmxuyog̓ʷa [Ethel (Hanyus) Alfred]. We did the same thing for her.

I just wanted to reveal the history of the giving of our dowries to the tribes. It is our custom to reveal it. That is the reason why our highborn daughters are difficult to acquire. That is why we have what we have. Our ancestors never said, "We have no more kikəsʔuẃ,"or "Our house is empty." Our houses were overflowing with wealth when we acquired your dowries, Chiefs; when we conquered your wealth. That is how our huge house filled up again. It received all kinds of dowries. That is what was told to me, as I grew older. That is what was told to me, so that I would not forget. That is it, Chiefs of the ƛawiċis. That is it, Chiefs.

Let my child come forward. Come forward ʔIwanukʷ [Lorne Smith; the groom]. Come on your own, child. Come forward, you and your brothers. I am embarrassed for I cannot remember your Indian names. Come forward, kinsmen, so that you can receive your ceremonial outfits.

[The five Smith brothers approached to receive their blankets and aprons, and did so in the order of their birth, except for Lorne, who as the groom, came last: Alec Smith, Bert Smith, John Smith, Dennis Smith, Lorne Smith. Daisy took off her Chilkat blanket and put it on Lorne. She also gave him the button blanket that she made especially for him.]

Come forward, mothers; come forward, ƛiⱡa [Margaret Cook]. Come forward, the two Ǧʷəntilakʷ [Lorne's mother, May Smith, and Agnes Cranmer]. [They put capes on them.] Come forward, uncles [Tommy Hunt, Ernest Scow (i.e., May's brother)]. Come forward, kinsmen; make a turn, make a circle [around the fire]. My sister will take our ceremonial outfits off and put them on you. You will be now outfitted. This is from our tribe, the Qʷiqʷasutinux̌ʷ. [At this time they put the outfit on Ernie Scow, Lorne's uncle; it is decorated with the representation of the Q̓ulus, crest of the Qʷiqʷasutinux̌ʷ.]

Billie Sunday Willie
The ƛawiċis will dance and sing the wedding dance.
[Billie Sunday Willie is singing and the ƛawiċis are dancing.]

Tommy Hunt
Pay attention, Chief ʔAmawiyus! Pay attention, ʔAmawiyus [Jimmy Sewid], and ʔUdᶻistalis [Henry Bell]! What do you wish to do with your Copper?

Henry Bell
I have told you before that I wanted to keep it. But now I have decided that I do not want it returned to us. It should be given to you outright.[12]

Billie Sunday Willie
[Incomprehensible.]

Arthur Dick (ƛawiċis)
What are you going to do with your Copper, Kʷaxsistala [Jimmy Dick]?

Jimmy Dick
I am going to buy it back from you for $1,000.

Tommy Hunt
Thank you, Chief. Pay attention, kinsmen, to what has been said by Chief Kʷaxsistala.

Arthur Dick
Pay attention!

Tommy Hunt
He said he is going to pay $1,000 to buy back his Copper. This is the Copper that we are now licensed to use.[13]

Arthur Dick
Pay attention, ƛawiċis to what they have done!
Pay attention, ʔAmawiyus! What do you wish to do with your Copper?

Jimmy Sewid
I value it. So let it return. I let it return. I let it return. Now you will pay attention, tribesmen! For what my uncle and I have to say. Thank you, ʔUdᶻistalis. Thank you, father of the ńamaẏam [descent group], for giving your Copper outright to my son-in-law [negʷəmp] ʔIwanukʷ. They have given it to you out right, ƛawiċis.

He is able to do this because he is very wealthy. Then it was your turn, Kʷaxsistala [Jimmy Dick], Nənwaqawēẏ. It was your turn, father. So you have paid $1,000 for your Copper to return. Thank you, father. I wish to thank my tribesmen. Now we will go to my x̱ax̱asiqʷəlla side. Thank you for what you gave, kinsman. You have revealed my position. That is what was told to me by my grandfather. We will now go to you, kinsman, x̱aqʷagila [Adam Dick]. Thank you for helping your niece [referring to his contribution to the dowry]. Also to all the relatives who have contributed to increase her dowry. Also Məmxuẇ, eldest of my children, whom I refer to as Bobby. He also gave a certain amount of money. It is supposed to be made public, Chiefs, to a gathering such as this one. So here it is, x̱aqʷagila. So pay attention, Chiefs! You have heard my father ʔUdᶻistalis. I never told my daughter what to do; she decided to do what she has done on her own [he refers to the work involved in preparing wedding regalia]. She worked on these things on her own, buying things. All the things that she is going to bring to you, Chiefs [Smith] cost $3,000 in jewellery for the women. Now you see the way my daughter is outfitted with abalone shells; this is our Indian jewellery. This is the way my Head Chief was outfitted among the Qʷiqʷasutinuxʷ, as I belong to Ḡʷayasdəms [Gilford Island]. This is the way my Head Chief was outfitted among the Wiʔumasǧəm [a descent group of the Maṁaliliqəlla]. All the women wore abalone shell earrings. That is the way it is. The jewellery, which is going to be distributed among the women, is worth $3,000. My daughter recorded everything that she did, Chiefs. Take, for example, what you are wearing. Consider what it is worth, the material and the labour.[14]

[Someone in the background says,] "That is correct."

This is what we have used as payment for our Coppers to be returned. It has never been done; it has never been done in this way before. This is it, Chiefs. This is what you have acquired from me. This is what you have acquired from me. That is what was told to me by my Chief, my grandfather Max̱ʷalagəlis, when he said that I am a good father.

[Someone in the background says,] "That is correct."

They were in a different category, the Chiefs of the old days. The value of my Copper will now increase because of all the goods mentioned, and also because of Kʷaxsistala's Copper. That is it, Chiefs. We have now completed the transaction. I will now go home to where I come from. "Goodbye, now." ["Goodbye, now" said In English. People are laughing.]

Tommy Hunt
We will now show our appreciation, x̱awiċis. You have all heard what the Chiefs had to say.

[In the background Chief Jimmy King says,] "That is the way it is."

The dowry is what every man dreams of.
All your courtship has now achieved its goals. So we will now bring the bride over.
Come forward.

Jimmy Sewid
Come forward, and get the cash, Chiefs. Come forward.
[In a joking manner,] "Do not go to the pub with it!" [Laughter.]

Tommy Hunt
Thank you! Thank you!
Just show your appreciation for me.
Let us show them how much we appreciate the dowry, which came over,
so that we could bring it all home.

[Tommy Hunt sings the appreciation song using his Chief's Raven rattle.]

It is appreciated. You know the song that I just chanted, people. That is the chant
from ꞌUmxꞌid [Tom Omxid (English name) at Fort Rupert; he was married to
Tommy Hunt's sister].

[In the background Chief Jimmy King says,] "That is it indeed."
We were kinsmen, ꞌUmxꞌid and I. His name was ꞌUmxꞌid.

Arthur Dick
Thank you, tribesmen! Thank you!
We x̱awiċis are wealthier now for having taken your respected one. We are truly in
that position. We cannot help but appreciate all the overflowing wealth that you
have given to the house of Sewidanakʷəla [Smith]. It is of great value. We wish to
thank you.

Tommy Hunt
Thank you!

Arthur Dick
What else could I say? We surely appreciated it. Come forward, x̱aqʷagila [Jim
King], so that you also can show your appreciation. That is what our ancestors
used to do. We all are supposed to show our appreciation. Come forward, for you
are a better speaker than I am.

Jimmy King
Greetings to you, people!
My father, Ɏaquλas, was a kinsman of Sewidanakʷəla [the late Peter Smith]. They
were of one blood.

Also Məllidᶻas [Lorne's father, who was also called Scotty Smith].

Also my uncle ƛaquλas.

This is how I am related to my children [Smith]. I would like to show my appreciation, for this also has benefited me.

[Addressing the Smiths,] Listen, children!

[Jimmy King sings his appreciation song using his rattle.]

That is what my grandfather said when he was fortunate to get a Copper from the Copper House.

That is why grandfathers were chiefs from generation to generation. They received all this wealth and names from their father's side and their mother's side. My grandfather was fortunate to receive this huge Copper. What was the name of it? I am like that too. I forgot the name of it. Do not laugh! [Laughter.]

It was ƛaqʷəlamas. It was used as a mast[15] by ʔIwanukʷ when he received his dowry at Ǵʷaʔi [Kingcome].

I will sing this.

[Jimmy King sings a second appreciation song using his rattle.]

That is the appreciation song where I come from.

That is what my own ancestral tradition says.

[He finishes the song.]

That is all I have to say for now. I will continue later on.

[He makes an allusion to the following potlatch.][16]

I am finished.

Arthur Dick

That is it, Chiefs.

We have now concluded, Chiefs. Everybody's heart is happy now, because we have received what we wanted. We have got it, ƛawiċis! It is to be appreciated. It has to be appreciated; we are finished! Do not go out, as we are going to begin the mourning ceremony. This is a part of the ceremony that should be appreciated and respected, the ways of our ancestors. The ceremony will comfort as it goes on. No man born is to remain in this world. All of us will some day go home. We will sing the mourning song to comfort our hearts. This is it. This is it. Thank you! Thank you, tribesmen! We are happy. Our hearts feel good.

[ʔAx̌uẇ took Daisy's hat off, detached the pieces of abalone shell that decorated it, and distributed them to the Chiefs, their wives, and the nobility.][17]

∾

APPENDIX E
Kinship Diagrams

The key symbols used to represent ʔAx̌uw̓'s genealogy are as follows:

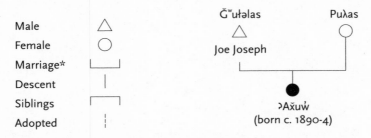

Male   △

Female   ○

Marriage*   └──┘

Descent   │

Siblings   ┌──┐

Adopted   ┊

Ḡʷułəlas   Puλas

△

Joe Joseph

●

ʔAx̌uw̓
(born c. 1890-4)

* 1 and 2 next to the symbol refer to first and second marriages.

DIAGRAM 1

Qʷiqʷasuṫinux̌ʷ
Died in BC raid*

Qʷiqʷasuṫinux̌ʷ
Ẏaquλas

Nəmǧis
Q̓ʷalaxəlogʷa

○ 1

△

○ 2

Q̓iqəx̌alla

Died in
BC raid

Died in
BC raid

Wikəlalisəmēy̓ǧa

Puλas

*Died in the Bella Coola massacre.

△

Dan Cranmer

●

ʔAx̌uw̓

Appendix E

DIAGRAM 2

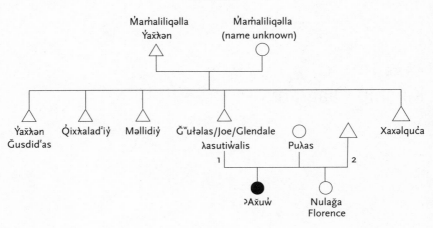

DIAGRAM 3

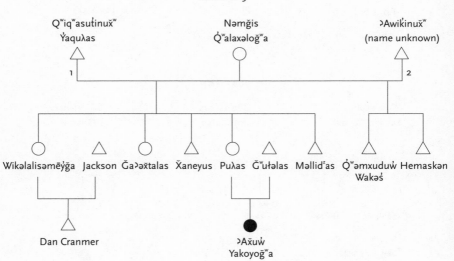

DIAGRAM 4

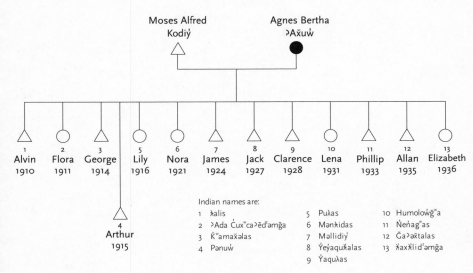

Moses Alfred
Kodiẏ

Agnes Bertha
ʔAx̌uẇ

| 1 Alvin 1910 | 2 Flora 1911 | 3 George 1914 | 5 Lily 1916 | 6 Nora 1921 | 7 James 1924 | 8 Jack 1927 | 9 Clarence 1928 | 10 Lena 1931 | 11 Phillip 1933 | 12 Allan 1935 | 13 Elizabeth 1936 |

4
Arthur
1915

Indian names are:

1 ƛalis
2 ʔAda Ċux̌ʷcaʔēdᶻəmğa
3 Ḱʷamax̌əlas
4 Pənuẇ
5 Puƛas
6 Mənƛidas
7 Məllidiẏ
8 Ẏeẏaqux̌alas
9 Ẏaquƛas
10 Humolowğʷa
11 Ńeṅagʷas
12 Ċaʔax̌talas
13 ƛax̌ƛidᶻəmğa

Note: Moses and ʔAx̌uẇ celebrated their Kʷakʷakəwakʷ wedding during the summer of 1908, and their Christian wedding at the Anglican Church during the winter of 1933.

DIAGRAM 5

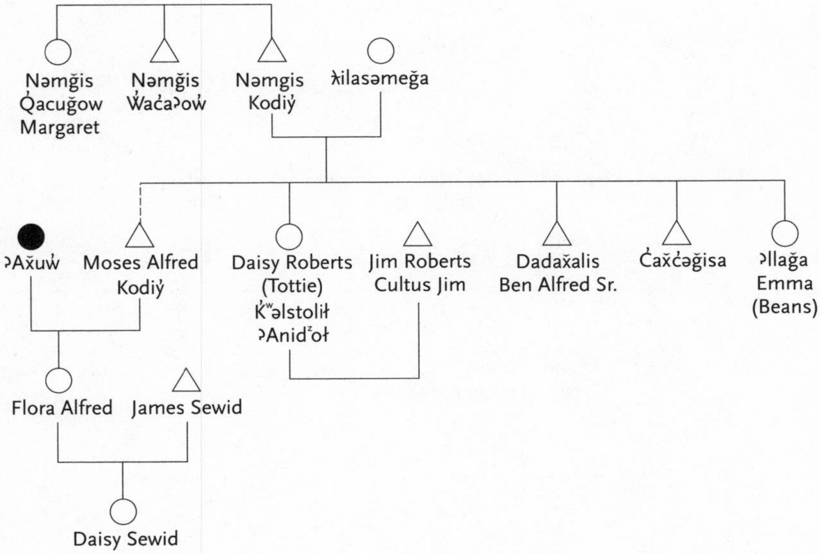

Nəmğis
Q̇acuğow
Margaret

Nəmğis
Ẇaċaʔoẇ

Nəmgis
Kodiẏ

x̌ilasəmeğa

ʔAx̌uẇ

Moses Alfred
Kodiẏ

Daisy Roberts
(Tottie)
Ḱʷəlstoliɫ
ʔAnidᶻoɫ

Jim Roberts
Cultus Jim

Dadax̌alis
Ben Alfred Sr.

Ċax̌ċəğisa

ʔllaǧa
Emma
(Beans)

Flora Alfred   James Sewid

Daisy Sewid

229

DIAGRAM 6

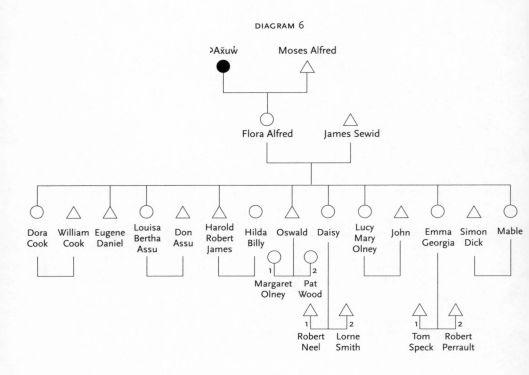

DIAGRAM 7

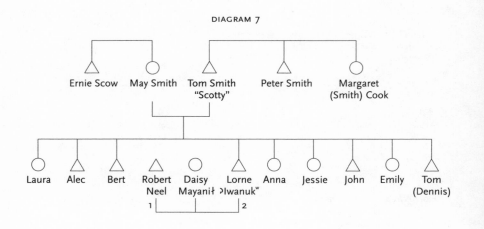

Notes

Preface

1 Dᶻunuq̓ʷa is a complex character in myth and in the Kʷakʷakəwakʷ dancing societies. She (although she is sometimes male) is a giantess who lives in the mountains and in the woods. She is usually described as black with bushy eyebrows and unkempt hair, and with a pursed mouth through which she utters her typical "Hu, hu!" cry. She carries on her back a basket in which to put the children she intends to steal. In myth, she is slow, sleepy, clumsy, and not particularly smart: the children outwit her. But she also controls the "water of life," a gift she bestows on a family that wrested her secrets from her. She brings wealth and fortune.

   The X̌ʷix̌ʷiẏ mask originated with the Salish Sx̌ʷayx̌ʷəy, which was an important crest mask worn during the rites of passage ceremonies. The mythic origin of the mask is deep within a lake, and it was associated with earthquakes. This mask's colour is predominantly white; its eyes are bulging and its tongue protruding.

   In a vast comparative study of the origin myths of Dᶻunuq̓ʷa (Kʷakʷakəwakʷ) and X̌ʷix̌ʷiẏ (Kʷakʷakəwakʷ) on the one hand, and the Sx̌ʷayx̌ʷəy (Salish) on the other, Claude Lévi-Strauss emphasized the parallelism linking the Copper and the Sx̌ʷayx̌ʷəy figure on both the sociological and the artistic, or aesthetic, levels. The results of his comparative works allowed him to go much further. Among the Salish, the Sx̌ʷayx̌ʷəy masks are interchangeable with the Copper since they have identical origin myths. Among the Kʷakʷakəwakʷ, the origin of the Copper goes back to Dᶻunuq̓ʷa, whose mask reverses the Sx̌ʷayx̌ʷəy mask from an aesthetic point of view, while both masks retain the same function from a semantic point of view. Furthermore, the semantic is reversed when one goes from the Salish Sx̌ʷayx̌ʷəy to the Kʷakʷakəwakʷ X̌ʷix̌ʷiẏ, but in this case the two masks are similar from a plastic point of view. (Lévi-Strauss, 1977: 112). For a summary of his conclusive remarks, see de Widerspach-Thor (1981: 164-5).

2 Born in 1903 (the daughter of Kenneth and Lucy Henderson) Mrs. Ferry, also known as Kitty Ferry, grew up at Blunden Harbour; she ran a workshop in Gastown, Vancouver, for twenty-nine years to help urban First Nations women cope with personal and social problems. (Later the name of the organization was changed to Saint James Workshop in recognition of the church's participation in this endeavour; see Neel [1992: 24-7].)

3 Yəlis: yəl comes from yəɬaɬa: having legs spread out; and lis: on the ground. Reference is made to the crescent-shaped island.

4 Chief James Sewid (1933-88), Poogleedee (as spelled by his biographer) has been the subject of an autobiography edited by anthropologist James Spradley (1969), which also provides an analysis of bicultural adaptation. In this important life story we are made aware of at least twelve names that Sewid received during his lifetime as well as their provenance (1969: 16-19).

5   George Hunt (1854-1933) was also known as Father of Yə̓gʷis; his ceremonial name
    was Nul'qulela (Boas 1966: 179-241; Berman 1996: 229).
6   For more information on the nature of the collaboration between Franz Boas and Dan
    Cranmer, see Codere (1966: xxv-xxvii).
7   A Nəmǧis origin myth tells how, after the Flood, there was only one survivor,
    Nəmugʷis, who landed on the back of the giant halibut (*nəmugʷ*: the only one; *gʷis*:
    land). Traditionally, the Nəmǧis lived at the mouth and along the banks of the
    Nimpkish River. For both historic and economic reasons, many Nəmǧis people who
    were part Kʷaguɫ moved to Yəlis on Cormorant Island in the 1870s and 1880s. As a
    result of this, Yəlis became the largest Kʷakʷakǝwakʷ settlement; it was known to
    non–First Nations people as Alert Bay. Before Yəlis became the home of the Nəmǧis
    Band it was populated by the Kʷaguɫ (who occupied its centre), the M̓aṁaliliqəlla (to
    the west), and the x̌awiċis (to the east). See Boas (1897: 331, 333); Dawson (1888: 72);
    Galois (1994: 309-10); Boas (2002: 305-12); Bouchard and Kennedy, eds., in Boas
    (2002: 305, n.1).
8   Dan Cranmer also worked with Boas after George Hunt's death. See Codere in Boas
    (1966: xv-xxvi).
9   *Nox̌sola* is a generic term that refers to the entire class of chiefs and the nobility. See
    Boas and Hunt (1921: 1416). It can also be translated as title-holder.
10 Julia Averkieva, a student of Boas, is said to have collected some life-history material
    from Kʷakʷakǝwakʷ women in the 1930s while recording genealogies (Rohner 1966:
    198). Her published work pertaining to these people, however, concerns mainly string
    figures and slavery. See Averkieva (1966 [1941], 1981); Averkieva and Sherman (1992).
11 See Reid (1984a).
12 For example, one such question had to do with women's relationships with masks.
    In the past, women who were actively involved in ceremonies and dancing could
    wear frontlets or headdresses, as they do today. Yet it seems that they never wore
    masks. Why was mask-wearing the prerogative only of men? I later had a chance to
    investigate this subject (Reid 1986a). Today a few women do wear masks, although
    only rarely.
13 See, for example, Buckley and Gottlieb (1988); Strathern (1972 and 1988); and
    Héritier (2002).
14 Name given to Daisy as an infant by her great-uncle ʔUd̓istalis Henry Bell, chief of
    the Q̓ad̓əgiwēy̓ descent group, among the M̓aṁaliliqəlla at M̓iṁkʷəmlis (Village
    Island).
15 Boas (1966: 372-6) documented a series of expressive and stereotyped gestures
    performed within the context of dances.
16 *baxʷkəm*, Indian; plural: *bibaxʷkəm*: First Nations people. (*Bibaxʷəs*: human beings.)

Introduction

1   An earlier version of this chapter was presented, under the title "Voices of One's
    Life," at the International Conference on Anthropology of the Northwest Coast:
    Assessments and New Perspectives, at the Collège de France, Paris, 2000. See Reid
    and Sewid-Smith (2003). We wish to thank Marie Mauzé, Michael Harkin, and Sergei
    Kan for their general comments; Dell Hymes for his editorial comments; and Judith
    Berman for her comments regarding Kʷak̓ʷala orthography.
2   See Weintraub (1978) on life episodes of the Greeks, and Georg Misch (1951) on the
    records of the deeds of Egyptian pharaohs. See also David Brumble III (1988: 4).

3   *The Confessions* by Jean-Jacques Rousseau (1889) is a good early model of the genre.
4   Kʷakʷ̓ala distinguishes between past, present, and future: in the past: x̌a galuɫ ɫe; today: x̌ʷanalax̌; the days to come: x̌a ʔaɫƙey ninalaɫ. See Bruner (1986: 6) for the distinction between reality, experience, and expressions; and Bruner (1984: 7) for distinction between life as lived, life as experience, and life as told. For a discussion of the concepts of tradition, continuity, and invention, see Mauzé (1997).
5   *Black Elk Speaks* by Neihardt (1972 [1932]) is equally well known.
6   For a feminist approach to women's lives, see Bridgeman, Cole, and Howard-Bobiwash (1999).
7   See also Clifford and Marcus (1986).
8   For a philosophical approach to autobiography, see Wolheim (1984).
9   We do know the reasons for the deletions and have decided to respect them.
10 "Kʷakʷ̓akǝwakʷ" aristocratic etiquette, for example, eschews maligning the past or others. To do so is a sign of a 'commoner'" (Saunders 1995: 61).
11 Theisz (1981) refers to narrated Indian autobiographies as bi-autobiographies (i.e., original bicultural compositions), distinguishing them from their two relatives, biography and autobiography.
12 See also Crapanzano (1977: vol. 2, pp. 3-7).
13 From a linguistic viewpoint – as this material emanates from only one source, one voice – the pace, the phrasing, and the dialectical inflections are constant. At a later date, linguists will be able to clearly define ʔAx̌uẃ's style from the transcripts.
14 For an analysis of the Baxʷbakʷ̓alanux̌ʷsiwēẏ myths and subsequent studies, see Reid (1981, 1984a); and de Widerspach-Thor (1981).
15 The trade language, Chinook jargon, not the "Chinook" spoken by Charles Cultee and others at the mouth of the Columbia River on its northern side, recorded in *Chinook Texts* by Boas (1894), and grammatically described in the first volume of *The Handbook of American Indian Languages* (Boas 1911a).
16 It might have been 26 January 1894, according to a date Moses Alfred had written in his Bible.
17 Kʷakʷ̓akǝwakʷ society was organized around a certain number of kin groups called ńǝmaẏǝm (descent groups), which were based upon descent from a common ancestor. An individual belonged to a ńǝmaẏǝm because either her/his father or her/his mother was a member of that ńǝmaẏǝm. This is what is known as a cognatic (or bilateral) rule of descent (i.e., individuals trace their descent through either males or females). A Kʷakʷ̓akǝwakʷ child can claim membership in both her/his mother's and her/his father's ńǝmaẏǝm. These descent groups functioned as corporate groups: they owned houses, fishing sites, berry-picking grounds, and hunting territories. The chiefs of a ńǝmaẏǝm acted as political leaders in potlatching and warfare. The ńǝmaẏǝm acted as a unit on ceremonial occasions (such as those performed around the marriage and repurchase of a bride). Kʷakʷ̓akǝwakʷ myths describe how the supernatural ancestors of present-day ńǝmaẏǝm acquired magical powers that were transmitted down the generations to their descendants.

According to Daisy Sewid-Smith, after the massacre of the Gilford Island people at Ǧʷayasdǝms, several Qʷiqʷ̓asutinux̌ʷ women, among them ʔAx̌uẃ, decided to emphasize their mother's side to demonstrate that some of the Qʷiqʷ̓asutinux̌ʷ had survived.

18 For a critical review of Boas's contribution to anthropology, see White (1963). See also Berman (1992: 125-62) for a reevaluation of some of Boas's translations.
19 Before the "Kʷaguɫ of Fort Rupert" came to be known as such, they existed as four distinct "tribes" (tribe: lǝǧʷax̌ɫēẏ) out of twenty-eight and lived in separate villages.

They were the Gʷitəlla (or Kʷix̣amut, "Those who received the blow"); the Q̓umuẏoʔiẏ (or Kʷix̣a, "Those who gave the blow," sometimes translated as "the Murderers"); the Walas Kʷaguɫ (the Great Kʷaguɫ); and the Q̓ʷəmk̓uɫəs (Rich in the Middle). For a detailed history of their move, see Sewid-Smith (1991: 24-5). See also Boas (1966: 39).

20   George Hunt was born from a high-ranking Tlingit woman (Mary Ebbetts Hunt; her Kʷak̓ʷala name was Musgəmxλala) and a Scottish father (Robert Hunt) and was raised among the Kʷaguɫ in Fort Rupert. For more on George Hunt, see Healy (n.d. 1958: 19); Berman (1996: 226-7).

21   A name alluding to the large amount of smoke billowing from the smoke-holes of potlatch houses. Boas (1897: 553) translated the term "Kwakiutl" as Smoke of the World.

22   For a reevaluation of the nature of the relationship between Boas and Hunt and the product of their collaboration, see Berman (1996: 215-56).

23   Personally, I have been struck by the way Kʷak̓ʷakəwakʷ elders revere books and how interested they are in knowing what they say (Martine Reid).

24   ʔAx̣uw̓ was so fond of that name that she gave it to her favourite cat.

25   In 1998, in recognition of devotion to the service of others and of the contribution to the fields of linguistics, Aboriginal justice, and cultural anthropology of the Kʷak̓ʷakəwakʷ, the University of Victoria conferred upon Daisy Sewid-Smith an honorary doctor of laws.

26   See de Widerspach-Thor (1978).

27   Boas and Hunt recorded family stories that span more than fifteen generations. It should be noted that generations were probably much shorter then than they are today.

28   For brilliant discussions of the problems of apprehending other cultures and of writing down other systems of thought, see Geertz (1988); Rubel and Rosman (2003); Yengoyan (2003); Silverstein (2003). For a discussion of the range of methods by which oral texts can be observed, collected, translated, and analyzed, see Finnegan (1992).

29   The quotative marker announces third-hand information not originating from the storyteller. For patterning with quotative markers, see Hymes (1990: 598). For more information on the linguistics of Kʷak̓ʷala and related subjects (such as translation and symbolic interpretation), see the recent works by Berman (1982; 1994; 1996).

30   For a discussion on the role of quotatives in oral literature, see Mishler (1981).

31   For a discussion of colloquial and ritual Seneca language, see Chafe (1981).

32   According to Daisy Sewid-Smith, Duda was Mrs. Peter Smith (born Glendale).

33   White man (m̓am̓aɫn̓a) is a Nootkan word meaning "people living on water," and it refers to the first European sailors.

34   The date of the first contact between Northwest Coast First Nations and Europeans is uncertain. We cannot rule out that early contacts may have taken place between North American Northwest Coast First Nations and people from Asia. There is evidence, for example, that survivors of a Manila galleon and other wrecks did reach the Oregon coast (Suttles 1990: 70; Cook 1973: 31-40). Speculations of other contacts have been advanced by McKechnie (1972: 7), who claims that a group of Buddhist priests were in what is now British Columbia in A.D. 458. These speculations, however, are not yet proven. The first recorded contact with the Kʷak̓ʷakəwakʷ occurred in 1786 in the person of British trader James Strange, who was "discovering" Queen Charlotte Strait (Strange 1929: 29-32; Fisher and Bumsted 1982: 130-1). The next recorded encounter was in 1792, when the Kʷak̓ʷakəwakʷ of the Queen Charlotte Strait were visited successively by Americans under Robert Gray (Howay 1941: 402-4); British under

George Vancouver (1798 vol. 1: 343-51) and Archibald Menzies (1923: 86-8), and Spanish under Galiano and Valdés (Wagner 1933). The Nəmǧis village of X̌ʷəlkʷ (meaning "crossed logs") located at the mouth of the Nimpkish River was visited by George Vancouver, whose report mentions muskets and other evidence of trade (see also Boas 1934: 36, 78). By the early nineteenth century contact was frequent. The village of Nahwitti at Cape Sutil was a favourite port of call, especially for Americans (Reynolds 1938: 22; Codere 1990: 360).

35 In 1843 the Hudson's Bay Company established Fort Victoria, which became a major trading post and an attraction for First Nations peoples living far north of the Kʷakʷakəwakʷ, who had to pass through Kʷakʷakəwakʷ territory to get there (Codere 1990: 360).

36 Since the 1830s the Hudson's Bay Company was active in the region, having established Fort Langley on the Fraser River in 1827 and Fort McLoughlin on Milbanke Sound in 1833. It also maintained ships to compete with the Americans.

37 For a geographical history of the Indian reserve in British Columbia, and the impact of reserves on First Nations lives and livelihoods, see Harris (2002).

38 According to Robert Galois (1994: 203), Robert Hunt bought the property in 1885 for $1,500.

39 Before the devastating smallpox epidemics of 1862, the Kʷakʷakəwakʷ had experienced epidemics in the 1770s and 1820s (smallpox) and in 1848 (measles) (Boyd 1990; Codere 1950: 53). In his recent book Robert Boyd (1999) details the introduction of infectious diseases among Northwest Coast First Nations and charts their effects upon the Aboriginal population.

40 One of the many ways of spelling Kʷaguɫ (synonym).

41 The long and unsuccessful attempt to eliminate the Kʷakʷakəwakʷ potlatching by law has been described by La Violette (1961); Codere (1950); Halliday (1935); and Sewid-Smith (1979).

42 Rivers Inlet, Alert Bay, and Steveston.

43 For language classification, see Laurence C. Thompson and Dale M. Kinkade (1990: 34).

44 There is a fair amount of literature on the "Kwakiutl" language, the bulk of which comes from Franz Boas: two grammars (Boas 1911b; 1947); notes on vocabulary and suffixes (Boas 1924; 1931); and text collections (Boas 1910; 1935-43; Boas and Hunt 1902-05; 1906). For treatment of Kwakiutl syntaxes, see Stephen Anderson (1984) and Robert Levine (1977; 1984). For dictionaries, see Neville Lincoln and John Rath (1980) and David Grubb (1977). For teaching manuals, refer to Daisy Sewid-Smith (1988) and Jay Powell, Vickie Jensen, Agnes Cranmer, and Margaret Cook (1990).

45 Among the Kʷakʷakəwakʷ people a baby will receive its first name at the age of ten months; at puberty (around twelve years old), the adolescent will receive his or her first adult name(s).

Chapter 1: Myth Time

1 A selection from *Indianishe Sagen* by Franz Boas has been arranged by the British Columbia Indian Language Project, and published under the title "Indian Folktales from British Columbia" in *Malahat Review* 60 (1981): 45-77. See also the most recent translation of the totality of *Indianishe Sagen*, under the new title *Indian Myths and Legends from the North Pacific Coast of America*, translated by Dietrich Bertz and edited by Randall Bouchard and Dorothy Kennedy, 2002. We would like to thank R. Bouchard and D. Kennedy for making available to us their Kʷakʷakəwakʷ material before it was published.

2 Bouchard and Kennedy (2002) mentioned several sporadic stories Franz Boas recorded from women: the "Oowekeeno" wife of a Hudson's Bay trader told him, while she was in Victoria, a story related to a haṁaċa mask (439), as well as "the story of the origin of the sun" (Rohner 1969: 25, 27; Bouchard and Kennedy 2002: 443-51). Bouchard and Kennedy kindly informed us that Oowekeeno stories 8 and 9 would also have been recorded by the same Oowekeeno woman. Some young Bella Coola women were also recorded by Boas when he was in Victoria (Rohner 1969: 27; Bouchard and Kennedy 2002, story 16, 535-7). Bouchard and Kennedy also mentioned a few stories told by Coast Salish and Tsimshian women.

3 Judith Berman (1996: 230) noted the same lack of precise information about George Hunt in what she called "an apparently deliberate concealment of Hunt's identity and of his sources." It is clear that most of the early information provided to Franz Boas by George Hunt, who was not Kʷaguł, came from his Kʷaguł female relatives. His first wife, Lucy (Homiskanis), was later credited by Boas (Boas and Hunt 1921: 45) as the source for much of her husband's writings on "cookery"; Hunt's second wife, Francine (or Tsukwani), who was Nakʷaxdaxʷ, provided many of the culinary recipes and some material pertaining to the sacred and ceremonial domain. See also Jacknis (1991: 181).

4 laǧała: singing the cry song; laǧʷaləm: crying song.

5 BPC: GH/FB 7/4/16, 10/14/16.

6 Boas (1966: 372-6) recorded a list of expressive gestures that accompany oratory and myth telling, as well as gestures expressing emotion.

7 Boas has translated ńuy̓əm variably as "myth," "tradition," "story," "legend." George Hunt used "historie" instead (see Hunt 1894; and Berman 1992: 127).

8 mił: inside a house.

9 See Boas (2002: 353-7) for a Kʷaguł myth with the Mink as principal character.

10 Q̇ani: flying; qilakʷ: looks like wings. According to Daisy Sewid-Smith, Q̇aniqilakʷ, who dresses in an outfit with outspread wings, is also referred to as Hiłatusila (from hiła: to fix, to repair things that are not right, whether they belong to the realm of humans or the realm of the environment); and tusila (coming downward, in a north-south direction). While the word "Q̇aniqilakʷ" refers to his appearance, the word "Hiłatusila" refers to the reason of his being at a particular place and/or his function.

11 Q̇aniqilakʷ is Transformation personified. According to Irving Goldman (1975: 247, n.2) one of his many powers involved the ability to "grind down the teeth in the vagina of Death-Bringing woman after he marries her."

12 Four is a sacred number. Four and its multiples are ritually significant – four ritual circuits around a fire; four ritual acts; four children in an ideal family; four moons (months) later; and so on. "Four moons later" is a common interval of time in Kʷakʷakəwakʷ narratives.

13 This weapon can take various forms, such as "baton, arrow, or quartz, that when pointed at people or objects causes instant destruction" (Boas 2002; Bouchard and Kennedy 2002: 297, n.7).

14 Boas (2002) recorded several versions of this myth: Nəmǧis (338-9); Kʷaguł (363-5); ꞌAwikinuxʷ (363-5, 466-8); Heiltsuk (494-7).

15 Berman (1992) has challenged Boas's translation. According to her, in Kʷakʷala the mouth of the river is not a mouth; rather, it is the river's entrance. Furthermore, there is a certain danger at using our own metaphors while translating texts that emanate from a different culture.

16 ṁiṁax̌ꞌinuxʷ (plural of ṁax̌ꞌinuxʷ; champion swimmer). It is said that the souls of sea mammal hunters go to the killer whales (Boas 1930: 257).

17 q̇aꞌy̓uł: "an event that has been heard of"; a belief.

18 Several versions of this myth or variations on its theme can be found in Boas (1910: 38-83); Boas (1930: 59); Boas (1935: 156-73); Boas (1966: 307). For interpretation see Lévi-Strauss (1982: 79-80); Goldman (1975: 228 and 235).

19 *Dᶻaq̓ʷa:* West Wind; for other myths pertaining to or about "prayers" to winds and weather, see Boas (1966: 163-6).

20 According to what ʔAx̌uw̓ and Daisy Sewid-Smith have seen on television, the rocks found on Maxʷa look like those that have been brought from space.

21 Lit., to go back and forth from end to end of the canoe (*la:* to go; *lalaba:* back and forth; *lalabəndala:* to go back and forth from end to end). See also Berman (1992: 128) "*hayəlbalisəla:* to go from one end of the earth to the other in a single day."

22 According to Daisy Sewid-Smith, *ƛawaẏuw̓* is a pole, which, when stuck in a river, indicates ownership of fish traps.

23 This myth and its main protagonist, Wawalis, who has been compared to Orpheus, seems to have a northern origin; it can be found among the Tsimshiam and the Haida. Boas's (1916) *Tsimshian Mythology* contains more than a dozen versions of this myth. For the Haida versions, see Swanton (1905) and Bringhurst (1999:145-8). For a Heiltsuk version, see Boas (2002: 486-9); and for a Bella Coola version, see Boas (2002: 523-7).

24 *ƛəmḡəẏuw̓:* female sawbill duck.

25 *ẏagəm:* monster; *ẏagis:* sea monster.

26 *sis, siƛəm:* serpent; *ċaliƚ:* coil.

27 A white sea otter is an albino. In mythology, occurrences of rare animals such as an albino of any species were considered omens for impending supernatural encounters. The white (or silver) sea otter also played an important role in Haida and Tsimshian mythology. See Reeves (1992) and Bringhurst (1999: 449-50).

28 ʔAx̌uw̓ says "Bible" in English.

29 *gisgas:* incest with in-law; adultery.

30 *ẏagəm:* lit., causing a problem, difficulty; a generic term for any kind of monster.

31 *ʔux̌ʷsuliẏ:* wild, green, "Indian," or false hellebore root. Synonymous with bitter; instigator of trouble. It was kept in canoes, in a special box, in case travellers encountered a monster.

32 This subtitle is ours.

33 An exclamation.

34 This myth was meant to educate, and it has a clear message: lazy children who stay in bed too long will have their bowels come out.

35 Nowadays, also known as the Animal Kingdom Dance.

36 Supernatural: *nawalakʷ;* house: *gukʷ.*

37 Bək̓ʷəs, or the Wild Man of the Woods, is a supernatural being who was human in form and lurked on the edges of the forest and its streams, where he tried to persuade humans to eat the food he offered them. If they did so, then they would become like him. He was associated with the spirits of people who had drowned and who hovered near him, and he was also linked with the underworld of the dead from which ghosts returned during the season of the winter dance. The mask of Bək̓ʷəs is skull-like, with deep round eye sockets, protuberant brow, and hollowed cheeks. See Hawthorn (1979: 29).

38 Every time A. Bondsound has performed this dance it has been during potlatch ceremonies hosted by the Qʷiqʷasuƚinux̌ʷ and as a member of the M̓im̓awiḡəm, or Wiʔumasḡəm, descent group.

39 ʔAnus was from the M̓im̓awiḡəm, or Wiʔumasḡəm, descent group of the Qʷiqʷasuƚinux̌ʷ.

40 ʔAx̌uw̓ disagreed with, and openly criticized, Daisy and the dance group for not including the Abalone Shell Covered House in the Animal Kingdom when they performed it. Daisy said that the dance was omitted because the performance, which was already quite lengthy, would have been even longer had it been left in.

41 ʔix̌c̓am: abalone shell; *haliotis* shell.

42 For another version of this myth, see Boas (1935: 212-19).

43 mig̱ʷat: seal; mig̱ʷat̓a: to go seal hunting.

44 həl: to search for; həlay̓uw̓: searching for.

45 *Hudis:* midget. The title is ours.

46 language: y̓aq̓əndas.

47 Killer whale rising on surface of water: ƛ̓aƚʔid.

48 For several versions of the same myth see, Boas (1897: 396-401); Boas and Hunt (1921: 1222-48); Boas and Hunt (1902-05); Boas (1910; 1928; 1935; and 1895 [trans. 2002]); Curtis (1915: 165-70); and Olson (1940: 192-3; 1954: 193).

49 George Glendale (no relation to ʔAx̌uw̓).

50 Duda was Mrs. Peter Smith.

51 Peter Smith.

52 q̓oyuwēy̓: in between.

53 N̓umas (Old Man) was Wakəs, Q̓ʷəmxuduw̓.

54 For a myth with a similar theme, see Boas (1966: 307).

55 This myth took place during the Flood.

56 k̓emux̌stəwak̓: box drum.

57 C̓ik̓ʷa: Seagull.

58 Copper scent: kəlṗala.

59 ʔalagəm is softened buckskin; ʔAlakilag̱amēy̓: the chief of the ʔAlagəm people.

60 According to Daisy Sewid-Smith, cəlwaqa (to praise) should not be confused with həwax̌ʔala (to pray or to plead) or ʔəm̓y̓ax̌a (to worship). Franz Boas translated cəlwaqa as "to pray." On prayers, see Boas (1966: 155-7).

61 In Boas (1930: 216) the seals are the dogs of Copper Maker.

62 Also known as the ƛəwəlax̌a among the ʔAwik̓inux̌ʷ.

63 The subtitle is ours.

64 David Gladstone is Northern K̓ʷak̓ʷakəwak̓ʷ, or Heiltsuk.

65 ʔAx̌uw̓'s first-born child, her son, Alvin.

66 To mourn: lag̱ʷat̓a. Literally, "crying for the dead"; mourning songs: g̱ʷ̓ayəms.

67 ʔAx̌uw̓ deliberately censured a passage that may have revealed some sexual content, as it referred to how the girl had been conceived (with the Raven's help). Northwest Coast mythology contained many stories that were overtly sexual. These stories now belong mostly to the male domain. It would be interesting to know what influences the missionaries had on this aspect of Northwest Coast oral tradition. Although ʔAx̌uw̓ may have related this passage of the story to a male listener, she was extremely careful not to reveal anything of that nature to her granddaughter or to me, regardless of our ages.

Chapter 2: War, Conflict, and Slavery

1 According to Boas (1966: 108), *wina* "includes not only fights between tribes or clans but also deeds of individuals who set out to kill a member or members of another group."

2 See also ʔAx̌uw̓'s recollections in Chapter 7.

3   For more information on war, warriors, and slavery on the Northwest Coast, see
     Avierkeva (1966); Donald (1997); Archer (1980); Ruyle (1973); and Ruby and Brown
     (1993); for warfare practised by the Liǧiɫdax̌ʷ (a division of the Kʷakʷakəwakʷ), see
     Taylor and Duff (1956); Hill-Tout (1907: 43-4); and Codere (1950: 104).
4   See Boas's accounts of previous raids (1966: 110-12).
5   According to Daisy Sewid-Smith, not long before the Campbell River potlatch took
     place, she, her father (James Sewid), and some representatives of the survivors'
     descendants went to Bella Coola and met with Bella Coola elders to discuss their
     motives for the raid at Ḡʷayasdəms. It seems that the reason offered was revenge:
     it is said that in the past some Bella Coola clam diggers had been attacked by the
     Dᶻawadaʔēnux̌ʷ and the Qʷiq̓asuɫinux̌ʷ causing the death of a Tallio (southern Bella
     Coola) princess. A slave might have led them deliberately to Gilford Island.
6   For a debate exposing different points of view concerning this later potlatch, see
     Wolcott (1996) and Sewid-Smith (1997).
7   The Kʷakʷakəwakʷ kinship system does not distinguish between siblings and first
     cousins but does use an age distinction for siblings and first cousins of the same sex.
     In one's own generation, all males (including parallel and cross cousins) are brothers
     and all females are sisters; therefore, they are designated by the same terms.
          Elder sibling of the same sex: *nula;* younger sibling of the same sex: *c̓aẏa*
          Blood sister and all female cross and parallel cousins: *nəmimaǧas*
          Blood brother and all cross and parallel cousins: *nəmimas*
          Sister and all female cross and parallel cousins: *w̓aq̓ʷa* (plural: *w̓iw̓aq̓ʷa*)
          Father's mother's sister: *ʔanis;* father's mother's brother: *qolei?ẏ*
          Father: *ʔump;* mother: *ʔabəmp;* grandparents: *gagəmp*

     In the parental generation, all males are fathers, and all females are mothers. A
     great-aunt is called grandmother. Max̌ʷaloǧʷa was ʔAx̌uw̓'s great-aunt. A great-uncle
     is called grandfather. For more kinship terminology (affines), see Boas (1966: 48-9)
     and Rohner (1967: 75).
8   According to Daisy Sewid-Smith, her name was ʔAbayoɫ. She was Billie Sunday
     Willie's grandmother. See picture of her daughter, Kʷənx̌ʷaloǧʷa, when she was very
     old (Plate 5). She was around four years old at the time of the massacre. ʔAbayoɫ was
     killed during the raid.
9   According to Daisy Sewid-Smith, the Tallio, Haida, and Chilcotin have sometimes
     been mentioned.
10   This person may have been a slave who was part Qʷiq̓asuɫinux̌ʷ.
11   Health Lagoon.
12   According to ʔAx̌uw̓ and Daisy Sewid-Smith, she must have been about four years
     old.
13   *Mənǧa* is a type of canoe identified as a war canoe, which had a long, narrow, heavy
     hull; a high flaring bow with two perforations; and a nearly vertical stern.
14   According to Daisy Sewid-Smith, she and ʔAx̌uw̓ listed all the survivors, who they
     were, where they went, and what happened to them.
15   According to Daisy Sewid-Smith, Q̓iqəxɬalla was captured during the so-called
     Bəlxʷəlla raid with the aid of their accomplices, the Haida and the Chilcotin. After the
     attack they divided the slaves and perhaps sold them to other groups. ʔAx̌uw̓'s aunt
     may have ended up among the Haida as they are mentioned several times in her
     narratives. Such is the case of Caribou Jack, who, according to the Kʷakʷakəwakʷ, had
     been taken by the Haida when in fact he was taken by the Chilcotin, to caribou
     country, thus resulting in his being named Caribou Jack.

According to Daisy, ꞬOlsiwidi's sister, Mary, was in her teens when the Gilford Island massacre took place. She was taken to Bəlxʷəlla. ꞬOlsiwidi saw her there and tried to get her to return home. By this time she was living with White Sam and had children with him. She was fearful for her children so refused to return home with her brother, ꞬOlsiwidi. She later left Bəlxʷəlla and went to Anahim. She disappeared into Chilcotin territory, and the search for her has continued to this day.

16 ꞬAx̌uw̓'s older half-sister [same mother], Florence Knox.

17 W̓aq̓ʷa, plural, w̓iw̓aq̓ʷa: female's brother or male's sister whether older or younger.

18 According to Daisy, the book is *Bella Coola* by Cliff Kopas (1970). Mary, ꞬOlsiwidi's sister, had been thought to have been killed in the massacre, but she was taken captive. ꞬOlsiwidi saw her during a revenge party that took place sometime after the raid. She was taken to Bella Coola and married White Sam.

19 Ƙug̓ʷid̓iy̓ or ꞬAbayoł was Daca's grandmother and Kʷənx̌alog̓ʷa's mother.

20 q̓akuw̓: slaves.

21 łil: to die; łiłəl: dead people; dead of feelings; without feelings.

22 ğağas: lit., your grandmother.

23 Y̓ax̌ʷəla: song used when dancing. According to Daisy Sewid-Smith, this song is used once the bride's dowry has been announced, after which time the groom's family performs the appreciation song/dance.

24 Some time ago ꞬAx̌uw̓ went to Bella Bella to attend a potlatch where some Bella Coola participants performed a dance that she believed was a reenactment of the massacre (q̓ʷaꞬalaxəla: to bring it out in a dance).

25 Among the Kʷakʷakəwakʷ all first cousins are considered to be brothers and sisters.

26 mu: four.

27 For an exploration of the relationship between cultural context, meaning, and aesthetic expressions in Northwest Coast art, see Reid (1987: 201-36; 1989: 219-52).

28 According to Audrey Hawthorn (1967: 148), "At naming ceremonies, a large ceremonial cradle (yałta) was constructed and hung from the beams at the front center of the house. The Copper was a 'blanket' to keep the child warm. A herald or other official stood at each corner of the cradle and shook his rattle four times, pretending there was a child in the cradle. A speech was then made naming the Copper and the child." According to Daisy Sewid-Smith, only the Mi̓ṁawiǧəm own this privilege.

29 According to Daisy Sewid-Smith, John Clark's mother was Qʷiq̓ʷasutinux̌ʷ. He married Emma Bell (Sewid), Jimmy Sewid's mother; Daisy's grandmother.

30 It is said that he actually escaped from his captivity and moved on to caribou country.

31 For the geographical names of the Gilford Island people, see Boas (1934, map 10-132).

32 See Boas (1934, map 13: 103).

33 See Boas (1934, map 14: 31).

34 For documentation of the Gilford Island traditional Qʷiq̓ʷasutinux̌ʷ village sites, see Boas (1934: maps 10, 13, 14); Rohner (1967: 32-5).

35 Mitła was a war dancer who usually wore a belt and carried a bow bearing the Sisayuł crest (see Hawthorn 1967: 47).

36 Ƙug̓ʷid̓iy̓, a potlatch name meaning Being Propped Up, or Standing Tall, could be worn either by a male or a female person.

37 It is interesting to note that a century ago similar expressions of joy were used by Kʷakʷakəwakʷ and recorded by Franz Boas, nearly word for word. In one case, it was said, "In olden times we fought so that the blood ran over the ground. Now we fight with button blankets and other kinds of property and we smile at each other! Oh, how good is the new time!" (Boas 1897: 580). And here is another remark, made by an old

man: "O, my dear! Your days, young men, are good, but our past ways were evil when we were all at war against one another. I mean you have no trouble nowadays" (Boas 1897: 425).

Chapter 3: Childhood

1   This chapter was told to Daisy Sewid-Smith and Martine Reid. All references to "you" and "your" are to Daisy.

2   The general rule was that the oldest male child whose father was a *haṁaċa* would inherit his father's privilege and have the right to be a *haṁaċa*. However, a younger male son could receive a *haṁaċa* dancing position from another relative.

3   According to Daisy Sewid-Smith, the boy's name was John; his sister was Mable Stanley, and his brother was Charley Peterson.

4   *Ṅaṅalalał:* "The embodiment of the personation of weather" (Hawthorn 1967: 31).

5   * x̱ax̱ax̌ʷas,* or Stone Body, was the fourth son of Ċeqaṁēẏ in one version of the myth of origin of the Qʷiqʷasut̓inux̌ʷ. According to Daisy Sewid-Smith, when the boy was born he was called x̱ax̱ax̌ʷas and then, after he was bathed in the blood of the Sisayuł, he was called Ṫisəmgiʔlakʷ, which means "Born To Be Stone-Bodied." Today, he is mainly known as Ṫisəmgid, "Stone Body." See Daisy Sewid-Smith, n.8, in Boas (2002: 344).

6   The Kʷakʷakəẇakʷ had a preference for patrilineal succession, and the ideal family should have had a first-born son and a second-born daughter (Boas 1925: 101). The first-born daughter of a chief of a descent group is called *k̓idił* – a term translated by Boas and Hunt as "princess," the equivalent of "heir apparent." Succession among the Kʷakʷakəẇakʷ followed the rule of unrestricted primogeniture, which meant that "house names" or "seats" went to the first-born male or female (Boas 1921: 831). However, the literature offers very few examples of female successions. Cases are mentioned where the chief's daughter's seat went to her eldest son or was held in trust for an expected son (Curtis 1915: 138-9). As Irving Goldman (1975: 39) points out "A woman as chief – even in male guise – upset traditional expectations by drawing men out of their *numema,* when in fact the aim of marriage was for men to draw women out of their place."

7   Physically fighting among themselves and killing.

8   Ethnologist at the Royal British Columbia Museum, Victoria.

9   According to Daisy Sewid-Smith, he is said to have been one of George Hunt's informants.

10 *k̓ʷak̓ʷicemēẏ:* you can attend all the feasts.

11 Not mentioned on the kinship diagram.

12 For more games documented by Franz Boas, see Boas (1966: 388-99; "*Lehal*" 391; and potlatch, 395; as property, 390; stick game, 392).

13 Covered with warts.

14 Western red cedar, *Thuja plicata.*

15 *Lysichiton americanus* Hultén and St. John.

16 *Rubus parviflorus* Nutt.

17 *Rubus spectabilis* Pursh.

18 The "button" of a clam is its muscular, fleshy foot.

19 See Stewart (1977) for methods of Indian fishing and the ways of preparing food. See also Boas and Hunt (1921), who documented more than 100 recipes for cooking fish and shellfish.

20 Bracken fern rhizome, (*Pteridium aquilinum*).

21 Sword fern rhizome, *Polystichum munitum* (Kaulf.) K. Presl.

22 Springbank clover, *Trifolium wormskjoldii* Lehm.

23 Pacific cinquefoil, *Argentina occidentalis* Howell.

24 See Turner and Kuhnlein (1982) for a description of the importance of cinquefoil and clover roots as food sources.

25 Two edible species of blue camas were used: common camas, *Camassia quamash* (Pursh) and great camas, *Camassia leichtlinii* (Baker) Wats. For a discussion of the importance of the camas as a food source for First Nations Peoples, see Turner and Kuhnlein (1983).

26 "Huckleberries" could be any of several edible *Vaccinium* species: mountain bilberry, *V. membranaceum* Doug. ex Hook.; oval-leaved blueberry, *V. ovalifolium* Smith; bog blueberry, *V. uliginosum* L.; or red huckleberry, *V. parvifolium* Smith.

27 Salmonberries, *Rubus spectabilis* Pursh.

28 "Contrary to the commonly held belief that Red Elderberries (*Sambucus racemosa* L.) are poisonous, the fruit was widely used as food by coastal First Peoples" (Turner 1995: 67-8).

29 "Salal berries (*Gaultheria shallon* Pursh) are without doubt the most plentiful and widely used fruit on the coast. All coastal indigenous groups ... used them in large quantities" (Turner 1995: 77-8).

30 Three species of "cranberries" were commonly used by the peoples of northern Vancouver Island: bog cranberries, *Vaccinium oxycoccus* L.; low-bush cranberry, *Vaccinium vitis-idaea* L. ssp. *minus* (Lodd) Hultén; and high-bush cranberry, *Viburnum edule* (Michx.) Raf.

31 Wild crabapple, *Malus fusca* Raf.

32 *Urtica dioica* L.

33 See photo of wife of Chief Wakəs holding ʔAx̌uw̓ (Plate 4).

34 These were called deadfall traps.

35 To harden the wooden hooks.

36 Like in a catamaran. For further documentation about Kʷakʷakəwak̓ technology, see Boas 1909.

Chapter 4: Becoming a Woman

1 This was made evident in the W̓aẃalis myth (M5) and other narratives.

2 Gloria is Daisy Sewid-Smith's daughter.

3 The sawmill was built in 1888.

4 k̓ʷak̓ʷəxtolił: squatting.

5 dᶻixdᶻəgʷił: to stretch.

6 q̓amsa: lazy; qamćax̌λa: a lazy person; q̓apix̌ała: to hold the blanket closely around you.

7 ʔaʔēkila: to take care of yourself; implies danger, seclusion, ritual purification; also used in the context of initiation.

8 ǧʷibałas: symbolic meaning.

9 Following the *kakənəla* (gathering of novices), the phases of an initiation ritual are:
   1. *Weliqa*: novices march through village and are fed in each home.
   2. *Kʷesa*: purification; novices cleansed by ritual bathing (sprinkling of water).
   3. *Qəxa*: novices go through cedar-bark ring four times; white down is sprinkled over all.
   4. *Wəłcəmliła*: novices enter, faces painted black. Masks are revealed.

10   Right foot going in first.
11   In Kʷakʷakəwakʷ thinking, weight is a metaphor for wealth.
12   Alvin Alfred was born in 1910.
13   *Sorbus sitchensis.*
14   She was also one of the survivors of the Bella Coola massacre.
15   "Soopolallie" in Chinook jargon. *Shepherdia canadensis* L. Nutt.
16   Pronounced "bada" in Chinook jargon.
17   Ǩag̱is, located near the mouth of the Nimpkish River.
18   According to Daisy Sewid-Smith, Joe Harris was one of the chiefs among the Nəmg̱is.

Chapter 5: Marrying Moses Alfred

1   For a good summary of a Kʷakʷakəwakʷ wedding ceremony, see Rosman and Rubel (1981: 24-30).
2   Daisy Roberts, or Tottie, was Daisy Sewid-Smith's mother's father's sister.
3   Very little is known about the lower-class Kʷakʷakəwakʷ.
4   ʔAx̱uw̓ referred to this practice during her own wedding ceremony in Chapter 5; see also Daisy's wedding in Appendix D.
5   See ʔAx̱uw̓s recollections of her ancestor who "married" several princesses for their dowries and names (Chapter 4).
6   According to Daisy Sewid-Smith, when the owner of a Copper gave it outright, he showed his deep love and respect for his daughter, the bride.
7   *sapid:* fast financial transaction resulting in boosting the value of a Copper that could also coincide with receiving cash or goods invested in it.
8   *pasʔaliɬ:* a metaphorical expression meaning "to collapse on the floor"; the containers holding the potlatch goods have collapsed because all the wealth that was in them has been invested in the *p̓asa.*
9   Flora (Alfred) Sewid did receive such a male name: Y̓ax̱ʎən.
10 Q̓agʷoɬ's big house at Alert Bay was one of the last to be demolished, therefore it was still in use at this time.
11 *ʔAʎlaqima:* "taken far away into the woods," or "taking back into the woods." This refers to a dancer who received and displayed a forest treasure. Boas (1921: 1193) mentions the names of thirty-four *ʔAʎlaqima* dances. *ʔAʎlaqima* dancers belong to the winter ceremonial and they bring treasures that originated from the forest. There were at least forty distinctive dancers, whose masks were made to be worn only for their brief four-day role and were burned at the end of the four-year dancing cycle. See also, Hawthorn (1967: 29).
12 When a dance was given as part of a dowry, it was usually performed by the groom's family. This was to establish which members of the groom's family would be given the privilege of performing it.
13 According to Codere (1966: xxvii), "Mrs. Stephen Cook [was] a formidable super-missionized woman who was a matriarch of a large household, lay preacher and interpreter of the Bible, and a person of great influence among the Indian women of Alert Bay. She was dead set against all Indian ways, none of which she knew much about. According to Agnes Cranmer and others, 'She talked our language just like a baby.'"
14 *p̓alx̱alasg̱am,* mountain goat furs and mountain goat-wool blankets; this term also refers to the colour of fog. After contact the mountain goat furs were replaced by the Hudson's Bay blankets, but they were still called *p̓alx̱alasg̱am.*

15 X̌ʷix̌ʷiý is said to have been introduced through marriage with the Salish and to shake the earth when it is performed. His dance is held to be a means of bringing back the *haṁaća* initiate (Boas 1897: 497).

16 *ƛ̓ugʷala*, or Wolf ritual, was held throughout the Nuu-chah-nulth area and was the most important ritual during the winter ceremonies. Possible historic connections between this ritual and the Kʷakʷakəẃakʷ winter ritual have been discussed by Boas (1897: 632-44).

17 The Sisayuł is a mythical being. According to Goldman (1975: 142-3), in mythology "the *Sisayuł* or Double-headed Serpent is commonly thought of as a canoe, a conveyor of the rainbow, the salmon, and the copper." Headdresses adorned with its representations are worn by warrior dancers; it was associated with Winalagilis, the War Spirit. It could be ridden and rowed like a canoe; its flesh was impervious to any spear; it could inflict instant death by its glance; and it could cause any enemy who looked upon it to be turned to stone, with all his/her joints turned backward (see also Hawthorn 1967: 154). Sisayuł can be worn on the headdresses of warrior dancers, on ceremonial belts, on clubs and knives, on cloaks and aprons, on feast dishes, on house fronts (see Plate 9), and on other ceremonial objects.

18 Ṅuṅuẃ was Mrs. James Knox, Nulaġa's daughter-in-law.

19 This Peace Dance headdress is now owned by Louise Assu, one of ʔAx̌uẃ's granddaughters.

20 According to Daisy Sewid-Smith, it is in the language spoken at Metlakatla by the Coast Tsimshian people.

21 Probably other First Nations people also had commercial fishing licences at that time, but ʔAx̌uẃ was perhaps referring to her own family.

22 Indian Agent William M. Halliday reported to the Chief Inspector of Indian Agencies W.E. Ditchburn, on 5 February 1919: "Several convictions were made where the Indians were drunk through purchasing cider on the reserve at Alert Bay. This cider was not sold by Moses Alfred himself, but by his partners in the concern and I have instructed them that no more cider may be sold on the reserve and I will warn the steam boat companies not to accept any more shipments of cider to any Indians in the agency as it will be laid before you, but you will see for yourself that it was absolutely necessary to do so." (Sewid-Smith 1979: 22).

Chapter 6: Ceremonies and Rituals

1 The source of the word "potlatch" is uncertain. The *Oxford English Dictionary* says that it derives from Nootkan, while *Webster's Third New International Dictionary* says that it derives from Chinook jargon – a trade patois of the region. In the early Nootkan vocabularies of Cook (Beaglehole 1967: 327) and of Moziño (1970: 108) *pa'chatle, pa'cheetle,* and *pachitle* are listed as meaning "to give." On the other hand, Sapir and Swadesh (1939: 261) list "potlatch" as an intrusion from Chinook jargon and *nahi* as the Nootkan word for "give." As Irving Goldman (1975: 245) points out, "even though the fur trade did not fully develop along the Northwest Coast until after Cook's visit in 1778, native trade may have been active before European contacts. The Spanish expedition of Pérez and La Bodega y Quadra of 1774-1775 coming up from the south and crossing Chinook territory, had already preceded Cook." See also Curtis (1915: 142).

2 As was mentioned earlier, our intention is not to provide new interpretations of Kʷakʷakəẃakʷ culture. However, for those interested in a selection of published

interpretations of the Kʷakʷakəwakʷ potlatch, Barbara Saunders's (1995: 54-6) preliminary listing is helpful. The potlatch has been seen as an expression of psychopathology (Benedict 1934); a form of economic redistribution and eco-survival (MacLeod 1925b; Suttles 1960; 1990; 1991b; Piddocke 1965; Vayda 1961); a type of social complementarity related to ranking (Barnett 1938; Drucker 1965; Drucker and Heizer 1967); a substitute for physical violence (Codere 1950); a symbolic rite of passage resolving hostility between groups joined in marriage and peace (Rosman and Rubel 1971 and 1972, inspired by Mauss 1967); as "total prestation," involving all dimensions of social, religious, aesthetic, moral, legal, and economic morphologies of Northwest Coast society (Goldman 1975; Kan 1989; also inspired by Mauss 1967); and as vital to reproduction and amplification of power relations (Böelscher 1988, inspired by Bourdieu 1977). For Mircea Eliade (1959: 34) the potlatch is "only the repetition of a practice introduced by ancestors in mythical times." Jean Baudrillard (1981: 30-1, 41) considers the potlatch to be a form of exchange – an exhibiting, provoking, competing, challenging rite destined to evince a hierarchy of values and the rules for being integrated within it.

For a discussion of the potlatch as a construction of colonialism and academic space, see Isabelle Schulte-Tenckhoff (1986); for conflicting interpretations of the Kʷakʷakəwakʷ potlatch, see Michaelson (1979); for a historical approach to the Kʷakʷakəwakʷ potlatch, see Cole (1991); and for a description of the contemporary potlatch, see Cranmer-Webster (1991).

For philosophically oriented approaches to the gift, see Bataille (1967). For an appreciation of the potlatch as an exuberant gift of excess energy (such as sunlight), see Derrida (1992a and 1992b). See the brilliant study of the "Potlatch Papers" by Christopher Bracken (1997), who observes not the First Nations but, rather, the Europeans vis-à-vis the institution of the potlatch.

3 According to Wayne Suttles (1990: 285), *pəsa* refers to the most general meaning of the term "potlatch." His terminology is in agreement with what ʔAx̱uw̓ says about the different kinds of situations during which property is given away. According to Boas (1935: 43; 1943: 41), *Walas pəsa* are great potlatches.

4 Boas (1897: 343) translated it as "flattening the name of a rival." A later translation is: "flattening of a soft basket from which objects had been removed" (Boas 1921, part 2, 1402, 1441, 1447; 1910, 435; see also Goldman 1975: 133-4).

5 According to Daisy Sewid-Smith, after the 1921-22 arrests at Village Island, Indian Agent Halliday's Indian informers refused to help him, and he asked for undercover police.

6 ʔAx̱uw̓ was not married at the time; but when she told the story Legix̱ was now her brother-in-law.

7 She is referring to a picture published in Daisy Sewid-Smith's book.

8 According to Robert Boyd (1999: 116, 142-3), there were several outbreaks of meningitis on the Northwest Coast, dating back to the 1830s – epidemics that were intensified later through increasing contact with newcomers. If ʔAx̱uw̓'s child did die of meningitis, then her disease does not seem to have been part of a large-scale outbreak; rather, it appears to have been an isolated case. According to Boyd (1999: 143), "meningitis is an inflammation of the outer membrane of the brain, and may be caused by any number of viral or bacterial agents. It is characterized by fever, intense headache; it is most common among children living under crowded conditions."

9 According to Daisy, he was around seven years old.

10 According to Mr. Frank Anfield's son, Anfield started building the school at Alert Bay in 1927. Personal communication.

11 See Boas (1966: 148-58). In anthropology it has become standard to use the word "sorcery" rather than "witchcraft" with regard to such practices as those described by Boas and ʔAx̌uw̓, where the emphasis is on a ritual act as well as a psychic intent (see Codere 1966: 148). Interestingly, however, the gloss ʔiqa is in Bella Bella dialect and means medicine. To "cure with medicine" is "to bewitch" (Boas 1932b: 245). Dawson (1888, in Boas 1966: 149) described some witchcraft situations. See also Boas (1930: Part 2, 279-81).

12 *D'əmid'əm:* buried under something. Potatoes would be steamed like clams, that is, "put under" a mat.

13 Salt water connotes purification, cleansing, and protection.

14 For *ƛasəla* or *welaxa*, Peace Dance or Healing Dance, see Boas (1897: 621-32).

15 Jimmy Sewid's father was Q̌wiq̌wasut̓inux̌w.

16 Today both the *ćeqa* and *ƛasəla* are combined. This is one of the most drastic changes in the Kwakʼwakʼwakʼwakʼw winter ritual. These were never performed at the same time and never in the same house. Important dancers in the *ćeqa* would not be allowed to enter the *ƛasəla* house. Today the *ƛasəla* dancers still follow the *ćeqa* dances; however, the same dancers perform in the same house and on the same night (as part of the same event). See also Holm (1977: 19).

17 Flora Sewid, on her father's side.

18 The welcome figure is now in the Cape Mudge Museum.

19 After potlatches were allowed, most of them took place in Alert Bay, along with other sports activities such as soccer tournaments and the annual weekend of sports-related activities that used to be scheduled in the spring, in the months of May or June.

20 Boas (1897: 594-8) described in detail the return of the *haṁaća* novice. For the Red Cedar-Bark Ceremony, see Boas (1930: 92-8, 121-33).

21 The terms "novice" and "initiate" are used interchangeably.

22 Winalagilis, "Making War All over the Earth," is the second high-ranking dancing order after the *haṁaća;* it is the spirit of war. See Hawthorn (1967: 47). Boas (1966: 173) translated Winalagilis as the Warrior-of-the-World. See also Goldman (1975: 108, 113, 148, 187, 189).

23 The *Lolinux̌w,* or ghost dancers, were associated with the war dancers. Ghosts had the power to return the dead to life.

24 Daisy was a ghost performer for her uncle Alfred.

25 Or Fire-Thrower, a being obsessed with fire.

26 "Rich Woman" is associated with the *haṁaća* ritual and feeds the *haṁaća* initiates.

27 *Tux̌wʔid* is a female war spirit dancer associated with Winalagilis; she performs many magical tricks and embodies invulnerability.

28 *Weliqa:* When the pubescent girl goes through the hoop made out of red cedar branches, she will go through it four times, right arm and right leg first. Each time she goes through the hoop, the ritual attendants say: "You will not steal"; "You will not have a bad temper"; "You will not be envious"; and so on. The *weliqa* is followed by the *kwesa.*

29 *Hawiṅalaƚ* is a war dancer, suspended from pierced skin.

30 *ʔutta:* to pierce with a needle or a hook.

31 Located at the back of the ceremonial house, above the singers.

32 See ʔAx̌uw̓'s recollection of this event in Chapter 2.

33 See Boas (1966: 165-7) for the wide range of meanings attributed to *nawalaǩw* (supernatural).

34 ʔAx̌uw̓ is discussing the literal meaning of these names; metaphorically, they mean "You are upholding your people."

35 Flora's father is actually ʔAx̱uw̓'s husband, Moses, and Daisy Sewid-Smith's grandfather. The recording was made in the presence of Flora.
36 Supernatural embodiment of the personification of the Weather. See Curtis (1915: 137).
37 For an analysis of the social organization of the Kʷakʷ̓akəw̓akʷ people, their principles of succession and inheritance, see Lévi-Strauss (1979: 163-87). He suggests that the ṅəmaýəm was a kind of noble "house" in the medieval European and Japanese sense. In accordance with the strict rule of primogeniture, the oldest Kʷakʷ̓akəw̓akʷ child succeeds to the highest position of either parent. Emblems of nobility were transmitted through the female line.
38 According to Turner (1995: 92-3), the Kʷakʷ̓akəw̓akʷ roasted and ate the rhizomes of the blue lupine, *Lupinus nootkatensis* Donn ex Sims., and possibly the seashore lupine, *Lupinus littoralis* Doug ex Lindl.: "Eating raw lupine rhizomes can cause dizziness ... This 'drunken' state is caused by toxic alkaloids ... Under some circumstances, the poison can be fatal." Steaming rhizomes thoroughly destroyed most of the toxic alkaloids.
39 People living around Cape Mudge and Campbell River to Salmon River.
40 See ʔAx̱uw̓'s own recollections in Chapter 5, as well as Boas (1966: 56) "parents advice to daughter."

Chapter 7: Fragments of Recollections

1 Sent by the Church Missionary Society in 1877, Mr. Hall began work at Fort Rupert, which had been abandoned by the Roman Catholics. George Hunt is said to have interpreted his sermons. However, it is reported in the literature that, although the Kʷakʷ̓akəw̓akʷ were eager to learn to read and write English, as far as religion was concerned, Hall met with no encouragement. By 1880 he had closed his Fort Rupert Mission because of resistance to conversion; he went, instead, to Alert Bay. The Fort Rupert Kʷaguɬ were, in the words of Indian Superintendent Dr. I.W. Powell, "too incorrigible for reformation" (Gough 1982: 86; Saunders 1995: 55). Hall's program grew into a residential school for girls, which ʔAx̱uw̓ attended for a very short time. On Hall's mission, see Healy (1958: 24-31); Halliday (1935: 229-32); Canada (1882: 171; 1883: 161; 1895: 158, 160); Codere (1990: 363).
2 Same tune as "Frère Jacques."
3 By 1888 Hall had built a sawmill at Alert Bay to provide employment and lumber for single-family houses.
4 Grandpa Moses, Daisy's grandpa.
5 *Babakʷ̓əmxsila*: an uninformed Indian or First Nations person; ignorant; unaware.
6 Čiċ̓ədanuw̓ means cracked, fractured; barley is cracked grain.
7 She says "our" grandfather because Daisy's father, James Sewid, is present during the recording.
8 The custom whereby a widow marries a brother of her deceased husband is called "levirate." According to Boas (1966: 50), "sexual relations between a man and his sister-in-law are considered particularly offensive, although after her husband's death, he may become her second husband, according to the levirate custom (*kwElo⁰s*; literally, they lie from one to the other)." Another example of such a marriage is mentioned in Boas (1921: 1077).
9 Gift is a synonym for property.
10 Haʔēλ̓əkʷ is Charlie Dick.

11 For incidents of warfare between the Bella Bella and the Kʷakʷakəwakʷ see Boas (1966: 114-16).

12 The ćeqa had religious connotations. ʔAx̌uw̓ is corroborating the fact that all active participants in the ritual were referred to as pipəx̌ala [shamans] (see Holm 1990: 384). According to Boas, there were several grades of shamans; the most powerful shaman had to disappear during his initiation and was said to have "gone through" (lax̌sa). This shaman could both cure disease and throw disease into someone's body. He was usually the assistant of chiefs as he would follow their orders and kill the chiefs' enemies. A second type of shaman, less powerful, could heal the sick but not throw disease. Still lower on the scale was the shaman who could locate a disease but could not extract it. Finally, there were people who had been cured by supernatural power but who had not received the gift of healing (Boas 1966: 120). For concepts of disease caused by material objects and the methods of removing them, see Boas (1966: 141-4); for "throwing" by the shaman, see Boas (1966: 120, 141, 148); for curing by shamans, see Boas (1966: 137-44).

13 For a different recollection of the same event, see Charles Nowell in Ford (1941: 96-7).

14 On Florence's father's side.

15 The area located near the residential school.

16 Examples of murder committed in order to "make others wail" or to procure a "pillow" for a relative are easily found in the literature. See Boas (1921: 1381).

17 One of the villages along the Nimpkish River.

18 For examples of the symbolic return of deceased chiefs, see Ford (1941: 222); Olson (1955: 235); Holm (1977: 12); Hawthorn (1967: 103). This ceremony was and still is (albeit rarely) practised during the brief mourning ritual period that introduces the ćeqa at the beginning of a memorial potlatch. It consists of the momentary return of the deceased chief represented by a dancer wearing a mask depicting one of his ancestral crest figures. These mourning masks were later represented by pictures of the deceased. See also Cranmer-Webster (1991: 236).

19 Rolling out the red carpet for her to walk on.

20 ʔawilpała: lit., to become discernable.

21 Florence Knox was among those who were arrested after the 1921 Cranmer potlatch, which took place at Village Island. She was afraid of the Europeans from that time on. She would hide under the bed when a European came to the door. She told her sister about the prison and, as a result, ʔAx̌uw̓ has always been afraid of Europeans.

22 Ẏakoyog̓ʷa: lit., "A woman lost at a sham war party during a wedding ritual." According to Daisy Sewid-Smith, it was Mrs. Jane Cook who told ʔAx̌uw̓ that her name meant "Lost to Gambling."

Eulogy for Granny ʔAx̌uw̓

1 This eulogy was written in 1992. See also the Introduction for another estimate of ʔAx̌uw̓'s age.

Epilogue

1 U'mista Cultural Centre, <http://www.umista.org> (August 2003).

Appendix A

1   Compiled after Grubb (1977); Smalley (1964) ; Sewid-Smith (1988).

Appendix B

1   Pieces of abalone shell (*haliotis*) used as decorative elements; indicative of wealth and beauty. For a commentary on concepts of beauty and abalone shell decoration on the Northwest Coast, see Mauzé (1999).
2   Helaṁolaǧa: swift.
3   He who takes the fat from his own body to fuel the fire.

Appendix C

1   The literature on the potlatch prohibition is quite large: Fisher (1977); Bracken (1997); Cole (1991: 135-68); La Violette (1961); Halliday (1935).
2   Pressure from Indian Agents, combined with pressure from missionaries, finally prompted the federal government to pass a law prohibiting potlatching. Section 3 of the 1884 Indian Act, which amends the 1880 Indian Act, became Section 114 in 1895 and Section 149 in 1913. The act states that "every Indian or other person who engages in or assists in celebrating the Indian festival known as the 'Potlatch' or in the Indian dance known as the 'Tamanawas' is guilty of a misdemeanor and shall be liable to imprisonment" (Canada, *Statutes*, "An Act Further to Amend 'The Indian Act,' 1880," 47 Vict. c. 27, *Statutes of Canada*, 1884).
3   Jean Baudrillard (1981: 31) saw the Protestant work ethic and the potlatch "prestation" (gift) as incompatible moral systems.
4   Besides five gas boats and twenty-five canoes, there were bracelets for women, gas-lights, violins, guitars, shirts, and sweaters for young people, 300 oak trunks, two pool tables, sewing machines, gramophones, and furniture.
5   For a detailed history of these events, see Sewid-Smith (1979).
6   As Saunders (1995: 57, note 31) pointed out: "An earlier agreement (1919) by the Indians to give up potlatching had not been honoured; tangible evidence of good faith was now required. It was suggested that the Indians of the whole Kwagiulth Agency make a voluntary surrender of all potlatch coppers, masks, headdresses, blankets, rattles, whistles and other paraphernalia used solely for potlatching purpose (Douglas Cole, 1985: 250). Some cite Donald Angerman (the RCMP) as the source of the idea of the confiscation of the potlatch regalia (U'mista Cultural Centre 1975 [film]), others accredit R. W. Ellis, a barrister (Forrest La Violette, 1973: 84). William Halliday (letter, 1 March 1922 to Duncan Campbell Scott, in Sewid-Smith, 1979) says the Indians suggested it themselves."
7   Among them were some chiefs of the Liǧiɫdax̌ʷ (Cape Mudge and Campbell River), Kʷix̌a (Phillips Arm), X̌ax̌amaċəs (Salmon River), Ṁaṁaliliqəlla (Village Island), and Nəmǧis (Alert Bay).
8   Now the Canadian Museum of Civilization.
9   For a survey of the numerous negotiations, see Greenfield (1986: 34).

Appendix D

1   That is, mind; I was just about to refuse.
2   Binas is Peter Smith's uncle; Chief Peter Smith was Lorne Smith's father's brother. (See Appendix E, kinship diagram 7).
3   His great-grandfather.
4   nəmuk" ʔum bəgʷanəm: lit., you are one man, one person.
5   The Maṁaq̓a (Death Thrower) Dance belonged to the winter ritual and was part of the Winalagilis ritual (war ritual). According to Hawthorn (1979: 47), "the Mamaka entered fiercely, looking about alertly for his 'secret,' a small tube that could expand to become quite long. This was his 'disease,' which he pretended to throw into the crowd while they ducked their heads and covered them with their blankets. By tele-scoping his tube, the Mamaka seemed to catch it again magically. Finally he appeared to drive it into himself and fell dead, after which he withdrew the disease, arose, and danced off. The Mamaka carried a Sisiutl staff and bow."
6   May Smith was May Scow; like James Sewid she comes from Gilford Island, Qʷiqʷasutinuxʷ.
7   When two cousins marry it is called ƚənƚag̓o. Far from being the norm, such marriages were intended to prevent the privileges from going out of the family. See Boas (1920); Lévi-Strauss (1979: 168-70).
8   Chief Tommy Hunt, because he is related to Margaret Cook. It should have been the late Peter Smith. Margaret Cook is Peter Smith's sister. Lorne's father was brother to Peter Smith and Margaret Cook.
9   The Copper was brought to Tommy Hunt because he is related to Margaret Cook.
10 The concept of weight, or heaviness, in Kʷakʷakəwakʷ thought is loaded with implicit meaning. It is a metaphor for wealth. The bride is made "heavy" (i.e., important) because of the weightiness of the names and Coppers she is receiving. According to Goldman (1975: 83), "an equation is implied between the weight of the immobilized bride and the formidable powers that overcome her. Kwakiutl equate the powers of rank with heaviness. The man elevating his son makes his son heavy. The bride for whom marriage to a chief completes her own elevation to the noble rank is perhaps heavy in like manner. In the case of the bride, however, the imagery of weightiness is refracted in several directions. In her heaviness the bride is seated on a mat, her 'marriage mat,' a euphemism for a quantity of property." The mat was usually valued in terms of slaves (Boas 1921: 1040), Coppers, or blankets. Her valuable blanket decorated with abalone shell is said to be her "heaviness." Transferring it to the groom gives him all that her heaviness implies. Chiefs are made great through their marriages, the Kʷakʷakəwakʷ people say.
11 To our chagrin, the speaker was elderly, far from the microphone, and very difficult to understand.
12 This was intentional. He knew beforehand what he wanted to do with it: he wanted to make it more difficult for the ƛawič̓is to obtain the bride. Only Henry Bell and James Sewid knew about it.
13 This is going to go to Lorne Smith in the forms of cash or goods for a total of $1,000 for his potlatch and increase the value of the Copper.
14 Daisy reported that the goods stored in the backroom were worth over $30,000. (Exactly $30,300; jewellery = $3,000, outfits = $4,300, miscellaneous goods = $23,000.) The amount of cash was over $5,000; Daisy's detailed list shows $5,150.
15 The language surrounding the usage of Coppers is highly metaphoric. Boas (1966: 85) described an elaborate ceremony during which a high-priced Copper was to be

purchased: "When the buyer is ready, he gives to the owner of the Copper blankets about one-sixth of the total value of the Copper. This is called 'making a pillow' for the Copper; or 'making a feather bed' or 'the harpoon line at which game is hanging,' meaning that in the same manner the Copper is attached to the long line of blankets; or 'taken in the hand, in order to lift the Copper.'" The "mast" may have referred to the considerable height of the piled blankets necessary to purchase the Copper.

16 On the morning of the wedding, Jane Cook (Chris Cook's mother) died. The Cook family will also give a potlatch.

17 The pieces of abalone shell ornaments were large, some old ones and some new ones cut in the shape of a Copper; these ornaments function as emblems of prestige and are transferrable. According to Boas (1897: 422), at a wedding the bride "wears a blanket set with abalone shells. A large abalone shell is fastened to her nose by strings which pass over her ears, as the shell is too heavy to be worn suspended from the septum. For the same reason her earrings are worn suspended from the hair. She performs a dance, after which her ornaments are given to her husband."

References

ANDERSON, STEPHEN R.
    1984   "Kwakwala Syntax and the Government-Binding Theory." In Eung-Do Cook
                and Donna B. Gerdts, eds., *The Syntax of Native American Languages*, 21-75.
                Orlando, FL: Academic Press.

ARCHER, CHRISTON I.
    1980   "Cannibalism in the Early History of the Northwest Coast: Enduring
                Myths and Neglected Realities." *Canadian Historical Review* 61: 453-79.

ASSU, HARRY, WITH JOY INGLIS
    1989   *Assu of Cape Mudge: Recollections of a Coastal Indian Chief.* Vancouver: UBC
                Press.

AUGÉ, MARC
    1982   *The Anthropological Circle: Symbol, Function, History.* Translated by Martin
                Thom. Cambridge and New York: Cambridge University Press.

AVERKIEVA, JULIA
    1966 [1941] *Slavery among the Indians of North America.* Translated (1957, revised
                1966) by G.R. Elliott. Victoria, BC: Victoria College.

    1981   "Son-in-Law: The Heir of Kwakiutl Indians." In Pieter Hovens, ed., *North
                American Indian Studies: European Contributions*, 59-65. Göttingen: Edition
                Herodot.

AVERKIEVA, JULIA, AND MARK A. SHERMAN
    1992   *Kwakiutl String Figures.* Seattle/New York/Vancouver: University of
                Washington Press/American Museum of Natural History/UBC Press.

BARBEAU, MARIUS
    1957   *Haida Carvers in Argillite.* Anthropological Series 38, National Museum of
                Canada Bulletin 139. Ottawa.

BARNETT, HOMER G.
    1938   "The Nature of the Potlatch." *American Anthropologist* 40 (3): 349-58.

BARTHES, ROLAND
    1994   *Roland Barthes by Roland Barthes.* Translated by Richard Howard. Berkeley:
                University of California Press.

BATAILLE, GEORGE
    1967   *La Part maudite.* Paris: Les Éditions de Minuit.

BATAILLE, GRETCHEN M., AND KATHLEEN M. SANDS
  1984   American Indian Women: Telling Their Lives. Lincoln, NB: University of
              Nebraska Press.

BAUDRILLARD, JEAN
  1981   For a Critique of the Political Economy of the Sign. Translated by C. Levine.
              St. Louis, MO: Telo Press.

BAUMAN, RICHARD
  1984   Verbal Art as Performance. Rowley, MA: Newbury House.

BEAGLEHOLE, JOHN C. (EDITOR)
  1967   The Journal of Captain James Cook on His Voyages of Discovery. 4 vols. Vol. 3:
              The Voyage of the Resolution and Discovery, 1776-1780. 2 pts. Cambridge,
              UK: Published for the Hakluyt Society at the University Press.

BENEDICT, RUTH
  1934   Patterns of Culture. Boston: Houghton Mifflin.

BERMAN, JUDITH
  1982   "Deictic Auxiliaries and Discourse Marking in Kwakw'ala Narrative." In
              Working Papers for the 27th International Conference on Salish and Neigh-
              boring Languages. 9-11 August. Portland State University, Portland, Oregon.

  1991   "The Seals' Sleeping Cave: The Interpretation of Boas' Kwakw'ala Texts."
              PhD diss., University of Pennsylvania.

  1992   "Oolachen-Woman's Robe: Fish, Blankets, Masks, and Meaning in Boas'
              Kwakw'ala Texts." In Brian Swann, ed., On The Translation of Native
              American Literatures, 125-62. Washington, DC: Smithsonian Institution
              Press.

  1994   "George Hunt and the Kwak'wala Texts." Anthropology Linguistics 36 (4):
              482-514.

  1996   "'The Culture as It Appears to the Indian Himself': Boas, George Hunt
              and the Methods of Ethnography." In George Stocking, ed., Volksgeist
              as Method and Ethic: Essays on Boasian Ethnography and the German
              Anthropological Tradition, 215-56. History of Anthropology 8. Madison,
              WI: University of Wisconsin Press.

BLACKMAN, MARGARET B.
  1981   "The Changing Status of Haida Women: An Ethnohistorical and Life
              History Approach." In Donald N. Abbott, ed., The World Is as Sharp as a
              Knife: An Anthology in Honour of Wilson Duff, 65-77. Victoria, BC: British
              Columbia Provincial Museum.

  1982   During My Time: Florence Edenshaw Davidson, a Haida Woman. Seattle/
              Vancouver: University of Washington Press/Douglas and McIntyre.

BOAS, FRANZ
  1887   "Census and Reservations of the Kwakiutl Indian Nation (with Map)."
              Bulletin of the American Geographical Society 19 (3): 225-32.

  1894   "Chinook Texts." Bureau of American Ethnology Bulletin 20. Washington.

  1895   Indianische Sagen von der nordpacifischen Küste Amerikas. Berlin: A. Asher.

1897 "The Social Organization and the Secret Societies of the Kwakiutl Indians." In *Report of the US National Museum for 1895*, 311-738. Washington.

1909 *The Kwakiutl of Vancouver Island*. Publications of the Jesup North Pacific Expedition; Memoir of the American Museum of Natural History 5. Part 2, 301-522. New York.

1910 *Kwakiutl Tales*. Columbia University Contributions to Anthropology 2. New York.

1911a "Chinook." In Vol. 1 of *Handbook of American Indian Languages*. Bureau of American Ethnology Bulletin 40, 559-677. Washington.

1911b "Kwakiutl." In Vol. 1 of *Handbook of American Indian Languages*. Bureau of American Ethnology Bulletin 40, 423-557. Washington.

1916 "Tsimshian Mythology: Based on Texts Recorded by Henry W. Tate." *31st Annual Report of the Bureau of American Ethnology for the Years 1909-1910*, 29-1037. Washington.

1920 "The Social Organization of the Kwakiutl." *American Anthropologist* 22 (2): 111-26. Reprinted in Franz Boas, ed., *Race, Language and Culture*, 356-69. New York: Macmillan, 1940. Page numbers are to the 1940 edition.

1921 "Ethnology of the Kwakiutl." *35th Annual Report of the Bureau of American Ethnology*. Parts 1 and 2. Washington, DC.

1924 "A Revised List of Kwakiutl Suffixes." *International Journal of American Linguistics* 3 (1): 117-31.

1928 *Bella Bella Texts*. Columbia University Contributions to Anthropology 5. New York.

1930 *The Religion of the Kwakiutl Indians*. Part 2: *Translations*. Columbia University Contributions to Anthropology 10. New York.

1931 "Notes on the Kwakiutl Vocabulary." *International Journal of American Linguistics* 6 (3-4): 163-78.

1932a *Bella Bella Tales*. Memoirs of the American Folk-Lore Society 25. New York.

1932b "Current Beliefs of the Kwakiutl Indians." *Journal of American Folklore* 45, 176: 177-260.

1934 *Geographical Names of the Kwakiutl Indians*. Columbia University Contributions to Anthropology 20. New York.

1935 *Kwakiutl Culture as Reflected in Mythology*. Memoirs of the American Folk-Lore Society 28. New York.

1935-43 *Kwakiutl Tales* (New series). Columbia University Contributions to Anthropology 26. Parts 1 and 2. New York.

1947 "Kwakiutl Grammar, with a Glossary of the Suffixes." In Helene Boas Yampolsky and Zellis S. Harris, eds., *Transactions of the American Philosophical Society* 37 (3): 201-377. Philadelphia.

1966 *Kwakiutl Ethnography*. Helen Codere, ed. Chicago: University of Chicago Press.

1981   "Indian Folktales from British Columbia." Translated for the BC Indian Language Project by Dietrich Bertz from *Indianische Sagen von der nordpacifischen Küste Amerikas*. In *The Malahat Review* no. 60. Victoria, BC: University of Victoria.

2002   *Indian Myths and Legends from the North Pacific Coast of America: A Translation of Franz Boas' 1895 Edition of Indianische Sagen von der nordpacifischen Küste Amerikas*. Edited by Randy Bouchard and Dorothy Kennedy. Translated by Dietrich Bertz. Vancouver: Talonbooks.

BOAS, FRANZ, AND GEORGE HUNT
1902- 5   *Kwakiutl Texts*. Publications of the Jesup North Pacific Expedition 3 (1-3); Memoirs of the American Museum of Natural History 5 (1-3). New York.

1906   *Kwakiutl Texts* (2nd. series). Publications of the Jesup North Pacific Expedition 10 (1); Memoirs of the American Museum of Natural History 14 (1): 1-269. New York.

1921   "Ethnology of the Kwakiutl (Based on Data Collected by George Hunt)." 2 parts. In *the 35th Annual Report of the Bureau of American Ethnology for the Years 1913-1914*, 43-1481. Washington.

BÖELSCHER, MARIANNE
1988   "The Potlatch in Anthropological Theory." *Abhandlungen der Volkerkundlichen Arbeitsgemeinschaft*. Heft 34, Nortorf.

BOUCHARD, RANDY, AND DOROTHY I.D. KENNEDY (EDITORS)
2002   See Boas, Franz. 2002

BOURDIEU, PIERRE
1977   *Outline of a Theory of Practice*. Cambridge and New York: Cambridge University Press.

BOYD, ROBERT
1990   "Demographic History, 1774-1874." In William C. Sturtevant, gen. ed., and Wayne Suttles, vol. ed., *Handbook of North American Indians* 7, 135-48. Washington, DC: Smithsonian Institution Press.

1999   *The Coming of the Spirit of Pestilence*. Vancouver/Seattle: UBC Press/ University of Washington Press.

BRACKEN, CHRISTOPHER
1997   *The Potlatch Papers: A Colonial History*. Chicago: University of Chicago Press.

BRIDGMAN, RAE, SALLY COLE, AND HEATHER HOWARD-BOBIWASH (EDITORS)
1999   *Feminist Fields: Ethnographic Insights*. Orchard Park, NY: Broadview Press.

BRINGHURST, ROBERT
1999   *A Story as Sharp as a Knife: The Classical Haida Mythtellers and Their World*. Vancouver: Douglas and McIntyre.

BRINGHURST, ROBERT (EDITOR)
2000   *Solitary Raven: Selected Writings of Bill Reid*. Vancouver: Douglas and McIntyre.

BRITISH ASSOCIATION FOR THE ADVANCEMENT OF SCIENCE
1891   Cited in Ronald Rohner 1967, 16-17.

BRUMBLE, H. DAVID, III
  1988   *American Indian Autobiography.* Berkeley: University of California Press.

BRUNER, EDWARD
  1984   *Text, Play, and Story: The Construction and Reconstruction of Self and Society.*
              Washington: American Ethnological Society.

  1986   "Experience and Its Expressions." In Victor W. Turner and Edward M.
              Bruner, eds., *The Anthropology of Experience*, 3-30. Urbana: University of
              Illinois Press.

BUCKLEY, THOMAS, AND ALMA GOTTLIEB
  1988   *Blood Magic: Explorations in the Anthropology of Menstruation.* Berkeley:
              University of California Press.

CAMPBELL, MARIA
  1973   *Halfbreed.* Toronto: McClelland and Stewart.

CANADA, DOMINION OF, DEPARTMENT OF INDIAN AFFAIRS
  1882   *Annual Report of the Department of Indian Affairs for the Year 1881*, p. 171.
              Ottawa.

  1883   *Annual Report of the Department of Indian Affairs for the Year 1882*, p. 161.
              Ottawa.

  1895   *Annual Report of the Department of Indian Affairs for the Year 1894*, pp.
              1958, 1960. Ottawa.

CANADA, DOMINION OF, STATUTES
  1876   "Indian Act, Section 149." NAC, vol. 3629, file 6244-2.

  1884   "An Act Further to Amend 'The Indian Act, 1880.'" *Statutes of Canada* 47
              Vict. c. 27.

CARPENTER, C.H.
  1981   "Secret, Precious Things: Repatriation of Potlatch Art." *Artmagazine* May/
              June: 64-70.

CHAFE, WALLACE
  1981   "Differences between Colloquial and Ritual Seneca, or How Oral
              Literature Is Literary." *Survey Reports: Survey of California and Other Indian
              Languages Report* 1: 131-45. Berkeley.

CLIFFORD, JAMES, AND GEORGE E. MARCUS (EDITORS)
  1986   *Writing Culture: The Poetics and Politics of Ethnography.* Berkeley: University
              of California Press.

CODERE, HELEN
  1950   *Fighting with Property: A Study of Kwakiutl Potlatching and Warfare,
              1792-1930.* Monographs of the American Ethnological Society 18. New
              York: J.J. Augustin.

  1961   "Kwakiutl." In Edward H. Spicer, ed., *Perspectives in American Indian
              Culture Change*, 431-516. Chicago: University of Chicago Press.

  1990   "Kwakiutl: Traditional Culture." In William C. Sturtevant, gen. ed., and
              Wayne Suttles, vol. ed., *Handbook of North American Indians* 7, 359-77.
              Washington, DC: Smithsonian Institution Press.

CODERE, HELEN (EDITOR)
1966   *Kwakiutl Ethnography* (by Franz Boas). Chicago: University of Chicago Press.

COLE, DOUGLAS
1985   *Captured Heritage: The Scramble for Northwest Coast Artifacts.* Seattle: University of Washington Press. (Reprinted 1995, Vancouver: UBC Press.)

1991   "The History of the Kwakiutl Potlatch." In Aldona Jonaitis, ed., *Chiefly Feasts: The Enduring Kwakiutl Potlatch,* 135-68. Vancouver: Douglas and McIntyre.

COLE, DOUGLAS, AND DAVID DARLING
1990   "History of the Early Period." In William C. Sturtevant, gen. ed., and Wayne Suttles, vol. ed., *Handbook of North American Indians* 7, 119-34. Washington, DC: Smithsonian Institution Press.

COOK, WARREN L.
1973   *Flood Tide of Empire: Spain and the Pacific Northwest, 1543-1819.* New Haven: Yale University Press.

CRANMER-WEBSTER, GLORIA
1985   "Kwakiutl." In J.H. Marsh, ed., *Canadian Encyclopedia,* vol. 2. Edmonton: Hartig. Online at www.thecanadianencyclopedia.com.

1990   "Kwakiutl Since 1980." In William C. Sturtevant, gen. ed., and Wayne Suttles, vol. ed., *Handbook of North American Indians* 7, 387-90. Washington, DC: Smithsonian Institution Press.

1991   "The Contemporary Potlatch." In Aldona Jonaitis, ed., *Chiefly Feasts: The Enduring Kwakiutl Potlatch,* 227-48. Vancouver: Douglas and McIntyre.

CRAPANZANO, VINCENT
1977   "The Life History in Anthropological Field Work." *Anthropology and Humanism Quarterly* 2: 3-7.

CRUIKSHANK, JULIE
1990   *Life Lived Like a Story: Life Stories of Three Yukon Native Elders.* Lincoln/ Vancouver: University of Nebraska Press/ UBC Press.

1998   *The Social Life of Stories: Narrative and Knowledge in the Yukon Territory.* Lincoln/Vancouver: University of Nebraska Press/ UBC Press.

CURTIS, EDWARD
1915   *The Kwakiutl.* Vol. 10 of *The North American Indian.* Edited by Frederick W. Hodge. Norwood, MA: Plimpton Press.

DAUENHAUER, NORA MARKS, AND RICHARD DAUENHAUER (EDITORS)
1987   *Haa Shuká, Our Ancestors: Tlingit Oral Narratives.* Seattle/Juneau: University of Washington Press/Sealaska Heritage Foundation.

1994   *Haa kusteeyi, Our Culture: Tlingit Life Stories.* Seattle: University of Washington Press.

1999   "The Paradox of Talking on the Page: Some Aspects of the Tlingit and Haida." In Laura J. Murray and Keren Rice, eds., *Talking on the Page: Editing Aboriginal Oral Texts,* 3-41. Toronto: University of Toronto Press.

DAWSON, GEORGE M.
 1888   "Notes and Observations on the Kwakiool People of the Northern Part of
         Vancouver Island and Adjacent Coasts, Made During the Summer of 1885;
         with a Vocabulary of About Seven Hundred Words." Montreal: Dawson
         Brothers. (Originally issued in 1887 in: *Transactions of the Royal Society of
         Canada* 5 [2]: 63-98.)

DERRIDA, JACQUES
 1992a   "Donner la mort." In Jean-Michel Rabaté and Michael Wezel, eds.,
         L'Éthique du don: Jacques Derrida et la pensée du don, 11-108. Paris:
         Métaillé-Transition.

 1992b   *Given Time: 1, Counterfeit Money.* Translated by Peggy Kamuf. Chicago:
         University of Chicago Press. (Originally published as *Donner le temps: 1,
         La fausse monnaie.* Paris: Galilée, 1991.)

DONALD, LELAND
 1997   *Aboriginal Slavery on the Northwest Coast of North America.* Berkeley:
         University of California Press.

DOUGLAS, G.
 1952   "Revenge at Guayasdums." *Beaver* 283: 6-9.

DRUCKER, PHILIP
 1965   *Cultures of the North Pacific Coast.* San Francisco: Chandler Publications.

DRUCKER, PHILIP, AND ROBERT F. HEIZER
 1967   *To Make My Name Good: A Reexamination of the Southern Kwakiutl
         Potlatch.* Berkeley: University of California Press.

DUFF, WILSON
 1964   *The Indian History of British Columbia.* Vol. 1: *The Impact of the White Man.*
         Anthropology in British Columbia. Memoir no. 5. Victoria, BC: Provincial
         Museum of British Columbia.

ELIADE, MIRCEA
 1959   *Cosmos and History: The Myth of the Eternal Return.* Translated by W.R.
         Trask. New York: Harper and Row.

FERGUSON, R. BRIAN
 1984   "A Re-examination of the Causes of Northwest Coast Warfare." In R. Brian
         Ferguson, ed., *Warfare, Culture, and Environment.* 267-328. Orlando, FL:
         Academic Press.

FINNEGAN, RUTH
 1992   *Oral Traditions and the Verbal Arts: A Guide to Research Practices.* London
         and New York: Routledge.

FISHER, MICHAEL M.J.
 1986   "Ethnicity and the Post-Modern Arts of Memory." In James Clifford and
         George E. Marcus, eds., *Writing Culture: the Poetics and Politics of
         Ethnography,* 194-233. Berkeley: University of California Press.

FISHER, ROBIN
 1977   *Contact and Conflict: Indian-European Relations in British Columbia,
         1774-1890.* Vancouver: UBC Press.

FISHER, ROBIN, AND J.M. BUMSTED (EDITORS)
    1982   *An Account of a Voyage to the North West Coast of America in 1785 and 1786
                by Alexander Walker.* Vancouver/Seattle: Douglas and McIntyre/University
                of Washington Press.

FORD, CLELLAN S.
    1941   *Smoke from Their Fires: The Life of a Kwakiutl Chief.* New Haven: Yale
                University Press.

GALOIS, ROBERT
    1994   *Kwakwaka'wakw Settlements, 1775-1920: A Geographical Analysis and
                Gazetteer.* With contributions from J.V. Powell and Gloria Cranmer-
                Webster. Vancouver: UBC Press.

GEERTZ, CLIFFORD
    1988   *Works and Lives: The Anthropologist as Author.* Stanford: Stanford
                University Press.

GOLDMAN, IRVING
    1975   *The Mouth of Heaven: An Introduction to Kwakiutl Religious Thought.* New
                York: John Wiley and Sons.

GOUGH, BARRY M.
    1982   "A Priest versus the Potlatch: The Reverend Alfred Hall and the Fort
                Rupert Kwakiutl, 1878-1880." *Journal of the Canadian Church Historical
                Society* 24 (2): 75-89.

GREENFIELD, J.
    1986   "The Return of Cultural Property." *Antiquity* 60: 29-35.

    1989   *The Return of Cultural Treasures.* Cambridge: Cambridge University Press.

GRUBB, DAVID McC.
    1977   *A Practical Writing System and Short Dictionary of Kwakw'ala (Kwakiutl).*
                National Museum of Man Mercury Series. Canadian Ethnology Service
                Paper 34. Ottawa: National Museums of Canada.

HALLIDAY, WILLIAM M.
    1922   Letter of 1 March to Duncan Campbell Scott. In Daisy Sewid-Smith,
                Prosecution or Persecution, 33-6. Cape Mudge, BC: Nu-yum-baleess Society.
    1935   *Potlatch and Totem, and the Recollections of an Indian Agent.* London and
                Toronto: J.M. Dent and Sons.

HARKIN, MICHAEL, SERGEI KAN, AND MARIE MAUZÉ (EDITORS)
    2003   *Coming to Shore: Northwest Coast Ethnology.* Norman: University of
                Nebraska Press.

HARRIS, R. COLE
    2002   *Making Native Space: Colonialism, Resistance, and Reserves in British
                Columbia.* Vancouver: UBC Press.

HAWTHORN, AUDREY
    1967   *Art of the Kwakiutl Indians and Other Northwest Coast Tribes.* Seattle:
                University of Washington Press.

    1979   *Kwakiutl Art.* Seattle: University of Washington Press.

HAWTHORN, HARRY B., C.S. BELSHAW, AND S.M. JAMIESON
1958   *The Indians of British Columbia: A Study of Contemporary Social Adjustment.*
         Berkeley: University of California Press.

HEALY, ELIZABETH (COMPILER)
1958   *History of Alert Bay District.* Vancouver: J.M. Bow for the Alert Bay
         Centennial Committee.

HEILBRUN, CAROLYN G.
1988   *Writing a Woman's Life.* New York: W.W. Norton and Company.

HENDRICKS, JANET WALL
1993   "Creating Meaning and Evoking Emotion through Repetition: Shuar War
         Stories." In Arnold Krupat, ed., *New Voices in Native American Literary
         Criticism*, 77-119.Washington, DC: Smithsonian Institution Press.

HÉRITIER, FRANÇOISE
2002   *Masculin/Féminin II: Dissoudre la hiérarchie.* Paris: Édition Odile Jacob.

HILL-TOUT, CHARLES
1907   "Report on the Ethnology of the South-Eastern Tribes of Vancouver Island,
         British Columbia." *Journal of the Royal Anthropological Institute of Great
         Britain and Ireland* 37: 306-74. London.

HILTON, SUZANNE, AND JOHN RATH
1982   "Objections to Franz Boas's Referring to Eating People in the Translation
         of Kwakw'ala Terms baxubakwelanuxusiwe and hamats!a." Working
         Papers for the Seventeenth International Conference on Salish and
         Neighboring Languages. 9-11 August. Portland State University, Portland,
         Oregon.

HOLM, BILL
1977   "Traditional and Contemporary Southern Kwakiutl Winter Dance." *Arctic
         Anthropology* 14 (1): 5-24.

1990   "Kwakiutl: Winter Ceremonies." In William C. Sturtevant, gen. ed., and
         Wayne Suttles, vol. ed., *Handbook of North American Indians* 7, 378-86.
         Washington, DC: Smithsonian Institution Press.

HOWARD-BOBIWASH, HEATHER
1999   "'Like Her Lips to My Ear': Reading Anishnaabekweg Lives and Aboriginal
         Cultural Continuity in the City." In Rae Bridgman, Sally Cole, and Heather
         Howard-Bobiwash, eds., *Feminist Fields: Ethnographic Insights*, 117-36.
         Orchard Park, NY: Broadview Press.

HOWAY, FREDERICK W.
1941   *Voyages of the Columbia to the Northwest Coast, 1787-1790 and 1790-1793.*
         Collections of the Massachusetts Historical Society, vol. 79. Boston.

HUNT, GEORGE
1894   Letter to Franz Boas, 7 February. Boas Professional Correspondence.
         American Philosophical Society's Boas Collection. Philadelphia.

1916   Letters to Franz Boas, 14 July and 14 October. Boas Professional
         Correspondence. *American Philosophical Society's Boas Collection.*
         Philadelphia.

HYMES, DELL

1977   "Discovering Oral Performance and Measured Verse in American Indian Narrative." *New Literary History* 8: 431-57.

1990   "Mythology." In William C. Sturtevant, gen. ed., and Wayne Suttles, vol. ed., *Handbook of North American Indians* 7, 593-601. Washington, DC: Smithsonian Institution Press.

INGLIS, JOY

1989   *Assu of Cape Mudge: Recollections of a Coastal Indian Chief.* Vancouver: UBC Press.

JACKNIS, IRA

1991   "George Hunt, Collector of Indian Specimens." In Aldona Jonaitis, ed., *Chiefly Feasts: the Enduring Kwakiutl Potlatch*, 177-224. Vancouver: Douglas and McIntyre.

JELINEK, ESTELLE

1980   "Women's Autobiography and the Male Tradition." In Estelle Jelinek, ed., *Women's Autobiography: Essays in Criticism*, 1-20. Bloomington: Indiana University Press.

JENNESS, DIAMOND

1955   *The Faith of a Coast Salish Indian*. Anthropology in British Columbia, Memoir 3, 1-92. Victoria, BC: British Columbia Provincial Museum.

KAN, SERGEI

1989   "Why the Aristocrats Were 'Heavy,' or How Ethnopsychology Legitimized Inequality among the Tlingit." *Dialectical Anthropology* 14 (2): 81-94.

KENNEDY, DOROTHY I.D., AND RANDALL T. BOUCHARD

1990   "Bella Coola." In William C. Sturtevant, gen. ed., and Wayne Suttles, vol. ed., *Handbook of North American Indians* 7, 323-39. Washington, DC: Smithsonian Institution Press.

KEW, MICHAEL

1990   "History of Coastal British Columbia Since 1849." In William C. Sturtevant, gen. ed., and Wayne Suttles, vol. ed., *Handbook of North American Indians* 7, 159-68. Washington, DC: Smithsonian Institution Press.

KLUCKHOHN, CLYDE

1945   "The Personal Document in Anthropological Science." In Louis Gottschalk, Clyde Kluckhohn, and Robert Angell, eds., *The Use of Personal Documents in History, Anthropology, and Sociology*. Social Sciences Research Council, Bulletin 53. New York.

KOPAS, CLIFF

1970   *Bella Coola*. Vancouver: Mitchell Press.

KRUPAT, ARNOLD

1985   *For Those Who Came After: A Study of Native American Autobiography*. Berkeley: University of California Press.

LANGNESS, LEWIS L.
1965   *The Life History in Anthropological Science.* New York: Holt, Rinehart and Winston.

LANGNESS, LEWIS L., AND GELYA FRANK
1981   *Lives: An Anthropological Approach to Biography.* Novato, CA: Chandler and Sharp.

LA VIOLETTE, FORREST E.
1961   *The Struggle for Survival: Indian Cultures and the Protestant Ethic in British Columbia.* (Rev. ed. 1973) Toronto: University of Toronto Press.

LEJEUNE, PHILIPPE
1975   *Le Pacte autobiographique.* Paris: Éditions du Seuil.

LEVINE, ROBERT D.
1977   "Kwakwala in Northwest Coast Texts." In Barry F. Carlson, ed., *Native American Texts Series*, 98-126. Chicago: University of Chicago Press.

1984   "Empty Categories, Rules of Grammar, and Kwakwala Complementation." In Eung-Do Cook and Donna B. Gerdts, eds., *The Syntax of Native American Languages*, 215-45. Orlando, FL: Academic Press.

LÉVI-STRAUSS, CLAUDE
1975   *La Voie des masques.* Genève: Éditions d'Art Albert Skira.

1977   "Les dessous d'un masque." *L'Homme* 17 (1): 5-27.

1979   *La Voie des masques.* Édition revue, augmentée et rallongée de Trois Excursions [Revised and expanded edition].

1982   *The Way of the Masks.* Translated by Sylvia Modelski. Vancouver: Douglas and McIntyre. (Reprinted 1999, Seattle/Vancouver: University of Washington Press/UBC Press.)

1989   *Des symboles et leurs doubles.* Paris: Plon.

LINCOLN, NEVILLE J., AND JOHN C. RATH
1980   *North Wakashan Comparative Root List.* National Museum of Man Mercury Series. Canadian Ethnology Service Paper 68. Ottawa: National Museum of Canada.

LURIE, NANCY O.
1961   *Mountain Wolf Woman, Sister of Crashing Thunder: Autobiography of a Winnebago Indian.* Ann Arbor: University of Michigan Press.

McCLUSKEY, SALLY
1972   "Black Elk Speaks, and So Does John Neihardt." *Western American Literature* 6: 231-42.

McFEAT, TOM (EDITOR)
1966   *Indians of the North Pacific Coast.* Seattle: University of Washington Press.

McKECHNIE, ROBERT E.
1972   *Strong Medicine: History of Healing on the Northwest Coast.* Vancouver: J.J. Douglas.

MacLeod, William C.

1925a   "Debtor and Chattel Slavery in Aboriginal North America." *American Anthropologist* 27 (3): 370-80.

1925b   "A Primitive Clearing House." *American Economic Review* 15: 453-6.

Mandel, Barrett

1968   "The Autobiographer's Art." *Journal of Aesthetics and Art Criticism* 27: 215-26.

Marriott, Alice Lee

1948   *Maria, the Potter of San Ildefonso.* Norman: University of Oklahoma Press.

Mauss, Marcel

1967 [1925]   *The Gift.* Translated by I. Cunnison from *Essai sur le don.* London: Cohen and West.

Mauzé, Marie

1999   "L'Éclat d'haliotide. De la conception du beau dans les sociétés de la côte Nord-Ouest." *Terrain* 32: 83-98.

Mauzé, Marie (editor)

1997   *Present Is Past. Some Uses of Tradition in Native Societies.* Lanham, MD: University Press of America.

Menzies, [Sir] Archibald

1923   *Menzies' Journal of Vancouver's Voyage, April to October, 1792.* Edited by C.F. Newcombe. Archives of British Columbia Memoirs 5. Victoria, BC: W.H. Cullen.

Michaelson, D.R.

1979   "From Ethnography to Ethnology: A Study of the Conflict of Interpretation of the Southern Kwakiutl Potlatch." PhD diss., New School of Social Research, New York.

Misch, Georg

1951   *A History of Autobiography in Antiquity.* 2 Vols. Cambridge: Harvard University Press.

Mishler, Craig

1981   "'He Said, They Say': The Uses of Reporting Speech in Native American Folk Narrative." *Fabula* 22: 239-49. Berlin: Moutonde de Gruyter.

Moziño, José Mariano

1970   *Noticias de Nutka: An Account of Nootka Sound in 1792.* Edited by Iris H. Wilson. American Ethnological Society Monograph 50. Seattle: University of Washington Press.

Neel, David

1992   *Our Chiefs and Elders: Words and Photographs of Native Leaders.* Vancouver: UBC Press.

Neihardt, John G.

1972 [1932]   *Black Elk Speaks: Being the Life Story of a Holy Man of the Oglala Sioux.* Norman: University of Nebraska Press.

OLSON, RONALD L.
1940   "The Social Organization of the Haisla of British Columbia." *University of California Anthropological Records* 2 (5): 169-200.

1954   "Social Life of the Owikeno Kwakiutl." *University of California Anthropological Records* 14 (3): 213-59.

1955   "Notes on the Bella Bella Kwakiutl." *University of California Anthropological Records* 14 (5): 319-48.

PASCAL, ROY
1960   *Design and Truth in Autobiography.* New York: Garland Publications.

PIDDOCKE, STUART
1965   "The Potlatch System of the Southern Kwakiutl: A New Perspective." *Southwestern Journal of Anthropology* 21 (3): 244-64.

POWELL, JAY V., VICKIE JENSEN, AGNES CRANMER, AND MARGARET COOK
1990   *Learning Kwak'wala.* Gloria Cranmer-Webster, series ed. Alert Bay, BC: U'mista Cultural Society.

POUILLON, JEAN
1997   "The Ambiguity of Tradition: Begetting the Father." In Marie Mauzé, ed., *Present Is Past: Some Uses of Tradition in Native Societies,* 17-21. Lanham, MD: University Press of America.

RADIN, PAUL (EDITOR)
1983 [1926]   *Crashing Thunder: The Autobiography of an American Indian.* Lincoln: University of Nebraska Press.

REEVES, HENRY
1992   *Adawga Gant Wilaaytga Gyetga Suwildook: Rituals of Respect and the Sea Otter Hunt.* Suwilaay'msa Na Gaa'niiyatgm 2. Prince Rupert, BC: Tsimshian Tribal Council.

REID, MARTINE J.
1981   "La cérémonie hamatsa des Kwagul: Approche structuraliste des rapports mythe-rituel." PhD diss., University of British Columbia.

1984a   "Le mythe de baxbakwalanuxsiwe: Une affaire de famille." *Recherches amérindiennes au Québec* 14 (2): 25-33.

1984b   *Review of the Council of the Tsimshian Nation Land Claims.* Submitted to the Office of Native Land Claims, Ministry of Indian and Northern Affairs, Ottawa. 180 pages.

1986a   "Women and Masks on the Northwest Coast: A Reappraisal." Presented at the First Conference of Native Art Studies Association of Canada, Victoria.

1986b   "The Significance of Colour among the Kwakiutl." In Doreen Jensen and Polly Sergent, eds., *Robes of Power: Totem Poles on Cloth,* 76-7. Vancouver: UBC Press.

1987   "Silent Speakers: Arts of the Northwest Coast." In *The Spirit Sings: Artistic Traditions of Canada's First Peoples* 1: 201-37. Toronto: McClelland and Stewart; Calgary: Glenbow Museum.

1989   "Le courage de l'art." In Claude Lévi-Strauss, ed., *Des symboles et leurs doubles*, 219-52. Paris: Plon.

1993   "In Search of Things Past, Remembered, Retraced and Reinvented: Contemporary Northwest Coast Indian Art." In *The Shadow of the Sun: Perspectives on Contemporary Art*. Mercury Series, Canadian Ethnology Service Paper 124, 71-92. Canadian Museum of Civilization, Ottawa.

2000   "Writing Aloud." In Robert Bringhurst, ed., *Solitary Raven: Selected Writings of Bill Reid*, 231-35. Vancouver: Douglas and McIntyre.

REID, MARTINE J., AND DAISY SEWID-SMITH
2003   "Voices of One's Life." In Michael Harkin, Sergei Kan, and Marie Mauzé, eds., *Coming to Shore: Northwest Coast Ethnology*. Norman: University of Nebraska Press.

REYNOLDS, STEPHEN W.
1938   *The Voyage of the "New Hazard" to the Northwest Coast, Hawaii, and China, 1810-1813, by Stephen Reynolds, a Member of the Crew*. Edited by F.W. Howay. Salem, MA: Peabody Museum.

ROHNER, RONALD P.
1966   "Franz Boas: Ethnographer on the Northwest Coast." In June Helm, ed., *Pioneers of American Anthropology: The Uses of Biography*, 149-212. Seattle: University of Washington Press.

1967   *The People of Gilford: A Contemporary Kwakiutl Village*. National Museum of Canada Bulletin 225. Anthropological Series 83. Ottawa: National Museum of Canada.

ROHNER, RONALD P. (EDITOR)
1969   *The Ethnography of Franz Boas: Letters and Diaries of Franz Boas on the Northwest Coast from 1886 to 1931*. Chicago: University of Chicago Press.

ROSMAN, ABRAHAM, AND PAULA G. RUBEL
1971   *Feasting with Mine Enemy: Rank and Exchange Among Northwest Coast Societies*. New York: Columbia University Press.

1972   "The Potlatch: A Structural Analysis." *American Anthropologist* 74 (3): 658-71.

1981   *The Tapestry of Culture: An Introduction to Cultural Anthropology*. Glenville, IL: Scott, Foresman, and Company.

ROUSSEAU, JEAN-JACQUES
1889   *Les Confessions (1782-1789)*. Livres I-XII. Paris: Édition H. Launette et cie.

RUBEL, PAULA G., AND ABRAHAM ROSMAN (EDITORS)
2003   *Translating Cultures: Perspectives on Translation and Anthropology*. Oxford and New York: Berg.

RUBY, ROBERT H., AND JOHN A. BROWN
1993   *Indian Slavery in the Pacific Northwest*. Spokane: Arthur H. Clark.

RUYLE, EUGENE E.
1973   "Slavery, Surplus and Stratification on the Northwest Coast: Ethnoenergetics of an Incipient Stratification System." *Current Anthropology* 14 (5): 603-31.

SAPIR, EDWARD
1921   "The Life of a Nootka Indian." *Queen's Quarterly* 28: 232-43, 351-67.

SAPIR, EDWARD, AND MORRIS SWADESH
1939   *Nootka Texts: Tales and Ethnological Narrative with Grammatical Notes and Lexical Material.* Philadelphia: University of Pennsylvania, Linguistic Society of America.

SARRIS, GREG
1993   *Keeping Slug Woman Alive: A Holistic Approach to American Indian Texts.* Berkeley: University of California Press.

SAUNDERS, BARBARA
1995   "Kwakwaka'wakw Museology." *Cultural Dynamics* 7 (1): 37-68. Thousand Oaks, CA: Sage Publications.

SCHULTE-TENCKHOFF, ISABELLE
1986   *Potlatch: Conquête et invention.* Lausanne: Édition d'en bas.

SEWID-SMITH, DAISY (MAYANIŁ)
1979   *Prosecution or Persecution.* Cape Mudge, BC: Nu-yum-baleess Society.

1988   *Liq̓ʷala/Kʷak̓ʷala Textbook.* Campbell River, BC: School District No. 72, First Nations Education Department.

1991   "In Time Immemorial." *BC Studies* 89: 16-32.

1996   "Child and Family from an Aboriginal Perspective." In Harold Coward and Philip Cook, eds., *Religious Dimensions of Child and Family Life: Reflections on the UN Convention on the Rights of the Child.* Victoria, BC: University of Victoria, Centre for Studies in Religion and Society.

1997   "The Continuing Reshaping of Our Ritual World by Academic Adjunct." *Anthropology and Education Quarterly* 28: 594-605.

SILVERSTEIN, MICHAEL
2003   "Translation, Transduction, Transformation: Skating 'Glossando' on Thin Semiotic Ice." In Paula G. Rubel and Abraham Rosman, eds., *Translating Cultures: Perspectives on Translation and Anthropology,* 75-105. Oxford and New York: Berg.

SMALLEY, WILLIAM A.
1964   *Manual of Articulatory Phonetics.* Tarrytown, NY: Practical Anthropology.

SPRADLEY, JAMES (EDITOR)
1969   *Guests Never Leave Hungry: The Autobiography of James Sewid, a Kwakiutl Indian.* New Haven: Yale University Press.

STEWART, HILARY
1977   *Indian Fishing: Early Methods on the Northwest Coast.* Vancouver/Seattle: J.J. Douglas/University of Washington Press.

STRANGE, JAMES
1929   *James Strange's Journal and Narrative of the Commercial Expedition from Bombay to the North-West Coast of America.* Madras, India: Government Press. (Reprinted: Shorey Book Store, Seattle, 1972.)

STRATHERN, MARILYN

1972 *Women in Between: Female Roles in a Male World: Mount Hagen, New Guinea.* New York and London: Seminar Press.

1988 *The Gender of the Gift: Problems with Women and Problems with Society in Melanesia.* Berkeley: University of California Press.

SUTTLES, WAYNE

1960 "Affinal Ties, Subsistence, and Prestige Among the Coast Salish." *American Anthropologist* 62 (2): 296-305.

1990 "History of Research: Early Sources." In William C. Sturtevant, gen. ed., and Wayne Suttles, vol. ed., *Handbook of North American Indians* 7, 70-2. Washington, DC: Smithsonian Institution Press.

1991a "The Spelling of Kwakwala." In Aldona Jonaitis, ed., *Chiefly Feasts: The Enduring Kwakiutl Potlatch*, 15-17. Vancouver: Douglas and McIntyre.

1991b "The Traditional Kwakiutl Potlatch." In Aldona Jonaitis, ed., *Chiefly Feasts: The Enduring Kwakiutl Potlatch*, 71-133. Vancouver: Douglas and McIntyre.

SUTTLES, WAYNE (VOLUME EDITOR)

1990 *Handbook of North American Indians* 7. William C. Sturtevant, gen. ed. Washington, DC: Smithsonian Institution Press.

SWANTON, JOHN

1905 *Haida Texts and Myths: Skidegate Dialect.* Bureau of American Ethnology Bulletin 29. Washington.

TAYLOR, HERBERT C., JR., AND WILSON DUFF

1956 "A Post-contact Southward Movement of the Kwakiutl." *Washington State College Research Studies* 24 (1): 55-66.

TAYLOR, ROBERT B.

1976 *Cultural Ways: A Compact Introduction to Cultural Anthropology.* Boston: Allyn and Bacon.

THEISZ, R.D.

1981 "The Critical Collaboration: Introductions as a Gateway to the Study of Native American Bi-Autobiography." *American Indian Research and Culture Journal* 5 (1): 65-92.

THOMPSON, LAURENCE C., AND DALE M. KINKADE

1990 "Languages." In William C. Sturtevant, gen. ed., and Wayne Suttles, vol. ed., *Handbook of North American Indians* 7, 30-51. Washington, DC: Smithsonian Institution Press.

TOLMIE, WILLIAM

1833-35 *Diary: August 11, 1833-December, 1835.* Unpublished manuscript. Victoria, BC: British Columbia Provincial Archives.

TURNER, NANCY J.

1995 *Food Plants of the Coastal First Peoples: A Royal British Columbia Museum Handbook.* Vancouver: UBC Press.

TURNER, NANCY J., AND HARRIET V. KUHNLEIN
1982   "Two Important 'Root' Foods of the Northwest Coast Indians: Springbank Clover (*Trifolium wormskjoldii*) and Pacific Silverweed (*Potentilla anserina* spp. *Pacifica*)." *Economic Botany* 36 (4): 411-32.

1983   "Camas (*Camassa* spp.) and Rice Root (*Fritillaria* spp.): Two Liliaceous 'Root' Foods of the Northwest Coast Indians." *Ecology of Food and Nutrition* 13: 199-219.

1998   "The Sacred Cedar Tree of the Kwakwaka'wakw People." Interview with Daisy Sewid-Smith (Mayanił) and Chief Adam Dick (Kʷaxsistala). In Marsha Bol, ed., *Stars Above, Earth Below: American Indians and Nature.* Niwot, CO/Pittsburgh, PA: Carnegie Museum of Natural History/Roberts Rinehart.

U'MISTA CULTURAL CENTRE
1975   *Potlatch: A Strict Law Bids Us Dance.* A motion picture produced with Anne Wheeler.

VANCOUVER, GEORGE
1798   *A Voyage of Discovery to the North Pacific Ocean and Round the World, in Which the Coast of North-West America Has Been Carefully Examined and Accurately Surveyed.* 3 vols. London: Printed for G.G. and J. Robinson.

VAYDA, ANDREW P.
1961   "A Re-examination of Northwest Coast Economic Systems." *Transactions of the New York Academy of Sciences* 23 (7): 618-24.

VIVELO, FRANK ROBERT
1978   *Cultural Anthropology Handbook: A Basic Introduction.* New York: McGraw-Hill Book Company.

WAGNER, HENRY R.
1933   *Spanish Exploration in the Strait of Juan de Fuca.* Santa Ana, CA: Fine Arts Press.

WALLAS, JAMES, WITH PAMELA WHITAKER
1981   *Kwakiutl Legends as Told to Pamela Whitaker.* North Vancouver, BC: Hancock House.

WASHBURNE, HELIUZ CHANDLER
1976   *Land of the Good Shadows: The Life Story of Anauta, an Eskimo Woman.* New York: AMS Press.

WEINTRAUB, KARL J.
1975   "Autobiography and Historical Consciousness." *Critical Inquiry* 1: 821-48.

1978   *The Value of the Individual: Self and Circumstance in Autobiography.* Chicago: University of Chicago Press.

WHITE, LESLIE
1963   "The Ethnography and Ethnology of Franz Boas." *Bulletin of the Texas Memorial Museum* 6. Austin.

WIDERSPACH-THOR, MARTINE DE (A.K.A. MARTINE REID)

1975   "Le saumon dans la vie des Indiens Kwakiutl de la Colombie-Britannique." Diplôme de L'École des Hautes Études en Sciences Sociales. Sorbonne, Paris.

1978   *Kwakiutl Marine Mythology. Translated from Kwak'wala to English.* Unpublished manuscript. National Museum of Man Archives. Urgent Ethnology Division. Ottawa.

1981   "The Equation of Copper." In Donald N. Abbott, ed. *The World Is as Sharp as a Knife*, 157-74. Victoria, BC: British Columbia Provincial Museum.

WILLIS, JANE

1973   *Geniesh: An Indian Girlhood.* Toronto: New Press.

WOLCOTT, HARRY F.

1996   "Peripheral Participation and the Kwakiutl Potlatch." *Anthropology and Education Quarterly* 27 (4): 467-92.

WOLHEIM, RICHARD

1984   *The Thread of Life.* Cambridge: Cambridge University Press.

WOODSTOCK, GEORGE

1980   "The Day the Treasures Came Home to Cape Mudge." *Saturday Night* (Canada) 95: 24-31.

YENGOYAN, ARAM A.

2003   "Lyotard and Wittgenstein and the Question of Translation." In Paula G. Rubel and Abraham Rosman, eds., *Translating Cultures: Perspectives on Translation and Anthropology.* 25-42. Oxford and New York: Berg.

Index

Note: Words beginning with a glottal stop (ʔ) are alphabetized according to the letter that follows the glottal stop.

Abalone shell: indicates wealth and beauty, 249n1, 250n10; jewellery, 78, 224; in myth, 5, 23, 26, 27, 192; names derived from, 26, 80, 192; on noble's hat, 226, 251n17

ʔAbayoł (Ḱugʷidᶻiẏ, grandmother of Billie Sunday Willie), 57, 58, 65, 239n8, 240n19

Abraham, 197, 198, 201

Abraham, Elsie, 174

Adax̄ʷəlis, 108

ʔAdoloł, 177

ʔAǧadiẏ, 169

ʔAlakilağamēẏ, myth of, 45, 46-7

Alert Bay (Yəlis): Apostolic Church, 118-19; Boas on, xxiv, 4; cannery, 171-2, 173, 175, 183; Chinese at, 171-2; description, viii, 137, 159; first electricity at, 120; First Nations at, 232n7; home of the Nəmǧis, xxv, xxxviii, 77, 78, 232n7; land sale at, 159-60; meaning of Yəlis, 231n3; pot-latches, viii, ix, xxxvi, 186, 246n19; residential school, xxxiv, 126, 177-8, 205, 245n10, 247n1; sawmill, xxxiv, 93, 158, 247n3; Sports Day, 135, 246n19; super-sedes Fort Rupert as centre, xxxii, xxxiv; telephone at, 179

Alfred, Agnes Bertha (ʔAx̄uẇ): at Alert Bay, x, xxviii, xxxiv, 108, 182; arrest of, xxiv, xxxiv, 183, 203-4; attitudes regarding alcohol, xxxiii, 100, 118, 175-6; big house of, 99, 107, 113, 120, 126, 137, 161, 183; birthdate, xxiv, 78-9, 182, 233n16; and childbirth, 96-8; childhood games, 83; children of, xiii, xxv, 82, 98, 100-1, 125-6,

161, 182-3; and Christianity, xxvi, xxxiv, 99-100, 118-19, 157-9, 161, 177, 182, 183-4, 185; and cookery, 83, 84-6, 87, 113, 172; and correct posture, 94, 95; dances of, 138, 198, 202, 208; death, 186; dowry, xxxv, 78, 79, 107, 113, 114, 115-16; dress, 112, 159, 161, 175, 182; education, xiii, xxxiii-xxxiv, 77, 88, 93, 94, 158, 162, 177-8, 247n1; employment, xxxiv, xxxv, 171-2, 173, 174-5, 183, 235n42; fears, 72, 88, 90, 98, 99, 114, 128, 131, 161, 167, 175, 248n21; and first European, 175; fishing, 86, 87, 113, 114; initiation, 79, 138; at logging camp, 113-14; marriage, 88, 94, 111, 112-13, 182, 183; and Max̄ʷalogʷa (great-aunt), 83, 85, 86; memorial potlatch for, 186; at Miṁkʷəmlis, 77, 89, 93-4, 124-5, 172, 178, 203; names, 79, 80, 81, 99, 153, 177, 248n22; noblewoman, ix; old-fashioned, 99, 178-9, 183; pets, 80, 88-9, 234n24; and potlatch, xiii, xxvii, xxxiv, 81, 122, 123-5, 186, 196, 206; puberty ritual, 92, 94-6, 138; as Qʷiqʷasutinux̄ʷ, xxvi, 74, 233n17; and silence, xxi, xxiv, xxvii, 53, 58, 75, 202, 238n67; solicits for Red Cross, 174-5; song of, 154; as storyteller, xxiii-xxiv, xxix-xxxi, 5, 184; styles of speech, xxix-xxx, 233n13; suitors, 112; time, concept of, xix, xxviii, xxx-xxxi; trapping, 88-9; and Village Island potlatch (1921), 183, 195, 197, 198, 202; and worldview, 5

Alfred, Allan (Ǧaʔəxtalas, son), 100, 182

Alfred, Alvin (ƛalis, ʔUdᶻistalis, son): 52, 126, 158, 162; and banjo, 120; birth, xxv, 96; at Daisy Sewid-Smith's wedding, 209,

Printed and bound in Canada by Friesens

Design: Echelon Design

Set in Weiss and ScalaSans by Artegraphica Design Co. Ltd.

Copy editor: Joanne Richardson

Proofreader and indexer: Deborah Kerr

Cartographer: Eric Leinberger